Peninsular Sketches

by

Actors on the Scene.

Edited by
W. H. Maxwell, Esq

Author of "The Life of the Duke of Wellington"
"Stories of Waterloo" etc.

Revised edition by S. Monick

IN TWO VOLUMES.

VOLUME I

Text © 2002 S. Monick
This edition © The Naval & Military Press Ltd 2002

First published in 2002 by
The Naval & Military Press Ltd
Unit 10, Ridgewood Industrial Park,
Uckfield, East Sussex TN22 5QE
www.naval-military-press.com

All rights reserved. No part of this book may be reproduced, stored in a retrieval system, or transmitted in any form or by any means without the prior written permission of the publisher, nor be otherwise circulated in any form of binding or cover other than that which it is published and without a similar condition being imposed on the subsequent publisher.

Printed and bound in Great Britain by Antony Rowe Ltd, Eastbourne

INTRODUCTION

The editor: William Hamilton Maxwell

The editor, William Hamilton Maxwell (1792-1850), was undoubtedly one of the more colourful characters of the 19th Century British literary establishment. Born at Newry, County Down, Ireland, in 1792, he was the son of James Maxwell, merchant, a descendant of the Maxwells of Caerlaverock, who had emigrated to Ireland from Nithsdale. His mother was the daughter of William Hamilton, a member of a well established family. William Hamilton Maxwell was educated at Dr Henderson's School and was admitted to Trinity College, Dublin, on 7 December 1807, aged only 15 years of age. He is probably identical with a student named as 'William Henry Maxwell', who is recorded as having graduated with a BA degree in 1812. Maxwell appears to have entered the Army prior to that date. However, not inconsiderable confusion surrounds his military career. A 'Hamilton Maxwell' is cited in the officer establishment of the 26th Regiment, in the rank of lieutenant, in the *Army List* of 1812. The same source records this individual as being a captain in the 42nd Regiment (*Army List* 1813,1814). He is possibly the individual referred to in the *Army List* of 1815, in which he is cited as 'Hamilton Bagwell', a captain in the 88th Regiment. He reputedly served in the last phases of the Peninsular War and at Waterloo. However, there is no concrete evidence to the effect that this individual ever served in these theatres. The Medal Roll for the Military General Service Medal 1793-1814, which recognizes service in the Peninsular War, does not mention any Maxwell, or Bagwell, under any of the regiments in which he is cited in the *Army List*; nor is he mentioned in the Medal Roll for the Waterloo Medal. The *Army List* of 1815 records a Capt Hamilton Maxwell, of the 42nd Regiment, as having been retired on half-pay. Whilst it may be assumed that the Hamilton Maxwell referred to above is the editor of the *Peninsular Sketches*, there is no record of active service in either the Peninsular War or at Waterloo.

On the demobilisation of the forces he returned to Newry and spent some years desultorily reading, hunting and shooting. He found himself in financial difficulties; having converted the income derived from certain leases granted by his father into ready money, and frustrated in his expectation of an aunt's fortune by the terms of her will. He applied for a commission in the Spanish service in South America, but the friend who was to have obtained it for him inopportunely died. However, he repaired his fortunes shortly afterwards through a profitable marriage, and took Holy Orders. In 1820 the Archbishop of Armagh gave him the living of Ballagh in Connemara, a place destitute of a congregation but abounding in game.

Whilst residing at a shooting lodge at Ballycroy, he wrote his first novel, *O'Hara, or 1798* (the story of a landowner who becomes involved with the Irish nationalists) which was published anonymously, and proved a failure. The Marquis of Sligo, with whom he was on friendly terms, gave him a house rent free to ensure that he remained at Ballagh (his restless disposition having manifested itself once again). Maxwell's *Wild sports of the west* (1832) acquired for him a certain reputation as a writer of sporting and military anecdotes. He next published his most widely known work, *Stories from Waterloo* (1834). In addition to contributing to *Bentley's Miscellany* and the *Dublin University Magazine*, he wrote a variety of sketches and novels; principally relating to military and sporting subjects. In addition to *O'Hara*, his works of fiction include: *The dark lady of Doona* (a gothic tale set in 17th Century Ireland) (1834); *Captain Blake, or my life* (1835); *The fortunes of Hector O'Halloran and his man Mark Antony O'Toole* (1842-1843); and *Captain O'Sullivan; or, adventures, civil and military, and matrimonial, of a gentleman on half-pay* (1846). Maxwell originated a colourful fiction associated particularly with Charles James Lever (1806-1872), who also contributed much of his early work to the *Dublin University Magazine*, which that author edited during the period 1842-1845. Lever's vivid pen-portraits of military life and of the hard-drinking, fox-hunting Irish gentry of his time were very popular. Maxwell exemplifies a dying tradition in English Literature; the vogue for military and nautical adventures of bluff soldier and naval types, in the picaresque tradition, having become exhausted by the 1840s, as also was the case with the comic Irish mode.

In 1839-1841 his *Life of the Duke of Wellington* was published and was repeatedly reprinted, sometimes in condensed form. His numerous works of non-fiction, in addition to those cited above, include: *Wanderings in the Highlands and Islands, with sketches taken on the Scottish border* (2 vols, 1844) (a sequel to *Wild sports of the west*); *The field book, or sports and pastimes of the United Kingdom* (1833); *The bivouac, or stories of the Peninsular War* (3 vols, 1837); *The expedition of Major Ap Owen to the lakes of Killarney* (1841); *Rambling recollections of a soldier of fortune* (1842); *Hints to a soldier on service* (2 vols, 1845); *Hillside and border tales (sketches), with legends of the Cheviots and Lemmermuir* (2 vols, 1847); *The Irish Movement...*(1846); *Erin-go-bragh, or Irish life pictures* (2 vols, 1859); and *History of the Rebellion of 1798* (1845). In addition, he edited the *Military and Naval Almanac* for 1840, the two volumes of *Peninsular Sketches* (1844-1845), and contributed to a volume entitled *Sporting* (1830), edited by 'Nimrod' (ie Charles James Apperley).

Maxwell's literary career is of direct relevance to the selection of material included in *Peninsular Sketches* in two important respects. First, the personalised anecdotal approach which informs many of the passages generate an urgency and dramatic immediacy which undoubtedly appealed to Maxwell's journalistic bent; continuing the individualised impressions of war contained in *Bivouac* and *Stories of Waterloo*. Second, *Peninsular Sketches* strongly exemplify the picaresque tradition in English literature, fused with travel narrative, which Maxwell clearly absorbed in his work. Both facets will be discussed in greater detail below. There is, indeed, a curious triple relationship between Maxwell's life, his literary career, and the Peninsular sketches. For his personal history exhibits a markedly adventurous, cavalier and roguish bent which was undoubtedly susceptible to the picaresque tradition (cf below) and which so closely informs his literary creations and which exert such a strong impress upon *Peninsular sketches*.

Maxwell is said to have been deprived of his living in 1844 for non-residence. Having made no financial provisions for his future, and after spending several years in ill-health and distress, he retired to Musselburgh, near Edinburgh, where he died on 29 December 1850. *The Dictionary of National Biography* describes him as 'clever and sociable'. *The Illustrated London News*, in the edition dated 25 January 1851, responded to Maxwell's death with the following eulogistic commentary (p 51):

> 'The spirited and lively writer, whose Wild sports of the West and Victories of the British Army were so deservedly well known, was originally an officer in the 88th. He there attained the rank of captain, and was, as may be supposed, a general favourite with his regiment, the delight of its mess room, and of all its social circles. He participated in the final achievements of the Peninsular campaigns, and was present at Waterloo...

Maxwell's name may be placed among those of the leaders of that humorous and yet romantic and sentimental school of novels which he and his powerful competitor, Charles Lever, have rendered famous. *The story of my life, Wild sports of the West* and a hundred tales and sketches, all excellent in their way, make his departure a loss to literature; and his many sterling virtues cause it to be most widely deplored.'

[As discussed above, the biographical details contained in the above extract, with reference to Maxwell's military career, are subject to debate].

Historical background

Peninsular Sketches consists essentially of a miscellany of impressions relating to the Peninsular War by participants. However, the connecting threads in this tapestry - the development and phases of the war itself - is not furnished to the reader. The generation which formed the audience for the work were fully acquainted with so recent an experience in the nation's historical memory (especially with regard to the work's middle-aged readers). However, such an assumption cannot be made with regard to the modern non-specialist lay persons. For this reason, the historical backdrop to the *Sketches* is furnished.

General overview of the Peninsular campaign

The Peninsular War (1808-1814) provided the scenario for Britain's major military contribution in the war against Napoleon and exercised a continual drain upon French resources and morale (the 'Spanish ulcer', to coin Napoleon's phrase). The war originated in Napoleon's desire to expand the 'Continental System' (the embargo upon British trade) throughout Europe. After the Treaty of Tilsit (1807), only Portugal remained an open market for British imports. Napoleon determined to seal this breach by invading Portugal via Spain, and simultaneously to extend his power over the entire Iberian Peninsula. (In the event, the Continental System was a total failure. Conversely, the British economic blockade of the Napoleonic empire proved to be a spectacular success, due to British naval supremacy). In November/December 1807 General Androche Junot led a French army through Spain and into Portugal. Lisbon was occupied (1 December) and the Portuguese royal family fled to their Brazilian colony; leaving the government in the hands of a Council of Regency.

1807-1808: The seeds of the War are planted

In 1807 the Council of Regency appealed to the British for assistance in extirpating the French. The situation in the

Iberian Peninsula deteriorated still further in 1808. In March of that year Murat led a massive French army into Spain; the ineffectual King Charles IV and his equally inept son, Ferdinand, were taken as virtual prisoners to France. Napoleon imposed his brother, Joseph (then King of Naples and Sicily) upon the Spanish as their king. This precipitated a nation-wide rebellion, commencing in May 1808, which activated British intervention.

A small expeditionary force, commanded by Lt Gen Sir Arthur Wellesley (as he then was) was sent to co-operate with the Portuguese and Spanish commanders; although, at that point in time, the Portuguese forces had virtually disintegrated. The British force reached Oporto on 28 July 1808, having been refused a landing by the Spanish at Corunna. Almost immediately, its strength was considerably increased and a number of officers senior to Wellington also arrived, generating a thoroughly unsatisfactory command situation. Nevertheless, tactical control remained in Wellington's hands and within a month he had inflicted a heavy defeat on General Junot at Vimiero (21 August 1808); the defeat being so heavy that Junot offered to withdraw into Portugal. The withdrawal was negotiated in the Convention of Cintra; by which it was agreed that the French should be transferred to La Rochelle in British ships. This agreement was very ill-received by the home establishment, and resulted in the withdrawal of the senior officers (including Wellington).

In October 1808 the British Government decided to commit a force of some 30 000 infantry and 5 000 cavalry to northern Spain, under the command of Lt Gen Sir John Moore, who was already in Portugal. The bulk of the force was based in Portugal, with a further 10 000 men arriving at Corunna from England. The two elements would meet in the general area of the River Ebro and conduct operations against the French in conjunction with the Spanish. However, the (predictable) rout of the Spanish by the French and the fall of Madrid, aggravated by the total lack of co-operation from the Spanish Junta and its senior officers, left Moore with no option but to withdraw his forces from the country, for he realized that he had to confront the entire strength of the French army, commanded by Napoleon himself. With great skill and determination, harrassed by Marshal Soult and plagued by appalling weather conditions, he withdrew up the difficult route to Corunna. There, despite his losses en route and the desperate state of his starving and weary troops, he defeated Soult in battle (16 January 1809), losing his life in the process. The remnants of the army were evacuated to England. Napoleon's strategy in the Peninsula had been seriously disrupted, as the result of the obstruction presented by Moore, which had prevented the total suppression of the Spanish resistance.

1809-1810
The British re-enter the camapaign: Despite Moore's withdrawal, British command of the sea furnished a secure base of operations at Lisbon, to which supplies could be landed from Britain, and Wellesley returned to command the British Army in Portugal in 1809. He was eventually greatly assisted by the Portuguese army, reorganised by Marshal Sir William Beresford, under British Army control. In the spring of 1809 Soult invaded Portugal but was driven back into Spain when Wellesley crossed the Douro and defeated the French at Oporto (12 May 1809).

Wellington forced into a posture of defence: Wellesley then advanced into Spain, to collaborate with the Spanish. They, and especially their superannuated and totally corrupt and vicious general, Cuesta, proved treacherousa allies from the outset. The Spanish forces totally reneged on their obligation to assist the British when the latter were attacked by Joseph Bonaparte and Marshal Victor at Talavera (28 July 1809); Welllington gaining the victory only after a desperate struggle. Co-operation with the Spanish had proved clearly impossible. The conduct of the Spanish in the Talavera campaign marked a seminal point in Wellington's conduct of the war in 1809. Up to that point he had expected to act offensively, as an ally of the Spanish. He now realised that to continue on this strategic basis would be disastrous. The small British force must attempt to hold as much of Portugal as possible, whilst consolidating its strength. The Spanish had to concentate on holding Andalusia in southern Spain. However, such logic failed to impress the Spanish Junta, which continued to harbour absurdly grandiose schemes, centred on the recovery of Madrid.

Wellesley (thereafter titled Wellington, which name he retained through successive elevations to the Peerage, until he was created Duke in 1814), commanding the Anglo-Portuguese army, emerged as the sole force capable of contesting French contol in Spain. Cuesta's successor, General Areizago, was crushed at Ocana by the forces of Soult and Joseph (19 November 1809), and the remnants of the Spanish army concentrated on the defence of the capital of independent Spain, Cadiz. Realizing that it was impossible to control all Portugal, Wellington ordered the construction of a double line of impenetrable fortifications to isolate the Lisbon peninsula. The preservation of Lisbon was vital; the Tagus estuary being the guarantee of supplies and reinforcements arriving from Britain. The Royal Navy's control of the sea prevented the French from ever threatening the former's supply route and, provided that Lisbon was secure, the British Army in Portugal could be kept continually provisioned. The chain of fortifications defending the Lisbon peninsula was known as the 'lines of Torres Vedras' and were constructed under the auspices of Col Richard Fletcher, RE, supervised by 17 sapper officers built by some 10 000 locally recruited labourers.

The French take the offensive: At the beginning of 1810 the French deployed two armies on the frontier of Portugal; viz the Army of Portugal (under Marshal Andre Massena) and Soult's Army of Andalusia; although personal animosity between the two commanders prevented the effective collaboration of the two armies. In July 1810 Massena invaded Portual, representing the most determined French campaign to date to drive the British from Portugal. Massena, with some

70 000 men, seized the border fortresses of Cuidad Rodrigo and Almeida, and advanced towards Lisbon. Wellington awaited the French at Busaco, a natural defensive position, and inflicted a severe defeat upon Massena (27 September 1810). Wellington then withdrew to the lines of Torres Vedras, which fully exploited every natural feature and obstacle. Wellington had adopted a scorched earth policy along the route that the French had been bound to follow. Massena was then confronted with an impotent siege position, with his army facing starvation.

1811-1812: A decisive turning point in the war

In March 1811, having lost 25 000 men, Massena retreated back into Spain; a withdrawal that marked a decisive turning point in the war. The French encountered no more success in their endeavours to capture Cadiz. Sir Thomas Graham's small British force won a notable victory at Barrosa (5 March 1811).

Almeida evacuated by the French: Massena's withdrawal left the French with only a single foothold in Portual. This was the small fortress town of Almeida. On 11 April 1811 Wellington established a blockade of the garrison, the blockading force comprising the 5th and 6th Divisions and a brigade of Portuguese militia; the besieging force being under the overall command of Maj Gen Dennis Pack. Massena, who had by then established his headquarters at Cuidad Rodrigo, was determined to relieve Almeida, and advanced on the besieged fortress with some 48 000 men. Upon learning of this approach, Wellington deployed a much smaller force around the village of Fuentes d'Onor. After a fierce battle which raged for several days, and during which the village changed hands twice, Massena was defeated and withdrew on 7 May 1811. This defeat led to Marshal Marmont succeeding him as commander. Even as the battle was being fought Wellington had been compelled to reduce the strength of the blockade in order to empower his forces. Although the French garrison was determined in its resistance, the French defeat at Fuentes d'Onor left them with no option but to evacuate Almeida. Having blown up the magazine, they filtered through the sleeping pickets of the 6th Division and effected their escape. Wellington was incensed and never gave the divisional commander, Maj Gen Alexander Campbell, another command.

Allied reverses: The French enjoyed more success in southern Spain, where Marshal Louis Suchet captured Tarragona (28 July) and Valencia (9 January 1812), defeating a combination of Spanish regular forces and guerrilla militia formations. Meanwhile, in the south, Beresford had invested Badajoz on 4 May, but was forced to raise the siege by the return of Soult to the area in some strength. Having defeated Soult at Albuera on 16 May 1811, Beresford returned to Badajoz, and renewed the siege on 25 May, only to learn that Marmont was en route to join Soult, so once again the siege was raised. At the end of 1811, therefore, the French still controlled the gateways to southern Spain; viz Cuidad Rodrigo and Badajoz. Despite these reverses on the part of the allies, however, the year 1811 marked the turning point in the Peninsular War, when a French victory became permanently beyond Napoleon's grasp. The year saw the irreversible consolidation of allied strength in Portual. The Anglo-Portuguese could thus depend upon a continual and untrammelled flow of supplies from Britain; guaranteed by British naval supremacy and the security of the Lisbon peninsula. From such a vantage point, a British victory was inevitable; whilst the French had to suffer tortuous and besieged lines of communication, allied with a ferocious partisan disruption of their forces.

A divided French command: By the middle of the year (July 1811), the French troops in Spain numbered 354 461; in addition to a further 8 298 held in reserve at Bayonne. These troops were contained within six armies: the Army of the South (Soult); the Army of the Centre (Joseph); the Army of Portual (commanded by Marshal Auguste Marmont (1774-1852), who had replaced Massena; the Army of the North (General Dorsenne); and the Army of Catalonia (Marshal Jacques Macdonald). These armies were occupied in holding down the territories to which their designations applied; and in fighting both the Spanish 'regular' forces (never completely conquered) and the guerrilla war. These armies were never able to fully co-ordinate their activities. This was partially due to the acrimonious relations between the commanders and partly to the treacherous nature of the terrain, allied with the distance between the main theatres of war. In contrast, to the French, Wellington enjoyed a 'unity of command; inaccessible to his enemies; being in sole command of the allied army (including the Portuguese). (The role of the Spanish forces was marginalised, save when they served under his direct command). Moreover, whilst the morale of the French was being increasingly eroded by the debilitating guerrilla war, the allied forces were approaching the peak of their efficiency ('probably the most complete machine for its number now existing in Europe', as he was able to write in November 1813), although still deficient in siege train, engineers, artillery and commissariat.

1812: Wellington takes the offensive

Wellington decided to move north to invest Cuidad Rodrigo, which fell in January 1812. As soon as the flooding of the northern rivers rendered the French invasion of northern Portugal impractical, he marched south again and re-opened the siege of Badajoz, which was captured on 7 April; followed by indescribable atrocities on the part of the British. With both Cuidad Rodrigo and Badajoz in his hands, Wellington now controlled the northern and southern approaches from Spain into Portugal.

His army now numbering some 56 000 men, Wellington marched north again on 13 June and entered Salamanca on the 17th of that month. Marmont, now reinforced, resumed the offensive, but was crushingly defeated by Wellington at Salamanca (22 July 1812). Marmont was severely wounded in that battle and superseded by Marshal Clausel. Wellington pursued the French through Valladolid to Madrid, from whence King Joseph had fled. The city was open for Wellington's unopposed entry on 12 August 1812. Leaving two divisions in Madrid, Wellington turned north again with four divisions to set siege to Burgos.

By the end of 1812 Clausel had restored the strength of the French army. As Wellington advanced with his four divisions from Madrid, Clausel withdrew through Burgos, leaving the fortress to face Wellington's siege unaided. At that point in time it was mid-September. Burgos, a very strong and well garrisoned fortress, proved too powerful for Welllington to storm, as he lacked adequate siege artillery. He learned that Massena, whom Napoleon had now restored to favour, and now commanded all French forces in the north of the Peninsula, had replaced Clausel with Souham and had ordered the latter, whom he had reinforced with 12 000 fresh troops, to relieve Burgos. Wellington raised the siege on 15 October and began to retreat towards the River Douro, Hill being directed down the valley of the Tagus. The two allied forces met on 8 November 1812 and took up positions on the River Tormes.

Wellington marched north again on 13 June and entered Salamanca on the 17th of that month. Marmont, now reinforced, resumed the offensive, but was crushingly defeated in the battle of Salamanca on 22 July 1812. Marmont was severely wounded in the engagement and superseded by Marshal Clausel. With northern Spain under his control, Wellington pursued the French through Valladolid to Madrid, from whence King Joseph Bonaparte had fled. The city was open for Wellington's unopposed entry on 12 August 1812. Leaving two divisions in Madrid, Wellington turned north again with four divisions, to set siege to Burgos.

British reverses: By the end of August 1812 Clausel had restored the strength of the French army. As Wellington advanced with his four divisions from Madrid, Clausel withdrew through Burgos, leaving the fortress to face Wellington's siege unaided. At that time it was mid-September. Burgos, a very strong and well garrisoned fortress, proved too powerful for Wellington to capture, as he lacked adequate siege artillery. He learned that Massena, whom

Napoleon had restored to favour and now commanded all the French forces in the north of the Peninsula, had replaced Clausel with Souham and had ordered the latter, whom he had reinforced with 12 000 fresh troops, to relieve Burgos. Wellington raised the siege on 15 October and began to retreat towards the river Duoro, Hill being directed down the valley of the Tagus. The two forces met on 8 November 1812 and took up positions on the River Tormes. Meanwhile, Souham had been joined by Soult, who now outflanked the allies crossing the upper reaches of the river; forcing Wellington to retreat yet again. By 17 December the allied forces were positioned behind the Portuguese frontier and went into winter quarters.

Despite the inauspicious end to a successful year, the tide in the Peninsular War had turned irreversibly against the French. Wellington spent the winter of 1812-1813 in the region of Cuidad Rodrigo; rebuilding his army with welcome reinforcements from England and planning his next offensive.

1813: Desperation of the French

In 1813 the situation became desperate for the French, as increasing numbers of their troops were withdrawn from the war in Germany. Soult was also recalled and Wellington now prepared to finally expel the French from the Peninsula, as he wrote to Lord Bathurst (Secretary for War) on 11 May:

'...I shall not be stronger throughout the campaign, or more efficient ...I cannot have a better opportunity for trying the fate of battle'.

A fortnight later the allied army was once again on the march, advancing in three columns. The field army then numbered 52 434 British and 28 792 Portuguese, in addition to some 46 000 Spanish troops under his command. The left and largest column, under Graham, consisted of six British divisions, two British brigades and a strong force of cavalry. In the centre, under Wellington's personal command, were two British divisions and one Spanish with supporting cavalry. Hill was placed on the right with two British divisions. Graham turned the French flank on the Couro, forcing the enemy, under Joseph Bonaparte's personal command, to withdraw to the Ebro, Burgos falling to the allies without opposition Graham's task had been greatly facilitated by the fact that, although the French retained numerical superiority, their forces had been gravely attenuated - in terms of both quantity and quality - because Napoleon had withdrawn the most experienced troops into France to compensate for the appalling lossess in Russia in 1812, which were tantamount to the effective annihilation of the *Grand Armee*. Moreover, the process of refurbishment and reinforcement which the allies had enjoyed in the winter had considerably enhanced both the efficiency and morale of Wellington's forces.

On 14-15 June 1813 Wellington crossed the Ebro and, by the 20th of that month, having concentrated his army, was facing Joseph at Vittoria, where he attacked on 21 June; utterly routing the French, capturing most of their guns and all their baggage train. In recognition of this great victor, he was created Duke of Vittoria by the Spanish and promoted to field marshal by the home government. Despite a deplorable record of failure of eastern Spain by Gen Murray, who had raised the siege of Tarragona for some inexplicable reason, Wellington now closed his approach to the French frontier.

Soult was given overall command of the remnants of the French forces in Spain, Joseph being finally permitted to abdicate. Soult's objective was now to deny access to southern France, and he performed prodigies. Joseph had managed to salvage some 50 000 men and one howitzer from Wellington's triumph at Salamanca. To this force Soult added the garrison of northern Spain and assembled the 'Army of Spain', consisting of 79 000 men and 140 guns. (Old and meaningless titles such as the 'Army of Portugal' were now discarded). Two fortresses barred the route through the Pyrenees into France; San Sebastian and Pamplona.

Wellington blockaded the latter and commenced

operations in late June 1813 against St Sebastian, which afforded an excellent harbour for the delivery of supplies. His major problem was the mountainous terrain, rendering the rapid transfer of troops extremely difficult. As a result, Soult was able to achieve superiority against any part of Wellington's line extending across the Pyrenees and outmanoeuvre these fragmented forces in detail. When Soult attacked the passes of Maya and Roncesvalles on Wellington's right, the latter regarded it as a feint. He assumed so as he believed that Soult would first attack San Sebastian, already subject to the first phases of a siege. However, Wellington was incorrect in this assessment, for Soult had massed his entire strength, achieving a 'local superiority' in the endeavour to reach Pamplona; realizing that this had to be swifty realized before his supplies were exhausted. Accordingly, Soult now advanced in strength on 24 July to relieve the fortresses of St Sebastian and Pamplona. Near Sorauren, Soult was defeated by the British (28 July 1813). He extracted his army only with the greatest difficulty, having lost 13 000 men in a battle of which Wellington wrote:

> 'I never saw such fighting as we have had here...the battle of the 28th was fair bludgeon work.'

San Sebastian fell to the allies on 31 August 1813 following a ferocious assault which cost 1 696 British and 577 Portuguese casualties, and the unfortunate city was then sacked. After a determined defence the garrson capitulated on 8 September. Soult's attempt to relieve the city on the day of the assault was repelled by the Spanish (who were, surprisingly, unaided) at San Marcial.

1814: Final victory in the Peninsula; across the Pyrenees

Pamplona finally fell to Wellington on 31 October 1813. His troops had already crossed the Bidassoa on 7 October, and thus were deployed on French soil before the end of 1813. As Napoleon's defeat in Germany was signalled at Leipzig, and was about to begin the fighting withdrawal that would culminate outside Paris, Wellington commenced his advance towards Bayonne, which would maintain a gallant defence for several months. He was vigorously resisted by Soult who, despite being defeated on the Nive and at St Pierre, refused to surrender, even when he learned in Toulouse of Napoleon's first abdication on 6 April 1814. However, following another hard-fought battle Toulouse fell on 11 April, Soult having managed to withdraw to the south.

Despite a most determined sortie by the garrison, which took the British by surprise and almost ended in disaster for them, Bayonne capitulated on 27 April and the last shots in the Peninsular War had been fired.

Main factors underpinning the allied victory in the Peninsular War

The main factors which were instrumental in Wellington's victory in the Peninsular War were:

— The undoubted genius of Wellington, expressed in both his strategic and tactical insight. The former was clearly revealed in his judicious decisions regarding the adoption of the defensive posture when the manifest weaknesses of his Spanish allies became apparent in 1810; following by the wisdom of his decision to assume the offensive in Spain after allied control of Portugal had been consolidated.   Wellington's tactical expertise is apparent in the numerous battles which he fought in the Peninsula, eg at Talavera and Salamanca.

— British naval supremacy was unquestionably a major factor in the allied victory. This ensured a constant and uninterrupted stream of supplies to Lisbon. In this respect, Wellington's construction of the defences which guaranteed the security of Lisbon (the lines of Torres Vedras) was a vital complement to British command of the sea.

— The reverse of the British advantage in terms of

communications was the logistical position of the French, beset with increasing problems as the war progressed. The two major aspects of these problems were the distances to be traversed (and hence the acute problem of supplies) and the disruption of those communications by the guerrillas. This latter facet introduces the final major factor in the French defeat; viz the impact of the partisan war.

— There is no doubt that the fierce and uncompromising resistance of the civilian population, expressed in the guerrilla war, profoundly aggravated the French disabilities in the Peninsular War. Wellington's sage policy towards the provisioning of his army (ie his draconian refusals to countenance looting and pillage, in marked contrast to the French) undoubtedly played a major role in harnessing this resistance in the allied cause.

However, the decisive factors were beyond dispute: the military genius of Wellington and the outstanding calibre of the Anglo-Portuguese army that he commanded. Neither the gallant resistance of the civilian population nor innate logistical problems could alone have extirpated the French from the Peninsula. Wellington acknowledged the services of the Anglo-Portuguese army in a General Order of 21 April 1814, annnouncing the cessation of hostilities and returning 'his best thanks for their uniform discipline and gallantry in the field, and for their conciliating conduct towards the inhabitants of the country.'

He trusted that he they would leave 'with a lasting reputation, not less creditable to their gallantry in the field than to their regularity and good conduct in quarters and camp.'

It is a remarkable feature of Wellington's Peninsular army that, in a century which has witnessed a markedly inconoclastic attitude with regard to military reputations (a movement which was intitiated as a reaction to the First World War), the reputation to which Wellington referred (as well as his own) has remained totally intact and unblemished.

Central features of *Peninsular Sketches*

Immediacy deriving from felt experience

Peninsular Sketches was published in two volumes (Vol I in 1844 and Vol II in 1845). To reiterate, it consists of diverse personal experiences (as opposed to memoirs angled from a single viewpoint). The work is testimony to the enormous popularity of literature relating to the Peninsular War and Waterloo. Capt William Siborne's *Waterloo letters* was published at a virtually identical point in time (1844).

To reiterate a point made above, a most striking feature of the *Peninsular Sketches* is the vigour and energy with which the accounts are related. The key to this trait is the dramatic immediacy which derives from oral testimony (in the sense of personal reminiscence). One is in danger of overlooking the highly innovative and original approach adopted by Maxwell in compiling the *Peninsular Sketches*. For he focused upon an historical source which, in the absence of its transliteration into the printed word, would have been lost to subsequent generations; viz oral history, the value of which has been rediscovered in the succeeding century. Although occasionally supplemented by written sources - such as journals and despatches (which, indeed, disrupt and fragment the flow of the narrative), personal reminiscence remains the key feature of these accounts. The writer of the section relating to the storming of Badajoz speaks for his fellow contributors when he states (Vol I, p 242):

> 'I describe matters, not technically, but exactly according to the impressions they made at the moment and which are still fresh in my recollection'.

In this respect, the work embodies a vital contribution to our understanding of the Peninsular War; in so far as the work graphically captures the tempo and mood of the participants (admittedly confined to officers, in all but one instance). *Peninsular Sketches* exerts an immediate impact upon the reader through the medium of the eye-witness accounts which the editor presents to us. The reader is dramatically thrust into contact with the deeply felt experience of the involved parties. The work thus furnishes an extreme contrast with the featureless prose which distinguishes, for example, the British official history of the First World War, the editors of which, to quote John Keegan, 'have achieved the remarkable feat of writing an exhaustive account of one of the world's greatest tragedies without the display of any emotion at all.' [1] Such an objective, unemotional approach, obviously impoverishes a subject which is profoundly rooted in, and deeply redolent of, human suffering.

There are numerous instances of dramatic immediacy furnished by this individualised approach. For example, in the section entitled, *The capture of Cuidad Rodrigo* (Vol I), we read (pp 245-248):

'The situation in which were were placed was one of extreme danger and embarrassment. Instead of falling into the rear of a column supposed to have already carried the breach, exposed to a tremendous fire of grape and musketry from its defences, while we were in danger of being assaulted in the rear by a sortie through the sally-port in the ditch already mentioned. For a minute we seemed destined to be sacrificed by some mistake as the hour of attack, but suddenly we heard a cheer from a body of men who, crowning the summit of the counterscarp, flung down bags filled with heather to break their fall, and leaped on them into the ditch. It was the old Scotch brigade, which, like us, having been intended as a support, was true to its time, and was consequently placed in the same predicament as ourselves. On the appearance of the 94th, the fire of the garrison was redoubled - and after a moment's consultation between the seniors, it was decided that it was better to die like men in the breach, than like dogs in the ditch, and instantly, with a wild hurra, all sprang upwards, absolutely eating fire. I think the breach must have been seventy or eighty feet wide…

It was now seven o'clock, the breach was carried and the town virtually ours. A voice was heard to shout above the uproar, "They run, they run!" All crowded on the summit of the breach, and some spoke of forming the men on the ramparts; but on that spot there was no safety, for we had rarely attained it, when a deadly fire was opened on us from a breastwork about twenty yards distant and beneath, formed from the ruins of some houses, of loose stones, and lined with men. Many of our people threw themselves on their faces, and that position returned the fire with good effect, as I observed on the following, more than forty of the garrison, lying dead behind the breastwork, shot through their heads - the only part of them exposed to our fire.'

In this chapter the writer vividly recreates the extremely tense atmosphere enveloping the initial approach to the breach (p 240):

'It was a time of thrilling excitement as we made our way by the right; at first preserving the distance of eleven or twelve hundred yards from the town, then bending in towards the convent of Santa Cruz and the river, and gradually narrowing the space betwixt us and the fortifications. The awful stillness of the hour was unbroken save by the soft measured tread of our little columns as we passed over the green turf, or by the occasional report of a cannon from the walls, and the rush and hiss of its ball as it flew past us, or striking short, bounded from the earth over our heads, receiving our most respectful, though involuntary, salaams'.

A striking feature of the accounts relating to the assaults on Badajoz and Cuidad Rodrigo is the vivid recapturing of the claustrophobic atmosphere invariably attendant upon the closely confined physical context of such battle scenarios. In the chapter dealing with the assault on Badajoz (Vol I), we read (pp 277-279):

> 'Whilst descending the ladders into the ditch, a soldier of the 52nd in a hurry growled out a hearty curse, and was very angry at my preceding him, and furious blows were exchanged amongst the troops in their eagerness to go forward; while the grape-shot and musketry fire tore open their ranks. The first officer I happened to see down was Captain Fergusson, who had led on our storming party here, and at Rodrigo; he was lying to the right of our ladders, with a wound on the head, and holding a bloody handkerchief in his grasp. I snatched it out of his hand, and tied it round his head. The French were then handing over the fire-balls, which produced a sort of revolving light. The ditch was very wide, and when I arrived at the foot of the centre breach, eighty or ninety men were formed. One cried out, "Who will lead?" This was the work of a moment. Death, and the most dreadful sounds and cries, encompassed us. It was volcano! Up we went; some killed, and others impaled on the bayonets of their own comrades, or hurled headlong amongst the outrageous crowd...
> When within a yard of the top, my sensations were most extraordinary; I felt half strangled, and fell from a blow that deprived me of sensation. I only recollect feeling a soldier pulling me out of the water, where so many men were drowned...I looked towards the breach. It was shining and empty! Fire balls were in plenty, and the French troops standing upon the walls, taunting, and inviting our men to come up and try again. What a crisis! What a military misery! Some of the finest troops in the world prostrate - humbled to the dust!'

Such impressionistic, subjective writing is highly suggestive of the prose and poetry associated with the personal reminiscences of the Western Front of World War I.

The analogy with the memoirs of the Western Front suggests an important aspect of the above quoted extracts; viz we are immersed in the impressions and reactions of small groups of soldiers. This is an extremely important dimension of military history, as is attested to by John Keegan [2]:

> 'The introduction of the concept of "small groups"…deals a body blow to the assumptions underlying the "win/lose" approach. For if one once admits that the behaviour of a group of soldiers on any part of the battlefield ought to be understood in terms of their corporate mood, or of the conditions there prevailing at the time, indeed in terms of anything but their willingness to do as duty, discipline and orders demand, then the whole idea of the outcome of a battle being determined by one commander's defter manipulation of his masses against his opponents crumbles…[The] relative importance [of such groups] is an unresolved question, and since we appear to know a great deal more about generalship than we do about how ordinary soldiers fight, a diversion of historical effort from the rear to the front of the battlelfield would seem considerably overdue.'

Indeed, the evocative power of the battle scenes described in *Peninsular Sketches* is associated with the work's description of engagements fought between small groups. The scenes relating to the storming of Badajoz and Cuidad Rodrigo clearly exemplifies this point; as also does the incident relating to the capture of the French picket at Blanchez Sanchez (*Capture of the enemy's picket at Blanchez Sanches*, by Sgt Maj William Hanley; Vol II, pp 380-388). In contrast, the description of the set battle pieces, focusing upon the movements of large formations (divisions and brigades) suffer from a definite stereotyped dramatic ritual; a point discussed in greater detail below.

In point of fact, the *Peninsular Sketches*, by effecting this 'diversion of historical effort from the rear to the front of the battlefield' [ie by focusing upon the reactions and responses of the participants in the front line] does provide important clues to those aspects of the soldiers' psychology which were instrumental to the British victories. A vital element in this psychology was the sense of close cameraderie binding commissioned officers to ordinary soldiers, to which numerous anecdotes in the *Sketches* bear witness. Second, one notes an implicit faith in the senior commanders, consistently reiterated, possibly a further symptom of this cameraderie; in this instance deriving, not from the cementing bonds of the regimental tradition, but from the participation of general officers in commonly shared dangers. The incidence of death and wounds suffered by senior commanders is frequently referred to. It may with justice be argued that the *Peninsular Sketches* furnishes a further insight into factors which cemented the morale of British troops, albeit unwittingly. This psychological element relates to the marked lack of introspective thought. The reminiscences of conflict are concentrated on external details and not upon inward reflection. This approach suggests a constructive suppression of the imaginative faculties, in order to reinforce the individual psychology in confronting the terrors of being placed on the extreme borders of extinction.

One must not assume that the time that had elapsed between the original experience and its memory recall necessarily impoverished the quality of the recollection. In this respect, the *Peninsular Sketches* exemplify an important aspect of memory; viz that memories which deeply scar the psychological landscape are retained with great precision, enabling them to be recaptured with fidelity and vividness after the lapse of many years. In his work, *Heroes' twilight: a study of the literature of the Great War* (1965), Bernard Bergonzi incisively remarks on the power of total recall. Discussing Henry Williamson's series of novels relating to World War I (*How dear is life* (1954), *A fox under my cloak* (1955), *The golden virgin* (1957), *Love and the loveless* (1958) and *A test to destruction* (1960), collectively titled *Chronicles of ancient sunlight*) he writes (pp 215-216,218-219):

> 'In fact his [Williamson's] narrative resembles an act of total recall by a patient undergoing analysis. The reader is all but swamped in a flood of indiscriminate detail, with the important and the trivial thoroughly mixed together...Williamson's novel [sequence]...is an impressive work. It is completely readable, and, more important, its unremitting saturation in the atmosphere and material detail of life both in the Army and on the Home Front does leave an accumulative sense of 'felt life', prodigally unselective though it may be...the minuteness of detail of the wartime volumes of Williamson's Chronicle give them an unforgettable quality.'

The above critique of Williamson's novels suggests important points of convergence with the *Peninsular Sketches*; especially the dual impact of felt experience and highly detailed reminiscence. Bergonzi's criticism, in discussing the superfluity of detail, highlights the avoidance of this flaw in the *Sketches*. By relating the reminiscence to a specific limited action, the detail is focused upon an isolated incident, thus eliminating superfluous material in the memory recall. Moreover, Bergonzi's reference to the 'patient undergoing analysis' suggests the psychologically therapeutic value implicit in such memory recall.

Visual power

A notable and striking feature of the *Peninsular Sketches* is what might be termed their painterly quality; viz the work's ability to evoke graphic pictures in the mind of the reader. A notable example of this feature is the account of the aftermath of the battle of Albuera, contained in Vol II (pp 233-234):

> 'Before us lay the appalling sight of upwards of 6000

men, dead, and mostly stark-naked, having, as we were informed, been stripped by the Spaniards during the night; their bodies disfigured with dirt and clotted blood, and torn with the deadly gashes inflicted by the bullet, bayonet, sword or lance, that had terminated their mortal existence. Those who had been killed outright, appeared merely in the palled sleep of death, while others, whose wounds had been less suddenly fatal, from the agonies of their last struggle, exhibited a fearful distortion of features. Near our arms was a small stream almost choked with bodies of the dead, and from the deep traces of blood on its miry margin, it was evident that many of them had crawled hither to allay their last thirst. The waters of this oozing stream were so deeply tinged, that it seemed actually to run blood. A few perches distant was a draw well, above which were collected several hundreds of those severely wounded, who had crept or been carried thither. They were sitting, or lying, in the puddle, and each time the bucket reached the surface with its scanty supply, there was a clamorous and heart-rending confusion, the cries for water resounding in at least ten languages, while a kindness of feeling was visible in the manner this beverage was passed to each other. Turning from this painful scene of tumultuous misery, we again strolled among the mangled bodies. The bodies were seldom scattered about, as witnessed in former battles, but lying in rows and heaps, in several places whole subdivisions [ie units within a battalion] appear to have been frustrated by one tremendous charge or volley'.

The vivid pen portrait of the dead crowded around the river is suggestive of murals relating to the aftermath of the nuclear bombs dropped on Japan, which feature thousands of victims swarming into rivers to allay the desperate thirst induced by radiation.

Central to this painterly quality is the evocation of vivid and concrete detail, clearly exemplified by the above quoted passages. Those details which are thrust upon our inner eye include the pathetic group of wounded feverishly clustered around the draw well; the corpses choking the water, tinged with their blood; the naked corpses, despoiled on the battlefield; the enemy illuminated by the fireballs; Capt Fergusson clasping the blood stained handkerchief in his grasp; the cannon ball ricocheting above the heads of the assaulting party; the soldiers impaled upon the bayonets of their comrades in the oppressive and claustrophobic atmosphere of the breach at Badajoz. Such a literary approach presages the intervention of the photographer in the wars of the present century. *Peninsular Sketches* furnishes the reader with pen portraits that are highly suggestive of the close angled focus of the camera lens, in its recreation of vivid and memorable detail.

Realism

In the above quoted passages, we are presented with a grimly evocative picture of war which, in its intensely realistic detail, is far more akin to the works of Goya or Hogarth than the romanticised illustrations of Victorian artists of the stamp of Lady Butler, Veriker M Hamilton or Caton Woodville.

In this respect, we are introduced to a further important facet of the work; viz the realistic presentation of war. The presentation of war in *Peninsular Sketches* is far removed from the highly romanticised, ritually dramatic approach which moulded historical writing after Waterloo. Such an approach is clearly evident in the conclusion to Capt William Siborne's *History of the war in France and Belgium in 1815* (1844), which concludes:

> 'Such the termination of this ever memorable Battle - a Battle remarkable for the spectacle it afforded, on the one hand of a bravery the most noble and undaunted; of a passive endurance, the most calm, dignified and sublime, of a loyalty and patriotism the most stern and

inflexible: and on the other, of a gallantry in assault the most daring and reckless; of a devotion to their Chief, the most zealous and unbounded; and, lastly, of a physical overthrow and moral annihilation unexampled in the history of modern warfare.
Such was the consummation of a victory, the most brilliant in its development, the most decisive in its operation, and the most comprehensive in its result, of any that has occurred since the bringing to the termination so long and so ardently desired by the suffering and indignant nations of Europe.' [3]

Siborne's impeccably researched, if ponderous, history, thus concludes with a 'sunburst of adjectives' (to quote John Keegan [4]; reflective of the hollow rhetoric and romanticised gloss that was to characterise both the literature and visual arts in relation to military events during the mid- and late-Victorian periods. As John Keegan writes:

'The visual imagination of writer and reader was meanwhile fed by an outpouring of brightly coloured canvases from the studios of an army of successful salon painters - Dighton, Philippoteaux, Raffer, Bellange, Caton Woodville - paintings which by their combination of photographic observation of detail with defiance of physical laws anticipate the work of the Surrealists. Much of the prose imagery of the constantly retold story of Waterloo - flashing sabres, dissolving squares and torrents of horseflesh - has its counterparts, often, one suspects, its origin, in the vision of artists who saw the battlefield, if at all, only as tourists.' [5]

The literary apotheosis of this illusory attitude towards war is embodied in the self-parodying poem, *Charge of the Light Brigade*, by Alfred, Lord Tennyson; in which he writes with a supreme and totally naive confidence of the state of mind of the unhappy cavalrymen forced to charge the Russian guns in the suicidal assaault:

> 'Forward the Light Brigade!
> Was there a man dismay'd?
> Not tho' the soldier knew
> Someone had blunder'd...'

The phrase 'Someone had blunder'd' lacks any ironic implication; the blunder merely renders the glory of the fallen heroes the more spectacular.

The *Peninsular Sketches*, however, is refreshingly free from the shallow artificiality of such military iconography. In contrast, one frequently encounters a grim realism in these pages. This is evident in the passages quoted above, and is also strikingly exemplified in the chapter entitled, *Seven weeks captivity in St. Sebastian in 1813*, by Lt Col Harvey Jones (Vol II, pp 286-311), in which we read (pp 305-306):

> 'After the capture of the town, a heavy bombardment of the castle took place, by salvos of shells from upward of sixty pieces of artillery: the short interval of time which elapsed between the report of the discharge of the guns and mortars, and the noise of the descent of the shell was that of a few seconds only. The effect of these salvos by day, terrific and destructive as they proved, was little heeded in comparison with the nightly discharge. Those of the wounded and mutilated who were fortunate enough to have found temporary relief from their sufferings by sleep, were awakened to all the horrors and misery of their situation by the crash of ten or a dozen shells falling upon and around the building, and whose fuses threw a lurid light into the interior of the ward: the silence within, broken by the hissing of the burning composition; the agonized feelings of the wounded during these few moments of suspense are not to be described. No one could feel assured of escaping the

destruction which was a certain attendant upon the explosion, to be immediately succeeded by the cries and groans of those who were again wounded.

Many an unfortunate soldier was brought to the amputation table to undergo a second operation; and in the discharge of this painful duty the medical men were engaged nearly the entire night...The legs and arms, as soon as amputated, were carried out, and thrown away on the rocks. It was a novel and by no means an agreeable sight, but one which I was daily compelled to witness.'

At an earlier point in this passage, the writer comments (pp 303-304):

'In an instant the ward was crowded with the wounded and maimed; the amputation table again brought into play; and until nearly daylight the following morning the surgeons were increasingly at work. To have such a scene passing at the foot of my bed, was sufficiently painful; added to this, the agonizing shrieks and groans, and the appearance of the grenadiers and sappers, who had been blown up by the explosions on the breach - their uniforms nearly burnt off, and their skins blackened and scorched by gunpowder - was truly appalling, the recollection of which can never be effaced from the memories of those whose ill fate compelled them to witness it. The appearance of these men resembled anything but human beings: death soon put an end to their sufferings, and relieved us from these distressing sights. Of all wounds, whether of fractured limbs or otherwise, those occasioned by burns from gunpowder appeared to be accompanied with the most excruciating pain and suffering.'

The images of the death agonies of the blackened, scorched

victims of the siege of St Sebastian, their amputated limbs thrown out of the windows of the hospital onto the rocks beneath, whilst the wounded inmates of the ward cower beneath the terrifying nightly bombardment - propelling shells into the hospital ward, illuminated by the fuzes - affords a most powerful and graphic contrast to the conventional stereotyped treatment of war current in Victorian art and literature.

The *Peninsular Sketches* thus dramatically undermines the illusory heroic attitude towards war. In this respect, one is reminded of Stendahl's classic, *La Chatreuse de Parma*, a superbly written novel which features Fabrice del Dongo's misadventures on the field of Waterloo. Overflowing with martial aspirations and eager for a place in the fight, Fabrice plunges into the battle and encounters a scene of inextricable confusion. Neither he nor anyone else can grasp the pattern of events, and there is little opportunity to perform the role of hero. Fabrice daydreams of glory and is thrilled to catch a sight of florid Marshal Ney, one of his heroes. But Stendahl ironically contrasts his state of mind with the reality that surrounds him; the carnage and spreading disorder of an army in retreat. The author provides the sharply observed and bloody detail that one more readily associated with writers of the Great War, of the stamp of Barbusse's *Under fire* or Remarque's *All quiet on the Western Front*:

> 'What most impressed him was the mud on the feet of the corpse, which had been stripped of its shoes and of everything else, indeed, except a wretched pair of blood-stained trousers…The corpse was hideously disfigured. A bullet had entered near the nose and passed out at the opposite temple. One eye was open and staring.'

We are instantly reminded of the naked, bloodstained corpses encountered on the field of Albuera, referred to above. A little later, Fabrice encounters a wounded horse, its hooves entangled in its own entrails, and reflects: 'Well, I am under fire at last. Now I am a real soldier!'. The analogy with

Stendahl's novel underlines two important features of *Peninsular Sketches*. First, the graphic prose style of the latter is clearly suggestive of the intervention of the accomplished novelist. Second, one is alerted to the interrelated character of certain central features of the *Sketches*. The realistic vision of war presented to us is inseparable from the evocation of - frequently harrowing - vivid detail which generates, in turn, the dramatic immediacy of events and painterly qualities discussed above.

The set battle piece

The weakest elements in *Peninsular Sketches* are those relating to set battle pieces; notably Albuera, Arroyo de Molinos, Salamanca, and Vittoria. The reason for this is the loss of the individualised vantage point which is a major characteristic of the work, as has been discussed in detail above. This statement does not imply, however, that such passages are devoid of impact or power. They manifest a thunderous rhythm and are tremendously powerful in emotional impact, virtually vibrating on the page. For example, we read in Vol II (*The battle of Vittoria*, pp 48-49):

> 'We closed up to them, behind a bank; when with loud huzzas they rushed from behind it, into the village of Ariyez, with fixed bayonets, amidst flashing small arms and rolling artillery, and after a bloody struggle carried it. The enemy's artillery was within two hundred yards of us, ploughing the ground in our rear: fotunately, the bank nearly covered us, during the time it was necessary to remain active, to support the attack if necessary...For ten minutes..., what with dust and smoke, it was impossible to distinguish any objects in front, save the shadows of the French artillerymen serving the guns, and the shouts of the troops while forcing their way into the village. The smoke had no sooner cleared away, than we came upon the bodies of many dead and grasping soldiers

> stretched in the dust. The sharp fire of musketry and artillery in the centre announced it to be the point of contest. The advance of the second division had been severely handled on the mountains of our right, but they were now getting on as speedily as the nature of the ground would admit; it being composed of deep ravines, and such natural obstacles as almost to delay their progress unopposed...
>
> The different divisions in the centre were exposed to a desultory fire, while passing the villages of Gomecha and Luazu de Alva, and over broken ground, forming lines, columns, or threading the windings of difficult paths, according to the nature of the country, or the opposition of the enemy.'

The text captures, with admirable effect, the rhythm of the troops' advance, evoking with great effect the tempo and atmosphere of the action and concisely indicating the tactical positions with total clarity. However, such passages, with the exception of isolated instances focusing upon individual participants - as in the case of the Spanish guide being decapitated by a cannon ball, related at an earlier point in this chapter, or the description of the Portuguese officer who falls weeping into the arms of another officer (p 45 and pp 48-49 respectively) - submerge the role of the eye-witness observer to a mere cypher; the inevitable consequence of the focus being directed upon the movement of compact masses of soldiers. (Maxwell clearly lacked the tremendous imaginative power of Tolstoy, whose great battle scenes in *War and Peace* - focusing upon Borodino (1812), the Russian equivalent of Waterloo in its impact upon the historical memory - combine Stendahl's cruel detail and awareness of confusion with a vast panoramic overview that dwarfs all the participants - whether generals or ordinary soldiers - reducing them to mere agents of the irreversible historical process. Also in the Tolstoyan manner - albeit on a far smaller scale - is Stephen Crane's astonishing recreation of a war that he had never experienced, in *The red badge of courage*).

This process is synonymous with the process whereby the editor assumes total control of the text, the necessary balance between 'actors on the scene' (to quote the sub-title of *Peninsular Sketches*) and editorial intervention being destroyed. One may effectively demonstrate this point by a comparison with extracts quoted above, relating to the accounts of Badajoz, Cuidad Rodrigo and St Sebastian. One may surmise that Maxwell extensively edited his sources (be they in the form of written documents or oral communication). However, despite this fact, the highly individualised reactions and responses are starkly highlighted in such accounts. But, to reiterate, the description of the set battle piece invariably develops into an exercise in that military inconography discussed above. (One should nevertheless note that Maxwell's style is never entirely free of stereotyped cliches, as in the use of such phrases as 'measured tread'). The essence of the sketch (to adopt the metaphor embodied in the title) is its highly individualised interpretation. In the battle scenes, however (to pursue this artistic metaphor) the sketch is supplanted by the salon painting. The editor is no longer the literary vehicle of the 'actors on the scene' but, rather, the receptacle of the style of established historians. In Maxwell's case this model is, obviously, Lt Gen Sir William Napier, whose epochal *History of the war in the Peninsula and the south of France* is referred to at several points in the text. The kinship with Napier becomes immediately apparent when one studies that historian's description of the advance of the Fusilier Brigade (7th Royal Fusiliers and 23rd Royal Welsh Fusiliers) at the battle of Albuera (16 May 1811). This advance is generally regarded as the crucial moment in the battle (of which Napier was not an eye-witness, having been wounded at Fuentes d'Onor a fortnight previously):

> 'Such a gallant line, issuing from the midst of the smoke and rapidly separating itself from the confused and broken multitude, startled the enemy's masses, then augmenting and pressing forward as to an assured

victory; they wavered, hesitated and, vomiting forth a storm of fire, hastily endeavoured to enlarge their front, while a fearful discharge of grape from their artillery whistled through the British ranks. Myers was killed, Cole, the three colonels, Ellis, Blakeney and Hawkshaw, fell wounded, and the fusilier battalions, struck by the iron tempest, reeled and staggered like sinking ships: but suddenly and sternly recovering, they closed on their terrible enemies, and then was seen with what strength and majesty the British soldier fights. In vain did Soult with voice and gesture animate the Frenchmen; in vain did the hardiest veterans, breaking from the crowded columns, sacrifice their lives to gain time for the mass to open out on such a far field; in vain did the mass itself bear up, and fiercely striving fire indiscriminately upon friends and foes, while the horsemen hovering on the flank threatened to charge the advancing line. Nothing could stop that advancing infantry. No sudden burst of undisciplined valour, no nervous enthusiasm weakened the stability of their order, their flashing eyes were bent on the dark columns in the front, their measured tread shook the ground, their dreadful volleys swept away the head of every formation, deafening shouts overpowered the dissonant cries that broke from all parts of the tumultuous crowds, as slowly and with as horrid carnage it was pushed by the incessant vigour of the attack to the farthest edge of the height. There the French reserve, mixing with the struggling multitude, endeavoured to restore the fight but only augmented the irremediable disorder, and the mighty mass, giving way like a loosened cliff, went headlong down the steep: the rain flowed after in streams discoloured with blood, and eighteen hundred unwounded men, the remnant of six thousand British soldiers, stood triumphant on the fatal hill.' [6]

INTRODUCTION

It is instructive to compare the above quoted passage with the account of the same battle - Albuera - contained in *Peninsular Sketches, Vol II (Recollections of the late war in Spain and Portugal,* by J Emerson, pp 243-242), in which we read (pp 237-238):

'About eight o'clock on the morning of the 16th, the enemy began to move from the wood seen in front, which till that time had concealed their numbers. Soon after, several columns advanced towards the river, one of which immediately crossed on the right, and commenced a vigorous attack on the Spaniards, while others attempted to pass at fords and at the bridge. The Spaniards, consisting of the united corps of Generals Blake, Castonos, and Ballasteros, defended themselves with the utmost bravery, but were at length driven from their position, leaving behind them ample and indubitable proofs of the obstinate valour by which it had been maintained. From this post the enemy's artillery was now enabled to rake the field, and scattered death throughout our line. Before attempting its recovery, it became necessary to change our front, and while executing this manoeuvre, a large body of French lancers, which had for some time been hovering about, dashed between the open divisions, and in the confusion that ensued, a dreadful havoc was made before they could be expelled.'

It is further instructive to quote the passage from *Peninsular Sketches* relating to the battle of Vittoria (Vol II, pp 28-54), in which we read (pp 48-49):

'We closed up to them, behind a bank; when with loud huzzas they rushed from behind it, into the village of Ariyez, with fixed bayonets, amidst flashing small arms and rolling artillery, and after a bloody struggle carried it. The enemy's artillery was within two hundred yards of us, ploughing the ground in our rear: fortunately, the bank nearly covered us during the time it was necessary to remain inactive, to support the front attack if needful. A Portuguese regiment, attached to our brigade, had been detached for a short time, and rejoined in close column; but just before they reached the cover, some round shot tore open their centre, and knocked over many men; and such was the alarm of a Portuguese officer, by the whizzing of balls and bursting of field shells, that he fell into an officer's arms, weeping bitterly. For ten minutes at this point what with dust and smoke, it was impossible to distinguish any objects in Front, save the shadows of the French artillerymen serving the guns, and the shouts of the troops while forcing their way into the village.'

All three passages clearly reflect the strong impress of Romantic prose, rich in imagery and thunderous in rhythm. Napier's 'deafening shouts' and the 'dissonant cries' of the French soldiers are literal sound effects that have their clear echoes in the 'loud huzzas' and 'shouts of the soldiers' relating to Maxwell's account of Vittoria, quoted above. The 'vigorous attack', 'utmost bravery' and the 'obstinate valour' mentioned in Maxwell's account of Albuera is reflected in the 'disciplined valour', 'stability', 'order' cited in Napier's description. One also encounters the predilection for romantic similes: 'vomiting forth a storm of fire', 'fearful discharge of grape', and 'iron tempest' of Napier's account having its counterpart in the description of Vittoria ('flashing small arms', 'rolling artillery', 'bloody struggle' and 'ploughing the ground') and the 'scattered death' of Maxwell's version of Albuera.

Moreover, in addition to this important question of the balance between editor and contributor, one must broach the question of the accuracy of such accounts. Does, for example, a body of men advancing under heavy musketry and artillery fire, engaged in a 'bloody struggle' in which a high proportion would suffer wounds and death as a result of their actions, suffer no hestitation whatsoever (albeit trained soldiers)? Can their reactions be adequately summarised in terms of 'obstinate valour' and 'utmost bravery'? Moreover, in the account of Vittoria, we are led to ask: How, precisely, were the villages captured - by the push of the bayonet? by virtue of superior numbers? by hand to hand fighting? by panic erupting among the ranks of the French? The same questions apply to Napier's narrative. Precisely how, we are tempted to ask, did the 'mighty mass' yield 'like a loosened cliff'?

The impact of the picaresque

As stated above, the tradition of the picaresque novel is a highly significant feature of Maxwell's literary career, and exercises a strong impress upon the *Peninsular Sketches*. The term 'picaresque' derives from the Spanish 'picaro', a disreputable character who lived on his wits. The form of novel which features the wily trickster first appeared in 16th Century Spain, with the anonymous, *Lazarillo de Tormes* (1553) and Aleman's *Guzman de Alfarache* (1599-1604). The latter work relates the histories of ingenuous rogues, the servants of several masters who eventually repent the error of their ways. The term 'picaro' came to be extended to any character who did not conform to society's norms. The picaresque novel - characterized by an episodic narrative describing the adventures of the picaro - was eventually to appear in the mainstream of all western European literature. *Don Quixote*, (Part I, 1605; Part II, 1615) for example, is told in the picaresque form. Le Sage's *Gil Blais* (1715-1735) (to which there is a reference in *Peninsular Sketches*) and Hans Jacob Christophe's von Grimmelhausen's *Simplicissimus* (1669) are futher illustrations of this genre. In English literature, the tradition is initiated in Thomas Nashe's *The unfortunate traveller* (1594). Examples in the English literary tradition would be *Moll Flanders* (1722) (Daniel Defoe), *Tom Jones* (1749) (Henry Fielding) and *Roderick Random* (1748) (Tobias Smollett). *Roderick Random* is an almost perfect embodiment of the picaresque novel, in the tradition of *Gil Blais*. Smollett's novel comprises a series of episodes, told with vigour and vividness, loosely connected with the theme of the selfish and unprincipled hero, who relates the incidents. Its chief interest is the picture that it provides, drawn from personal experience, of the British Navy and the British sailor of the day. Much of the story is repulsive. The kinship with Maxwell's fiction is apparent. The term 'picaresque' first appears in English usage during the 19th Century. To a certain extent the novels of Dickens (especially the *Pickwick Papers* (1837) exemplifies the picaresque tradition. In the English literary tradition, the picaresque novel eventually attained the form of an episodic story involving a journey. William Makepeace Thackeray's *Barry Lyndon* (1844) is a further Victorian exemplar of this genre. (Most appropriately, it is set in the 18th Century). In the United States the picaresque novel exercised an obvious influence on Mark Twain's *The adventures of Tom Sawyer* (1876), *The adventures of Huckleberry Finn* (1884) and many later works describing the adventures of the open road. *The golden ass of Apuleius* by Apuleius (born circa 124 AD) is generally regarded as the forerunner of the picaresque novel.

As intimated above, the picaresque tradition – focused upon the episodic narrative centred upon a journey – closely informs Maxwell's literary career. Indeed, one notes the curious fact that Maxwell, in his personal life, personifies the picaresque tradition, in two important respects. First, he was clearly of an adventurous disposition. One notes his service in the Army, and the contemplation of mercenary service in South America; and, as we have seen, adventurousness is a marked feature of the picaresque hero. Second, the roguish element in the traditional picaro is certainly not absent in Maxwell's life. One gains the impression of an opportunist (marrying for financial security, the acceptance of a living in order to develop his sporting inclinations). A certain fecklessness – also characteristic of the picaresque hero – is a further marked feature of his life. That life, indeed, conformed to the fate of the hero of the picaresque novel, of the stamp of *Barry*

Lyndon); two squandered inheritances (that of his father and wife) ending in destitution. His novels, of the stamp of *Captain O'Sullivan* and *The fortunes of Hector O'Halloran* clearly echo the heritage bequeathed by Defoe, Fielding and Smollett, in the episodic character of the narrative. The fragmentary experiences encountered by officers serving in the Peninsula - which forms a consistent motif of the *Peninsular Sketches* (and, indeed, constitutes one of its most charming aspects) - is, essentially, a non-fiction embodiment of the traveller encountering various disconnected adventures, which shapes the picaresque novel. There are numerous instances of such experiences in the *Sketches*. One has, for example, the incident of the child rescued from the well, who is subsequently adopted by a wealthy British officer (*Venturinho Do Poco*, Vol II, pp 367-372); the experiences of an officer in the course of a night's journey (*A night in the Peninsular War*, by Dr James Byron Bradley: Vol II, pp 187-204); *Dolores: an incident in the Peninsular War* (Vol II, pp 260-269), which recounts the familiar (and timeless) story of the 'native girl' betrayed by a soldier with false promises of marriage (the theme of Puccini's *Madam Butterfly*). A typically striking illustration is the piece entitled, *Marshal Beresford* (Vol II, pp 337-343), which provides a grimly detailed anecodate centring upon the surgical practices of the time. One almost flinches as one feels the surgeon's fingers entering the wound, probing for the bullet. A further illustration of the picaresque tradition is contained in a piece entitled, *Santarem* (Vol II, pp 359-367), in which the writer relates his increasingly desperate efforts to procure transport for three Portuguese girls who wish to convey their bed-ridden grandmother to safety by leaving Santarem. Such incidents furnish charming cameos of the Portuguese and Spanish people with whom the British Army came into contact; albeit the tone of the writing may well appear alien to the modern reader, being couched in the romanticised idealism ('sensibility') evident in the early 19th Century novel. A further notable illustration is that of the case of Pte Evans (*Military retribution*, Vol II, pp 349-356). Pte Jones, a veteran, bayonets a severely wounded casualty of the French force, after the latter had pleaded for water. It transpires that the wounded man was in fact a Pte Evans, who had deserted the night before the battle of Corunna. One also reads of the silently grieving dog at the grave of General Rousseau; the pet being adopted by Gen Sir Thomas Graham, and the dog residing for many years with the general in his new home (*Anecdote of Barossa*, Vol II, pp 356-357).

The tradition of the travel narrative

The picaresque tradition of the English literary heritage - focused upon the journey and the experiences of the wanderer encountered in its progress - serves as a natural vehicle for the travel narrative, which exerted a dominant impress upon English literature during the 18th and early 19th Centuries. Henry Fielding embodies the fusion of the two traditions of the travel narrative and the picaresque novel. His work, *The journal of a voyage to Lisbon* (1755) is a sharply observed but unavoidably depressing account of his final travels. The vogue for travel literature was a marked feature of the 18th Century reading public. Especially noteworthy works in this genre were James Cooks's *A voyage towards the South Pole and round the world*, published in 1777; and *A voyage to the Pacific Ocean*, by the same author, published in 1784. Both works enjoyed a continuing appeal in the succeeding century. (Indeed, this interest greatly captured the Romantic imagination, and pervaded the poetry of the period (as in Coleridge's *Rime of the ancient mariner* (1798)).

The interest fired by Cook was continued in Captain William Bligh's *Narrative of the mutiny on board the Bounty* (1790) and *A voyage to the South Sea* (1792). These works which disclose numerous classical themes: the drama of the mutiny; the long hazard of the open-boat voyage; the recurrent individual tragedies and the privations and contrivances that eventually brought the survivors to land. Probably one of the finest achievements of 18th Century travel literature is Samuel Johnson's *Journey to the western islands of Scotland* (published in 1775), the record of a journey which he undertook to this region in conjunction with James Boswell in 1775. The latter's separate account of the tour (*Journal of a tour to the Hebrides with Samuel Johnson* (1785)) is casual and anecdotal. Johnson, in contrast, offers to the reader a formal survey. He journeys to Scotland with the hope of exploring the variety and extent of nature, particularly human nature. Daniel Defoe's *A tour thro' the whole island of Great Britain* (3 vols, 1724-1727) is an outstanding evocative guide.

The influence of this genre exerted a strong impress on the literary career of Maxwell, as his travel books, cited above, clearly bear witness. The genre forms a strong shaping influence on the *Peninsular Sketches*, which serves as a vehicle for picturesque and vivid recreations of the geography - both human and physical - of the Iberian Peninsula. Its landscape - so often traversed by the contending armies - is memorably explored by the wanderers in that terrain; exposing the multifarious aspects of the people. The poverty of the Portuguese peasantry exerted a strong impression upon the British observers (*Recollections of the late war in Spain and Portugal*, by J Emerson: Vol II, pp 205-242):

> 'They are deficient in the most common necessaries of household use. In all our wanderings in either kingdom, we never saw an iron pot, pan, bellows, spinning wheel...Throughout the country towns and villages of Portugal, especially in the northern provinces, the common people were sunk in the utmost poverty. In their miserable hovels were rarely any beds, the people lying on mats, without any covering except the filthy rags they wore during the day. Their chief food was coarse bread, and of rye or Indian meal, kidney beans, picked olive-berries, dried figs or grapes, and sometimes a few potatoes.'

The urban centres are portrayed with no less graphic detail.

The section entitled, *Leaves from the journal of a veteran*, by Maj Patterson (Vol I, pp 21-50) graphically evokes the atmosphere and social tempo of Coruna:

> 'The streets, like those of other walled towns, are regularly planned, and were, though narrow, paved throughout with large flag stones, which were kept in the cleanest order by criminals, who were marched out daily from the prisons, chained in pairs, for that service, and whose iron fetters, clanking upon the ear with a somewhat dismal sound, producing a degree of melancholy in the strangers' mind.'

This section is characterised by detailed observation of individuals, suggestive of a Hogarth print:

> 'Amongst the convicts were a male and female linked together by the ankles, with a chain about a yard in length, which they dragged after them apparently with considerable pain while drudging at their task; the man working away with a scraper as far as the limit of his chain permitted, the woman with a broom.' (p 23)

A dominant impression formed by the observers of the Spanish people is one of primitive cruelty, illustrated in the following extract from the above quoted chapter, relating to Castello Branco (p 33):

> 'A Spanish nobleman...was doomed to an awful and cruel death. His body, after strangulation, was cut in quarters, each of which being fixed on lofty gibbets, adorned, or rather disgraced, the four extremities of the fortress; the mutilated remnants of the Marquis hung in this way, a prey to vultures and bleaching in the wind.'

The impression of a latent cruelty in the Spanish character is shared by another observer, Lt Col Wilkie, who authors the section entitled, *Recollections of the Peninsula* (Vol II, pp 246-259). Lt Col Wilkie regards the bull fight as exemplifying this trait. He writes (p 255):

> 'On occasions of great festivals, this plaza [of Salamanca] is converted into an amphitheatre for that barbarous amusement of the Spaniards, the bull-fight...administering to that innate love of cruelty which forms so large an ingredient in the character of the Spaniard.'

He writes of 'the torment and death of a poor animal, and the interesting spectacle of horses gored by the beast in its excited rage moving about the arena with their bowels trailing on the ground'.

In this evocation of mindless cruelty - embodied in the indelible impression of the mutilated animals - we are transported into the uncompromising world of Goya. The Spanish, marked by a deep hostility to the British, are most unfavourably contrasted with the Portuguese, in terms of both military prowess and disposition.

The vivid descriptions of the Peninsula are widely variegated, encompassing the hospitality received in the various religious institutions and farming methods, the primitiveness of the latter being detailed in the section entitled, *Recollections of the late war in Spain and Portugal*, by J Emerson, Vol II, pp 205-242):

> 'The agriculture of these countries appeared universally defective; the most common implements of tillage were either unknown, or of the rudest description; and the soil, though sandy, or of a loose mould, was so imperfectly cultivated, that the surface seemed merely scratched. Their ploughs were without iron, or any other metal, having only one handle, and so truly

> simple, as to resemble a branch lopped off a tree, with the end for turning over the earth with a hatchet or knife...Their harrows are entirely of wood; we never observed either spade, shovel, gripe or any implements likely to answer for similar purposes.' (p 217)

The daily toil of the peasantry is rendered with characteristically concrete detail:

> 'We often witnessed men going out to labour, carrying the ploughs under their arm, and driving before them the bullock or cow...In a few places in the northern parts of Spain, when the earth was heavy, they turned it over with a kind of hoe, and in one instance, a number of men were seen raising a rich loamy ground, with iron prongs fastened on a pole, about three feet in length. Those persons struck down their forks together into the earth, and turned over the soil with the like union of strength. They were followed by women, who, with wooden mallets, broke the large lumps or clods thus cast over. The process of separating the grain from the straw was performed in an equally primitive manner, being trodden out by the feet of cattle.'

We are thus presented with the image of an extremely backward, 'third world' society, plunged in ignorance and, in the case of Spain, an inherent cruelty. It is, of course, impossible to ascertain the extent to which these judgements are coloured by the sub-conscious prejudices of a society which is predominantly Protestant, confronted with peoples who represent a bastion of Catholicism. However, the vivid nature with which the societies of the Iberian Peninsula are portrayed suggest that these judgements are fundamentally free of pre-determined prejudice and essentially impartial. The alien character of the societies of the Peninsula was, indeed, probably the major source of the work's appeal with regard to the dimension of the travel narrative.

Maxwell as editor

It has to be admitted that Maxwell undertook his role as editor in an undeniably cavalier fashion (to employ the most charitable phrase). There are numerous instances of an undeniably feckless approach to the editorial task; manifested in the following areas:

— With regard to historical detail, the text presents a decided lack of clarity. For example, in Vol I, both Lord Paget and General Paget are referred to (cf entries in Index to Vol I and accompanying note). The two individuals are distinct (Gen Edward Paget and Lord Henry Paget) and both served in the Peninsula during the period 1808-1809 (although only the former served in the war subsequently). Yet the editor makes no distinction between the two, and the non-specialist reader could be excused for assuming the references refer to the same person.

— With regard to regimental designations, one finds the reference to the 1st Hussars. In actual fact, the Light Dragoon (subsequently Hussar) regiments were numbered from 7 upwards. The confusion arises from the fact that the 7th Light Dragoons were the first such regiment to be converted to Hussars. One also notes the reference to the '1st Rifles', in fact referring to the 1st Bn of the 95th Rifles (Vol II, p 45). Further, there are numerous references to units which the reader finds it difficult to identify other than by inference, through consulting the previous or succeeding text. Thus, the contributors frequently refer to 'the division', 'our regiment', etc, and the reader must construe the formation being referred to. For example, in Vol I, the writer of the section entitled, *Events subsequent to the battle, and advance from Salamamca* (pp 349-389) may be construed as a member of a unit contained within the Light Division (ie the 52nd Regiment). One may thus assume, with a certain degree of confidence, that the Light Division is being referred to in the first section of the succeeding volume, as it would appear to be a continuation of the final chapter of Vol I.

— The confusion is compounded by the fact that different titles are accorded to the final section of Vol I, and the first chapter of Vol II. However, whilst Vol II continues the final chapter of Vol II, there is no editorial comment to inform the reader that this is in fact the case, which must be inferred. This instance alerts us to a central weakness in the structure of the book; viz the dispersal of material. This dispersal is manifest both spatially and chronologically. With regard to the spatial dispersal of material, one notes that the battle of Albuera is described on pp 237-238 of Vol II (cf above) (*Recollections of the late war in Spain and Portugal*). Yet a further description of the battle, featuring the 29th Regiment, is contained in the same volume, entitled *The twenty-ninth at Albuera*. Moreover, an anecdote relating to Sir William Inglis is contained in a separate section (Vol II, pp 358-359). Similarly, in Vol II one has a section entitled, *The Heavy Cavalry at Salamanca* (pp 373-380), separated from a section entitled, *The British cavalry in the Peninsula* (Vol I, pp 197-132). Further, the section relating to the Heavy Cavalry at Salamanca is separated from the discussion of the battle of Salamanca, which occurs in Vol I (pp 321-348). In terms of chronology, the discussion of the battle of Albuera (which appears in Vol II) succeeds campaigns and battles fought at later points in time (Cuidad Rodrigo, Badajoz and Salamanca), and which appear in Vol I. In Vol II the description of the siege of St Sebastian (1813) immediately precedes the battle of Arroyo de Molinos (1811). It is possible that the matereial contained in Vol II became accessible after the publication of Vol I, which would excuse the dispersal of related material over two volumes. However, one should note that each volume consists of exactly 389 pages; suggesting that the subject matter contained in both was accessible at one point in time, and that the publisher (Henry Colburn) decided to stagger publication over two years; in which case the editorial culpability for the poor organisation of material cannot be dismissed. Further, even if the material contained in Vol II was not available at the time of the publication of Vol I, it cannot excuse both the chronological and spatial dispersal of material contained within the same volume.

This faulty organisation of material underlines the isolated character and fragmentation of the accounts. The episodic approach characteristic of the picaresque novel can prove a frustrating device when applied to the study of military history. Thus, in reading the *Peninsular Sketches* one cannot avoid the impression of a serious lack of continuity; that absence of a connecting thread, referred to above.

— The various bibliographical sources referred to are invariably vague. Thus, on p 8 of Vol I a source is simply attributed to 'Southey'. We may infer that the authority referred to is Robert Southey, but no title is cited. We are left to speculate as to which of Southey's numerous publications (eg *Letters written in Spain and Portugal* (1797), *History of the Peninsular War* (1823-1832)) is being referred to. One may assume it to be the *History of the Peninsular War*, but one cannot be absolutely certain on this point. Similarly, one finds in both volumes references to 'Jones', the author of 'Journal of Sieges', referring to the work by Maj Gen Sir John Thomas Jones, entitled *Journals of the sieges undertaken by the Allies in Spain* (1814). In a similar vein, we are not informed that the work, *Victories of the British Army* was authored by Maxwell. Lord Londonderry's work, *Narrative of the Peninsular War from 1808-1813* (1828). Details of such publications would no doubt have been readily available to Maxwell.

— There is no standardised spelling, especially with regard to place names, which often vary not only in different volumes, but sometimes within the same chapter. Thus, one has reference to both St Jean du Port and St John du Port, and St Jean de Luz and St John de Luz within Vol II. Similarly, the place 'Echelar' is sometimes spelt 'Etchelar'.

— It is readily apparent that the majority of contributors to the *Sketches* are anonymous. One is tempted to speculate whether Maxwell is in fact the author of these sections.

— The total absence of maps is to be regretted in a text which records the movements of armies and the topography of the Iberian Peninsula, often in considerable detail.

It is generally conceded that Maxwell was a careless writer, and this trait is clearly evident in his editorial role. The current edition has sought to overcome certain of the problems discussed above. The lack of continuity, symptomatic of the dispersed and fragmented material, is compensated for by the element in the Introductory Essay which seeks to provide an overview of the Peninsular War. The index indicates variations in the spelling of place names and individuals, and also seeks to clarify potential confusions relating to personalities (as in the case of the Paget brothers) and regimental designations; as well as providing full bibliographical details of sources referred to in the text.

However, despite this undoubtedly flawed approach to the material, this cannot obscure the essential intrinsic appeal and vibrancy of the subject matter itself. Indeed, the undeniably feckless approach to the editorial task - so vastly distanced from the rigorous demands of modern scholarship - constitutes a certain charm within itself.

Concluding observations

To reiterate, the strength and value of the *Peninsular Sketches* resides within a specific context; viz the power of personal reminiscences and anecdotes to capture the tempo and atmosphere of war. It is for this reason that the description of the set battle pieces represent the weakest and least enduring aspects of the work. For the *Peninsular Sketches* encapsulates the unique contribution of oral history (ie records conveyed through memory recall), whilst the descriptions of the set battle pieces have been recapitulated - often without variation - on countless occasions, both previous to the book's publication and subsequently. The value of the work is thus anchored in the sphere of individualised impressions. Such responses and reactions project the images and atmosphere of conflict with an often terrifying immediacy; often through the impression of grimly realistic detail upon the reader's consciousness. As intimated above, the source of personal reminiscence generates the central, memorable features of the work. The infusion of deeply felt experience into the descriptive passages create the interrelated features of dramatic immediacy, powerful visual detail and a grim realism. In these respects, the work possesses a curious modernity, expressed through its convergence with the literature of the Great War. At the heart of that convergence is the subjective impressions relating the movement of small bodies of troops, experienced in the psychologically therapeutic act of total recall. However, in another respect *Peninsular Sketches* is a striking exemplar of the 18th Century literary tradition. For the work is shaped by the literary heritage of the picaresque novel and the travel narrative. There is a curious paradox at the heart of *Peninsular Sketches*, implicit in its essential modernity, referred to above. Despite its obvious historical context, that of the Peninsular War, one is impressed by the timelessness of the reminiscences. The discussion of tactics and weapons technology which are manifestly antiquated in the modern world (eg the muzzle loading artillery, bayonet, etc), and the description of set battle pieces in terms of the stereotyped imagery of Romantic prose, cannot, ultimately, obscure this essential modernity. A further intriguing feature of the *Sketches* is the manner in which the material reflects both the literary personality and biographical profile of the editor. With regard to the former, the picaresque tradition which strongly shaped his fiction is translated into the novelettish experiences and episodic narrative form encountered in the *Sketches*; whilst his feckless personality is both a personification of that tradition and a determining factor in his role of editor.

S. Monick
May 2001

Bibliographical sources referred to above

(1) Keegan, John. *The face of battle: a study of Agincourt, Waterloo and the Somme.* London: Barrie & Jenkins, 1988, p 30.

(2) Op cit item (1) above, p 46.

(3) Op cit item (1) above, p 104.

(4) Op cit item (1) above, p 103.

(5) Op cit item (1) above, p 104.

(6) Op cit item (1) above, p 35.

CONTENTS

OF

THE FIRST VOLUME.

	PAGE
INTRODUCTION	v
THE ENGLISH IN SPAIN	1
LEAVES FROM THE JOURNAL OF A VETERAN	21
THE BRITISH CAVALRY ON THE PENINSULA	51
THE BRITISH CAMPAIGN OF 1809, UNDER SIR ARTHUR WELLESLEY	64
RECOLLECTIONS IN QUARTERS	218
THE CAPTURE OF CIUDAD RODRIGO	225
THE STORMING OF BADAJOZ	267, 304
THE BATTLE OF SALAMANCA	321
EVENTS SUBSEQUENT TO THE BATTLE, AND ADVANCE FROM SALAMANCA	349

INTRODUCTION.

THIRTY years have elapsed since the last of the events recorded in the following pages took place, and the British colours, after floating triumphantly over many a glorious battle-field, were cased in honourable peace, upon the banks of the Adour. In the stream of time, the names of those who were busy actors in those stirring scenes are fading fast away. The chief "rests under the grey stone"—the soldier finds an humbler grave—veteran after veteran disappears—the hero of Aire —the glorious old man of Barossa, have gone to their accounts. Of those whose onward stride to victory, fortress could not stay nor mountain bar, a few alone are left, and in that honoured number, thank God!

"He, the chieftain of them all,"

fortunately for his country, is still included.

If ever there was in European history an epoch of all engrossing interest, it was that stormy interval occurring between the landing of a British army in the Mondego, and its embarkation, the fifth year afterwards, in the Garonne. During that eventful era the Continent was in a blaze; every hamlet, from Paris to the Kremlin, had trembled at the roar of "red artillery," and from the descendant of the Cæsars to the little potentate—"royal but in name,"—all had felt the iron rod, and bent, in turn, to the conqueror.

One happier land boasted a proud immunity, and no foeman's foot had crossed the sea-girthed barrier of England. When all besides were prostrate at Napoleon's feet, whence came her security? Her appeal to arms had been made under another sky, and to preserve "happy homes and altars free," her sons had freely bled. Her marvellous resources lavishly, but wisely dispensed,* encou-

* "Within twelve months from the commencement of the war, she sent over to the Spanish armies (besides £2,000,000) 150 pieces of field artillery, 42,000 rounds of ammunition, 200,000 muskets, 61,000 swords, 79,000 pikes, 23,000,000 ball cartridges, 6,000,000 leaden balls, 15,000 barrels of gunpowder, 92,000 suits of clothing, 356,000 sets of accoutrements and pouches, 310,000 pairs of shoes, 37,000 pairs of boots, 40,000 tents, 250,000 yards of cloth, 10,000 sets of camp equipage, 118,000 yards of linen, 50,000 great coats, 50,000 canteens, 54,000 havresacks, with a variety of other stores, far too numerous to be recapitulated."—JONES'S ACCOUNT OF THE WAR.

raged the bold, re-animated the despairing, and made the influence of the island-empire felt and feared, wide as the world of waters itself; or, as Talleyrand so happily expressed it — "wherever there was water to float a frigate, there English dominion extended."

The arduous struggle to which we have alluded, and one that achieved the deliverance of the Continent, from the opening action of Roliça to the crowning victory at Toulouse, may be found, in most of its important occurrences, faithfully described in the present volumes; which, for the first time, give the details of those past events in a collected form to the world—while without the dry formality of history, many of these documents will strike the reader, as possessing a fresh and graphic power of description which more learned writers labour at in vain.

Narratives descriptive of the glorious and protracted contest in the Peninsula,—for the most part from the pens of the *gallant actors who took a prominent part in the war*, and who have portrayed the stirring events that successively took place under their own immediate observation,—such records of British valour and daring, although sometimes as it were constituting mere episodes in war, and therefore not detailed in any history of the period, *must, it is conceived, prove cordially welcome to* every one who rejoices in the name of Englishman.

On almost every contribution the author can look back and affix the stamp of veracity, and, as he describes a passing scene, lift his head proudly and exclaim, "Pars fui!" He who sketches the varying fortunes of "the heady fight," from the scientific field of Salamanca, to "the bludgeon-fought" contests of the Pyrenees, himself, sword in hand, pointed out the path to victory; and now, from the quiet of a peaceful retirement, the veteran recalls his glorious reminiscences, and, in vivid fancy, crowns the breach anew, or

"Shoulders his crutch, and shews how fields were won."

A few connecting or illustrative notes have been introduced by the editor, to link up the broken chain of desultory narrative, and thus save the reader the trouble of a reference.

LONDON, 1st July, 1844.

PENINSULAR SKETCHES.

THE ENGLISH IN SPAIN.*

THERE are few events in ancient or modern history that have occasioned more surprise, or a greater degree of excitement, than the resistance given by the Spanish people to the ruler of the French Empire, when he endeavoured to place the yoke upon their necks; and the interest taken by this country in an event so unlooked-for, which opened a gleam of hope to the nations of Europe, naturally gave rise to a variety of speculations and dreams for the future.

As we sent an army immediately to co-operate with those who were thus endeavouring to assert their national rights, and break asunder the chains that had been forged for their subjugation, it fol-

* By Lieut.-Colonel Wilkie.

lowed, that the greatest possible curiosity would be brought into play, to ascertain what success might attend our efforts in this novel interference in the affairs of the Continent. The official gazettes and private correspondence at the time, did not in any degree serve to abate the inquiry; new versions of the same thing were called for with the greatest avidity, during a long period of time; and among contributions thrown out to appease this appetite of inquiry, the events gave rise to, and formed the basis, of a military history, rarely if ever surpassed, that reflects equal honour on the writer and his country.

I had made some notes from memory on these events, but by the time they were ready, the ground was already filled by different writers, and the interest, by the lapse of time, had considerably abated; under these circumstances, my memoranda were laid on the shelf, where they have ever since remained, unnoticed in their dust.

Taking up one of those papers the other day, to ascertain a doubtful point, I ran over that and one or two others, and had reason to be satisfied that they were not published at the time, from being written in haste. Some of the remarks were raw and *jejune;* while in military observations on the operations, although, generally, my opinion is in no way changed, I might have given offence to those whose opinions I respect, although I differ from their views.

As the two first campaigns in the Peninsula,

although of less value as military examples, were of greater interest as regarded the novelty of the objects, I thought something might still be gleaned, by relating incidents quite personal, and giving occasionally some sketches of the people and country, as they appeared to me at the time; putting aside the military details and speculations, only in so far as they served as a locomotive power that removed us from the shores of the Tagus to the mountains of Gallicia.

The troops under Sir Arthur Wellesley, joined by the division of General Spencer, were landed, by the assistance of country boats, near the mouth of the Mondego, on a beautiful day in August, 1808:* from thence, they marched to a small place called Lavos, about four miles from the shore, where it was understood they were to halt until the artillery and stores joined. On this supposition, and having some business on board one of the ships, I got leave to return to the anchorage. The gentle breeze that had assisted our landing, had died

* "It was a fortunate circumstance that the mouth of the Mondego was open, for the Fort of Figueras had been taken by the partisan Zagalo, and was now occupied by a detachment of English marines. On the 1st of August the landing commenced, and on the fifth it was effected with but a few casualties, as the weather had continued favourable. As the last brigade was leaving the transports for the shore, Spencer's division most opportunely came to anchor. The whole were disembarked on the fourth evening; and the gallant divisions formed their first bivouac upon the beach, and mustered about 13,000 effective men."—MAXWELL'S LIFE OF WELLINGTON, vol. i. p. 298.

away; the surface of the sea was smooth as glass, but a heavy ground swell had set in from the Atlantic, causing the ships to roll so heavily, that it was a matter of great difficulty either to get on board or to leave them. I have been on board a light transport in a heavy gale of wind, but the rolling was not to my recollection near so heavy as that the ships were undergoing in Mondego Bay in a perfect calm. Having completed my errand, I returned to the place where I had left the regiment; but the birds had flown, and it had become nearly dark; there was nothing, therefore, but to follow up the chase. After walking for about five or six miles, there appeared in front some large dark object in motion, which it was very difficult to make out; at first I thought it was a woman on a donkey, but a nearer approach convinced me that there were only two legs in motion, and that they carried some large uncouth mass, which I at last discovered to be a very tall and corpulent friar doing duty as a patrol. He had his coats tucked up and strapped round his huge paunch, the *capucin*, with its sharp termination, pulled over his head, and across his shoulder was a firelock. On getting near this formidable-looking personage, I asked what he was doing, his reply was, that he was guarding the highway; he looked more like the Colossus of *roads*, than the god Terminus. He assured me the troops were only a short way in front; but "Hope told a flattering tale." I only got sight of them at daybreak, and then they were just leaving their bivouac, and taking a fresh departure.

Our second halt was on an elevated plateau, parallel to the great road, and near to it; on our left, the ground descended rapidly, and was broken into several deep ravines. After dispatching the provisions we carried with us, the wigwams for our night's repose were soon put into requisition. One of our officers, who had volunteered from the Militia, and who made his first appearance as a campaigner, declared it was impossible to get any sleep so near the noise of the ungreased axles of the horrible Portuguese cars, that were continually moving along the road; he therefore retreated into one of the ravines already alluded to, where, having chosen a snug nook, his servant fitted him up a hut with boughs of trees, that was a perfect picture of military felicity; he had his cloak spread nicely for repose, and his shaving and dressing things all spread on a napkin ready for the morning toilette. We left him in this terrestrial paradise, and retired to our own shake-downs with good appetite for a sleep after our march.

About twelve at night a heavy storm of thunder and lightning began, accompanied by torrents of rain that soon penetrated our leafy coverings, and left no hope of security against the wet: we therefore sate up, wrapped in our blankets, and did "as they do in Spain when it rains—let it rain." We had about five hours of this shower-bath; as the weather broke up about daylight, we looked like a set of half-drowned rats. When we had our laugh at each other, some one thought of asking for our happy friend of the ravine : he was not to be found in the place where we had left him, but was at last discovered at the bottom of the hill, looking amongst the rubbish swept down by the torrent for his goods and chattels, which were nowhere to be found. The thunder had awakened him, and he heard the pattering of the rain on the leaves of the trees, but he was sheltered by the projecting ground above his head, and he lay in fancied security, until the water, accumulated on the upper ground, rushed down into the very heart of his nest, half choked him with mud and water, and when he started on his feet to avoid the threatened fate, he left a clear course for the speedy disappearance of his *traps*. It was a lesson for the future not to make his dormitory in a ravine, however snug it might look.

The approach to Leira is pleasing, along an avenue of trees, and the general situation is cheerful and picturesque, to which the position of the Bishop's palace on rising ground gives additional effect. Here we first saw a specimen of the enemy in the shape of four Swiss soldiers in scarlet, who were left behind by mistake in the prison ; and here also we saw the French method of picking a lock, by putting the point of the bayonet into the keyhole, and then firing the musket with ball. It was at Leira also that the Portuguese General Freire, who had accompanied us thus far, took his leave, promising to give us 1700 men to aid the future operations.

The following day the march was continued to Las Caldas; the day was exceedingly hot, and the road dusty, which made us anticipate with pleasure the delights of a warm bath. The springs, from whence the place derives its name, furnish a pretty steady supply of warm water, strongly impregnated with sulphur, which is conveyed into one large bath of an oblong form; the bottom is of a clear white sand; the water is about two and a half feet in depth, and has a slightly greenish tinge, similar to that of the sea, but is perfectly transparent, and only smells in a trifling degree of the mineral with which it is so strongly impregnated. We enjoyed the luxury of warm water without any inconvenience from this cause, but the next day, when on the march, and under the influence of a hot sun, the sulphur came out strong, and the odour could scarcely have been greater that attached to the " gentleman in black," when "he left his brimstone bed at break of day, to see how his farm on earth was going on."

Not far from Las Caldas our Riflemen first touched on the advanced picket of the French at Obidos, which, after a skirmish, retreated. A little further in advance brought us in view of the French position at Roleia (or Roliça),* which at a distance

* "The view from these heights is singularly beautiful, presenting just such objects as Gaspar Poussin delighted in painting, and in such combination as he would have placed

put me much in mind of the range of hills that overhang the valley of the Severn, near Gloucester. Below this range was a detached hill that bore the appearance of a landslip, and on this the enemy had posted a portion of their force. Before leaving Caldas we had been joined by the promised Portuguese, who were posted on the right. What they did there I never exactly heard, but I can speak for a small detachment we had on the left of the centre, about 300, who were called light troops, but were chiefly formed of the students of Coimbra whom the fire of patriotism had started from their academical benches. They were armed with fowling-pieces, *escopetas*, carbines, and other such deadly engines. The centre had halted to give time for the operations on the flanks, but our Portuguese friends seemed anxious for the fray, as they passed on in front without any orders, and the moment they got sight of the French on the lower plateau, began blazing away with great vigour. While thus employed, and before the enemy had deigned to reply by a single shot, one of these heroes came limping to the place where I stood. He was deadly pale; he could talk a little English, and said he

them—rocks and hills rising in the valley, open groves, churches with their old galilees, and houses with all the picturesque verandahs and porticoes, which bespeak a genial climate. Obidos, with its walls and towers, upon an eminence in middle distance, and its aqueduct stretching across the country as far as the eye could follow it; Monte Junto far to the east; and on the west the Atlantic."—SOUTHEY.

was badly wounded, although there was no appearance of anything of that kind. Serjeant Bowdler of my company, who was standing close by, said, "Yes, my good fellow, I see you are badly wounded, and it is in the worst place, in your heart." This sally produced a grand explosion of laughter among our men, under which the Coimbrese continued his retreat with anything but flying colours.

The ascent of the ground on which the chief position of the enemy rested, was an operation of no little difficulty—for the hill was as steep as that at Malvern, and covered with loose pebbles, having only a few stunted shrubs here and there to give security to the footing. To use the phrase of the *fancy*, there was "great cry of bellows to mend;" and had the French, in place of volleys, favoured us with a song, they might have used with propriety that one from *Il Matrimonio, Si fiato in corpo avete*. The exertion caused the death of an old friend of mine, Captain Payne, of the 45th. He had been shot through the lungs, the preceding year, at Buenos Ayres, and had made a wonderful recovery, but was still unfit for active service; his zeal, however, would not allow him to remain behind his regiment: he came out to Portugal, and was getting on tolerably well, when he attempted to mount this hill, a feat far beyond his strength; he was obliged to give way, and go in the rear, and survived but a short time.

Laborde made a gallant defence of his position,

and, when obliged to retreat, he effected it in a very masterly style.* He took up a second position at a village, with a name nearly as long as itself, (Zambageira,) which he defended for some time, and then retreated in excellent order. Whether from the fire of artillery, or that it was done purposely to check the pursuit, the village was burnt to the ground, offering one of the common spectacles of war, the inhabitants standing in the street with every mark of grief and despair, as they looked at the blazing rafters of their dwellings. It was said that Laborde's division was chiefly composed of conscripts; if so, they deserved much credit for quickly learning their business. I saw them retreat across the plain, after they abandoned the village, and their movements were made with as much precision as on a parade, retiring by files from the right of companies, wheeling up occasionally round their pivot, giving their volley to the light troops in pursuit, and then resuming their former order of march.

* Roliça, sometimes termed Roleia, was the first of the Duke of Wellington's Peninsular victories. The action takes its name from a pretty village, situated in a wild romantic country, stretching for many miles along the coast.

Roliça was fought on the 17th of August, 1808—the allies having the advantage in numbers, the French in position. Laborde held his ground obstinately, and when driven from his first position, rallied at Zambageira, from which he was ultimately deforced, with heavy loss. Although but a part of the troops came fairly into action, the casualties on both sides were severe; that of the French amounting to 700, and the British to 480.—ED.

Nothing of any moment occurred on the march to take up our ground at Vimiera, a position which, although defective in itself, was the only one that could have covered the communication with our floating reserves; a small cove gave the means of landing fresh supplies of ammunition, provisions, stores, &c.; and also our maritime reservoirs furnished us with reinforcements of troops, some of whom landed during the action, and had hardly time to prime and load before they were in the thick of it.

When the French were repulsed and we were in full pursuit, no little surprise was exhibited when the word halt was given, and we returned to the place from whence we came; the cause, however, soon transpired. There had been too many head-cooks; but fortunately the broth was not quite spoiled. We heard of a flag of truce, and the rest naturally followed. The following day we marched, and passing through the verdant defiles of Torres Vedras, took up our ground on the plain of Bucellas. After the convention was signed, and consequent cessation of hostilities, another officer and myself obtained leave to go down to Cascaes, where the transports had arrived, taking with us sundry small commissions for execution. The day was extremely hot, and the road in the first part difficult and indirect. As we passed through a village, we observed the curate at his door, who kindly invited us to take some refreshment and bait the horses; this we accepted. Introduced into his house, a large supply of very fine fruit, and some bread and wine, were placed before us; at the same time, there also alighted a Portuguese officer, dressed in French-grey, with a profusion of silver lace. He said he belonged to the Lusitanian Legion, or some such designation, and he began directly to question us, from whence we came— where we were going—what regiment and brigade we belonged to, &c. We laughed outright at this kind of catechism, which rather disconcerted our inquisitive friend. He had been evidently trying to do the great man, and to give us an idea that he was authorized to stop all travellers until they gave an account of themselves; he accordingly finished by saying, that all was correct, glancing at the same time to the padre with a look of conscious power, and that we might proceed on our journey. To this we replied with another loud laugh, which so discomposed the hero that he mounted his horse and rode off.

The ride proved longer than was expected. We could not have reached Cascaes in time to get on board ship that night; we therefore turned to the right, and took up our abode at the hotel in Cintra, kept at that time by an Irishwoman, whose name I forget. A good dinner and a bottle of wine had been discussed, when our landlady made her appearance, and asked if we would not like to walk out and see the illuminations. Fortunately, curiosity got the better of laziness, for I have seldom witnessed a more pleasing scene. Whatever was the discontent and disappointment elsewhere on the subject of the Convention of Cintra, there was not the smallest symptom of that feeling in the place itself; all was gaiety and hilarity ; groups of men and women in their holiday clothes parading up and down, laughing and talking ; rows of young men, with their arms on each other's shoulders, marching along the road, singing their national airs ; while, in favourable spots, parties had formed dances. Those who have visited Cintra, can form some idea of what it might be when lighted up; to me the effect was almost magical. The lights from the quintas (country houses) partially screened by the shrubs that surrounded them, were sometimes reflected against the naked rock of some fantastic peak, or slightly illumined the upper foliage of a majestic pine, leaving all below in deeper shade; and the vast variety of sites on which these houses were perched, and their whiteness, with the abrupt turns and angles of the road, gave almost endless change of light and shade. I may truly say that it was quite a fairy-scene.

The next morning we pursued our journey by Penalonga to Praza d'Arcos, where communication with our heavy baggage was obtained. On returning to join the regiment, we found it had moved from its former ground, had approached nearer to Lisbon, and was in bivouac within a short distance of the palace of Queluz, where it remained until the embarkation of the French army was completed, and the entrance to Lisbon was the order of the day. That was indeed a splendid exhibition; from the entrance of Belem, the whole way to the Rocio-square, was a triumphal march. One might have supposed that the whole population of Lisbon had been thrown on the line—

"——————— Stalls, bulks, windows,
Were smother'd up, leads fill'd, and ridges horsed
With variable complexions."

The balconies and windows of all the better houses were filled with Portuguese ladies in their best attire, hailing us with continued *vivas*, and showering down garlands and flowers. Guns were firing, and bells ringing as we marched along the streets with flying colours, and band and drums in full activity. It was one of those exciting hours that compensate the soldier for weeks of privation and fatigue.

The quarters destined for our regiment were in a large convent near the Rocio-square; and a Spanish battalion that had occupied it was just turning out to be embarked with the other troops of that nation that had been in the French service, to be sent to Cadiz. The men were dressed in white, and formed a very fine body of troops: for their numbers, I think they would have covered more ground than any regiment I ever saw. They were tolerably clean in their persons, but had never learnt " to set their house in order." Anything so abominably filthy, serving as a habitation for human beings, I never had seen before. It required the incessant labour of pioneers, fatigue parties, and Lisbon scavengers, before the place could be made tolerably decent. I have heard from officers who served lately on the coast of Spain, that this propensity to filth was equally to be found among the Spanish soldiers there, whether in cantonments or on board ship. The convent had, most likely, served previously as a French barrack, as there were several scraps of writing on the walls, not very complimentary to the great Emperor. *L'homme de Corse— Le Nain jaune—Petit Caporal.* On one of the landing-places there was written in pencil on the wall, the qualifications necessary to form a good soldier; which I have quoted elsewhere.

> "Le courage d'un lion,
> La force d'un cheval,
> L'appetit d'un souris,
> Et l'humanité d'une bête."

When Junot marched to attack our position at Vimiero,* he left in the capital about 1200 men, many of whom were invalids, as a garrison: the craven population dared not to attack this handful of men, but the moment the French troops were embarked, and there was no danger of reprisal, this *canaille* proclaimed war to the knife against every

* Vimiero was fought four days after Roliça, (August 21, 1808,) the French, commanded by Duc d'Abrantes, assailing the English position. The strength of the rival armies was tolerably equal—Sir Arthur having about 16,000 men, of all arms, with 18 guns; Junot, 14,000, and 23 pieces of cannon. The French guns, though more numerous, were of lighter calibre than the British, while in infantry Junot was inferior to his rival, but in cavalry decidedly superior.—ED.

Frenchman, of whatever trade or profession. Several attempts had been made at assassination, and more were expected. The evening after our arrival I was sent with the outlying piquet to strengthen the main-guard. I had hardly arrived there when a Frenchman came running to the guard-room to claim protection, and presently two more appeared, followed up by a large mob. I had the guard and piquet turned out, left room for the fugitives to pass, and stopped the pursuers; who, calling out *Viva los Ingleses*, said that the runaways were Frenchmen, and expected they would be given up directly to their vengeance. It was in vain to argue with such persons; they kept pressing on the men, so that I feared they would get within our bayonets' points. I ordered three men to load with ball-cartridge, and told the mob that I would shoot any one who endeavoured to force his way. This had the desired effect: they drew off, broke into groups, and kept moving about, in the hope of catching their prey; but I expected their patience would tire out before morning. I had the three Frenchmen into the officers' guard-room, offered them some wine and bread; but their alarm was too great to allow them to partake of it, and I could hardly get any account from them. It turned out, however, that the first arrival was a merchant, who had resided fifteen years in Lisbon; the second was a barber, of the same period of residence; and the only one connected with the arrival of the French army was the last of the three, who had been a waiter in a coffee-house in the Rocio-square. I offered to guarantee their safety during the night, and, as soon as it was daylight in the morning, to send them down with sufficient escort to the beach, and see them safely embarked. This would have been very grateful to them under other circumstances, but two of them had families they could not abandon, and they said that if they could get unnoticed into a street not far distant, they could get shelter in the house of a Portuguese friend, on whom they could depend. About half-past one in the morning I directed the patrols to look out if there were any crowds or knots of people collected anywhere. At two o'clock they returned, and reported that "the coast was clear." To avoid notice I took the refugees under my charge, dropping only two or three men at intervals to give an alarm, and with palpitating hearts the three Frenchmen followed me. We proceeded without any interruption, and apparently unnoticed, until we gained the corner of a street, when one of the trio stooping down, stretched out his neck, and taking a lengthened look up and down the street, whispered to his friends that all was clear, and away they scuttled, stooping their heads as they ran. I could not help laughing at the ridiculous appearance of the race.

In returning to my post I took a different turn, to avoid observation of any persons who might have been on the look-out, and unexpectedly fell upon a pack of the half-wild dogs that prowl about the streets of Lisbon. These animals seemed to rejoice in their new-found liberty, and in the absence of their French enemies; probably they took me for one, as I was attacked directly. They seemed, however, to have an instinctive knowledge of sharp tools, for none of them came within the reach of the sword's point. Whatever faults may have been laid to the doors of the French, they had done much to improve the cleanliness of Lisbon. They made the people cleanse the streets, have watchmen at night, and they killed hundreds of these dogs,— the greatest nuisance in the place. Indifferent as the police was then, I was struck with the contrast which it afforded to my last visit, twelve years previously. At that time Lisbon was not only the dirtiest, but most unsafe large town in Europe; the streets were left unguarded day and night, and there was no light, except a candle stuck up in front of the Virgin, at very long intervals. Assassination for the sake of plunder was of nightly occurrence; and dogs and dirt were in high favour. Although forty-one years had passed after the earthquake, its ravages had not been completely obliterated; a large portion of the buildings in what is now the best part of the town were incomplete, and the streets unpaved. We lodged at that time at Williams's English hotel at Buenos Ayres; from whence it was not safe to move out, except in a carriage. Those who could not afford that luxury were obliged to keep a sharp look-out in going to or returning from the Opera. If you went close to the houses you ran the double danger of the assassins aforesaid, and having an ungenial shower on your head, administered without the premonitory "*gare de l'eau.*" In the middle of the street there was the chance of being run over, or the more frequent one of being up to the knee in mud. The people swept up the filth opposite to their houses into heaps in the middle of the road, to be carried off at the perfect leisure of the scavengers, if they existed, or to be swept off by the autumnal rains.

At this period the old Queen was alive, but insane; she was not allowed to interfere in the affairs of the government, but was indulged in many of her whims and caprices. Among these she took an objection to having female performers on the stage of the Italian Opera, and the only way to meet this fancy was, the importation from Italy of the required number of *soprani*. To look at these great ungainly creatures in petticoats striding over the stage was quite ridiculous. An Irish officer in the regiment with me, unaware of the nature of the animals, made a remark about them that served as a standing joke against him for many years.

To return to 1808: I mentioned that a small division of Portuguese had joined us on the march, and had been employed, attached to our right flank, at the affair of Roliça. The officers and men of this detachment were directed to wear on the left arm a bit of white linen, or a pocket-handkerchief tied round, to distinguish them from the French. I should conceive that the number of officers was under forty: a few days after we got to Lisbon at least a hundred officers appeared in the streets in new uniforms, with each a broad white satin riband on the arm, surmounted by a cockade, like that in a baby's cap; thus transforming a distinguishing mark, set up to save them from sudden death, into a badge of distinction.

It is needless to say that great rejoicings took place in Lisbon on the late events, religious processions to the churches to sing *Te Deum*, illuminations, firing of rockets, &c. A new piece was got up at the theatre, in honour of the Commander-in-Chief; the principal *artistes* had, however, accompanied the French army, and what remained were very indifferent. All the amusements to be found in a capital had been gone through, when our attention was called more to matters of business, the army was freshly organized in brigades and divisions, and received orders to march to Spain, under the command of Sir John Moore.

LEAVES FROM THE JOURNAL
OF A VETERAN.*

We sailed from Portsmouth, under convoy of some ships of war. The transport in which I was embarked, I had almost said entombed, originally flourished in the occupation of a collier, trading from Newcastle to the Thames, the worst, or most unseaworthy of which, after being pensioned off that service, were hired by Government for the shipment of the troops, and a more wretched, crazy, or worn-out flotilla, could scarcely be imagined,—so miserably crank and leaky, that in the adverse gales which afterwards set in, while endeavouring to cross the Bay of Biscay, many of them, with all hands on board, had foundered, while few, if any, escaped shipwreck on the coast. Happy was he whose better fate led him safely to

* By Major Patterson, late of the 50th, or Queen's Own Regiment.

any destination. Mine was for Falmouth, at all times a refuge for the destitute, where part of the tempest-tossed fleet found shelter, and where we remained for several weeks, anticipating, with no small degree of horror, even though bound for service, our return once more to those frail and time-worn relics of antiquity in which we had been so lately captives.

After a quick though stormy passage across the well-known Bay, we put into the harbour of Coruña, when we went on shore, not only to recruit our sea-stock, but to see the "lions," if any there might be, in a place having otherwise but few attractions, or possessing but little to interest the stranger. In the progress of our various ramblings through the town, one of our officers recollected that a distant relation of his wife's was Consul there, when perceiving a group of natives at some distance in the street, he ventured to address himself to one of them in English, inquiring for his friend. This individual, who, from his long residence, his dusky aspect, and his dress, might well have been taken for a Spaniard, proved to be the identical person of whom he was in search. Not unmindful of the hospitable customs of his country,—for the Consul was an Irishman, —he gave us all a cordial welcome, and entertained us generously at his house, attending us, moreover, to whatever theatrical or other amusements the town afforded.

Coruña was, at the period of which I write, the

scene of peace, and its inhabitants were both numerous and respectable,—well disposed towards the English, who, by this time, were crowding to their shores in aid of their independence, and of their resistance to enslavement by a foreign power.

The streets, like those of other walled towns, are regularly planned, and were, though narrow, paved throughout with large flag stones, which were kept in the cleanest order by criminals, who were marched out daily from the prisons, chained in pairs, for that service, and whose iron fetters, clanking upon the ear with a somewhat dismal sound, produced a degree of melancholy on the stranger's mind, by no means favourable to the continuance of any agreeable impression that might previously have existed there.

Amongst the convicts were a male and female linked together by the ankles, with a chain about a yard in length, which they dragged after them apparently with considerable pain, while drudging at their task; the man working away with a scraper as far as the limit of his chain permitted, the woman with a broom. What their object was in thus fastening together two of opposite sexes, I could not ascertain, nor could I even imagine its intention, unless the woman was placed there either to console her wretched partner in crime and sorrow, under his misfortunes, or keep him from being refractory, should such appear to be the case during the performance of his toil. It is a custom very general throughout Spain thus to employ the prisoners who may have been found guilty of any crimes: but poor, emaciated, ill-fed creatures, as they almost always are, it would seem a matter of great cruelty to append the burden of a chain, or thus to load them with accumulated oppression, for between the lynx-eyed vigilance of a hardened taskmaster and their own enfeebled state, there needs but little fear of even the slightest effort to escape. Miserable, unhappy wretches! — " the iron entered into their very souls,"— but in proportion as countries are uncivilized, in the same ratio is the treatment of their criminals.

In the midst of our enjoyments and convivialities at Coruña, orders came; when, to our extreme delight, we bade farewell to our luckless transport, and embarked on board a frigate, which sailed immediately for Lisbon. With a fair and moderate wind, we soon lost sight of the dark, iron-bound coast of Spain, and found ourselves abreast of the more pleasant shores of Portugal, — the land of dark eyes, fruits, and flowers. Gliding almost imperceptibly along, for the sea was smooth as glass, it was truly delicious to inhale so sweet—so mild an atmosphere. There is not in the wide world a climate so fine as that of Portugal, where every wind that blows breathes health and animation, where, with all the softness of the balmy south, is combined the refreshing breeze, that both enlivens and invigorates the frame.

Could it be possible, or could we imagine any circumstances under which a life at sea might be associated with the idea of an agreeable state of being, this our present voyage might well be remembered as one to favour such impression; for, entertained as we were by the hospitalities of the captain and officers on board, and our time spent in every variety of agreeable occupation, there was scarcely anything left to wish for. In succession, the various picturesque and beautiful objects on the coast floated, as it were, in review before us; for, in quickly sailing past, they, instead of the vessel, appeared to move. So varied was the scenery, that it was difficult to fix the eye on one more exquisite than the other. Churches, convents, windmills, orange groves, vineyards, and richly-planted fields, seemed to glide on with the effect of a moving panorama, while, here and there, the green hills and deeply-seated valleys, speckled with milk-white cottages and quintas, relieved in the distance by those richly-covered mountains, their natural barrier, produced on the whole, it might almost be said, a " tableau vivant" hardly to be surpassed by the scenery of any country in the world.

Many a lovely prospect reminded us of scenes at home; but how much more was the loveliness here enhanced by the verdant shadows of the coast, as reflected in the deep blue waters of the ocean, and warmed by the brilliant rays of a glowing sun.

As soon as we came to anchor in the Tagus, a large boat, with one of those great lateen sails, came alongside, well laden with every variety of fruit and vegetables, a little aqua ardente, and tobacco for the sailors. The sunburnt countenances of the crew, with the singularly picturesque costume they wore, soon reminded us of our near approach to—shall I say sweet Lisbon? No, I dare not; for, by every voyager, from Columbus down, it has been pronounced a city of "villanous odour." Preserve me from a visit to its narrow streets, or from the pungency of its non-ambrosial gales!

Amongst the heterogeneous group who stood upon the gunwale of the boat, waiting to board the frigate, was a money-changer, and two of his wretched syrens, decked out in all the finery of May-day sweeps. Signior, without the smallest ceremony, proceeded to the quarter-deck, accompanied by the aforesaid damsels, and from thence descended to the ward-room, assuming in his progress an air of much importance. Having extracted from his pocket-book sundry certificates of his honour and respectability, (which we greatly doubted,) he ordered, by way of an overture to his performances, his syrens to pour forth their strains. These strains, however, proving but sorry and doleful ditties, there was but little evidence of applause; when, at length, finding no customers, he returned with his merchandise and his syrens to the boat. But misfortune pursued him even here; for, extending his hand to grasp his bag of dollars from a sailor, in order to exchange them for our English money, he missed his grasp, and his treasure slipped between them to the bottom of the sea; amid the splash from which, accompanied by threats of vengeance from the Don, (who raved out loudly,) and by invocations from the sailor to his patron saint,—increased by this time to an uproar, — the party rowed off quickly to the shore.

Parting from our friends on board the frigate with much regret, and with mutual feelings of esteem, we landed on the steps ascending to the Black Horse Square, from whence we at once proceeded to the hôtel of Mrs. O'Donnel, in Rua——
. . . . . A splendid breakfast, consisting of tea, coffee, eggs, dried meats, fruit, &c. &c., was soon disposed of, when we sauntered about to view the far-famed city. Having passed most of our first day on shore in this way, exploring all that could be witnessed in that short space of time, we returned to dine at Mr. Bunker's English hotel, where we were assured of finding cleanliness and the best accommodation, and we were not disappointed. In proof of their desire to make us comfortable, the platform, or flat roof of the building, was cleared of all encumbrance, and here we enjoyed our evening lounge and glass, while we had a view of the magnificent prospect extending on every side.

Our preparations for the field being at length

concluded, we proceeded to the camp at Monte Santa, in the neighbourhood of Belem, where we joined our regiment, which, composing part of Sir John Moore's army, marched in a few days after, on the route to Salamanca.

The first town of any respectability that we passed through, on leaving Lisbon, was Villa Franca, from whence we pursued our journey to Santarem. In this city, where we halted for a little time, were twenty-seven convents, relating to one of which a ludicrous incident occurred, which not only varied the dull sameness of our route, but afforded much amusement to those promoters and lovers of fun who were with us at the time.

A young officer, who had lately been imported from one of our fashionable towns in England, anxious, perhaps, to become eminent as a gallant chevalier, was sauntering past the largest of those convents, making the best use of his visual organs for the discovery of some of those black-eyed houris whose charms he had so often pictured to himself. On the point of turning in despair, he was suddenly arrested by the sight of a figure in white, apparently watching his movements from a distant window in the building.

Imagination was on fire. All the romance he had ever dreamed of was at length about to be realized. He readily invested the lovely form before him with every attribute attendant on youth, beauty, and perfection, which his romantic and ardent turn of mind could fancy. Alas for the maddening distance that intervened to dim the vision of so rich a prize!—but imagination filled up the blank. His rapturous signs of admiration were returned at first with apparent shyness; but, encouraged by the immaculate patience of our hero, the youthful figure at the window, at last throwing off all restraint, bowed and kissed her hand with the most angelic grace. To express some place of rendezvous was more quickly thought of than understood by signs, although to the imaginative swain the maiden must be as desirous of a meeting as himself; but how this was to be accomplished was more difficult to decide.

To scale the wall was to him but the work of an instant,—but it must be under cover of the shades of night. To enlist one of his brother-officers in his service was the next consideration; when, acting on this thought, his rapid strides quickly brought him to his friend, who cheerfully offered all that friendship could,— his services when needed.

The enamoured youth observed not the scarcely stifled laugh that ever and anon played round the features of his friend. His object gained, he was already in Elysium. With a promise that he should not be betrayed, he hastened off to prepare, as far as his agitated feelings would allow, for the desired elopement. Meanwhile his confidant, free from all restraint, now gave vent to merriment among his own companions; and well aware that the convent was of the order of Santa Cruz, and the imaginary "Hebe" a corpulent old friar, rounds of convulsive and uproarious laughter proclaimed their enjoyment of the scene.

While this was going forward, and the impetuous lover waiting the issue in tremulous suspense, orders came for the troops to march; not only thus cruelly throwing a damper on his flame, but upsetting all those shadowy castles that floated in his brain; while, to add still more to his confusion and misfortune,—for

> The course of true love never did run smooth,—

it was very currently rumoured that before he marched, a letter* was written by the abbot of the convent, stating, " that he was informed by one of the fraternity, of the youth's perambulations, and expressive *signs* of true repentance, and of his desire to enter the sacred gate; from which, he felt assured, the penitent was alone restrained by that modesty natural to the saints on their first visitation and conversion; he would invite him, in the name of all the saints, to fly immediately to receive the affectionate and holy kiss of the ninety brotherhood, and this before the evil spirit could again possess him."

* The desponding influence of such a letter upon the ensign's mind, perhaps induced him, in after times, to sing, by way of consolation, the following ditty:—

> Hast thou forgot the magic tie
>   That once endeared thy soul to mine?
> The impassioned gaze, the burning sigh,
>   That told me all my soul was thine?

Our hero, it was also said, having received this letter, it would be difficult to express his feelings on the tender subject. The reader must, therefore, be left to form his own conclusion on the condition of the love-lorn youth, who, we have little doubt, profited by the strange adventure in his early life, and would most likely, in future years, mistake not shadows for realities.

Previously to our arrival at Santarem, we crossed the Tagus at Abrantes, when we entered upon a wild and almost uninhabited country. In some places our route lay over a deserted tract, where scarcely a human being ever crossed our path; added to which, the dreary aspect of the cork and olive forests would have rendered our journey both tedious and disheartening, were it not for the relief occasioned by the pleasant converse of some lively fellows of our party. We came to different halting places on the wide and extensive plains, before we again crossed the Tagus; and after some days' weary marching, we ascended to Castello Branco, where we enjoyed a hospitable reception, which we experienced not only here, but in most of the towns and villages on our way to Salamanca.

Castello Branco has little in itself to boast of on the score of interior or exterior beauty; but the kindness and generous disposition of the people more than compensated for all deficiencies, and gave us reason to regret the shortness of our stay among them.

I was billeted, with one or two others, at the

house of a worthy medico, who provided sumptuously for our entertainment, his wife and family likewise lending their aid to make us comfortable. One of his sons, a lad about sixteen, asked me the usual question,—If I was a Catholic?—when, being answered in the negative, he very emphatically observed, looking to the ceiling, "Ah! Catholic go up, but Protestant go down," pointing smartly downwards. Though these sentiments were, no doubt, the father's, yet he did not express them; and his kindness fully recompensed for the imprudence of the son. A dishful of boiled chickens was placed upon the table, when the doctor, with a fork and his fingers, tore them asunder, to display his skill in their dissection; plates and dishes were replenished faster than the guests could clear them, while copas of generous wines were filled out with equal liberality. In taking leave of our worthy entertainer, the medico expressed his regret at the necessity for our departure to meet the enemy, as well as his grateful reliance on the British army for the preservation of his country.

Most of our old campaigners, who travelled along that route, will remember, with sentiments of esteem, many such instances of liberal feeling on the side of their patrons. So much, however, cannot be said of Ciudad Rodrigo: for a more traitorous set of people never existed than those who inhabited that city; many of whom, being in the French interest, and corrupted by their spies, displayed their treachery in every possible way, whenever the

English appeared within their gates; but an instance of this treachery among themselves was punished in a most vindictive and remarkable manner. A Spanish nobleman being suspected of such conduct, and of tampering with the interests of the city, or perhaps obnoxious to the civic power, was doomed to an awful and cruel death. His body, after strangulation, was cut in quarters, each of which being fixed on lofty gibbets, adorned, or rather disgraced, the four extremities of the fortress; and while the mutilated remnants of the Marquis hung in this way, a prey to vultures, and bleaching in the wind, there was none to be found among the sanguinary and repassing crowds, who had commiseration or heart enough to heave one sigh for the unfortunate noble's fate.

We were all horrified at such an exhibition, which at once stamped the character and customs of the people, who, from this circumstance alone, were held in so much detestation, that all were rejoiced to leave their gates, and shed but few tears on the downfall of their walls in three years after, when Wellington, with his artillery, brought them tumbling about their ears. I had almost overlooked the town of Guarda, a few days' march to the west of Rodrigo.

Here I was billeted on a venerable padre—and a jolly soul to wit, who received me with a cordial welcome, and a no less cordial *grasp of his right hand;* proving farther, in a more substantial way, the sincerity of his purpose, by causing his pretty niece to set before me, chocolate, fruit, viands, and sundry delicacies, always to be found within the cupboard of a priest. The innocent girl smiled as she laid the salver down, with "todos para servir usta seignor," and following the example of the holy father, she was most attentive to our wants while we remained.

After going the rounds of everything worth seeing, upon our arrival at the various towns through which we passed, it was usually the custom to finish our rambles by a visit to the nunneries and convents—and these were pretty numerous—where we never failed to meet with some pleasant adventure, either in carousing with the jolly fat friars, or in holding soft parlance with the nuns. With two others, who were with myself in search of some hidden treasure, I visited the nunnery of Santa Clara—a large and most imposing edifice in the town of Guarda, above referred to—where nuns from noble families only were admitted. I can scarcely think of any way in which an evening could be passed more pleasantly, nay, it might be said more profitably, than in one of those too fleeting visits, for whatever was gained by the gentle conversation of the eyes, we gained much more by the eloquent language of the "little unruly member," improperly so called, so pure and beautiful was the Spanish, or Portuguese, of the fair secluded ones, that we were sure to become proficient; indeed, with such teachers, he must have been dull of intellect that failed. There was something so musical in their words, that we were left at a loss which to admire the most—the being who gave expression to them, or the tones.

In the visit I now speak of, we were received in the most gracious manner by three superiors, who, leaving us in the reception-chamber to amuse ourselves as best we might, assured us, as they parted, that they would send a few of the sisters to our comfort. " One at a time, Seignora, if you please !" we uttered; but this had scarcely passed our lips, when the entrance of three as fair penitents as ever took the veil broke on the tenor of our contemplations. I am quite sure there was no sincerity in their vows, for the mischief that lurked beneath the most beautifully-pencilled eyebrows and sparkling eyes I ever saw, betrayed another tale. They smiled benevolently as they took their seat beside the " grating"—" alas, for the villanous grating !" and said the world had done with them : but they now were guarded from the world, and all its vain pursuits, by this their friendly grating—nothing less than iron bars could guard the innocent lambs who sighed within from the wolves that prowled without the gates. They inquired of us, with pitying anxiety, if we were married, as if with a horror of what is called the " happy state"—of our country, religion, our names and surnames—all of which was truly replied to, much to the gratification of the nuns, who, by way of rewarding us for our affecting stories, played on the spinnet, singing in accompaniment with plaintive sweetness, that made us almost forget the past and all its cares, and wish that here might be our future resting-place. To get, if possible, still more into their good graces, one of the officers presented his sword-knot for their acceptance, and the other two their feathers, when, presently, they served us with cakes, liquors, and sweetmeats, passed to us through the revolving shelves. During the repast, the nuns became more animated; when, after a round of lively conversation, the approach of midnight, and the tolling of the convent bells, reminded us that time was hastening on, and that our regiment was to march the following morning; so, bidding a last and affectionate farewell to those kind and gentle sisters of the veil, we turned from the visiting-chamber, not without a lingering hope that fate or fortune would, at another period of our lives, conduct us to the gates of the peaceful Santa Clara.

Not only before we entered the gates of Salamanca, but previous to our entry into every other town or city, the inhabitants came out in crowds to meet the troops; men, women, and children, shaking hands with and embracing officers and soldiers, while, as they escorted them, the air was rent with their loud and enthusiastic acclamations —" Viva los Ingleses!" "Mueran los Francessa!" issued from every quarter. At Salamanca, the city guard turned out, with a non-military display of court dresses, rather soiled, of different reigns and fashions, and armed with various weapons, like the city of London train-bands. They felt themselves highly honoured and much gratified on being relieved by a British guard, to whom the city keys were with all due ceremony confided.

On the centre of the bridge, a small square structure, having but one room, to which the only access was by a ladder, was erected on pillars. From one of the windows of this dismal-looking fabric was suspended, from a short iron bracket, the head of a criminal; which, as it swung to and fro with the wind, seemed to warn, with ghastly frown, the passengers below to take good care to keep their heads upon their shoulders.

I was billeted at the caza of a true disciple of Sangrado—one of the most soup-meagre-featured dons whose acquaintance I was ever honoured with, and who, together with his numerous and equally cadaverous family, assembled in a group round the table where I was discussing my frugal rations: subsisting themselves entirely on Indian corn bread, sopped in a kind of soup made of water enriched with garlic, some kail, oil, pepper, and salt,—it was an affair of much astonishment to them how I could contrive to dispose of so much provender, while, as before said, sharp misery appearing in their bones, they exclaimed, at every morsel that I took, "O Maria! que mucho vacca. O hombre que mucho!"

Besides the multitude of convents, nunneries, and chapels, there were many large and splendid buildings at Salamanca; a circumstance not so remarkable in such a city, for even in the meanest towns the houses of the higher class were of substantial and elaborate dimensions. In Spain, they measure your respectability by the size and grandeur of your dwelling. However poor the proprietor may be, he seeks his last and chief comfort and consolation in the amplitude of his spacious halls and galleries—in the solid workmanship of his balcos, gates, and doors—the strength and thickness of his bolts and bars. Their houses, therefore, may well be compared to prisons, where often, amid the dreary vastness of his chambers, well festooned with cobwebs, the poor attenuated don, or proud hidalgo, wanders about in splendid misery; or in the dark recesses of a cold alcoba, he sits in spectral solitude.

The Grand Plaza was the general resort and promenade — one where our gallants sought a relief from war's alarms in joining the fair seignoras there, as they pursued their daily ambulations. It was, on those fine evenings of November, a lively scene: all that could constitute the animation of a promenade, served to render it the favourite haunt of civilians as well as military; while the music of the various bands contributed, in a great measure, not only to the gaiety of the paseo, but in attracting to the windows around the square a luminous display of beauty.

The social disposition of the Spaniards is a peculiar and amiable feature in their character. They are fond of assembling together to enjoy the chit-chat, the laugh, the cheerfulness of the promenade. In the delicious climate of Castile, where the harsh frowns of winter are scarcely ever known—where the voice of storm or tempest is seldom heard—they may well enjoy that scene—they may well indulge that happiness of soul, that warm benevolence of feeling, without which no pleasure can exist, no enjoyment can be perfect.

Amongst our friends in the square was the principal of the Irish convent; an office he had filled, as he informed us, for twenty-seven years. His kind-hearted, friendly manner, gained our esteem; but he was more valued for the zeal he manifested in our cause, and for the information and advice he gave us. It was, in fact, unfortunate for himself, poor man, that he was so beneficial to the British army, for the French, well aware of the interest he took against them, resolved on his destruction, and, two days after the departure of the English troops, they unmercifully caused him to be hanged.

The army marched from Salamanca for Valladolid, through the kingdom of Leon—a country that seemed to be one immeasurable plain, the soil consisting of fine loam, without a single tree, bush, hedge, bank, or ditch; the fields or land of each proprietor being divided by unploughed stripes of ground, and the entire of this vast surface sown with corn as far as the boundaries of sight.

Whatever might have been the fertility of the soil, their advancement in agricultural pursuits was anything but rapid; a curious instance of which we noticed on marching through the country. Close to the road by which we passed, a pig and donkey were yoked together by a straight pole, fastened across their necks, and attached to a plough, which consisted merely of a long, heavy, crooked billet. This grotesque and extraordinary team, rendered still more so by the different stature of the animals, and the oblique position of the pole upon their necks, was attended only by one person, the ploughman, so called, who, holding the straight end of the pole, guided the other; while, notwithstanding the opposite natures of the ass and his companion, the shallow furrows, although of no great length, were perfectly in a line.

Arrived at Toro, the quartermasters were despatched to Valladolid to prepare for the ensuing march, when, on approaching that city, they discovered the enemy already in full possession of it. They, therefore, with the same speed, rejoined their corps.

In the prison of Toro were some French soldiers, taken by General Stewart, near Alaejos. Hearing that another party of the enemy, who were captured by General Paget, had entered the town, escorted to the prison, I went to witness the meeting of both parties on the occasion; where the affectionate interview which took place between the comrades of many a battle, assured me, more plainly than any language could convey, that the harsh visage of war had not wholly stifled in those poor fellows the amiable and finer feelings of their nature.

Other nations, even the English, have been accused of using the prisoners of war with undue severity; but nothing could be worse than the cruelty under which those captives suffered from the Spaniards. In this prison was a cell, with a window, near the portico, which, besides being strongly barred, was covered by a plate, or iron shutter, pierced with holes, and an aperture only sufficient to admit a small drinking-cup, and a glimmering of light. The entrance was by a door of massive iron bars, four feet in height, which, being a-jar, I forced open on its grating hinges, to the full extent, and entered. The apartment, or dungeon, was about ten feet square, and five and a half feet high. At the furthest end was a block of stone for a seat, with an iron collar for the neck, fixed by a short chain in the wall, and near this a similar collar for the body. At the foot of the seat was grooved a chain of massive links, with a clasp to confine the leg.

Upon inquiry, I was informed that all those dreadful clasps and shackles, evidently much worn, were continually locked upon the prisoner, except when permitted, as a great indulgence, to receive at the window his scanty allowance of bread and water. Again were the chains replaced, constraining the wretched victim to a sitting posture, and often hasting him to a miserable, though welcome, death.

* * * * * * *

The cold weather, and appearances of approaching winter, had set in before our departure from Salamanca. The whole country was at this time mantled with a slight covering of snow, but the roads were pretty clear of this, and were crisped in a pleasant state for marching by a hard bracing frost, so that, notwithstanding the keenness of the air, we got over the ground with comparatively less fatigue than on many previous journeys. Nearing the district of Castro Novo, we entered a country of a totally different aspect from that we had lately traversed. The snow had partially cleared away, disclosing with more effect the barrenness of a tract that might with truth be called a wilderness, the only discernible objects above its cheerless surface being the villages, scattered so irregularly, as to give the idea of their having come down in a fall of snow. The whole of our previous line of march afforded no supplies beyond what our havresacks contained, but we could in every case get forage; here, however, we could neither get provender for men or animals, and, as for fuel to warm us, or to cook whatever little food we had, that indeed was a stranger to our eyes, for all around was void of tree or shrub, and, with the exception of the solitary beam which an old house now and then presented, there was nothing, as before said, to gladden us with a fire.

At a distance the chapels, rising high above the hovels that surrounded them, seemed as landmarks to guide us in our progress, and would lead one to form a good opinion of the hamlet, but on a close inspection the illusion vanished; what we imagined a respectable good-sized place turning out no better than straggling mud walls, and houses to correspond, all of one dull shade, and scarcely distinguishable from the brown colour of the soil on which they stood. It would be difficult to imagine anything more devoid of interest or beauty than those villages, where the staring peasantry, of the same ochreous hue, were perfectly in keeping with their dwellings. I had almost forgot to say, that we had, at the worst of times, chopped straw to make a blaze under our tea-kettle, and to supply the mules. All of which, with any other luxuries we might pick up betimes, carried us on to Sahagun, where we remained in check of Napoleon's army for some days.

No veteran of that day can ever think of Sahagun with any degree of patience; it was in every sense a place of evil omen. Wretched and miserable as the town was in reality, and poverty-struck as were its people, the country round was still more wretched, while the prospect of a long cheerless march, in the very depth of winter, through the wildest of all wild mountain-roads, and that which to a soldier's heart is chilling, a *retreat* before us —ill-clad, and badly off for food—it was truly a dispiriting affair, and brings the recollection of that halting-place, associated with the idea of every misery, privation, and calamity that the mind can possibly conceive.

Here the whole of Sir John Moore's army being assembled, as before observed, the French generals reconnoitred our position, during which I was standing, with another officer, on the margin of a field in front of the line, watching the enemy's staff. A silent anxiety prevailed on both sides, when at this moment a French sharpshooter, perhaps to try his skill on our elevated and advanced position, crept behind a tree, and, from a considerable distance, fired on us. The shot struck a stone upon which my hand was placed, and, while we were remarking on the attempt, and the accuracy of his aim, the soldier fired again, and hit the same stone, when, it not being necessary to prove his third attempt, and not being particularly anxious to make our exit from the world at that period, we moved to a more respectful distance ; otherwise, I am quite convinced, so determined did the rifleman appear, that I should not be living now to tell the story.

All were by this time prepared for combat, and every eye was intently fixed on the enemy's manœuvres, but the challenge which we offered them being declined, the troops were shortly in rapid movement to the rear.

This change of scene produced a considerable alteration in our affairs : instead of being the assailants, or ourselves assailed, in the open field,— where with fair play there is always something encouraging to hope for,—we were forced to defend ourselves against superior numbers in a country of truly Alpine wildness; pent up, formed in files or sections, within the limits of a narrow, rugged, and hilly road, in many parts almost impassable by huge projecting rocks, between whose craggy fissures the mountain torrents rushed with fearful violence,—at every step we took the winding route became more desolate. We also had to defend ourselves against the elements, which conspired to render our sufferings complete. After crossing, or rather wading through, the numerous deep and rapid rivers, the rain, sleet, and snow came down alternately, while the piercing wind, blowing in gusts through every crevice in the rocks, or through the defiles, in loud and successive squalls, made the very earth tremble beneath our feet, and this for many weeks,—it were vain to attempt even a faint outline of the scene so often, yet so imperfectly, described.* Let but the miserable and calamitous

* In describing the confusion that reigned around, Leith Hay gives the following graphic sketch of Lugo at nightfall:—"There might be seen the conductors of baggage toiling through the streets, their laden mules almost sinking under the weight of ill-arranged burdens swinging from side to side; while the persons, in whose charge they had followed the divisions, appeared undecided which to execrate most, the roads, the mules, the Spaniards, or the weather. These were succeeded by the dull, heavy sound of the passing artillery; then came the Spanish fugitives from the desolating line of the armies. Detachments with sick or lamed horses scrambled through the mud, while, at intervals, the report of a horse pistol, knelled the termination to the sufferings of an animal, that a few days previously, full of life, and high in blood, had borne its rider not against, but over

events of war for years gone by be recapitulated, all summed up together would fail to bear comparison with that retreat; and yet there are those who would heap down calumnies on the brave and devoted officer who commanded. The very circumstance of his having led his gallant troops through difficulties so unparalleled to the end,—to a battle, and that a victory,—shielding their fame and honour from reproach by his own glorious fall, is of itself enough to refute and crush the vilest calumny, and elevate the hero to a pinnacle, which his revilers can never by any possibility attain.

At Benevente, the duke's splendid palace was entered at midnight by the English soldiers, who forced the gates; and so urgent were the times, so extreme were the wants and sufferings of the men, and their long exposure to the most rigorous cold, that, however much to be deplored, the necessities of war left no alternative, and they were compelled to kindle fires on the beautiful marble staircases, to the utter destruction of the fabric.

From these and other appearances of slender discipline, which, as before observed, arose, the would-be politicians of the day, either to hide or excuse their own blundering incapacity, threw a considerable degree of odium upon the army, for

the ranks of Gallic chivalry. The effect of this scene was rendered more striking by the distant report of cannon and musketry, and more gloomy by torrents of rain, and a degree of cold worthy of a Polish winter."

plundering, disorder, want of discipline, and so forth, which those wiseacres chose to say were the origin of all the failure, loss of life, and misfortune which subsequently occurred; professing to be borne out in this, by a general order, said to be reflecting on the conduct of the troops, issued on the route by Sir John Moore, without even considering the circumstances under which that order emanated, and in which the troops were placed. The faction wished to make the whole campaign an unpopular affair, in this way getting up the cry of discontent; until at length, the good sense and better feeling of the English nation, always alive to justice, led them to see the matter in its true and reasonable bearing; when joining no longer in the discordant cry, a clamour so ill attuned to generosity of mind, they forgot, in admiring the heroism of Moore, and the valour of his soldiers, whatever his enemies had reproached them for,—they honoured and revered his memory, and received, with a warm and generous welcome, his gallant followers on their shores.

It may be well to talk of want of discipline on such occasions; and people at their firesides at home, when all goes smooth with them, may speak at random on these so-called excesses; but when the harassing events, to which allusion has been made, are patiently considered, and when all the disheartening circumstances of the retreat are borne in mind, none but the most determinately rigid will fail to judge with a temper of forbearance. If they will not, however, deal in a tone of moderation with the measures and results of the campaign, let them at least give the worn-out soldiers credit for their fortitude and steadiness when called on to meet the disasters incident to a long and wintry march, for their bravery and coolness when summoned to meet the enemy, and not by one sweeping calumny accuse them of crimes they never committed, and lay to their charge that for which unforeseen misfortunes and the elements were alone to blame.

Such, however, is the inconsistency of human nature—the world—our fellow-beings, look darkly on us when we are overtaken by misfortune or by faults; they will scan with microscopic eye our smallest peccadillos, sifting them till not a grain is left unsifted; but our merits, however praiseworthy, are light in the balance of their scrutiny, they are analyzed but to detect the mote, they are scarce worthy of a thought breathing of approval of one poor remembrance, and are blown like chaff to the winds of heaven.

At the hour of midnight, during the course of that dismal route, when struggling on against the pitiless pelting of the storm, which raged with its usual violence, and when the black clouds that gathered round our heads poured down in torrents, we entered Bembibre, a small and truly wretched place, buried amid the recesses of the wildest mountain scenery.

The quarter-masters had preceded their regiments as usual, and apportioned the cantonments, where the cheerless habitations, each consisting of one small room below, with a ladder conducting to another of the same dimensions above, were all deserted, the doors being locked and fastened as securely as almost to defy the power of entrance. In distributing my own company, I met with the same difficulty in my efforts to obtain admission, for after knocking loud enough to awake the inmates, had such been there, or even the dead if necessary, I was with others compelled to use more violence, when at last the door giving way sufficiently to admit one person, we found, to our disappointment and surprise, that the domicile of our promised rest, and the reward of so much labour, was no other than a wine-store, filled with casks and barrels piled up close to the only entrance.

By the approach of dawn next morning I went round the quarters to get the men under arms, when I discovered that this wine-store, with many others, had been ransacked during the night; the wine-casks scattered about the streets, the wine spilled in all directions, a number of men lying drunk in the streets and in the houses, several totally unable to move. In an upper room, a soldier of the 42nd regiment was laid across the embers of a wood fire, which his pressure fortunately had almost extinguished, when fearing, should the fire rekindle up, from the combustible nature of the rum, or any other intoxicating drink the man had taken, that an explosion might take place, I turned him out of the way of danger on the other side.

The troops, meanwhile, were formed ready for the march, the arms and accoutrements of the men unfit to move were placed upon the baggage waggons, and the unfortunate victims to brutal and disgraceful drunkenness, abandoned to its fearful consequences, became soon after an easy prey to the pursuing enemy.*

---

* " The rain came down upon us in torrents; men and horses were foundering at every step; the former fairly worn out through fatigue and want of nutriment, the latter sinking under their loads, and dying upon the spot. Nor was it only among the baggage animals that an absolute inability to proceed further began to show itself; the shoes of the cavalry horses dropped off, and the horses themselves soon became useless. It was a sad spectacle to behold these fine creatures urged and goaded on till their strength utterly failed them, and then shot to death by their riders, in order to prevent them from falling into the hands of the enemy. Then, again, the few ammunition wagons which had hitherto kept up, fell one by one to the rear; the ammunition was immediately destroyed, and the wagons abandoned. Thus were misfortunes accumulating upon us as we proceeded; and it appeared extremely improbable, should our present system of forced marches be persisted in, that one-half of the army would ever reach the coast."—*Lord Londonderry's Narrative.*

THE BRITISH CAVALRY ON THE PENINSULA.*

At the commencement of the war on the Peninsula, there remained in the army but few who had witnessed an active campaign. From the time of the breaking out of the revolutionary war, nothing of great importance had been executed by the British army. Part of the infantry had occasionally been employed in desultory warfare, and on several occasions had an opportunity to evince the bravery and discipline of British soldiers. Among these feats of war, Alexandria and Maida must always be claimed as brilliant examples of British valour and skill. In the different expeditions which were undertaken, as diversions, the difficulty of transporting dragoons had induced the chiefs to forego the use of that arm, while the field of operation was frequently of too small extent to admit of the movements of cavalry. During the

* By a Retired Officer.

war previous to 1808, we can only call to mind one affair of cavalry at all worthy of notice—that of Villars en Couché, where the 15th light dragoons defeated a very superior body of the enemy, and having rescued the Emperor of Austria, the order of Maria Theresa was conferred on every officer present on that memorable occasion.

During this uninteresting epoch, the British army was little esteemed by the continental powers. The part of the French army opposed to our troops in Egypt, was ready to acknowledge the valour of the *red wall* of Britain. Alexandria and Maida were known to all as scenes of British glory; but these were slender achievements for so large an army, and indeed were known to great part of the continent only through the garbled medium of the *Moniteur*, while Europe was kept in continued excitement by the campaigns of the French in Italy, Austria, and Prussia. The cavalry was nearly confined to the British islands; the equipment and discipline were not neglected, but never employed. It appeared as a useless appendage to the army, which might have been dispensed with,—save the labours of the men as orderlies, and the officers as a glittering addition to the county ball-room. We remember communicating to a waiter in a county town, where, at the head of a recruiting party, we had for some months been playing *l'aimable*, that we had received an order to proceed forthwith to Portsmouth for embarkation. Dick's immediate answer was, "But *you'll* buy off!"

We really had some little military ardour, but found it quite hopeless to convince him of the napkin of the expediency of the proposed change. From the year 1808, we must date a new epoch in British military annals: although the army had been inactive, the boar was whetting his tusks, and while the greatest pains were bestowed on the organization of the troops, a general was being formed on the plains of Hindostan, whose talents and foresight had been surpassed by none, and who has ever been most willing to ascribe to the troops under his command, an ample share of the merit assigned to himself.

Sir A. Wellesley landed on the coast of Portugal in the month of August 1808, totally unprovided with cavalry; but shortly afterwards he was joined by two hundred of the 20th light dragoons, who came from Sicily, under the command of Lieut.-Colonel Taylor. The battle of Vimiera was fought on the 21st. The French force was somewhat inferior to ours, and the weak effort they made, in consequence of dividing their force into three columns of attack, never allowed them even a momentary hope of success. The French were very superior in horsemen. General Margaron, by the French account, was at the head of 1200 cavalry, the greatest part of which were heavy dragoons. Little could be expected from the British dragoons; an opportunity, however, did offer, and was seized on by Colonel Taylor, who, observing that Laborde's division was in confusion from the heavy fire it had sustained, rushed forward, and fiercely charging the infantry, completed their rout, and made numerous prisoners. Having done so much, they were unable to resist the attack of a large body of French dragoons, and the 20th retired, leaving their gallant chief among the slain. The French cavalry were of material use to their infantry in this battle, as they formed a gallant front to cover their formation after their repulse; but thirteen guns remained in our hands, and we heard of no attempt on the part of the French horsemen to retake them. Thiebault speaks of many brilliant charges made by the French cavalry, but as they came into collision with our troops on no occasion except the one mentioned, when they repulsed the victorious 20th light dragoons, we are inclined to believe, that when the French speak of their troops *executant de belles charges*, they mean little more than what we technically name *demonstrations*.

The convention of Cintra having accomplished the first object for which a British army had been sent to the Peninsula, viz. the deliverance of Portugal, including the surrender of its fortresses, all of which were in the hands of the French, the active operations of the army were at an end. It is no part of our intention to write an account of the war, nor even to take a military or political view of the subject; so far we must venture to intrude our opinion as to say, that General Junot richly deserved to be hanged for making a treaty by which he surrendered two fortresses which he might have retained till they were relieved by the Emperor, which could have been accomplished by Napoleon in less than three months, probably with little loss to the French army, save the stores of plunder which they had amassed, and which the convention allowed them quietly to carry off. The writer is ashamed to say that he has not yet seen Sir Hew Dalrymple's published memoir, in which he no doubt amply justifies his conduct: the best excuse we can make is, that no justification is necessary.

Early in October, an army for the assistance of the Spanish patriots was committed to Sir John Moore, and before the middle of that month, the different corps were on the march to Salamanca, which had been selected as the place of rendezvous. It had been deemed necessary, in consequence of the information received at Lisbon, to send the cavalry round by Escurial, and it was not till the 20th of December that the British cavalry was united at Toro, under the command of Lord Paget. It was composed of the 7th, 10th, 15th, and 18th British hussars, and the 3rd hussars of the German legion, and formed a body of about 2400 sabres.

No more perplexing situation can be imagined than that of the British cavalry. The French were greatly superior in number, flushed by recent success, and commanded by able and experienced officers: it is only necessary to mention General Franceschi, who was decidedly one of the most able officers in the French army. Lord Paget and his gallant troops do not appear to have been awed by these circumstances. The General lost no time in asserting his superiority: having received information that 700 *chasseurs à cheval* were at Sahagun, under the command of General Debelle, Lord Paget marched to attack them at the head of the 10th and 15th hussars, and so confident was his lordship of success, that he sent the 10th round the town to cut off the retreat of the enemy, while he attacked them in front with the 15th. The French picket was surprised and taken, with the exception of one or two men, who, having escaped, gave the alarm, and allowed time to the French brigade to form, which they accomplished under very favourable circumstances, having a ravine in their front; and the ground being covered with snow, rendered the attack more perplexing; Lord Paget, however, ordered the charge, which was made with the greatest vigour. The chasseurs, who received the charge without advancing to meet their antagonists, were completely overthrown; many were killed and wounded, and 157 prisoners, including two colonels and eleven or twelve inferior officers, were secured. One French author states Debelle's loss at 200; but at the lowest calculation, 157 is an enormous number of prisoners for one regiment to make, and must appear so to those who have witnessed the difficulty of securing cavalry prisoners; even when they are utterly destroyed as a body, small parties and single horsemen escape their conquerors.

We can confidently assert, that on many occasions not one-half of the prisoners who had surrendered have been eventually secured. The loss of the 15th on this occasion was very trifling, not exceeding thirty in killed and wounded, and some even of that small number were wounded by chance, in the French scuffle of retiring. We remember one hussar of the 15th, whose horse had fallen in the snow; while he was in the act of remounting, a French trooper, escaping from the throng, passed him, and seizing the fair occasion, by a cut of his sabre extended the mouth to the ear on each side: the wound speedily healed, and the man long continued in the regiment, though his personal charms were not enhanced by the application of the French cosmetic.

On the commencement of the retreat which occurred only three days after the gallant affair at Sahagun, the French pushed forward strong bodies of cavalry, which was the occasion of numerous combats, all of which terminated most gloriously for the British. At Villa Franca, a strong detachment of French cavalry was attacked by Colonel Leigh, under the direction of Lord Paget, with two squadrons of the 10th hussars; the French were posted on a steep hill; the soil, a heavy clay, saturated with wet from the incessant rains, rendered the attack more difficult; the 10th overcame those difficulties, and completely overthrew the French, killing twenty of their number, and making a hundred prisoners. Another instance is mentioned in the narrative of Sir John Moore's campaign, from which the foregoing anecdote is copied:—"The 18th dragoons had signalized themselves in several former skirmishes; they were successful in six different attacks. Captain Jones, when at Palencia, ventured to charge a hundred French dragoons with only thirty British; fourteen of the enemy were killed and six made prisoners." In a letter addressed to Lord Castlereagh by Sir John Moore, dated December 28th, after recounting the affair of Sahagun, Sir John adds, " there have been taken by the cavalry since our march from Salamanca, from 400 to 500, besides a considerable number of killed; our cavalry is very superior in quality to any the French have, and the right spirit has been infused into them by the example and instruction of their two leaders, Lord Paget and Brigadier-General Stewart."

The last opportunity afforded to Lord Paget of evincing his superiority occurred on the 29th: the main body of infantry having left Benevente, General Lefebre, thinking that nothing remained but the cavalry pickets, which were posted near the Esla, distant about a mile from the town, crossed that river with the chasseurs of the imperial guard, which we have repeatedly heard mentioned by French officers as the best cavalry in the service. The affair which followed is thus described in Sir John Moore's Narrative:—

" At nine o'clock A.M. 500 or 600 of the imperial guard plunged into the river and crossed over; they were immediately opposed by the pickets under Colonel Otway, which, when united, amounted only to 220 men. They retired slowly before the enemy, bravely disputing every inch of ground, and, upon the pickets being reinforced by a small body of the 3rd dragoons, they charged with so much fury, that the first squadron broke through, and was, for a time, surrounded by the enemy: wheeling up, they extricated themselves by charging back through the enemy. Lord Paget soon reached the field with the 10th hussars, and having drawn the French from the river, he charged; but before the British could close, the chasseurs wheeled about and fled to the ford, leaving on the field fifty-five killed and wounded, and seventy prisoners, among whom was General Lefebre. The imperial guards shewed themselves much superior to any cavalry which the British had before engaged; they fought gallantly, and killed or wounded near fifty of our dragoons."

The number of wounded who escaped was very large. Baron Larrey, in his narrative, mentions the number, many of them very severely injured, and describes the cases of several of them who died in the hospital. They are curious, and prove that the old light dragoon sabre, much as we disapprove of it, might be applied to some purpose. In this affair, the conduct of the pickets was admirable indeed, as they checked a brave enemy treble their number. When joined by the 10th hussars, the British force fully equalled that of the French, when no farther opposition was offered. The circumstances of this gallant affair are well known, and it would be needless to detail them farther. The French army does not appear to have regretted this humiliation of the chasseurs, who, since Austerlitz, had claimed the title of Invincible. There appears to have been an overbearing spirit among the French cavalry towards their infantry. We remember a ridiculous display of that feeling. Shortly after the peace of 1814, a captain of French *chasseurs à cheval* was supping with a small party of British officers, when he addressed himself to an officer of dragoons present, " Brave captain of hussars, my fellow soldier, I pledge you to a glass of wine;" and then, turning to two very fine young men, who were officers of a distinguished infantry corps, he said, in a most superciliously condescending manner, " and, *Messieurs d'infanterie*, I am not proud ; the *fantassin* is good in his line, and I am willing that you should join us. *Mon camarade! nous buvons, Messieurs d'infanterie, à votre santé.*"

In all the encounters during this short but brilliant period, Lord Paget appears to have been present : it is quite impossible that during a long campaign his lordship could have shared in every affair of post, nor would it have been necessary. He had set the example and encouraged the spirit; he had established a confidence of superiority which would not have been obliterated ; and it is deeply to be lamented that an officer who evinced so much bravery, skill, and self-possession in his first campaign, was doomed to take no farther share in the Peninsular war. The British cavalry was infinitely inferior in number to that of the French, which was also commanded by experienced officers, who had frequently distinguished themselves, and, being placed under the eye of the Emperor, were certain of immediate reward: the legion of honour, whose crosses were liberally bestowed on the brave, was of itself a great stimulus to exertion; nevertheless, the British cavalry, without that incentive, at once asserted its superiority, and lost no opportunity to establish its claim.

In most cases, the object of the occupation of ground might have been accomplished without coming to the *arme blanche*, as at Sahagun. Debelle and his chasseurs might have been skirmished out of the latter place, and as far as regards the occupation of the town, the object of the general-in-chief would have been equally attained, but without establishing the valour of the British cavalry. Lord Paget wisely avoided half measures, which would have left each party uncertain as to their intrinsic merit.

After the affair of Benevente, the army retired rapidly to Astorga, and soon afterwards, from the want of shoes, or, as we have heard, of nails, the cavalry became absolutely non-effective. It is natural that a corps hurried out of England, and at once brought into active service, to which they were quite unused, should have been deficiently equipped. We remember a striking instance of the necessity of practice to inform us of our wants:— in the staff of a general, whose table, on opening the campaign, was supplied with every comfort, and even luxuries, on sitting down to their first dinner, it was discovered that among the supply of condiments, &c. the simple omission of salt rendered their feast a very unsavoury one. On the retreat, it was frequently necessary to shoot a number of the cavalry horses, which could not proceed for want of shoes; and, in the morning, numerous shots were frequently heard, which proved to be the destruction of horses.

We think it was at Herrerias, that the reserve had turned out, after a short repose, to continue the retreat; a number of shots were heard in the front, and the general sent his aide-de-camp to inquire into the cause; he returned with the answer, "It is only shooting horses." The plot, however, thickened; the aide-de-camp was again dispatched, and again returned with the answer, "Only shooting horses." The general, however, only replied, "Nonsense, there has been firing enough to shoot all the horses in the army." The posts had, in fact, been attacked.

A great part of the retreat, after leaving Villa Franca, was through a country perfectly unsuited to cavalry. The hussars continued to render any assistance in their power, and on many occasions were useful. When the reserve retired in the night from the position above Constantino, a party of the 15th remained and kept up the fires, by which means the French were prevented molesting the retreat, which they might have done in the open country, through which the road to Lugo lay, and which the reserve had traversed with perfect safety by good time on the following morning.

THE BRITISH CAMPAIGN OF 1809, UNDER SIR A. WELLESLEY.*

On the 18th of January, 1809, when the last transport, containing the rear guard of Sir J. Moore's army, sailed from the harbour of Corunna, the British little foresaw that the Peninsula was still to be the arena for their conquests and renown. None were so sanguine as to hope that their splendid successes and example should yet cause Europe to regain the moral feelings she had lost under the long victorious career of France, or that the latter country was finally to sink under their exertions.

No more did Buonaparte suspect, when halting on the confines of the Gallician mountains, and leaving to Soult the easy duty of " driving the leo-

* From the revised journal of an Officer on the staff of the army.

pard into the sea," that his legions were soon to be checked and defeated; or that his vaunted representation of the broken-hearted and dismayed state of the British army, should, by the repulse of his troops, within a few days after, in a set battle, become a severe reflection on the conduct of his own soldiery. Neither Soult nor the Frenchmen under his command could have supposed, at the same period, how early the fate of war would create a total reverse in their hitherto prosperous campaigns; or that their corps, which had led the advance to Corunna, should soon become the *pursued*, and in a far more disastrous retreat than that they had just witnessed. But Buonaparte ever miscalculated, and at this time was wholly unacquainted with the perseverance of our national character, or the power of England; and when he compared her apparent means with that of France, by showing she had not a million of infantry, or one hundred thousand cavalry, to oppose her rival, he had to learn the extent of her vast and boundless resources, and the determined character of her people.*

When this boastful and triumphant comparison

* This was not greatly exaggerated, if the artillery, the regular foreign regiments in the French service, and those of the various countries of Europe, at Buonaparte's disposal, are included. "Sous le titre modeste de protecteur, Napoléon envahit l'argent et les soldats d'une moitié de l'Allemagne," says Foy, speaking of the Confederation of the Rhine; and besides, he had the armies of Italy, Naples, and Holland, at his command.

was made, the ruler of France little feared that the refutation of England's inadequacy to cope with his power, would be proved, within seven years, by her hurling him from the throne, by leading him a captive at her chariot wheels, or that he should end his days in one of her distant colonies, in confinement and obscurity! Buonaparte considered the army expelled from Spain as the utmost extent of the means and exertion of the English as a military people, and that they could not again appear on the continent. He naturally deduced from this, that the subjection of both Spain and Portugal was the inevitable consequence of his success in Galicia, and that it only required the time necessary for their occupation, to secure them under Gallic sway.*

At the moment when Buonaparte thought the Peninsula at his feet, the seeds of discontent, sown by that restless ambition which was urging him on to his ruin, began to develop themselves in a distant and northern nation. Their growth to maturity was as rapid as opportune, and created a powerful diversion in favour of those countries to the southward, suffering under his yoke.

* Cependant parce que les Anglois s'étaient embarqués à a Corogne, Napoléon se complut dans l'idée qu'ils ne reparaitraient point sur le Continent, et que les Portugais perdant tout espoir d'en être secourus, reçevraient les Français en amis—telle était son aveugle confiance, que les mouvemens de l'armée étaient tracés par dates. *Mémoires sur les Operations Militaires des Français en Gallice, en Portugal, et dans le Vallée du Tage, en* 1809.

The perhaps necessary employment of the French nation, and of the military feeling and spirit grown up since the revolution, which Napoleon fostered, had twice, previously to his invasion of Spain, caused him to direct his conquests against his most powerful military neighbour—Austria.

The last campaign of 1806 left the family of Hapsburgh indignant at its reverses, and on their vanquisher becoming entangled by his unjust aggression of Spain, they hoped a fit opportunity was offered for redeeming their character and importance in Europe. If the bold advance of Sir J. Moore into the heart of Spain, and his demonstration on Carion, had made Buonaparte divert the most considerable portion of his armies on the front or flanks of the English, thus interrupting, for a time, in other quarters, the rapidity of conquest, not less did the Austrian declaration of war, drawing off a portion of the resources of France, tend materially to the ultimate advantage of the rightful cause. Buonaparte was not only personally arrested from overrunning Spain by his return to France, but from directing a just combination among his dispersed marshals, which circumstance fortunately allowed England to regain a firm footing in the Peninsula, and, by the events of the succeeding campaign, an opportunity of renewing a good feeling and confidence in the people. Considering the re-organized Austrian as a more dangerous enemy than the broken Spaniards or expelled English, Buonaparte, on withdrawing from Astorga, only passed through Madrid and returned to Paris. He, however, left (with the exception of the imperial guard, about 15,000 of whom had accompanied him across the Pyrenees) his armies entire, under the command of his various marshals, to complete the subjugation of Spain.

Of these eight *corps d'armée*, (each equal to the whole British army,) which had crossed the frontier, five had co-operated directly or otherwise against Sir J. Moore. The sixth, commanded by the gallant Ney,* was ordered to remain, and

---

* As the French generals are occasionally designated sometimes by name, and at others by their titles, a list of both is annexed.—ED.

BERTHIER . Prince of Neufchatel; a particular favourite of Napoleon; was chief of the emperor's staff, and major-general of the French army.

MURAT ... Grand Duke of Berg, and afterwards King of Naples; the best cavalry officer of the day. He was married to the sister of Napoleon.

MASSENA . Prince of Essling, and Duke of Rivoli.
NEY ..... Prince of Moskwa, and Duke of Elchingen.
SOULT.... Duke of Dalmatia.
VICTOR ... Duke of Belluno.
BESSIERS.. Duke of Istria.
MONCEY .. Duke of Corregliano.
LEFEBRE.. Duke of Dantzic.
MORTIER . Duke of Treviso.
JUNOT.... Duke of Abrantes.
MARMONT . Duke of Ragusa.
SUCHET... Duke of Albufera.
LANNES... Duke of Montebello.
AUGEREAU, Duke of Castiglione.
JOURDAN.. Marshal of France.

reduce Galicia and the Asturias. The fourth, under Mortier, with a vast body of cavalry, commanded by Kellerman, was directed to overawe Leon and Castile; while Victor, with the first corps, was at once to complete the ruin of the beaten Spanish armies, and to threaten the line of the Tagus, the south of Portugal, and eventually its capital. The eighth corps, which had, under Junot, served in 1807-8 in Portugal, and, according to the convention of Cintra, been carried to Rochelle, and subsequently recrossed Spain, and met their old antagonists before Corunna, was broken up, and its *debris* added to the second corps under Soult.*

This force was intended to take the active part of the campaign against Portugal, which country was to be immediately attacked, the orders to that effect being received within ten days after the embarkation of the British. So certain was Buonaparte of Soult's conquest, that he fixed the 5th of February for the arrival of his troops at Oporto—and the 16th of the same month for his triumphant entrance into Lisbon!

The army under Soult consisted of 23,500 men, of which 4,000 were cavalry, divided into ten regi-

---

* At Corunna, a soldier's wife, taken in the retreat, was sent in by Junot. She brought his compliments to the general officers he had known the preceding year, and a message that he and his corps were opposite them, ready to "*pay off old scores.*"

ments. It was accompanied by fifty-six pieces of cannon. Besides these troops, a division under General Lapisse was to be pushed south from Salamanca, to invade Portugal, by the way of Almeida, at the same time becoming a point of communication between the corps of Victor and Soult. The army of the latter general advanced to the southward, through Galicia, by several routes, but the principal part, with the artillery, marched through St. Jago. His directions were to invade Portugal along the sea-coast, and with that view, he attempted to cross the Minho, at Tuy —but failing, was forced to proceed up the right bank of the river as far as Orense, where he crossed that barrier. Besides the great loss of time from this disappointment and change of route, the army was much detained by the opposition of the peasantry, and the remains of Romana's dispersed army, and it was only on the 10th of March it was able to enter Portugal, by the valley of the Tamega.

Though Soult met considerable opposition from General Silveira,* the French army reached and captured Chaves on the 12th, and Braga on the 20th, after defeating a corps of Portuguese troops under Baron Eben; and nine days subsequent, forced the entrenched lines covering Oporto, having been more than seven times longer on their march than had been calculated by Buonaparte. The next

* This is the present Marquis de Chaves, who headed the insurrection in 1827, against the constitution.

day, General Franceschi, with several regiments of cavalry, was pushed on to the banks of the Vouga, where he established his posts opposite those of Colonel Trant, who had collected a few troops and ordenança, and a corps of volunteers, formed of the students of the university of Coimbra, who gave up their literary pursuits for the defence of their country. The division of General Mermet was cantoned in Villa Nova, with the 31st regiment in its front in support of the cavalry. Soult's corps had been diminished upwards of 3,000 men within the two months occupied in its march, having left great numbers of sick at Chaves and Braga. Although it had overcome all opposition, its chief found himself in an isolated position, shut out from all intercourse with the other French corps, and his difficulties increasing every day, as he was obliged to separate and detach a considerable portion of his force to subdue the country, and attempt to open his communication with Lapisse.

But however insecure and critical his post, it was likely to become more immediately endangered by the activity of the British, whose government, far from being discouraged at the result of the preceding year, was employed in preparation for a hearty prosecution of the contest. At the moment the British army withdrew from Corunna, the troops left in the Peninsula, including a brigade under Brigadier-General Cameron, (which had advanced to the north-east frontier of Portugal,) the 14th light dragoons, and the sick, convalescents, and stragglers of Sir J. Moore's army, did not consist of above 7,000 men, under the command of Sir J. Craddock, at Lisbon. The want of information was great, and the state of alarm so exaggerated, that the advance of the French on that capital was daily expected. The artillery and cavalry were embarked, and the forts of St. Julien and Bugio dismantled, to prevent their guns being turned upon the ships while going out of the Tagus.

The Portuguese felt the danger in which their country was placed, and the Regency called upon the people to rise *en masse*. They had little else than the populace to oppose the invader, as the same principle which had instigated the march of the Spanish corps under Romana to Denmark, had been acted upon with the only respectable part of the Portuguese army. These had been sent into France under the Marquis de Lorna, and suffered a harder fate than the Spanish troops, the greater part of whom, by aid of the English fleet, returned to fight their country's battles, while the miserable remnant of the Portuguese perished at Moscow, under the appellation of the " *Legion Portugaise.*" The remaining regular troops were scarcely to be considered as organized, and those under Silveira, though actuated by the best spirit, were little better than the rest. One regiment of two battalions, called the Lusitanian legion, raised by Sir R. Wilson at Oporto, was an exception to the general inefficiency, it having made considerable progress in discipline and order. Sir Robert had proceeded with the first battalion to the frontier opposite Ciudad Rodrigo, while the other, under Baron Eben, had been engaged in the defence of the Tras os Montes, and in the entrenchments around Oporto.

But this inefficient army had a probability of being regenerated. Scarce had the fleet returned from Corunna, when the British government evinced its conviction that the Spanish and Portuguese cause was not hopeless, and with a view to make the latter aid in their own defence, sent General Beresford, with twelve or fourteen officers, from England, to re-organize and form their army. This determination being made so soon after, and before the despondency of the failure at Corunna had worn off, was much ridiculed at the time as being too late, and doubts were expressed if Lisbon would not be in the possession of the enemy before they could reach the Tagus. This anticipation was not confirmed by events, and with the rank of a Portuguese marshal, General Beresford, on the 13th of March, issued a spirited address to that nation, in which he assured them, that they only required organization and discipline to make them equal to face the invader. How just were the Marshal's ideas of their latent martial character, is to be learned from their brilliant conduct in the ensuing war. Much, however, was to be done to raise from degradation the military profession in Portugal. Perhaps, in no age or country, had it fallen so low. Even among the Chinese, where civil and literary celebrity is ever sought before that of arms, it was never so despised, as it had been among our faithful allies since the war of succession.

In 1762-3, La Lippe had been called in by the Marquis de Pombal, who formed the army into twenty-four regiments of infantry, twelve of cavalry, and four of artillery, and which had continued, at least nominally, till the arrival of Junot. Few of his regulations were permanent or long respected. During the whole of the latter half of the eighteenth century, in all the short successive wars, though occasionally invigorated by fresh disciplinarians from foreign countries, the Portuguese army never rose above mediocrity. It is true, but few opportunities were offered of trial; but in 1801, at Aronches, the scandalous panic that seized the corps commanded by the Duke d'Alafoes, made them be considered worse than contemptible. Not that the people required either physical or moral qualities, as might be easily proved from their conflicts with the Spaniards, having ever placed themselves at least upon an equality, in courage and conduct, with their neighbours. The French in their progress through the Tras os Montes, drew a favourable comparison of their bravery with that of the Spaniards, while it was impossible to see the peasantry and not be convinced of their bodily strength and capability of bearing fatigue.

The difficulty of creating a Portuguese army lay not with the men, but with the officers, who had sunk so low in the estimation of the country, of themselves, and of their men, as to be little superior to the degrading and menial offices, which (as when La Lippe arrived in 1762) they once filled, of servants in the houses of the nobility; and no cause of improvement had offered since those disgraceful times, which had naturally placed them on terms of the greatest familiarity and equality with their men. It was no uncommon spectacle to find them in a common *cabaret,* gambling, if not cheating the soldiers out of the pay they had just made over to them. It was not less to counteract this deteriorating cause, than to organize the soldiers, that General Beresford had taken officers with him from England, whose numbers were subsequently greatly increased. Those who accompanied him in the first instance, and some who afterwards joined him, were, with the view to place British captains in command of battalions, first raised a step of rank in their own service, and received another in that of the Portuguese, when appointed to regiments.

The Marshal established his head-quarters at Thomar, and fairly grappled with all the prominent difficulties, and, aided by the example and conduct of the officers placed under his orders, at once did away the causes of the want of respect and confidence of the men. The interior economy was strictly investigated, and the regiments made efficient, not only by British arms and equipments, but by being subsidized to fight their own battles by the money of England.

Without going farther into detail, it will be sufficient to remark, that the arrangement and system of the Marshal were so good, and improvement so rapid in the Portuguese army, that within two months from the date of his first order, a battalion of the 16th regiment was brought into collision with the enemy; and if it did not distinguish itself as much as it did on so many subsequent occasions, it neither evinced confusion nor dismay. Eighteen months after, the general conduct of the whole Portuguese army was marked by traits of discipline and bravery, and even of individual gallantry, which continued on the increase to the end of the war, and which were most unquestionably shown on many subsequent occasions, by overthrowing the veterans of France with the bayonet. The twenty-four regiments of the line formed by La Lippe, had been broken into two battalions each, in 1797, and were continued at that establishment, as were the twelve regiments of cavalry, of which not above one-third had been ever mounted. The artillery was placed under British officers, as well as the other arms. To this the whole population was to be added, though as irregulars or ordenança, rather than militia. This force was increased in the course of the next year, by six regiments of caçadores, which were, at a later period during the war, doubled, on their value being duly appreciated. But England was not less active in sending reinforcements of her own troops to the Peninsula. Doubts had been once entertained, whether future operations should be carried on from the south of Spain, rather than from Portugal, and the first convoy of troops was directed to Cadiz. On its reaching that port, the besotted Spaniards hesitated, as they had the year before, when Sir D. Baird arrived at Corunna, respecting the disembarkation of the troops. After some futile negotiations, and (in consequence of the slow advance of the French) in the revived hope of saving Lisbon, the British troops fortunately passed to the latter place, as the frontier and statistics of Portugal are better calculated for military operations than those of Andalusia.

The first reinforcement that reached the Tagus early in March was commanded by Lieutenant-General Sherbrooke, which was followed in the beginning of April by another, under Major-General Hill, together increasing the army to 13,000 men. The arrival allayed much the fears, and not only allowed Sir J. Craddock to take up a position out of Lisbon, and cover the great roads that led upon it, with the right on Santarem, and the left on the sea, but even to contemplate offensive operations, and in the middle of April to push the army in advance towards the north.

In the meantime, the administration at home had determined to give the command of the army for the defence of Portugal to the same general officer who had so successfully attacked it the year before, and in order to make room for him, Sir J. Craddock was appointed to be Governor of Gibraltar.

Sir A. Wellesley sailed on the 16th of April on board the Surveillant frigate, Sir George Collier, from Portsmouth, to which place or to England he did not again return, until 1814, as Duke of Wellington,—when, on his first arrival from the south of France, his Grace proceeded direct to the same town, where the Prince Regent was showing to the Emperor of Russia and the King of Prussia the arsenal and fleet. The same night the frigate was nearly lost, off St. Catherine's Head, in the Isle of Wight: so imminent was the danger, and so close the ship to the breakers, that Sir G. Collier desired Sir Arthur to dress, and thinking the loss of the vessel certain, advised him to stay by the wreck as long as possible, this being considered a more probable means of escape than a premature attempt to reach the shore. The frigate missed stays more than once, but a fortunate shift of wind carried her off the land. Even had all escaped with life, but for this shift of wind (or rather the never-failing happy destiny of Sir

Arthur, who might have desired Sir G. Collier not to despair, while he had (not Cæsar) but Wellesley and his fortunes on board—much valuable time would have been lost, not only in striking the blow at Soult, but by allowing fresh combinations between the distant French marshals, and perhaps not giving the opportunity of opposing them in detail.

The entrance of the Surveillant into the Tagus was an interesting event, when at a distance of twenty years it is considered that she bore in her bosom the regeneration of England's military fame, and that Europe was to date from it the positive commencement of that formidable and permanent position taken up by our armies, which allowed its nations to breathe, and subsequently, by our victories over the common enemy, to break the spell of gloomy conviction, becoming daily universal, that the French armies were invincible.

Sir Arthur's landing at Lisbon on the 22nd of April was strongly marked by the gratifying expression of the people's feeling; they hailed him as their former deliverer, and evinced their gratitude by illuminating the city during his stay. On the 25th, Sir J. Craddock, in a farewell address, bade adieu to the army, and two days subsequent Sir Arthur took the command, and in his first order changed its staff, placing Brigadier-General Stewart at the head of the adjutant-general's, and Colonel Murray, 3rd guards, at that of the quartermaster-general's department. The same day his excellency went in procession with the royal carriages, escorted by a squadron of the 16th dragoons, to be introduced to the Regency, at the palace of the Inquisition in the Roçio, on his receiving from them the rank of Marshal-General.

The state of affairs in the Peninsula at this time was neither satisfactory nor encouraging. Although Buonaparte had withdrawn from Spain, his legions, which had passed through Madrid, and witnessed the replacing Joseph on the throne, had subsequently overthrown all the Spanish armies. The advance guard of the Duke del Infantado's army, under Vanegas, had been beaten at Ucles, in January, and the army of Cartojal had met a defeat at Ciudad Real. Cuesta, with the main Spanish army, after retiring across the Tagus, and taking position at Almaraz, had allowed his flank to be turned by the bridge of Arzobispo, and was forced, in consequence, to retreat across the Guadiana, when, at Medellin, on its banks, he was on the 28th of March completely routed through the bad conduct of his cavalry. His infantry, who from their behaviour on this occasion deserved a better fate, were so completely,— not at the mercy, for none was shown,—but in the power of the enemy's cavalry, that their horsemen were worn out with slaughtering their easily routed victims; and it was reported, many wore their arms for several days in slings, from having had such opportunity of using their sabres. The remnant of the Spanish army took refuge in the Sierra

Morena, where attempts were made to recruit the infantry, the dastardly cavalry, not less disgraced in the action by their conduct, than after by the General's notice of it, scarcely requiring a man. While so little aid was to be expected for the British from these broken armies, Victor was left, with 22,000 men, in a position threatening the weakest part of Portugal, and, by the existence of the bridge of Alcantara, both banks of the Tagus.

But in the meantime Soult's position at Oporto had become more critical every day. Vigo had surrendered to the Spaniards, aided by some English ships, while Silveira had retaken Chaves, with 1300 sick, and continued his advance by Amarante to Penafiel. Lapisse had advanced as far as Ciudad Rodrigo, but on finding himself opposed by Sir R. Wilson and the Spanish troops, he made no attempt to communicate with, or join Soult, and after a little skirmishing, passed on to join Victor on the Tagus. Soult's communications were thus wholly destroyed, and his force had been much dispersed in trying to make them good, not less than between 6000 and 7000 men having been sent into the valley of the Tamega and other points. Thus, although Marshal Soult had not above half the number of men collected at Oporto that Victor's army consisted of, still the British army was not strong enough to oppose both at once. It became necessary, therefore, to act with vigour on one point, and the former army being the weakest, and in the Portuguese territory, and whose retreat was endangered, drew the more immediate attention of the British general. Lest Victor should be enabled to advance to the south of the Tagus, Sir Arthur lost no time at Lisbon, and after a stay of but six days, set out on the 23rd for the army, part of which had arrived at Coimbra. All the towns were illuminated on the road, and on his excellency's arrival at Coimbra on the 2nd, in addition to other demonstrations of joy, the ladies from the balconies covered him with roses and sugar-plums.

The army was fresh brigaded on the 4th of May.

Cavalry.
MAJOR-GENERAL COTTON.
14th Light Dragoons.
20th ,,   ,,
16th ,,   ,,
 3rd ,,   ,,   King's German Legion.

Infantry.
BRIGADIER-GENERAL H. CAMPBELL.
2 Battalions of Guards.
1 Company, 5th Battalion, 60th Reg. (Riflemen.)

First Brigade.
MAJOR-GENERAL HILL.
3rd, or Buffs.
66th Regiment.
48th   ,,
1 Company, 5th Battalion, 60th Regiment.

Third Brigade.
MAJOR-GENERAL TILSON.
5 Companies, 5th Battalion, 60th Regiment.
88th Regiment.
1 Battalion Portuguese Grenadiers.
87th Regiment.

PENINSULAR SKETCHES.

Fifth Brigade.
BRIGADIER-GENERAL A. CAMPBELL.
7th Fusileers.
1 Battalion 10th Portuguese Regiment.
53rd Regiment.
1 Company, 5th Battalion, 60th Regiment.

Seventh Brigade.
BRIGADIER-GENERAL CAMERON.
9th Regiment.
2nd Battalion 10th Portuguese Regiment.
83rd Regiment.
1 Company, 5th Battalion, 60th Regiment.

Sixth Brigade.
BRIGADIER-GENERAL STEWART.
1st Battalion Detachments.
1st Battalion 16th Portuguese Regiment.
20th Regiment.

Fourth Brigade.
BRIGADIER-GENERAL SONTAG.
2nd Battalion Detachments.
2nd Battalion 16th Portuguese Regiment.
97th Regiment.
1 Company, 5th Battalion, 60th Regiment.

Second Brigade.
MAJOR-GENERAL M'KENZIE.
27th Regiment.
45th   ,,
31st   ,,

King's German Legion.
MAJOR-GENERAL MURRAY.
1 Brigade (2 Regiments).
BRIGADIER-GENERAL LANGWORTH.
2 Brigades (2 Regiments).
BRIGADIER-GENERAL DRIBOURG.

It was subsequently divided into wings, under Lieutenant-Generals Sherbrooke and Paget, and the cavalry placed under Lieutenant-General Payne. The same reasons that pressed the departure of the commander of the forces from Lisbon, accelerated the preparations of the campaign, and the advance upon Oporto. A few days' delay were, however, necessary to complete the arrangements, according to the following plan of operations. While Sir Arthur advanced with the main force of the army on the enemy's front, a corps that quitted Coimbra on the 5th, was intended to move on the enemy's left flank and rear. This was to be under the orders of Marshal Beresford, and consisted of Major-General Tilson's brigade, and some cavalry. It was ordered to direct its march on Viseu, and across the Douro, to co-operate with Silveira. This officer was unfortunately driven from Amarante on the 2nd of May, the enemy thus opening to themselves a practicable route for carriage to the eastern frontier. Lisbon was to be covered, during these northern operations, by a corps of observation, under Major-General M'Kenzie, to watch Victor. It was posted at Santarem, consisting of the general's own brigade, a brigade of British heavy cavalry, and 7,000 Portuguese. In his front, at Alcantara, was Colonel Mayne, with a battalion of the Lusitanian legion.

On the 6th, opportunity was taken of inspecting that portion of the army around Coimbra, on some sands two miles from the town. The British troops appeared in excellent order, and the Portuguese regiments, though not so soldier-like as their allies, looked better than was expected, as it was the fashion of the day to hold them in utter contempt. Their dark olive complexions, and blue single-breasted coats, gave them a *sombre* appearance when in contrast with our countrymen, and it could not be denied that the comparison was to the advantage of the latter. It was a fine sight, although of the 21,000 British in Portugal, only 17,000 were present, on account of the detachment of two corps.*

On the 7th, part of these troops advanced in two columns on the main roads towards Oporto, by Adiga on the Vouga, and by the Bay of Aveiro to Ovar. On the 9th, the remainder of the army and head-quarters quitted Coimbra in the same direction. The advance of the French, under General Franceschi, had remained on the Vouga, and arrangements were made for surprising it on the 10th.† If the success of this *coup d'essai* was to be taken as a sample of our future proceedings, it would have been unfortunate, as between the neighing of the horses of the Portuguese cavalry, and the stupidity of the guides, the enemy were prepared, and the whole was a complete failure. But for the withdrawing of the French, and the capture of two

* The French called the British force with which we advanced against Oporto, 30,000 men.

† Franceschi was an old opponent of General Stewart, the adjutant-general having commanded the brigade, of which a portion had been surprised at Rueda, in Leon, a few months before, during the Corunna campaign.—ED.

four-pounders, we had little to boast in the scrambling skirmish it produced. We advanced to the spot where they had been encamped, which was as much chosen for beauty of situation as strength. We had here the first instance of the trouble the French took in embellishing their camps; in the centre of the front they were erecting a pretty wooden obelisk.

On the following day the army advanced on the great northern road, and, about twelve o'clock, a squadron of the enemy was seen on the skirts of a wood, in front of a little village. On some three-pounders and our cavalry advancing against them, they fell back, but showed some infantry, and our light troops were directed to attack them. This produced some skirmishing as we continued to advance. The country was much inclosed. The enemy clung longer to their ground than was expected, as we only supposed it an affair of posts; but a column of infantry, on a height over the village of Grijon, soon convinced us that it was at least a strong advanced guard. The road here crossed a ridge of hills at right angles, covered with olives and fir woods, which offered a strong position. The ground was not ill-chosen, though the left was without any *appui*. Brigadier-General Stewart's brigade formed in line to the support of the 16th Portuguese regiment, acting as skirmishers on the left of the road, while the German light infantry were engaged on the right. The four battalions of the German legion brought their left shoulders up, and marched diagonally across to turn the left, the enemy's weak point. The skirmishing was very sharp in the woods, and the 29th regiment was forced to support the Portuguese, who were once obliged to fall back. At this moment they pushed a column of infantry down the road through the village of Grijon, which being reported to Sir Arthur, he replied, in the most quiet manner, "Order the battalion of detachments to charge them with the bayonet if they come any farther."

The officers of the staff, many of them at that time young soldiers, could not help evincing strong feeling on hearing the simple and distinct manner in which this order was given, but before some months had passed over their heads, they had opportunities of not only hearing similar orders repeated, but of seeing them carried into execution. On this occasion, the alternative mentioned by Sir Arthur did not occur, as on their flank being turned, and finding our whole force on their front, about two o'clock they retired from the position. Our guns were brought up to bear upon them in their retreat, and Brigadier-General Stewart put himself at the head of two squadrons, and trotted after the enemy, who withdrew their troops with astonishing rapidity. The country was much inclosed and intersected, and on nearing the enemy's rear-guard, the cavalry entered a deep ravine, closely wooded. The French lined the sides with their light infantry, who opened a close and sharp fire, which, for a moment, created some confusion, and checked the advance; but on coming in sight of five companies, drawn up in line in a wider space, by the exertion and example of the general, he led them to the charge, broke through the enemy, and made above one hundred prisoners. This rapid movement threw the 31st French regiment off the road of retreat, and they fell back on Ovar, where finding Major-General Hill, they withdrew, after some skirmishing, to Oporto, during the night. Thus ended the operations of this day, which were beautiful in their prosecution, and satisfactory in the result.

The enemy's corps (besides the cavalry engaged the day before on the Vouga) consisted of four or five thousand infantry of the division of Mermet, which had been pushed on to this ground from Villa Nova on the 8th, on Soult's hearing of our probable advance. It was the 47ᵉ *de line* that was charged on the retreat, and however valiantly they may have acted, cannot be praised for prudence or judgment in forming in line to receive cavalry.* Instead of this, had they vaulted over the enclosures, or scrambled up the banks, they might have killed every man of the cavalry without endangering a soldier. One of the privates was very loud in his attempts to draw notice, and by his vociferation, that he was the son of a marquis, proved the aristocratic feeling not quite deadened by the revolution, though the conscription has reached and levelled

* In the French account of this campaign, published at Paris, 1821, the author represents le 47ᵉ de line, when covering this retreat, as "se conduisant valeureusement."

all ranks of society. Our loss was under one hundred men: one officer of the 16th dragoons received no less than three balls, though, happily, none proved mortal.

Our first progress to the front, on the morning of the 12th, showed us the horrors produced by a war of invasion. Beyond Grijon nine bodies of unfortunate Portuguese peasants were seen hanging on trees by the side of the road, blackened in the sun. The common people, naturally considering the enemy as *hors de la loi*, sought every means, open or otherwise, for their destruction. This brought on them that retaliation produced by the military ideas of a regular army, who conceived they had only a right to be opposed by *soldiers*, and not by the unclothed and unorganized population. These they considered as insurgents and brigands, and shot and hung, with as little compassion as we should a burglar. The exasperation of the French was not wholly uncalled for, as the atrocities committed on the stragglers and sick were horrible, amounting often, besides shocking lingering deaths, to frightful mutilations. A hair-dresser who escaped from Oporto in the night, had brought in, soon after day-break, the intelligence that the enemy had destroyed the bridge of boats over the Douro at one o'clock; and, in addition, the still more disagreeable information, that all the boats were secured on the other side the Douro. On the fugitive barber being taken to Sir Arthur by Colonel Waters, of the adjutant-general's department, that officer was instructed to proceed immediately to the banks of the river, and directed to procure boats, *coute qui coute.*

As we advanced on the high road to Oporto, this report of the destruction of the bridge was confirmed, and doubts came fast and thick upon us, respecting the passage of the Douro in the face of an enemy. On our arrival at Villa Nova, we found General Hill's brigade arrived from Ovar, and with the troops of the centre column choking the streets; through these Sir Arthur threaded his way, and took post on the right of the town, in the garden of the convent of Serra. From this elevated spot the whole city was visible, like a panorama, and nothing that passed within it could be hidden from the view of the British general. The French guards and sentries were seen in the various parts of the town, but no bustle was evinced, or even apparent curiosity. No groups were noticed looking at us, which was afterwards accounted for, by learning that the French were ordered to remain in their quarters ready to turn out, and the Portuguese not allowed to appear beyond the walls of their houses. There were a few sentries in the quays, but none without the limits or above the town. A line of baggage discovered retiring beyond the town, across the distant hills, was the sole indication of our threatening neighbourhood.

The passage of a river, in the front of an enemy, is allowed to be the most difficult of military operations; and when it became obvious, from the collection of boats on the other bank, that precautions had been taken to secure them from us, the barrier appeared insurmountable. General Murray had been directed to march in the morning to try and cross the river, about five miles up, at Aventas, but having only four battalions and two squadrons, unless we could aid his successful passage, he would lie open to defeat; and in consequence our anxiety was very great to establish ourselves on the opposite bank. In the meanwhile, Colonel Waters (who has since become so distinguished for his intelligence and activity) had passed up the left bank of the river, searching for means to cross it, and about two miles above the city, found a small boat lying in the mud. The peasantry demurred at going over to the other side to procure some larger boats seen on the opposite bank; but the colonel (from speaking Portuguese like a native) learned that the Prior of Amarante was not distant from the spot, and hoped by his influence to attain his object. This patriotic priest, on learning the desire of the British, joined with Colonel Waters in inducing the peasants, after some persuasion, to accompany the colonel across, who brought back four boats.

When our doubts and fears were at the highest, this agreeable information arrived, and was received by all with the greatest satisfaction, and three companies of the Buffs, accompanied by General Paget, were immediately conveyed to the other side.

The spot at which they passed over and landed was about half a mile above the city, at the foot of a steep cliff, up which a zigzag road, or wide path, led to a vast, unfinished brick building, standing on the brink. This was intended for a new residence for the bishop, and placed in the Prado, being surrounded by a wall, with a large iron gate, opening on the road to Vallongo. It was a strong post, and the three companies, on gaining the summit, threw themselves into it, as it at once covered the place of disembarkation, and was for themselves a good means of defence. Our artillery was posted on the high bank, on the other side, completely commanding the Prado and the Vallongo road.

Soult had his quarters on the side of the city near the sea, and having collected all the boats, as he supposed, on the right bank, considered himself in perfect security. He thought if we made any attempt to cross, it would be in conjunction with our ships lying off the bar, and all his attention was devoted to that quarter. He even turned into ridicule the first report of our having crossed, and discredited the fact to the last, until it was incontestably proved by our firing. The boats had made more than one trip before any one in the town appeared to notice it. Foy has the credit of being the first to discover our having passed, and instantly ordered the nearest battalion to beat the *general*. We heard the drums rolling when nearly the whole of the Buffs had crossed, and soon saw symptoms of bustle and confusion in the town, and the French regiments forming on their parades. This was an anxious moment; and just as the whole of the Buffs had landed, a battalion was observed moving down a road towards them. This was the 17th, brought down by Foy, and which was quickly supported by the 70th. The first made an attack on the Buffs, who stood their ground, giving a tremendous fire, while our artillery from the opposite side killed and wounded a great number of the enemy.

More boats, in the meantime, were brought across, and more troops; the 48th, 66th, and a Portuguese battalion, landed, and not only defended themselves successfully, but even drove the enemy from the walls between the town and the bishop's palace. This petty success was seen by Sir Arthur and his staff, who cheered our soldiery as they chased the enemy from the various posts. The enemy's troops now came through the town in great numbers, and obliged our troops to confine themselves to the enclosure. They continued running along the road towards and beyond the iron gate, while our shells and shot were whizzing through the trees and between the houses into the road as they passed. They brought up a gun through the gate to batter the house; but this proved an unfortunate experiment, as our troops, increasing in number by fresh embarkations, though General Paget was wounded, charged and captured it. They also brought some guns to bear from the open spaces in the town, but they were tamely, if not badly served. But General Murray had made good his position on the north bank of the river, and we soon descried him making as much show as possible, marching with his ranks open towards the Vallongo road, thus threatening the communication of the enemy with Loison. He was not, however, strong enough to interrupt the retreat of 10,000 desperate men; for the French now began to think of nothing else, and directed their march toward Amarante. On their deserting the quays, the Portuguese jumped into the boats, which soon transported across (amidst the cheers of the people, and the waving of pocket-handkerchiefs by the women from the windows) the Guards and General Stewart's brigade, who proceeded through the town with the greatest speed.

The Buffs, in the meantime, had dashed into the city, and cut off a battery of light artillery in retreat, which, becoming jammed between that regiment and the 29th, received the fire of both, and was captured. The flight of the enemy was continued, but they were overtaken by the two squadrons which had passed with General Murray, led by Brigadier-General Stewart, who charged the rear and made 200 prisoners. Major Hervey, who commanded the dragoons, lost his arm. The enemy collected their scattered troops at some distance, but continued their retreat towards Amarante in the night. Our loss did not exceed 120 men, while the enemy, besides killed and wounded, left in our hands 500 prisoners and 1000 sick in the hospitals, and several pieces of cannon. The city was illuminated at night, and Sir Arthur, without allowing himself any rest, the same evening gave out an order of thanks to the army. The operations of the three preceding days had been most gratifying, and the quickness with which the enemy had been forced from his various positions and pursued, seldom equalled. The army had advanced eighty miles in four days, three of which were in constant presence of the enemy.

Sir Arthur had completely surprised in his quarters one of the most distinguished French marshals, and consummated in his face the most difficult operation in war—that of crossing a deep and rapid river before an enemy. Nothing can relieve Soult from the disgrace of this day; and all that has been, or whatever may be, written in his defence, can but palliate his want of precaution and fatal security. The rapidity of Sir Arthur's own movements had been wonderful; for within twenty-six days of leaving Portsmouth, Oporto was captured and the enemy in full retreat. Captain Fitzroy Stanhope, one of the commander-of-the-forces' aides-de-camp, was sent to England, with the despatches of this success, by one of the ships cruising off the port, whose crews from the sea had seen the smoke of the firing during the actions of the 11th and 12th.

The retreat of the enemy was directed upon Amarante, the seizure of which place from Silveira by Loison, ten days before, having opened them a loop-hole for escape. But Marshal Beresford, after crossing the Douro at Pedro de Regoa, had joined Silveira, and on the 11th drove Loison out of Amarante, and thus closed the road and the enemy's hopes in that direction. Loison fell back on Guimaraens by the good carriage-road that led to Chaves, sending information of his movement to Soult at Oporto. Soult, on his arrival at Penafiel on the night of the 12th, received this disagreeable news, and finding himself pressed in so many directions, and no road open for carriages, determined at once to destroy the heavy materiel of his corps, and to join Loison across the Sierra de Santa Catherina, at Guimaraens. Captain Mellish, who was sent on the morning of the 13th to Penafiel, confirmed the report which had reached Oporto, of the destruction of their ammunition-wagons, guns, and carriages. The cannon had been placed mouth to mouth and discharged into each other, by trains laid communicating through the mass of baggage and ammunition-wagons.

Want of provisions and uncertainty of the enemy's route prevented the advance of the army on the 13th, but the Germans were pushed on with some six-pounders on the road of the enemy's retreat. On ascertaining that the enemy had given up the idea of retreating by Amarante, orders were sent to Marshal Beresford, to direct his march on Chaves, at which place he arrived on the 16th, detaching Silveira in the direction of the enemy's rear on Ruivaens. On the 14th, the army advanced half way on the road towards Braga. Soult collected his army (the garrison of Braga retiring on our advance) on the morning of the 15th, at Guimaraens; but finding our troops at Villa Nova, and aware that no road was open for cannon, he destroyed the baggage and the military chest of Loison's corps, and in despair took to the goatherds' paths across the mountain, trusting to the interest, aid, and information procured by the Bishop of Braga. Their army was in great confusion during the 13th, but the two following days it became totally disorganized. The paths were so narrow, that but one man could pass at a time, and the cavalry were obliged to lead their horses, while their column, thus distressingly lengthened, had the additional misery of incessant rain, that fell in torrents during the whole of this trying period. The peasantry, happy in revenging the horrors and atrocities of their enemy's advance, watched them like vultures, and failed not to dart upon all who sunk under fatigue; the stones they rolled on them swept whole files into the abysses, while single shots from the mountain tops slew soldiers in the column of march. Their sufferings met commiseration from the British alone, who had not suffered from the guilty acts for which they were now receiving retribution.

Their *déroute* was so complete, that Sir A. Wellesley thought it unnecessary to follow them with the whole army beyond Braga, which city he reached on the 16th. The probability of Victor's threatening the south was also to be taken into consideration, and he therefore contented himself in pursuing with some cavalry, the Guards, and Brigadier-General Cameron's brigade, while the Germans, following the enemy, even with three-pounders, across the Sierra de Santa Catherina, reached Guimaraens the same day. The French continued their retreat, and on the night of the 15th reached Salamonde, where their position was most alarming. They found one of the bridges on the Cavado, on the road to Ruivaens, destroyed and occupied, while that called Ponte Nova, only offered a single beam. They, however, surprised and killed the Portuguese who guarded the last, and which proved the safety of their army. They restored the troops into some order on the night between the 15th and 16th, while the bridge was being repaired, which was made passable by the morning, and allowed them to continue their march towards Montalegre, leaving a rear-guard at Salamonde. Our cavalry discovered them about half-past one o'clock, but the Guards did not arrive until late. The position of the enemy was behind a deep and wide ravine, accessible only by the road, with their right on the torrent, and the left upon a ridge of broken mountains. The light troops were directed to turn this point, and when sufficiently on their flank, about half-past six, the column and two three-pounder guns, which had joined from General Murray's column, were pushed along the road to attack in front. The enemy, who had placed their pickets, thinking the cavalry were the only troops up, and hoping to continue all night, instantly retired from the position, and, as it was almost dark, little advantage could be taken of the confusion in which they fled, farther than the guns firing on their columns, and the light infantry pressing them *en tirailleur*: a few prisoners were made, among whom was an officer. The rain continued incessant, and the miserable village scarcely allowed cover for a quarter of the troops.

The next morning, the disasters of the enemy in their flight of the night before were fully revealed, by the wreck left at and near the bridge over the Cavado. The bridge had been only partially repaired, and the infantry were obliged to file, and the cavalry to lead their horses across. The passage must have been ever hazardous, but the confusion occasioned by our pursuit and cannonade, and the darkness of the night, rendered it to a degree hazardous. The rocky torrent of the Cavado, in consequence, presented next morning an extraordinary spectacle. Men and horses, sumpter animals and baggage, had been precipitated into the river, and literally choked the course of the stream. Here, with these fatal accompaniments of death and dismay, was disgorged the last of the plunder of Oporto, and the other cities north of the Douro. All kinds of valuable goods were left on the road, while above three hundred horses sunk in the water, and mules laden with property fell into the hands of the grenadier and light companies of the Guards. These active-fingered gentry soon found that fishing for boxes and bodies out of the stream produced pieces of plate, and purses and belts full of gold and silver, and amidst scenes of death and destruction, arose shouts of the most noisy merriment.

Soult reached the pass of Ruivaens before Silveira, or his capture would have been certain; but at that place learning that Marshal Beresford had arrived at Chaves, he turned the head of his columns towards Montalegre. The British army, being greatly distressed from fatigue, want of provisions, and bad weather, only advanced a league on the 17th; but a squadron of cavalry and a battalion of Germans, were pushed to the bridge of Miscrele and Villa da Ponte. On the 18th, the Guards, Germans, and Brigadier-General Cameron's brigade, pushed on in pursuit of the enemy, whose track might have been found from the *débris* of baggage, dead and dying men, (worn down by fatigue and misery to skeletons,) houghed mules, and immense quantities of cartridges, which the wearied soldiery threw away to lighten themselves from even the weight of the balls.

Marshal Beresford had directed Silveira to march on Montalegre, but he arrived about two hours too late, the enemy having dragged their weary march along by that town and across the frontier, at twelve o'clock. This was witnessed by some of our officers, who had pushed on, and observed their distressed and miserable state. On our arrival at Montalegre, we saw their retiring columns in march fairly over the Spanish frontier, and a village on their route in flames. However, Colonel Talbot, of the 14th light dragoons, followed the enemy's route for some way, and made prisoners an officer and fifty men. Marshal Beresford crossed the frontier, but proceeded no farther than Ginso, on hearing that Sir Arthur had given up the pursuit. The commander-of-the-forces, from the advices received from General M'Kenzie, had become anxious respecting the line of the Tagus, and being content with seeing the enemy across the frontier, desisted from a more northern advance, and ordered the troops to be cantoned in the nearest villages, wherever the order might reach them.

Thus ended this short but active operation of twelve days, in which the disasters of the Corunna campaign were repaid on the corps of Soult with interest, and the distress and misery of the enemy were more considerable than we had suffered in the preceding January. Instead of the fine Gallician road of retreat, they were obliged to file through mule, and even goatherd paths, while the incessant rain was more distressing than the snow. The French had not stores and supplies to fall back upon, but, on the contrary, passed through the most unproductive wilds in the valleys and mountains. But the difference of the circumstances of the two retreats mark their degrees of misery. The peasantry, while friendly to us in Gallicia, evinced, in the Tras os Montes, every mark of hatred to the enemy, whose cruelties had well deserved severe retributive justice. This was carried to a distressing extent, and though it kept the French together, added greatly to the extent of their loss. Our army was never so disorganized in Gallicia as that of the French, who could not have attempted to fight a battle at Montalegre, as we did at Corunna. The loss of men (including Soult's invasion and retreat) seems to have been nearly equal; but the enemy, besides the military chest and baggage, (of which we only sacrificed a part,) left the whole of their artillery, while we embarked ours safely at Corunna. But Soult saw that his escape could be alone confined to his men, and barely avoided capture, if not destruction, by sacrificing the whole of his *materiel*. The fortunate chance of finding a traitor in the Bishop of Braga, tended to the safety of their retreat, which, as it were, had been constantly endangered, and would have been intercepted, had he continued his march from Salamonde, on Chaves instead of Montalegre.

Intelligence from the south of Victor's intention to invade Portugal, had induced Sir A. Wellesley to avoid pushing more troops beyond Braga than were absolutely necessary, in order that they should be as near and as ready as practicable, to proceed against Victor. This marshal, having been joined by Lapisse, hoping to create a diversion in favour of Soult, seized, with a corps of twelve to fourteen thousand men, the bridge of Alcantara, and pushed his patrols to Castello Branco. This movement required strict attention, and rendered necessary a more speedy retrograde movement from the northern frontier than would have been desired after the fatigues of the troops; but, only allowing two days' rest at Oporto, they were withdrawn to Coimbra, by the same routes by which they had advanced. Head-quarters were, on the 23rd, at Coimbra. Here the Portuguese regiments, which had acted with us in the Tras os Montes, were ordered to form the garrison of Oporto. These regiments had given some hopes of good promise, yet none were so sanguine at this time as to expect from them their subsequent bravery and efficiency.

Sir Arthur continued his route on the 5th, to Thomar, where we found the heavy brigade, consisting of the 3rd dragoon guards and 4th dragoons, which had disembarked while we were in the north, and appeared in excellent condition. Head-quarters were established at Abrantes on the 8th of June, from whence Major-General M'Kenzie, on our advance, had been pushed forward to Castello Branco; as Victor, finding that Soult's retreat had left Portugal free from danger in the north, considered his own position less tenable, had withdrawn from the north of the Tagus. The French army soon afterwards fell back from Caseres upon Merida and Medellin.

Although it was understood that Sir Arthur's orders only extended to the defence of Portugal, yet he felt that these stirring times required active exertions from all Europe, and that tranquillity was incompatible with the strides France was making to universal dominion. The cause of our allies on the spot, and of those more distant, struggling in Germany, pointed out the propriety of some attempt to create at least a diversion in their favour. It was evident that, could arrangements be made with the Spaniards, the disorganization of Soult's army offered an opportunity for striking a blow at Victor, and perhaps at the Spanish capital, particularly as Sebastiani was supposed to be fully employed in La Mancha. Sir Arthur, in consequence, offered to aid the Spaniards in a forward offensive movement into Spanish Estremadura. Such a step appeared the only means of re-establishing the war in the Peninsula, as the cause of Spain was fast sinking under the superior troops and management of the French, who, however they might dread the population, had learned that the armies were incapable of opposing their progress.* Much precious time was

* The Author of the "Voyage en Espagne, et des Lettres Philosophiques," says, at this time, " Les Espagnoles ne pouvoient plus rien par eux-mêmes : ils n'avoient à opposer que des partis mal armés, mal equipés, mal aguerris, et plus mal commandés encore."—ED.

wasted in the arrangements for the necessary co-operation of the two armies, which, but for the pride and obstinacy of Cuesta, might have been more usefully employed. It was only after considerable *negotiation*, (an expression perfectly applicable to the intercourse between ourselves and our allies, though we had only in view the saving their country,) that it was determined to make a simultaneous advance into Spanish Estremadura.

In the meanwhile, Victor had retreated from the Guadiana, and withdrawn his army across the Tagus, evidently falling back to receive aid from Madrid and La Mancha. The plan for this forward movement, was the advance of both armies along each bank of the Tagus, and a junction of the allies in front of the enemy in the plain of Estremadura. The British were to march to the north of the river, by Coria and Placentia, turning Almaraz and the enemy's posts facing Cuesta, while the latter was to cross at Almaraz, and to co-operate with our advancing column. It was necessary to secure the frontier of Portugal to the north and north-east, and the passes along the frontier of that country leading from Castile and Leon, as two *corps d'armée*, besides that of Soult, were in the north of Spain.

Marshal Beresford, posted near Almeida, was to undertake the first with the Portuguese army, while Cuesta promised to occupy the Banos pass, leading direct from Salamanca upon Placentia. The Spaniards engaged to find means of collecting and furnishing us with provisions. On the 27th June, head-quarters left Abrantes for Villa del Rey; on the 28th, they reached Cortesada; the 29th, Sarzedas, and Castello Branco on the following day, and halted the 1st of July. They continued their march on the 2nd to Zobreira; and the 3rd, passed the frontier to Zarza Mayor, where they crossed upon the route of the captured General Franceschi, who, after reaching Spain with Soult's army, had been taken in Leon, and was being carried to Seville, fated to die incarcerated within the walls of Grenada. He was a distinguished officer of light cavalry, and had been opposed to us not only six weeks before on the Vouga, but the like number of months antecedent on the plain of Leon. He was dressed in a hussar's uniform, and decorated with a star, bearing an emblem similar to the arms of the Isle of Man—three legs diverging from a common centre.

The army was here joined by the Lusitanian legion under Sir R. Wilson, and after halting on the 4th, reached Coria on the 5th, Galestad on the 7th, and Placentia on the 8th. The approach to this city drew forth the admiration of all. The bishop's palace and cathedral tower above the houses, which rise from a bed of verdure, bordered by the river, while the whole is backed with the most splendid mountains, with tops silvered by perpetual snow. The river above this city is divided into two branches, which form an island, covered with the finest trees.

The several reinforcements received antecedent to, and during our short stay at Placentia, rendered necessary a new distribution of the regiments and brigades. The cavalry were divided into three brigades: the first, of the 14th and 16th light dragoons, under Sir Stapleton Cotton; the second, commanded by General Fane, consisted of the 3rd dragoon guards and 4th dragoons; and the third, of the first German hussars, and 23rd light dragoons, led by General Anson.

The infantry was divided into four divisions:—

1st DIVISION.—Lieut.-Gen. SHERBROOKE.

Brig.-Gen. H. CAMPBELL, Guards, and 1 Comp. 5th Batt. 60th Regiment.
Brig.-Gen. CAMERON, 61st, 83rd Regiments, 1 Comp. 5th Batt. 60th Regiment.
Brig.-Gen. LANGWORTH, 2 Batt. King's German Legion.
Brig.-Gen. LOWE, 2 Batt. King's German Legion.

2nd DIVISION.—Major-Gen. HILL.

Brig.-Gen. STEWART, 29th, 48th Regiments, 1 Batt. Detachment.
Major-Gen. TILSON, Buffs, 48th, 66th Regiments.

3rd DIVISION.—Major-Gen. M'KENZIE.

1st Brigade, 24th, 31st, 45th Regiments.
Col. DONKIN's Brigade, 5 Comps. 5 Batt. 60th Regiment, and 87th, 88th Regiments.

4th DIVISION.—Brig.-Gen. A. CAMPBELL.

1st Brigade, 7th, 53rd Regiments, 1 Comp. 5 Batt. 60th Regiment.
2nd Brigade, 2 Batt. Detachment, 97th Regiment, 1 Company, 5th Batt. 60th Regiment.

To these was to be added, the Lusitanian legion, under Sir R. Wilson, being the only Portuguese troops employed in this operation.

This distribution into divisions was the first step to the gradual growth of these corps into little armies, complete in themselves, like the Roman legions, being (with the sole exception of cavalry) about their strength. The light companies of the regiments composing them were formed into a battalion, which, under some intelligent officer, ever marched at its head, and to which was added a company or more of the deadly riflemen of the foreign corps, the 60th. These were the Velites, while the battalions were all worthy to be considered as Triarii, or Principes. They had subsequently artillery, spare ammunition, and engineer, medical, and commissariat staff attached to them; and when each was increased, in 1810, by a Portuguese brigade, consisting of a battalion of light infantry, and two line battalions, they became, in themselves, superior in numbers to some of the petty expeditions in which England has often placed her hope, while they have only wasted her strength. Our whole force of British did not consist of eighteen thousand men, principally of men raised by the voluntary enrolment of the militia.

We learned at Placentia, that the French occupied Talavera de la Reyna, and were supposed to be waiting for reinforcements from Madrid and La Mancha. During the concentration of the army at Placentia, Sir Arthur had his first personal communication with Cuesta, at Casa del Puertos. His excellency passed in review the Spanish army, and definitively settled the plan of the campaign.

The British army was to cross the Teitar, and

direct its march upon Oropesa, where it was to form a junction with the Spanish army from Almaraz, and to advance on Talavera de la Reyna. The cavalry of the Spaniards under the Duke of Albuquerque, and the division of infantry commanded by Ballasteros, were to continue and move on the left bank of the Tagus, and cross that river at the Puente del Arzobispo.

To diminish and separate the enemy's force, and distract their attention, General Vanegas, from La Mancha, was to threaten Aranjuez; while Sir R. Wilson, who was already on the Teitar, was to have, besides his own corps, some few Spanish troops, and to act upon their other flank, and by pushing to and beyond Escalona, make them uneasy respecting the capital.

Sir Arthur, after having halted eight days at Placentia, moved on the 17th to Talaquela; on the 18th to Majedas; and on the following day, to Casa de Centinela, across vast plains, occasionally covered with forests of cork trees. These quarters of the 19th, as the name indicates, consisted of a single house, which offered such miserable accommodation, that Sir Arthur, as well as the rest of the staff, preferred sleeping in wigwams, made with boughs of trees. On the 20th, while the army pushed on to Oropesa, the heat and the want of water was so great, that the troops suffered exceedingly, and several men sunk under exhaustion. Here we became an allied army, forming a junction with the Spaniards, from whom we hoped, however we might doubt, to receive support and assistance. But the first view of the infantry considerably damped our expectations, though we were assured their cavalry, moving across at Arzobispo, were to appearance (for we had not forgotten their conduct at Medellin) the best of the army. On further acquaintance, however, our conclusions respecting even this part of the army were not more favourable than that we had formed of their sister arm the first day we joined them, as they wanted in spirit and conduct, what the foot soldiers required in appointments and organization.

The army of Spain, before the breaking out of the Revolution, though not so degraded as that of Portugal, had been long in a declining state. Although the army intended for the coast of Barbary assembled under General Count O'Reilly, as late as 1788, was in an efficient state, it had greatly altered for the worse within the last twenty years. Instead of keeping pace with the rest of Europe in improvements in the art of war, Spain had considerably retrograded; and while the two last years had shaken to pieces the old establishment, the officers educated under it were incapable of forming a new army.

Although the men were the same as those who, three centuries before, had raised the Spanish name to the height of celebrity it so well deserved and so long maintained, they were no longer led by a chivalrous nobility and gentry. The officers taken from these classes in the beginning of the nineteenth century, evinced in their character the debasing state of the court and government.

In July, 1809, it was but the remnant of an organized army, and even this was only evinced, except in a few regiments, in the appellation of the corps known to be of long standing. A portion of the *garde du corps* accompanied this army—the sole remains of the court establishment of the past Bourbons, whether of France or Spain. It had been created by Philip V., on taking possession of the throne of Spain at the beginning of the last century, and consisted entirely of officers. Those with Cuèsta bore cartouch belts of green leather and silver. Some of the heavy cavalry looked respectable, particularly the Regimento del Rey, the first of dragoons, which, commanded by a relation of Cuesta, would have passed muster in any army.

The carabineers, a part of the royal guard, and who bore a better character for conduct in the field than the other regiments of cavalry, were efficient both in men and horse, as well as in appointments.

A brigade of two regiments of heavy dragoons, one of which was the regiment of Saguntum, attracted the attention of the British officers, from being dressed in yellow, with cocked hats, and who looked better than would be supposed from so singular a costume.

Their light cavalry consisted of hussars (*usares*) and chasseurs, dressed in all the colours of the rainbow. Little judgment seemed to have been employed in proportioning the size of the horse to the light or heavy cavalry, though it must be allowed the Spanish horses offer little choice, being universally slight, and not so well adapted for the shock of a charge as an eastern irregular kind of warfare.

The Spanish cavalry had a means of turning their jackets and sleeved waistcoats into a stable dress, by the sleeves taking off at the shoulders, from being only laced on with a different coloured cord to that of the coat; thus, besides being useful, having a good appearance. Their mode of riding was new to the English; the stirrup leathers were so long, that they could only touch them with their toe, while the carabine, hanging perpendicularly along the valise, was equally novel. Boots were far from universal, and many had, in their stead, a kind of leather legging, stiff, fitting buttoned tight to the limbs, and formed like a gaiter, coming over the shoe. Many horsemen, however, were devoid of covering for the legs or feet, and the naked toe was seen, peeping through a sandal, touching the stirrup. Of the infantry, the Walloon guards, (consisting principally of foreigners,) and the Irish brigade, were in the best order. The first, in two or more battalions, were dressed in dark blue, and broad white lace, while the uniforms of the latter were light blue. These consisted of the regiments of Yrlanda, Ultonia, and Hibernia, being the remains of the Irish Catholic regiments. At this time, although they had no privates, there were still among them some few officers of that nation. The white Bourbon uniform had entirely disappeared, and circumstances and economy had changed the colour of the principal part of the infantry into a deep chocolate.

But several battalions were, with the exception of the British arms, little better in appearance than peasantry; and though the major part of them had chaccos, many could only boast a kind of sandal instead of shoes, and in lieu of cross, waist-belts, from which hung tubes, lined with tin, each containing a cartridge. Few had great coats, the generality having blankets, with a hole in the middle for the head to pass through, hanging loose about their person.

Their artillery was good, from attention having been given to it before the breaking out of the war, but the train was unlike any other in modern armies, the guns and ammunition-wagons being drawn by mules, not two abreast, but in teams like cart-horses, without reins, and under no farther command than the voice of their conductors, who ran on foot on the side of the road. Their guns were heavy, and among the field batteries were several of twelve-pounders.

Their *materiel* for provisions, stores, and baggage were perfectly inadequate to their army, and ill adapted for their country. Instead of a large proportion of sumpter mules, they were accompanied by a vast train of tilted two-wheeled carts, carrying little, and with long teams of mules, lengthening to inconvenience the line of march.

The whole army was said to consist of seven thousand cavalry and thirty-one thousand infantry.

But we should not have been dissatisfied with our allies, *malgré* their appearance, or even their rags, had we felt any reason to confide in them. The men were evidently capable of "all that men dare," but the appearance of their officers at once bespoke their not being fit to lead them to the attempt. These not only did not look like soldiers, but not even like gentlemen; and it was difficult, from their mean and abject appearance, particularly among the infantry, to guess from what class of society they could have been taken. Few troops will behave well if those to whom they ought to look up are undeserving respect; and on this principle we might, at Oropesa, have predicted coming events, as far as the conduct of the Spanish soldiers were concerned. But besides their general inefficiency, we found their moral feeling different from what we expected. The preceding two years had made a great alteration in the feelings of the nation; the burst of enthusiasm was but momentary, and being only fed by accidental victory, soon subsided on a reverse of fortune. Far from their army evincing devotion, or even the most common courage in their country's cause, they were more often guilty, individually and collectively, of the most disgraceful cowardice.

The inefficiency of the officers spread to the staff,

and we hourly regretted that the revolution had not occasioned a more complete *bouleversement*, so as to bring forward fresh and vigorous talents from all classes. The proof that this opinion was just, was evinced by none of the regular military showing themselves worthy of command. Indeed, with the exception of a few self-made soldiers among the guerillas, who had risen from among the farmers and peasantry, it would be difficult to point out during the whole war any officer, whose opinion, even in his own department, or on the most trivial military subject, was worthy of being asked.

The Cortes ruling for Ferdinand, and continuing the old system, was one of the causes of the want of success of the Spaniards. They had to meet the youthful generals and the fresh energies of France, with all the improvements of modern warfare, by old besotted and prejudiced generals, whose armies were formed on obsolete principles, while the system of an *ancien regime* of a decrepit government continued to cramp every step to improvement. To these were added that blind pride and self vanity, which made them still consider themselves what history and tradition had represented their forefathers and nation. No proofs of inferiority would open their eyes, and without reflection or consideration they rushed from one error and misfortune unto others, benefiting by no experience, and disdaining to seek aid or improvement from those capable of restoring them to efficiency.

Had they placed their armies at our disposal, and

allowed the introduction of the active and intelligent British officers into command, their regular army might have become as celebrated in afterages for the defence of the Peninsula, as the Portuguese or their own guerillas; while at present, with the exception of their irregular warfare and defence of cities, their military character, during a period so brilliant for their allies, both Portuguese and British, appears absolutely contemptible. The army which we joined at Oropesa, in addition to its other drawbacks, was headed by a general as decrepit in mind as body. To abilities not superior to the most common intellect, he united the greatest fault in a commander of an army, that of indecision, while every act bespoke his suspicion and jealousy of his allies and their commander.

Attached to this army was an example, in the person of Lord Macduff, of one of those gallant spirits, who occasionally, shaking off the indolence of wealth, volunteer to aid some soul-stirring cause. His lordship had the rank of a Spanish colonel.

On the 21st, the two commanders-in-chief dined together, and in return for the military spectacle Cuesta had given to Sir Arthur at Casa de Puertos, when he went to see him from Placentia, the British troops, with the exception of General M'Kenzie's division on the advance, were drawn out in the evening for his inspection. The mounting on horseback to proceed to the review, showed how ill-fitted was Cuesta for the activity of war. He was lifted on his horse by two grenadiers, while one of his aides-de-camp was ready on the other side to conduct his right leg over the horse's croup, and place it in the stirrup! Remarks were whispered at this moment, that if his mental energy and activity did not compensate for his bodily infirmity, Sir Arthur would find him but an incapable coadjutor. The Spanish general passed along the line from left to right, just as the night fell, and we saw him put comfortably into an antiquated square-cornered coach, drawn by nine mules, to proceed to his quarters.

On the morning of the 22nd, we came in sight of the town of Talavera de la Reyna, which has since become so celebrated in English history. The town, seen about three miles distant, was embosomed in trees and inclosures, while the scarped hills on the right marked the course of the Tagus. The inclosures ended about a mile to the left of the town, joining some low, open, undulating hills, which stretchèd to some valleys and higher ridges. This open country communicated with an extensive plain in front of the town, across which passed the road from Oropesa, being gradually lost as it approached Talavera in the vineyards and woods. In the midst of this plain were posted about eight hundred or one thousand French cavalry, who, with the utmost indifference, were dismounted, feeling assured that a few skirmishes would check the advance of the Spanish cavalry in their front. These, under the Duke d'Albuquerque, had crossed the Tagus at the Puente del Arzobispo, and had arrived early opposite the French advance. Instead of being anxious to show their allies their activity when at so little cost, being five or six times more numerous than the enemy, they made no attempt to drive them in, but contented themselves with deploying into several long lines, making a very formidable appearance. With feelings of astonishment we rode on to the skirmishers, who consisted of mounted guerillas, dressed like the farmers of the country. We expected to see them closely and successfully engaged, having heard they were peculiarly adapted for petty warfare; but we found them utterly incapable of coping with the enemy's *tirailleurs*, who were driving them almost into a circle. They were so careless and inexpert in the use of their arms, that one of them nearly shot, by accident, an English officer near him.

The Spaniards, from the commencement, thus continued skirmishing for four hours,* until General Anson's brigade arrived, which they allowed at once, and as a matter of course, without any reference or notice, to pass through the intervals of their squadrons; at the same time these heroes notified their own want of efficiency and spirit, by acknowledging and paying tribute to both in their allies, by a profusion of *vivas!*

On our advancing, the French drew off to the

---

* In the author's original copy of his journal, written a few days after, he finds the conduct of the Spaniards on this occasion thus noticed,—" and it is my belief they would have continued till *now*, if we had not aided them."

left of the town along the open ground, skirting the inclosures, and exchanging shots with our skirmishers. The Spaniards kept to the right along the great road, and could scarcely be brought by the intercession of British officers to enter the town, from whence they learned a body of four or five hundred infantry had just retired. General Stewart, the adjutant-general, who happened to be on the spot, persuaded their officers to follow their retreat along the fine Madrid road, which was one hundred and fifty yards wide. The enemy were overtaken retiring in two small columns, and to the attack of one General Stewart led the Spanish cavalry. The result, as indeed all we saw on this day of our allies, was a proof of their total want, not only of discipline, but of courage. On this and two succeeding attempts, (to which the English general headed them,) on receiving the enemy's fire, when the principal danger was past, they pulled up and fled in every direction; yet in Cuesta's account of this affair, he called it an "*intrepid charge.*"

Cruelty and cowardice are ever combined, and these same Spaniards, who had thus avoided closing with the unmaimed enemy, murdered in cold blood a few wounded and dying men their column left in the road when they retired, who were struck down by the artillery which was brought up after the cavalry's repulse. Their barbarity was even heightened by accompanying each stab with invectives and comments on their victims never again seeing their homes or Paris. On the left the enemy retired before our cavalry, about four miles beyond the town. Anson's brigade made an attempt to charge about 1500 of their cavalry, but they were found unassailable, having taken post beyond the bed of the Alberche, which, running for about two miles at right angles with the Tagus, empties itself into that river. The enemy allowed them to come close, and then opened a fire of four guns and two howitzers, which occasioned some small loss before they could withdraw out of fire. One of the horses of this brigade, the hip and leg of which was carried off, and its entrails trailing on the ground, recovered itself on three legs, and tried to take its place again in squadron.

The enemy had tirailleurs in the underwood near the river, and were very jealous of its banks, opening a fire of artillery on all who showed themselves. Sir Arthur and head-quarter staff came unexpectedly in the afternoon, under a fire of some light guns, on the right in front of the Spaniards, and one, of several four-pound shots, whizzed close over the general's head. The troops were ordered to bivouac in the neighbourhood of Talavera, and General M'Kenzie's division was pushed on to the front in the neighbourhood of an old ruined building, at the angle of the Alberche, where it turned east. It was evident that the enemy were in force on the opposite side of the river, and a ridge of hills, above eight hundred yards from the bank, sloping towards it, offered them a very suitable defensive position.

Its left rested on the Tagus, and its right was secured by the turning of the Alberche, and some difficult wooded ridges beyond. Their strength could not exceed 23,000 men, being the troops which had fallen back from the south of the Tagus, not having been joined by any troops from Madrid or Aranjuez.

We fully expected a battle on the following day, and about twelve o'clock on the 23rd, the first and third division got under arms, and advanced in the direction of the enemy's right, while the rest of the army were ready to move at a moment's notice; but, unfortunately, Sir Arthur had to overcome the wavering conduct of his confederate general, who appeared quite unaware of the use of time or opportunity in military operations.* He could not be brought so to decide on attack, that Sir Arthur could feel secure of the Spaniards making a simultaneous attack with his army, or that the British might not be left to gain the day alone. The bivouac of Cuesta was on the road to Madrid, about three-quarters of a mile from the Alberche, where, on the cushions taken out of his carriage, he sat, the picture of mental and physical inability.

* The writer of this journal has since served in India, and has often been inclined to compare the conduct of Cuesta to that of the Sirdars of the native armies. After conducting their armies into the field or before the enemy, they are seized with an apathetic infatuation, that causes them to trust for the result, not to their own plans or exertions, but to the decrees of fate or any fortuitous circumstances—both bad auxiliaries when opposed by an enterprizing enemy.

Two soldiers stood near to aid or support him in any little necessary operation, and the scene would have been ridiculous had it not been painful, as we saw the tide, which, " when taken at its flood," might, nay, would "lead us on to fortune" and victory, fast ebbing, without our taking advantage of it. After considerable suspense, it was universally reported throughout the army, that on being pressed and driven to his last excuse, Cuesta pleaded that it was Sunday, at the same time promising to attack at daylight the next morning, and our troops were in consequence ordered back to their bivouacs. It may be fairly considered that pride had considerable weight on this occasion. Cuesta was a true Spaniard, and disliked the suggestions of an English general in his own country, and, with recollections of two hundred and fifty years before, could not bring his ideas down to present changes and circumstances. These feelings were national, and ever evinced, and it was only very late in the war, after the Spaniards found they had not an officer to lead their armies, and they despaired of finding one, that they consented to place Sir Arthur at their head. Sir Arthur deserves as much credit for keeping his temper during his six years' intercourse with the Spanish government and officers, as in the general conduct of the war. When we reflect on promises broken, and engagements violated, involving the safety of his army, the honour of his character, and his credit as an officer, and yet know of no quarrel that extended (if any existed) beyond correspondence or negotiation, future ages are bound to give our commander credit for unbounded placidity of temperament.

Though sorely annoyed by this determination, the officers could not let pass without ridicule the incongruity we had observed within the last three days in the old gentleman's proceedings. It was impossible not to notice the Spanish general going out to battle, to within half a mile of the advanced posts, in a carriage drawn by nine mules, and the precautions to preserve him from the rheumatism, like those taken by delicate ladies, in our humid climate, at a *fête champêtre*, in placing the carriage cushions on the grass. To these the Spanish commander-in-chief was supported by two grenadiers, and on which he was let drop, as his knees were too feeble to attempt reclining without the chance, nay certainty, of a fall. Yet this was the man to whom the Cortes had intrusted their armies, but who ought (if he did not himself feel his own inability,) to have been removed without a moment's delay after the first trial. They had only one excuse; the year before had made common honesty a virtue, and they forgot every other requisite, in a desire to avoid treachery.

We began, however, to have some hope on the evening of the 23rd, when orders were delivered out for attack the next morning at daylight. General Sherbrooke was to move at two in the morning, while the remainder of the army was to rendezvous in rear of the third division, at the angle of the

Alberche. The British column of attack, with the third division at its head, supported by General Anson's brigade, and followed by the first, second, and fourth divisions, was to attack the enemy's right, the Spaniards were to force the troops on the heights crossed by the road to Madrid, while the remainder of the British, and the whole of the Spanish cavalry were to cross the river on the open ground in the enemy's front. No drums or trumpets were to sound. The columns for attack were formed before daybreak on the 24th, and the left column, which was to cross the river and ascend the heights round the enemy's right, and opposite the village of Casalegas, was already on its march, when it was discovered the enemy had retired during the night.

While this event proved the effect of procrastination in warfare, it was to be deeply lamented on every account. The enemy, the day before, not consisting of above twenty-two thousand men, had most imprudently offered us battle before the reinforcements from Madrid or La Mancha had reached him, and if he had been attacked, must have been annihilated. We had near eighteen thousand British and thirty-six thousand Spaniards, of which ten thousand were horse, and the position once forced, they would have had to retire across an open plain of many leagues, pursued by a victorious enemy, and a superior cavalry.

Colonel Delancey had gained and continued in the rear of the enemy all night, and joined us at daylight with a French officer he had taken. We entered their various hutted camps across the river, which we found arranged with comfort and taste. Their army, on arriving from the line òf the Tagus, had found the ripe wheat standing, and regardless of its value, had not only thatched, but made whole huts, with the corn in the ear, which, hanging down, shed the grain on the ground as we passed along and between them. They had built with boughs of trees an immense *salle de spectacle*, and formed, by cutting down and removing the largest olive trees, and sticking their pointed ends into the ground, an avenue, leading up to it, of some length—an act more wanton and reprehensible than that of taking the unthrashed corn, as the fruit of the olive is not produced under several years' growth.

Shy as Cuesta was of coming to blows with the enemy when in his front, he became most anxious for his pursuit when at a distance and in retreat. Without considering that Victor was only falling back on reinforcements, he ordered his army to advance, (as if the French were in full retreat for the Ebro), and established his posts on the 25th at Torrijos. Had not the English general taken quite a different view of the subject, it would have been most imprudent, if not impossible to advance, as provisions began to fail us. The Spaniards, far from aiding our commissariat, took no precautions whatever to prepare food for 18,000 additional mouths, and our position threatened to be untenable for want of food.

Sir Arthur, in consequence, declined making any forward movement, and contented himself with pushing two divisions of infantry across the Alberche, and posting them at Casaleguas. In the meanwhile the enemy were concentrating their various corps. The reserve, and the guards from Madrid, left that capital with King Joseph, on the 22nd, at night, and joined the 4th *corps d'armée*, under Sebastiani, at Toledo. These united on the 25th, between Torrijos and Toledo, with the corps under Victor, and formed an army of 45,000 to 48,000 men, after a garrison of 2,000 had been left in Toledo. This small force was sufficient to cover any advance of the Spaniards from La Mancha, as Vanegas frittered away the time to no purpose, while Madrid was overawed by General Belliard, entrenched in the Retiro.

On the junction of these armies, Cuesta saw too late his mistake in so inconsiderately advancing from the neighbourhood of the British, and before he could withdraw his most advanced corps, became engaged with the enemy. The regiment of Villa Viçosa, drawn up in an enclosure surrounded by a deep ditch, with but one means of egress, was hemmed in by the enemy and cut to pieces, without a possibility of escape. A British officer of engineers saved himself by his English horse taking at a leap the barrier which surrounded the Spaniards, and which their horses were incapable of clearing. The Spaniards, on the 26th, fell back towards the Alberche and Talavera, in such confusion that it can only be compared to a flight, while the enemy followed with the evident intention of bringing the allies to battle.

Every one now felt its approach, and some little preparations were made to strengthen a position which Sir Arthur had selected, resting on Talavera. These consisted in placing some of the Spanish heavy guns in battery on the main road, in front of the Madrid gate, and throwing up some barricades on the different approaches to the town. A breastwork was commenced on a small rising ground in a little plain, at the spot where the flanks of the British and Spanish would unite, about the centre of the allied army. These were the only attempts at entrenchment, and the last was not completed. All the troops were ordered to hold themselves in readiness to move at a moment's notice.

On the 27th the British cavalry were ordered to the front, to cover the retreat of the Spaniards and of our own divisions across the Alberche. About mid-day the enemy's army began to show itself, and while our cavalry withdrew to the right bank of the river, in the open ground, the 5th division fell back from Caselaguas, through a woody country, to the same spot, near an old ruined house, the Casa de Salinas, which they had occupied before the enemy retreated. Before re-crossing the Alberche, they set fire to the old hutted camps of the enemy, the smoke from which rose so thick as to completely hide from view the country beyond and to the west of the village of Casaleguas. The two brigades of the 5th division lay upon their arms in front of this ruin, the highest part of which overlooked the surrounding trees, offering a view of the country. Sir Arthur dismounted, and leaving his horse standing below, scrambled with some difficulty up the broken building, to reconnoitre the advancing enemy. Though ever as gallant, we were by no means such good soldiers in those days as succeeding campaigns made us, and sufficient precautions had not been taken to ascertain what was passing within the wood, (on the skirt of which the division was posted,) and between it and the ford below Casalegas.

But the enemy had crossed, under cover of the smoke from the burning huts, a very large force of infantry, and, gradually advancing, opened a fire so suddenly on our troops lying on the ground, that several men were killed without rising from it. This unexpected attack threatened the greatest confusion, little short of dismay, but the steadiness of the troops, particularly the 31st, prevented disorder, and gave time for Sir Arthur and his staff to withdraw from the house and mount their horses. Sir Arthur's escape may, however, be considered most providential. The troops were withdrawn from the wood into the plain, but after we had lost many officers and men. As this was the enemy's first attack, and might, by our withdrawing, be considered successful, it was peculiarly unfortunate, from adding to the enemy's confidence in attacking our army. These two brigades, being supported by General Anson's cavalry, gradually fell back towards our army.

The enemy now crowded the heights, extending from Casalegas to the Tagus, with vast bodies of troops, accompanied with quantities of artillery. These crossed at the various fords on the Alberche, to the plain west of it; while some of their cavalry, in the loosest order, came in crowds through the woods, following our advanced corps as they gradually withdrew to our position, of which, as we approached the chosen ground, the principal features began to show themselves. Their horse artillery soon overtook us in our retreat, and opened a heavy and constant fire, particularly of shells, under which the troops formed on their ground. As the enemy closed on our position, our different divisions were seen hurrying to the post assigned them, which formed the left wing of the allies; and some anxiety was felt for the arrival of the troops who were to defend a towering height, which, it was evident, would be the key of the position.

The men, as they formed and faced the enemy, looked pale, but the officers riding along their line, only of two deep, on which all our hopes depended, observed they appeared not less cool and tranquil than determined. In the meanwhile the departing sun showed by his rays the immense masses moving towards us, while the last glimmering of twilight proved their direction to be across our front, towards the left, leaving a sensation of anxiety and doubt if they would not be able to attack that point even before our troops, which had not yet arrived, were up. The darkness, only broken in upon by the bursting shells and flashes of the guns, closed quickly upon us, and it was the opinion of many that the enemy would rest till morning. But this was soon placed beyond doubt, by the summit of the height on our left being suddenly covered with fire, and for an instant it was evident the enemy had nearly, if not completely, made a lodgment in our line. This attack was made by three regiments of the division of Ruffin—the 24th, 96th, and 9th, but of which the enemy say, the last only reached the summit, the very citadel of our position.

They marched, without halting, up the rise of the hill, and came upon the German legion, who, having been informed they were to the rear of General Hill's division, had, believing they were in a second line, lain down on their arms, and when the enemy topped the hill, *en masse*, many were asleep. But General Hill's corps had not arrived, and the Germans were first roused by the enemy seizing them as prisoners, or firing into them at *brule-pourpoint*. The flashes of the retiring fire of the broken and surprised Germans marked the enemy's success, and the imminent danger of our army. General Sherbrooke, posted in the centre, with the promptitude required in such an emergency, ordered the regiments of the brigade next to the Germans to wheel into open column, and then, facing them about, was preparing to storm the hill, with the rear-rank in front, when the happy arrival of General Hill's brigade restored the height to its proper owner.

The 48th, the first battalion of detachments, and the 29th regiment, advanced with the bayonet, and drove the French from the top of the hill into the valley, with immense loss, and the colonel of the 9th regiment terribly wounded. There was some alarm and fear that the enemy, when the Germans had been driven back, had carried off the only heavy guns we had with our army; but fortunately they had been withdrawn at dusk from the brow of the hill. Major Fordice, of the adjutant-general's department, an officer of great promise, fell in retaking these heights, with many valuable officers and men.

After this attack was repulsed, the enemy remained quiet, awaiting the morn which was to decide the fate of the battle. The British light infantry was thrown out to the front, with sentries still more advanced towards the enemy. This necessary precaution, coupled with the inexperience of our troops, principally militia-men, produced a heavy loss, from the jealousy they felt of all in their front, after this night attack. This was increased by the constant word "*stand up*" being passed along the line; and on more than one occasion it led to an individual soldier firing at some object in his front, which was taken up by the next, and so passed, like, and to appearance resembling, a running wildfire, down the front of one or more regiments, till stopped by the officers. In this, the troops unfortunately forgot their light infantry in front, and many brave officers and men fell a sacrifice to the fire of their comrades; amongst them was Colonel Ross, of the Guards.

The Spaniards were not less on the alert than ourselves, but their anxiety not only extended to firing musketry, but in salvos of the cannon placed in front of Talavera. On one occasion this was said to have originated from a cow having got loose and cantered up to their line. Our troops, however, stood firm to their ground, while regiments of the Spaniards, after giving a volley, quitted their position and fled through the gardens and enclosures, bearing down all before them, and were only brought into line again by degrees. One of these alarms, about midnight, in front of Talavera, was so great, that a large portion of the troops posted in the front, left their ground, and rushed through the town, and in the midst of the crowd of fugitives was seen a certain square-cornered coach, the nine mules attached to it being urged to the utmost, implying that its inmate was as anxious to escape as the meanest in the army.

Sir Arthur, surrounded by his staff, slept, wrapped in his cloak, on the open ground, in rear of the second line, about the centre of the British army. A hasty doze was occasionally taken, as more continued rest was disturbed by alarm of different kinds, while the reflections of others kept them waking. The bustle of the day had prevented a review of our situation, but on being left to our own thoughts, it was impossible not to reflect on the awfully approaching crisis. We could not but feel that here was to be another trial of the ancient military rivalry of England and France; that the cool, constitutional, persevering courage of the former was again to be pitted against the more artificial, however chivalrous, though not less praiseworthy, bravery of the latter. This view of the relative valour of the two nations cannot be questioned, if we consider that the reminding the British of this moral quality is wholly unnecessary, and instead of language of excitement being constantly applied to our soldiery, that of control, obedience, and composure is solely recommended; while our ancient opponents are obliged incessantly to drive into the ears of their men, that they are nationally and individually the bravest of the human race. Hearing nothing else so flattering to their unbounded vanity, they become so puffed up by this eternal stimulant, as to be fully convinced of its truth, which, in consequence, makes their first attack tremendous.

Buonaparte, being aware of this weak point in

their character, fed it in every way, and the object of wearing a paltry piece of enamel gained him many battles. But this sort of created courage is not capable of standing a severe test, and the French have always been, in their military character, more Gauls than Franks; and what Cæsar said of the former, eighteen centuries ago, is still applicable to the races now occupying their fine country. If stoutly opposed at first, this spurious kind of courage not only diminishes but evaporates, and has, does, and will, ever fail before that of the British. As soldiers, taking the expression in its widest sense, they are equal, if not superior, to us in many points, but on one, that of individual courage, we rise far superior to them. It is remarkable how often they evince a knowledge of this; and in nothing more than their subterfuges of all kinds to keep it from resting on their minds. All France, aware of this inferiority, by all species of casuistry attempt to conceal it; and in order not to shock their national vanity, blame every unsuccessful officer opposed to us, even should his dispositions be ever so good, and which might, but for the courage of our men, have succeeded.

Buonaparte's conduct after Vittoria, was directed to work on this feeling, and by sacrificing the officers to the self-vanity of the troops, established for a time the *moral* of the army, by making those who had fled like sheep at Vittoria, fight us again, though unsuccessfully, with renewed spirit. Besides the bravery of the two nations, no less was the plain of Talavera to try the merit of two systems, and prove the value of different means and education in forming a powerful and efficient military. It was not only to be shown if a chivalrous enthusiasm, and a confidence founded on vanity was to overcome natural and patriotic courage, but if a sense of duty, inculcated by a real discipline, was to sink under feelings created by an absence of control and a long train of excess and military licence. It was whether an organized army, worthy of a civilized period and state of warfare, should not overcome a military cast grown up in the heart of Europe, (from the peculiarity of the times and circumstances,) little better than the bandits, led by Bourbon to the walls of Rome in the sixteenth century. The system on which the French armies were formed was so demoralizing and pernicious in its effects, that the army of Buonaparte ought not to be considered as the national force of France, but that of a conqueror, like Ghenghis Khan, or Tamerlane, of a more civilized age and quarter of the world. Like those scourges, the ruler of the French existed by upholding that soldiery the times had first created, and which his ambition subsequently fostered, and in perpetuating their attachment to his person by leading them to victory and plunder. In consequence, robbery was not only overlooked, but permitted, and an encomiast of the French army has since dared in print to excuse its atrocities. This, it is true, is written by one of the revolutionary school, but it will be (as long as the work is read) a perpetual disgrace to the army whose acts he records.* All discipline sunk under this state of things. Coercion was neither necessary nor prudent, where the views of all were directed to the same lawless objects; and the military code was rather a bond of union and companionship, fostering a spurious glory or ambition, and a thirst and hope of reward in unshackled military licence and execution, than in an observance of laws respecting the rights and claims of human nature.

The quickness and intelligence of the French soldiery, pointed out the necessity of an obedience to their officers, whom they considered as leading them to objects equally desirable to all; and thus actuated, far from having to receive orders, they readily anticipated them. A Bedouin robber does not require the positive commands of his chief to do his utmost to destroy the guards, or to plunder the camels of a caravan; and no more did the French, with gain or impure military fame in view, require farther stimulus or direction.

But these various causes so suited the French, that they had the effect, since the Revolution, of raising their armies to the summit of fame, while their successes over the continental troops had made them universally dreaded. They felt this, which increased their confidence; and the army before us, sleeping on the opposite side of the ravine, was

* It is needless to say, this alludes to Foy's Introduction to the War of the Peninsula.

strongly embued with this impression, being formed of the fine regiments of the Italian army, who had so often conquered under Buonaparte, and subsequently marched from one victory to another. Neither the corps of Victor nor of Sebastiani, nor the guard or reserve under Desolles, from Madrid, had formed parts of the armies defeated by us at Vimiera or Corunna, and had no recollections of our prowess to shake that good opinion of themselves, in which the principal strength of the French armies consists.

Though no fears could be entertained for the result, dependent on the brave fellows lying around us, we could not but regret that they were not composed of troops as fine as those who accompanied Sir J. Moore.

We could not hide from ourselves that our ranks were filled with young soldiers, being principally the second battalions of those English regiments who had embarked at Corunna, and consisting of draughts from the militia that had never seen an enemy. With the exception of the Guards and a few others, there were more knapsacks with the names of militia regiments upon them, than of numbered regular regiments. Indeed, we felt no contrast could be stronger than that of the two armies. The ideas of England have never run wild on military glory. We more soberly consider our army rather as a necessary evil than an ornament and boast; and as an appeal to brute force and arms are proofs of barbarism, so ought the general diffusion of the former sentiment in a community to be viewed as conclusive evidence of advance to civilization and intelligence; and instead of directing the talents, or drawing forth the best blood of a people to be wasted in the field, a well-wisher to his country ought to desire them to be retained at home for the general advantage. But, however secure in ourselves, we recollected that we formed but one-third of the allied army, and that thirty-six thousand men lay in the same line, every action of whom had led us to consider them as more likely to occasion some common reverse than a happy termination to our operations. We were convinced, that if attacked, even in their strong and almost impregnable position, it was most likely to be attended by their immediate flight, which would leave the whole of the enemy to direct his efforts upon us single-handed. In addition, a certain degree of coolness had grown up between the two commanders; and Sir Arthur must have felt that the weakness of his ally by his side was not less to be dreaded than the strength of his enemy in his front. The prospect on the eve of the 28th July, 1809, was thus, though far from hopeless, by no means one of encouragement or sanguine expectation.

The rest of all the officers lying around Sir Arthur was hasty and broken, and interrupted by the uneasiness of the horses held at a distance, and the arrival of deserters, a few of whom came over during the night. They generally informed us, that we were to be attacked at day-light, and that the corps that stormed the hill had consisted of six thousand men. Our glances were constantly directed towards the point from whence the sun was to rise for the last time on many hundreds who were here assembled within a mile around, while Sir Arthur, occasionally asking the hour, shewed he looked for daylight with as much anxiety as any of us. Just before day, we quietly mounted our horses and rode slowly towards the height, where we arrived just as the light allowed us to see the opposite side of the ravine beneath us covered with black indistinct masses. Every instant rendered them more visible, and the first rays of the sun showed us Sebastiani's division opposite our centre, Victor's three divisions at our feet; with the reserve, guard, and cavalry extending backward to the wood near the Alberche. Our eyes were, however, principally attracted by an immense solid column opposite, but rather to the left of the hill, evidently intended for attack. Its front was already covered with tirailleurs, ready to advance at the word, and who saw before them the dead bodies of their comrades, who had fallen the night before, strewing the ground. The gray of the morning was not broke in upon by a single shot from either side, and we had time to observe our position, (which had not been completely occupied before dark on the preceding eve,) and how the troops were posted.

The distance from the Tagus to the height on

our left, which overlooked a deep valley, bounded beyond by some sharp and rugged hills, was little less than two miles. The right of the allied army rested on the town of Talavera and the river. About half the ground from our right to a little beyond the centre was flat, and covered with woods and vineyards, but where these ceased, the remainder of the country was open, and gradually rose to the foot of our important conical hill on the left.

A rill ran along the whole front of our line, and in that part of the ground which was open and undulating, it passed through a ravine, the brow of which was taken advantage of in posting our troops. The Spaniards, from being incapable of moving, were posted in heavy columns in the most difficult country, till they joined our right, which was in an open space, though in its front and rear were enclosures. At this point had been commenced a little redoubt, which, however, remained imperfect, and was the only "*rentranchement*" of which the French, in their accounts, as an excuse for their defeat, have so liberally strengthened our line. But as every thing is sacrificed by them to vanity, truth cannot be expected alone to escape.

On the right of the British was posted the fourth division, under Sir A. Campbell, supported by Sir S. Cotton's brigade of cavalry; on their left commenced the first division, of which the Guards were on the right. The remainder of this division, consisting of Brigadier-General Cameron's brigade and the Germans, extended across the most open ground, and joined on the left to the second division, clustered round the height for its defence. The two brigades of General M'Kenzie were placed in the second line, his own brigade in rear of the Guards, and that of Colonel Donkin behind the centre. The remainder of the cavalry had bivouacked at some distance to the rear, and were not come up. The enemy were employed from daylight in placing opposite our centre thirty pieces of cannon on the opposite side of the ravine, but not a shot was fired on either side, and the whole looked as if the armies had met for a review. But the calm augured the coming storm, and the quiet evinced that all were aware of the great approaching struggle, and that it was useless to throw away a casual fire, or destroy individuals, where salvos alone and the death of thousands could decide the day. When the vast column we had seen in the dusk was considered ready, a single cannon shot from the centre of the enemy's batteries was the signal for its advance, and for the opening of all their guns. A shower of balls instantly fell on all parts of our position, and the smoke, the wind being east, and the damp of the morning preventing its rising, was blown across the ravine, and completely enveloped us in a dense fog. But we had seen the forward movement of the mass intended for our dislodgment, and knew that, under cover of this cannonade and smoke, it was advancing up the face of the hill. It consisted of a *colonne serrée de bataillons*, of the same division of Ruffin which had attacked the night before.

General Hill, with the brigades of Tilson and Stewart, which had already successfully tried their strength with these same troops, were ready to receive them. The Buffs, 48th, and 66th, advanced to the brow of the hill, wheeling round to meet them with their arms ported, ready to rush on the ascending foe as soon as perceived through the intense smoke. They were not long in suspense, and without a moment's hesitation, by a desperate volley and charge, they overthrew, as they topped the hill, the enemy, who fled in the utmost confusion and consternation, followed by our troops, even across the ravine. Here they rallied, and after an exchange of sharp firing, our regiments were withdrawn again to their vantage ground. Had the cavalry been present, the victory might have been completed at this early hour, but they had not come in from their bivouac. As the smoke and tumult cleared off, and the troops were seated behind the summit of the hill, we found our loss considerable, and that General Hill had been forced to quit the field from a shot in the head. The dead of the enemy lay in vast numbers on the face of the hill, and had been tall, healthy, fine young men, well-limbed, with good countenances; and as proof of their courage, (the head of their column having reached within a few yards of the top of the hill before being arrested,) the bodies lay close to our ranks. The face of the height was furrowed out into deep ravines by the water rushing down its steep sides during the rains, and the dead and wounded of both nations lay heaped in them.* Musketry almost ceased after this defeat, but the cannonade continued, our centre and right suffering considerably, though in the other parts of the line, as our shots were plunging, while theirs were directed upwards, it was not so deadly. It continued for above an hour after the repulse, and showed us the inferiority of our calibre. All our guns, with the exception of one brigade of heavy, were miserable *light* six-pounders, while the French returned our fire with eights and twelves.

As the weather was dreadfully hot, and it was impossible to know how long we should occupy this ground, orders were given to bury the men who had fallen the night before and in the morning attack, lying around the hill interspersed with the living.

The entrenching tools were thus employed, and it was curious to see the soldiers burying their fallen comrades, with the cannon shot falling around, and in the midst of them, leaving it pro-

* We were occupied after this attack in carrying away our wounded in blankets, by four or five soldiers, and within a short time the number of unfortunate men assembled round our field hospital, a small house and enclosure behind our centre, barely out of cannon shot, proved our heavy loss.

bable, that an individual might thus be employed digging his own grave. Gradually, however, the fire slackened, and at last wholly ceased, and war appeared as much suspended as, before daylight and previously to the attack of the morning. The troops on the advance talked together, and the thirsty of both armies met at the bottom of the ravine, and drank from the same stream. There was also a well at the foot of the hill to the left, where the same water was divided among the collected of both nations around its brink.

About nine it was evident that the enemy had no intention of disturbing us for some time, as their numerous fires proved they were not inclined to fight again on empty stomachs. This was a painful sight to us, who felt acutely for our starving soldiery, who began to feel the most pinching want. All the promises of the Spaniards had ended in naught. They had made no arrangements to act up to their word, and starvation began to stare us in the face. Generally, however, it was borne by our men with philosophy, but one hungry soldier became almost troublesome, and close to Sir Arthur and his staff, said, " It was very hard that they had nothing to eat, and wished that they might be let to go down and fight, for when engaged they forget their hunger." The poor fellow was, however, at last persuaded to retire. Till about eleven o'clock all remained quiet, but about that hour immense clouds of dust were seen rising above the woods towards the

Alberche opposite the centre of the allied army, implying movements of large bodies of troops. This indicated the preparing for a general assault, and was occasioned by Sebastiani's corps forming a column of attack.* As the enemy's troops approached, the cannonade was renewed, and our inferiority of metal was so evident, that a brigade of Spanish twelve-pounders was borrowed from Cuesta. The fellows attached to these guns shewed good spirit, and, posting their guns on the side of the hill, were found most effective. The French, at times, had the most exact range of the height, and threw shot and shells upon it with terrible precision. One shell killed four horses, held by a man, who escaped uninjured. Their fuses, however, often burned too quick, exploding the shells high in the air, forming little clouds of smoke. It was curious that the enemy changed their fire from the troops to our artillery, or from our batteries to our line, whenever we gave them the example.

But the dust drew near in the woods, and a vast column was seen preparing to advance against Sir A. Cameron's brigade in the open ground. General Sherbrooke had cautioned his division to use the bayonet, and when the enemy came within about fifty yards of the guards, they advanced to meet them, but on attempting to close the enemy

* It is remarkable how the accounts differ respecting the hour of attack. Sir Arthur says, about twelve, another relater mentions two, and Jourdan, in his interesting letter, places it as late as four o'clock.

by a charge, they broke and fled. The regiment on their left, the 83rd, made a simultaneous movement, driving the enemy with immense loss before them; but the impetuosity of the guards led to endangering the day. The flying enemy led them on till they opened a battery on their flank, which occasioned so heavy a loss, that the ranks could not be formed after the disorder of pursuit, and on being ordered to resume their ground, produced confusion.

The enemy instantly rallied and followed them, and were so confident of victory, that their officers were heard to exclaim, "*Allons, mes enfans, ils sont touts nos prisonniers.*" But Sir Arthur had foreseen the probable difficulty into which the guards were likely to become entangled, and had ordered the 48th from the height to their support. This gallant regiment arrived in the rear of the guards at the moment when they were coming back in confusion, pressed by the enemy, on the line of position. They allowed the guards to pass through them, and then breaking in upon the enemy, gave them a second repulse. The guards quickly formed in the rear, and moved up into the position, and their spirit and appearance of good humour and determination, after having lost in twenty minutes five hundred men, were shewn by their giving a hurrah, as they took up their ground; and a report soon after that the enemy's cavalry was coming down upon them, was answered by a contemptuous laugh along their ranks.

The remainder of Sherbrooke's division, after repulsing the enemy, had retired to their former ground in excellent order. The enemy had made an attack at the same time on the fourth division; they accompanied this by a *ruse*, which nothing but the determination of our troops could have overcome. Trusting to the similarity of uniform, they advanced towards the 7th, 97th, and 53rd, crying out they were Spaniards, and repeating the Spanish cry of "*Vivan los Ingleses!*" Though this did not deceive our officers, it did the men, who, under this false impression, could not be brought to fire on them; this allowed their approaching quite close, when they gave their fire so unexpectedly, that it staggered our line, and even caused them to fall back. This was, however, only to exemplify the French proverb, *reculer pour mieux sauter*, as indignation and anger took place of surprise, and a spontaneous rush with the bayonet instantly threw the enemy into utter rout. A Spanish regiment of infantry on the right flank of the fusileers, broke and fled on this attack; but the King's regiment of horse, with great gallantry, dashed into the wood in co-operation with our troops in pursuit. Several pieces of cannon fell into the hands of General A. Campbell, and three were captured by the Spanish cavalry, while the flight of the enemy was so rapid, that several others were left in their retreat.

Besides these attacks, the enemy's endeavours and intentions were extended along the whole

British line, with the exception of the hill, which they did not again attack after the morning. We had not posted any troops in the valley, or on the hills on our left, the former being commanded, and the latter considered too distant, but it soon became evident that the enemy had turned their views to these points.

The Spanish division of General Bassecourt was, in consequence, borrowed from Cuesta, and sent across the valley to oppose the enemy's light troops on the distant ridge. The French soon after advanced two heavy columns into the valley, consisting of the divisions of Vilelle and Ruffin, and two-thirds of our cavalry were ordered to occupy the valley opposite them. General Anson's brigade arrived first, while the heavy brigade was moving from the rear of the centre to its support. The enemy's two columns advanced, supported by cavalry, threatened to turn our left, and orders, either positive or discretionary, were given, to charge them if opportunity offered; these were either interpreted into direct orders, or considered as definitive, under particular circumstances, and the 23rd regiment soon after advanced in line against one of the columns, the brigade of Laval, which had taken post with its flank against a house. This gallant regiment moved forward with great steadiness, and the squadron, for the width of only one could embrace the front of the column, on arriving within firing distance received a well-directed volley. It seemed to stop them in their career—the whole country was instantly covered with horses galloping back without riders, and men straggling to the rear without horses, while a dense spot seen from the hill marked where the slaughtered lay.

Though this squadron was annihilated, the others dashed on, passed between and round the columns, and fell upon a brigade of cavalry in the rear, broke through them, and rushed on a second brigade beyond. Of these, some cut their way back, while many were slain or taken. Though this desperate charge cost the 23rd two-thirds of its men and horses, it had the effect of astounding the enemy, who, seeing not only the 1st German, and the 3rd and 4th dragoons prepared for a similar act, but the Spanish cavalry moving into the valley in support, and their efforts unsuccessful elsewhere, not only gave up all further idea of penetrating in that quarter, but seemed satisfied that it was imprudent and hopeless any longer to continue the contest. But for being on the defensive, the gaps in our lines, which now forcibly shewed themselves, by the regiments not covering one-third of their former ground, would have made us come to a like conclusion; and it was no unpleasing sight to see them begin gradually to draw off their infantry, and bring forward, to cover their retreat, their cavalry, which had been all day in numerous *echellons*, extending back to the woods.

They formed several lines, and must have numbered not less than nine or ten thousand cavalry, dressed in all the colours of the rainbow.

But the views of the British were attracted to a new enemy which had threatened occasionally during the day, and had gained great head soon after the defeat on the right and centre. The ripe corn and dry grass took fire from the cartridges and wadding, and hundreds of acres were rapidly consumed, involving in their conflagrations the more severely wounded and helpless; adding a new and horrid character to the misery of war.

It was so general, that it was a consolation to the friends of officers slain, to learn that their bodies, when found, did not bear the marks of being scorched or burned in their last moments.

But the attention of all was directed till dusk to the enemy's evident preparations for retreat, and during the night they drew off behind the Alberche, which river they had all crossed by the daylight of the 29th; on which morning, Brigadier-General R. Crawford joined the army with three thousand men, and a troop of horse-artillery, and was pushed on to the old ruin, from which Sir Arthur had so narrowly escaped two days before. But these reinforcements, consisting of the 43rd, 52nd, and 95th, (the beginning of the celebrated light division,) did not make up for the heavy loss we had sustained during the 27th and 28th.

Out of 17,500 men, we had lost 5335, including General M'Kenzie and Langworth killed, and

General Hill, Sir H. Campbell, and Brigadier-General A. Campbell, wounded. This was two-sevenths of our force, and is, with the exception of Albuera, the heaviest list of casualties offered, for the men engaged, of any victorious army in modern war. The loss of the 23rd dragoons was remarkable from its extent; that fine regiment, which had only joined three weeks, being only able to assemble, after the action, one hundred men. Two officers and forty-six men and ninety-five horses were killed on the spot, and besides the numerous wounded, three officers, and about one hundred men were taken, in consequence of penetrating into the enemy's supporting cavalry. The whole regiment was so reduced, as to be sent home to England, on our return to the Portuguese frontier.

The Spanish returns gave between thirteen and fourteen hundred men, but this included their loss on the 25th in front of St. Ollala.*

The French army fell back across the Alberche, diminished not less than one-fifth, if not one-fourth of their effectives, their loss being indifferently rated from ten to fourteen thousand men. Some of the little enclosures in front of the right of the

* Nous pumes remarquer à l'occasion de ces deux affaires, le peu de cas que les Espagnols faisoient des Anglais; ils ne les surent aucun gré des efforts qu'ils firent à Talavera, et croyoient faire éloge de leur armée en disant qu'elle n'avoit essuyé presqu' aucune perte. Les Anglais de leur côté l'en meprisent souverainement et sont honteux de les avoir pour Alliés.—*MS. Journal of a French officer taken at Badajoz.*

British were choked with their dead, and in one little field more than four hundred bodies were counted.

Besides the innumerable dead, a vast number of wounded were left in our front; and many more stand of arms, than the most sanguine rated their loss, were abandoned on the field of battle.* Nineteen pieces of cannon remained in our possession as trophies of our victory.† Besides these, they left in our possession several silk standards, but whether they had borne eagles or not it was difficult to say; as, besides being much broken and torn when brought into head-quarters, the staff of one had been used as a poker to a bivouac fire. It was the custom of the French to unscrew their eagles, and for the eagle-bearers to conceal them about their person when in danger.

Having only one to a regiment, and there being five battalions to each, every eagle taken by us during the war, may be considered as equivalent to five stand of colours, and the trophies at Whitehall as ten times more numerous than they appear.

It is a remarkable and curious instance of the instability of human institutions, that these idols of the French armies for so many years, and

* It was said 17,000 were found.

† A noble peer, on the vote of thanks to the army, remarked, that the capture of these guns was no proof of a victory, as, he sagaciously observed, it might have been *convenient* for the enemy to leave them on the field of battle.

around which so much blood was spilt, only now exist but as trophies to their conquerors.

This hard-fought battle was remarkable from the circumstance of almost the entire efforts of an army being directed on the troops of one nation of their allied opponents. It is, perhaps, fortunate, that the rancour and vanity of the enemy led them to this conduct, as, had they forced the Spaniards from the difficult country on our right, our army would have been thrown from off the Tagus, and had to combat the whole French army, with its communications threatened, if not cut off.

With the exception of occupying the ground, the dash of the regiment of king's cavalry, and the employment of a few battalions in skirmishing on the hills on our left, the Spaniards did nothing whatever.* But their previous behaviour had tended to make us uneasy during the whole battle, and so disgusted was Cuesta with some of his troops, that he ordered several officers and men to be shot for cowardice the next day. This battle gave the character to all the subsequent actions in the Peninsula. They were ever almost entirely of infantry and artillery, while the cavalry, which acted with such effect on the continent, did not assert its power. However brilliant Vimiera and Corunna, still Talavera must be considered as the place where the military character of the two nations was

* " Les Espagnols seuls restaient paisibles spectateurs du combat," says a French author.

fairly brought to trial and proved. This battle proved the total want of firmness of the enemy in meeting our troops with the bayonet, and offered an example, followed by others on every occasion, of their best troops flying like chaff before the wind, on the hostile troops arriving within charging distance.

The French would ever expose themselves to fire at the smallest distance as long as ourselves, but a hurra and a rush with the bayonet, within reach, caused their instant flight.

With the exception of a few desperate men at the rear of a flying column, or from accidental circumstances, scarce any bayonet wounds were exchanged during the whole war; and their dread of closing was so strongly evinced in foggy weather, that a shout was sufficient, as at the pass of Maida, to disperse a forming column.

Indeed, our bayonets might as well have been of pasteboard, from their temper being so seldom tried, for the dread of them alone was sufficient to scatter the best troops of France. But it is a bad, if not useless weapon in their hands, and the Portuguese beat them with it on more than one occasion.

Brigadier-general Alexander Campbell had two horses shot under him, and though wounded through the thigh, continued on his horse till the close of the battle. Sir H. Campbell, who headed the brigade of guards, was wounded in the face, the ball entering the cheek and coming out behind the ear. Colonel Gordon, 83rd, was badly wounded in the neck, and when in the act of being removed to the rear, a shell fell into the blanket in which he was carried, and bursting, slew alike the wounded and his bearers. A man of the 87th, while lying down, was shot, the ball entering the head, and was alive five days after.

The incessant and terrible cannonade had created the most shocking wounds, and an unusual portion of wounded were not expected again to join the ranks. The standard of one of the regiments of Guards had three balls in its staff. The prisoners and deserters stated that during the action, a Westphalian regiment, in the enemy's service, mutinied, but that they were reduced to obedience and marched in the rear.

The morning after the battle was employed in removing our numerous and suffering wounded into the convents and churches, now converted into hospitals. By requisitions of beds and blankets, within three days, principally through the exertion of the head of the medical staff, Dr. Frank, no patient was without a mattress. Nurses and orderlies were selected to attend, and Sir Arthur visited the hospitals himself. The number of deaths from wounds that proved mortal, obliged immense burial parties to be employed during the first three or four days in removing the bodies from the hospitals. Even in the case of the officers, it was only through the attention of their brother officers, who read the service themselves, that the usual funeral forms were used, while the men were interred without prayers, being generally placed in ditches and the bank dug in upon them.

The heat of the weather rendered as necessary a proper attention to the dead of the enemy, and the Spaniards burned a vast number of the slain; but the weather was too rapid for all exertion, and the tainted air was fraught with every horror, and the quarters of some of the troops were forced to be changed. Though distressing to relate, it must not be overlooked, that the 29th was disgraced by the atrocious conduct of the Spaniards, in putting to death most of the enemy's wounded left in our front. The amount has been rated as high as one thousand, but it is certain several hundred were thus inhumanly butchered. One of our officers found a French officer badly wounded, and on offering to seek aid, the poor fellow remarked that he had no right to expect it, until our own numerous wounded were housed and dressed. But while seeking assistance, the Spaniards had passed the spot, and he was found stabbed to death!

Sir Arthur felt he could not too soon thank the army which had so nobly aided his efforts, and on the 29th his Excellency issued a long order to that effect, naming distinguished officers and regiments. The enemy continued a rear guard on the Alberche till the night of the 31st July, when they retired through St. Ollala, and our patroles passed through that town: here our officers learned some curious details of the enemies' bearing, under the different feelings of confidence of expected success and the discouragement of subsequent defeat, In the house where the king had lodged, an instance was given highly creditable to Joseph. A caricature was discovered of El Rey Pepé, which created great indignation in those around Joseph's person. accompanied by threats and ill-treatment. The king the next morning, on his departure, tendered his host a snuff-box, remarking, that he should be more careful of its contents than of the caricature; on its being opened, it was found to contain the king's miniature.

We were prevented from moving after the enemy, not only on account of our numerous wounded, but from want of provisions. Our difficulties on this head greatly increased after the battle, and were felt to so great an extent, that the army in part became disorganized, from the ravenous callings for food overpowering all other considerations. While it was said comparative plenty reigned in the Spanish camp, our troops were driven to seek and take provisions by force, wherever they could find them; this led to such straggling from the camp, that on the 2nd of August the rolls were ordered to be called every two hours. While our position was thus unsatisfactory, and even doubtful, news reached head-quarters that our rear was threatened by troops moving down from Castile and Leon. On the 30th, a rumour (however proved to be anticipated) spread that the French had arrived in Placentia, and the anxiety became universal.

Our information at this time was less perfect than it afterwards became, and the various reports left the impression that it was Soult's corps alone, of twelve to fifteen thousand men, that was thus menacing our communication with Portugal. This, however, did not make our position untenable, as our army of between fifteen and sixteen thousand, was capable of defeating his force, if Cuesta could be persuaded to hold his ground, and keep in check the lately defeated army, and thus cover our hospitals. To this Cuesta agreed, and ordering General Bassecourt's division to act as our advance, caused it to march to Oropesa on the 2nd. Arrangements were made respecting the hospitals, and Colonel M'Kinnon was left in their charge, with but thirty-four medical officers (all we could spare) to attend five thousand sick and wounded.

We left Talavera on the 3rd, under the full expectation of fighting the forces coming from the north, concentrating about Naval Moral. On our arrival at Oropesa on the evening of that day, Bassecourt was pushed on towards that place, and orders were given out implying active and immediate operations, by directing the troops to hold themselves in readiness to march by such orders as they might receive from the quarter-master-general.

But the course of the night changed all our

prospects. Sir Arthur received a despatch from Cuesta stating, that he had received information on which he could depend, that not only had Soult's corps moved from the north, but that it was accompanied by the two other corps, the 5th and 6th, and that he had, in consequence, determined to retire from Talavera. This implied the sacrifice to the enemy of all in our hospitals who had not the power of walking, as the Spaniards, on Colonel M'Kinnon applying to them for means of transport, furnished only ten or a dozen carts, while very many quitted the town empty. Colonel M'Kinnon, thus under the painful necessity of leaving near two thousand three hundred sick and wounded, gave directions for the rest to withdraw by a nearer road to the bridge of Arzobispo, than through Oropesa.*

This unexpected news added to Sir Arthur's difficulties; and while these were under consideration, they were greatly increased by the whole Spanish army coming in upon us, at daylight on the 4th, with their carts and baggage.

On this occasion the old gentleman had not wanted discretion, and within a few hours of taking his departure, the presence of himself and army proved its accomplishment.

The intelligence of Cuesta proved most true; a

* We had the satisfaction of hearing after, that Victor, on entering Talavera, behaved with the greatest attention and kindness to those who, by the chance of war, had thus been left to his mercy and care.

junction of the three corps had taken place, and the king, before he left Madrid, had sent them orders on the 22nd to advance on Placentia. The head-quarters of the 2nd, 5th, and 6th corps were at Salamanca on the 27th of July, and directing their march on three succeeding days to the south, forced all the weak passes and posts, and arrived, on the 1st of August, at Placentia, making prisoners three hundred sick in the hospitals.

The Spanish troops retiring before Soult, crossed the Tagus, and fortunately destroyed the bridge of boats at Almarez. But the enemy only thought of intercepting and surrounding the British, and their advance reached Naval Moral on the 3rd, but five leagues from Oropesa, thus cutting off the direct road, by Almarez to Portugal.

No time was now to be lost, as we were not only likely to be attacked from the west, but in consequence of the retreat of the Spaniards, threatened with the advance of King Joseph, and his defeated army at Talavera, within three or four days; in which case, we should have had, besides thirty-six to thirty-eight thousand from Madrid, thirty to thirty-four thousand from Placentia.

But Sir Arthur soon decided, and gave directions, at four o'clock on the 4th, for all the baggage to proceed across the bridge of Arzobispo. This was preparatory to a similar movement of the army; and recalling Bassecourt's division, the whole British force filed over to the left bank of the

Tagus, where the wounded had safely reached a short time before.

The Spaniards followed to the side of the river, but did not cross that evening. So nearly had the enemy intercepted our retreat, that at dusk his cavalry interchanged some shots with our advance-posts, close to Arzobispo, and carried off one of our videttes. The Spaniards did not cross the next day; but the British army proceeded down the river, by the same road the enemy had turned Cuesta's flank before the battle of Medellin, in the preceding spring. This was rendered the more necessary, as the occupation of Almarez could alone secure a retreat upon Portugal; and the pontoons, though removed, had been left in charge of some militia. Head-quarters on the 5th were near the village of Peretada de Gabern—and the 3rd division, which had been placed under the orders of General Crawford, with the light brigade, was pushed by narrow paths across the mountain, and reached a point within two leagues of the passage of the Tagus.

On the 6th, it reached Roman Gardo, which secured this important position, and head-quarters moved on to Messa de Ibor, (the spot of Cuesta's unsuccessful affair on the 17th of March,) and the following day to Deleytoza. It was possible now to halt with security, from the pass at Almarez having been secured—and in a large convent about a mile from the town a hospital was formed, when it was found that above 2000 wounded had accompanied the army. General A. Campbell had found his way, in a huckster's tilted-cart, with a bed made in it, across the most difficult passes in the mountain.

The roads, during three days' march, were scarcely capable of transport,—the greatest difficulty being experienced in conveying the artillery, and the troops were often halted to cover their retreat.

As we moved over the high ridges, we had a most extensive view across the place we had traversed a fortnight before from Placentia, and saw the glittering of the arms, and the rising dust of the French columns moving on Oropesa.

Colonel Waters and Captain Mellish crossed the river, and reconnoitered the last of these columns, and learned from the peasants that it was the third of the same size that had passed along that road within the preceding few days; thus fully confirming the information of the three corps having been directed on our rear.

Thus, as in the preceding year, the British had again drawn five *corps d'armée* of the eight in Spain upon them. Some of the troops from the north were not re-equipped after their losses in the north of Portugal, but the three corps had little short of thirty-five thousand effectives. However precipitate the retreat of Cuesta, it would have been eventually necessary—for, although we could have checked on the 5th, 6th, and 7th, the successive arriving columns of the enemy from Naval Moral, (allowing time for the very desirable transport of many more of our wounded beyond Arzobispo,) still our position would sooner or later have become untenable.

It may be conjectured that few armies have witnessed such vicissitudes as the French and English within the short period of eleven months. The two armies had more than once advanced and retired in the face of each other. Many of those we saw marching across the plain with the sanguine hope of intercepting our retreat, had been driven from Portugal and carried to France, had witnessed our embarkation from Corunna, and had since been expelled from the Tras os Montes, and now again were compelling us, by an immense superiority of numbers, to retrograde again.

After leaving the Spaniards at Arzobispo, the two armies were totally disunited, and little or no subsequent communication took place between them. We had seen enough of both officers and men to despise and distrust them, from the chief to the drummer, and to hope that we might never again be quartered in the same camp. They not only were incapable of acting as a military auxiliary, but were most remiss in fulfilling their promises, and instead of attempting to find us provisions, while plenty reigned in their camp, even our officers were destitute of bread. While our troops were on one occasion four days without this indispensable necessary, they had the shameless impudence to sell loaves to our starving soldiers at an immoderate price. So pressing were our wants, that one of our commissioners took from them by force one hundred bullocks and one hundred mule loads of bread. But if their conduct before us had been despicable, it no less at a distance deserved reprehension. Vanegas, who was to have made a powerful diversion from La Mancha on Toledo, completely failed, even to the extent of alarming the enemy, who felt satisfied that 2,000 men in that city were sufficient to keep in check his whole force, while the passes along the Portuguese and Spanish frontier were gained almost without a struggle.

But disasters quickly followed the Spaniards after our separation. On the 6th they crossed to the left bank of the Tagus—and on the following day Cuesta retired with his main force, leaving two divisions of infantry, and the cavalry with the artillery in battery to defend the bridge. The enemy showed themselves on the 6th on the opposite bank, and increased in number on the 7th, but the interposition of the river between them made the Spaniards consider themselves in perfect safety. On the 8th, the French brought up their artillery, and opened a fire on some redoubts constructed by the Spaniards, while they made preparations for crossing the river. The Spanish cavalry, devoid of all caution, were out in watering order, when 2,000 cavalry dashed into the river, above the bridge, at a good ford, and attacked the redoubts in the rear, at once enveloping the Spanish camp in confusion, dismay, and rout. They fled, some in the direction of Messa de Ibor, others to the southward, leaving their baggage and guns in the hands of the enemy. Those who fled by the former road, abandoned guns and ammunition-wagons several leagues beyond the point of pursuit; and Colonel Waters, sent from our head quarters with a flag of truce, finding them thus safe, persuaded the Spaniards, with difficulty, to return and bring back their deserted cannon.

This disgraceful affair was the climax of disaster to this army. It could not assemble, in a few days subsequently, 18,000 men, and the Duke of Albuquerque (against whose advice the Spanish cavalry had been left unprepared) quitted it in disgust, sending in charges to the Cortes against his commander. This was anticipated by Cuesta, who, on the plea of ill-health, resigned on the 13th the command of the army. To complete the sad picture presented by the Spaniards, Vanegas, without answering any purpose, committed himself so grossly on the Toledo side, that Sebastiani fell upon him at Almonaciadid, on the 10th, and routed him with considerable loss.

Want of forage and provisions continued to an alarming degree in the mountainous tract around Deleytosa and Almarez, and, still keeping the advance at the latter place, rendered necessary the army's moving more to the westward. Head quarters were, on the 11th, at Jarecejo, in order to be nearer Truxillo, where a large depôt was forming. Sir Arthur ordered, with justice, that the stoppage for the troops usually of sixpence a-day for their provisions, should be only threepence from the 27th of July till further orders, in reference to their want of regular supplies.* While the head quarters were at this place, the effects of want of food began to show themselves on the troops by sickness breaking out, though not at first to the alarming extent it did a month after on the Guadiana. But the road by Castelo Branco to Lisbon was only covered by a small force of four British regiments, which had been moving up under General C. Crawford, and it became necessary to place the army nearer to Portugal, in a position to cover both banks of the Tagus, should the enemy direct his march from Placentia. Although Crawford was soon joined by Marshal Beresford from the north, the army moved, on the 20th, from Jarecejo to Truxillo, and gradually withdrew towards the frontier head quarters, passing through Majadas, Medellin, Merida, to Badajoz, where Sir Arthur established himself on the

---

* It was not till the 12th of August that rations of spirits were delivered to the troops, and only on the 2nd of September that the regular delivery of provisions allowed the stoppage of sixpence per day.—ED.

3rd of September, with the troops cantoned as follows :—

First Division at { Badajos, Arroyo, Lobone, Almendralejo, Talavera la Real, and Santa Marta.

Second Division { Modtejo, La Mata, La Puebla de la Calsada, Gorravilla, and Torre Major.

Third Division { Campo Mayor, Villa de Rey.

Fourth Division { Olivenza, Badajos.

In the meantime, the enemy had not followed the defeated Spaniards, but, fearful of leaving the north of Spain without troops, as early as they had separated the two armies, and felt secure of the capital, the three corps set out on their return, on the 9th, towards Salamanca. Sir R. Wilson, whose advance to Escalona had not produced the supposed effect on the French army, or at Madrid, in retiring from his exposed situation, took post in the pass of Baños. This was the direct road for the enemy's returning columns, who, after a sharp affair on the 12th, forced the position, and continued their route, leaving Sir Robert to fall back on the frontier of Portugal.

Thus ended the campaign of 1809, which was not less brilliant than interesting, and tended greatly to the ultimate deliverance of Spain and Europe. Though no immediate results were produced from it, there can be no doubt it saved Andalusia for a time, which province would never have fallen into the enemy's power, had not the besotted Spaniards sought opportunities for defeat, and committed themselves, as at Ocana. In drawing the three corps from the north, it showed all that part of Spain that the struggle was continued with firmness in other quarters, and the very fact of relieving the country from the pressure of the enemy, allowed breathing time, and proved that their stay would not be permanent.

The battles of the 27th and 28th of July broke much of the enemy's confidence when opposed to us, and their repulse gave spirits not only to the Spaniards, but opened the eyes of Europe to the possibility of defeating the French; for it may be fearlessly advanced, that the *morale* of the European armies was restored by this and our succeeding campaigns in Spain.

* * * * *
* * * * *

The next period of the Peninsular war to which we propose to refer, is the retreat to the lines. A corps was left between the Coa and Agueda rivers, under the command of General Robert Crawford, The cavalry attached to that corps was small in number, compared to the host of horsemen opposed to it, and *this* was the more to be lamented as the district through which Crawford must retire was open, and peculiarly suited to cavalry movements. It was therefore of great importance to spare the dragoons as much as possible; nevertheless, two squadrons of the 14th Light Dragoons, under Colonel Talbot, were ordered to charge a body of two hundred French infantry. We have heard, and we believe on pretty good authority, that Talbot requested that the infantry might be broken by artillery, but having received for answer a taunt as to his shyness in charging, he led his men against the square, and fell among the French bayonets, while thirty-two of his followers were either killed or wounded, and the French were allowed to retire without further molestation. It is a well-established fact, that cavalry has a very bad chance of breaking a compactly-formed body of infantry, and therefore they ought not to be so employed, unless some advantage is expected beyond the mere destruction of the body attacked. The most advantageous opportunity, and the one in which an impression has been most frequently made by cavalry is, when a column of infantry is about to occupy an important position, the attainment of which object may be of great importance to them. If they are attacked by cavalry while in motion, there is a fair prospect of success; and even if the cavalry is repelled, the very formation to resist the attack may be of immense importance in gaining time, and in making the enemy's movement more timid. There can be no excuse for so gratuitous a sacrifice as the one just alluded to. A very gallant charge was made about the same time by Captain Krauchenberg — who, being posted at the bridge of

Marialva when it was attacked by a strong body of cavalry and infantry, with his single troop of hussars charged the head of the column, checked the enemy, and retired in safety. This affair was always mentioned among the cavalry in the highest terms—and Krauchenberg was universally allowed to be fitted for a much higher command than the one entrusted to him; but as the river was fordable and the British advance was not pressed for time, there was no object to be gained by the charge beyond the chivalrous feeling which it inculcated.

When Massena made his arrangements, after the fall of Rodrigo, he allotted 8,000 horsemen to that part of his army with which he proposed to pursue the British. Lord Wellington had not a third part of that number of British and German dragoons. Several affairs of posts occurred previous to the battle of Busaco, in which the British cavalry did well, but Lord Wellington naturally avoided squandering an arm with which he was so slenderly provided.

The morning after the battle of Busaco,* Sep-

* Busaco was fought on the 27th of September, 1810. The attack was made on two points, the height Antonio de Cantara, and the convent hill. Massena was bloodily repulsed, while, including the affairs on the 25th and 26th, when retreating, the allied loss amounted only to 1269. That sustained by the French has never been correctly ascertained. Jones sets it down at 2,000 killed, 300 prisoners, and 5,000 wounded; Napier only at 800 killed, and 3,700 wounded and missing.—ED.

tember 29th, the British cavalry retired early, but were soon overtaken by the French, who, being in very superior numbers, pressed them into the plain on the Mondego. They then found themselves on a plain, occasionally intersected with deep roads, with the river Mondego in their rear, which was passable only by one deep ford. Here was a situation in which the retiring force had scarcely a chance, had they been vigorously attacked; and considering their well-known inferiority in point of number, they should have been supported by infantry. With one of the light division battalions to aid them, their retreat was secure; as it was, their safety may be ascribed to a want of energy on the part of the French. The British rear-guard took advantage of a defile formed by a bridge over which they had passed; the ever ready horse artillery bore upon it, and the cavalry was formed upon the plain; and thus the enemy was checked, and the rear guard crossed the Mondego with trifling loss.

Here we have a day's work probably little known to the army, and little appreciated by those acquainted with it, yet involving one of the most difficult operations in war—viz., a rear guard opposed by a very superior force in front, and a river in their rear. The accomplishment of this object conferred great honour on the troops and the officer commanding them; and it is much to be regretted that some one of the officers present on this and other occasions has not devoted his time to justify the British cavalry, and, by a sketch of the different affairs of posts, to form not only an interesting, but a highly instructive elementary work. We could name several officers who, from having been actors in most of the scenes, and from a general knowledge of war, could do ample justice to the subject. The field is still open; the writer of these pages has little opportunity to collect information, and he will feel highly gratified if the cursory remarks he has made may be the means of stimulating some abler hand to take up the pen.

The early part of the day following the passage of the Mondego, was passed without molestation; and in the afternoon, the picket of the 16th retired before a superior force. On the following morning, probably the 1st of October, the French advanced with determination, and in a force which it was impossible to keep in check. The pickets were attacked, and would soon have been put to flight, when a squadron of the 16th, under Captain Cocks, came to their aid, and charging the enemy twice, made some prisoners, and effected a retreat without loss. But a new difficulty presented itself; the French were driving in the rear guard; a narrow bridge lay in the rear, and a narrow way beyond it. The bridge was passed with difficulty, and Lieutenant Hay of the 16th was left with five or six men to check the French, who, furnished with guns, were gaining upon the main body of the rear guard. That officer remained for a considerable time in his perilous post. The French skirmishers as they came up formed, and one gun opened on the bridge; when, having accomplished his object, Lieutenant Hay and his party retired at speed, and joined the support. We continue our narrative in the words of our informant, which would be injured by alteration.

"We soon saw Major Murray's squadron of the 16th advancing at a gallop to charge. The skirmishers joined this squadron, and they advanced to attack the three leading French squadrons— viz., two of hussars, and one of chasseurs, who were formed in three lines to receive them. The leading squadron of French hussars advanced at a walk, then halted, and no persuasion of the officers, who behaved most gallantly, could induce them to move. We were anything but compact, our files having been loosened by the inequality of the ground, and by a horse falling, and others falling over him, as we approached. Three French officers and one man dashed out to meet us; they were all cut down, and the whole fled in disorder: about thirty prisoners were secured. A squadron of the Royals then charged,* and with success; but Lieutenant Carden, who commanded the party, having had his horse shot while in the enemy's ranks, was made prisoner. They did not press us again, but showed a great force of cavalry,

* Our informant says a squadron; we are able to correct him—the party consisting of forty men, made up of the old and new pickets, the relief of which was going on.

and six or eight guns, of which they made little use; our artillery remained almost amongst the skirmishers, and kept them in check, knocking their supports about as soon as they came near enough. We encamped at Rio Mayor, and were almost drowned in rain. On the 2nd we were on picket with a squadron (Major Murray's of the 16th); the cook of a French general strayed into our line, and was sent as a present to head quarters. Our orders were positive, to keep the enemy in check *without engaging*. The French had not seen an infantry soldier since Busaco, and had evidently attempted the day before to discover where the army was. About twelve o'clock we saw a long line of cavalry advancing, apparently two or three regiments; the rain was incessant, and the French were cloaked; Major Murray and his squadron retired slowly before the enemy, who offered no active molestation. Major Murray sent an orderly to Alcoentré, to which place the British cavalry had retired—no answer was returned; a second messenger was dispatched, and no answer being received, an officer was sent, who found the cavalry and artillery in perfect tranquillity, watering their horses, and apparently unconscious of danger—the officer, very wisely, ordered the trumpet to sound, and returned to his squadron. The French had now commenced the attack, and although the uncloaking took a long time, still more time was required. Messengers were sent to our cavalry camp, to bring up the men first mounted. Lieutenants Tomkinson and Penrice of the 16th, with about forty men, were the first to come up; these were joined to the force already under Major Murray and Lieutenant Hay. As the French column was advancing into the main street, we charged them without a moment's hesitation; they went about at once, and we beat them back out of the town. An officer and a good many men were killed, and many prisoners secured, while others escaped down the cross streets, and it was impossible to follow them, as we were forced to stick close to the main body, to prevent their forming and turning on us. The guns were got out of the town. Captain Cock's squadron, which was on picket the following day, charged and made some prisoners. It was the 14th heavy dragoons which we met at Alcoentré, and they got a good dressing. General Montbrun was up, and in the immediate command."

At Alcoentré it is difficult to say what might not have been done. The whole British cavalry had established their camp, and had Montbrun dashed on, he might have destroyed the cavalry before they could have formed to resist him. The British horse, however, had done their duty so well as to leave the French in utter ignorance of the position of the army; the town of Alcoentré *might* have been full of infantry, and to this possibility we may, perhaps, ascribe the safety of the rear guard. The slackness in turning out appears to have arisen from an idea that the French would not come on that day, although Major Murray had sent *two* dispatches. The gallantry and determination of that officer, after all, saved the rear guard by the gallant charge, which we have given in the words of a gentleman who was present, and who, in telling his story, has not claimed the honour of the active share he took in the affray. Colonel Napier states that fifty or sixty dragoons were lost in passing the Mondego. We can only say, that our information is to be relied upon, and, perhaps, the loss subsequent to the passage of the river may have been mixed up with the previous losses in the Colonel's history.

Thus, although the French cavalry was immensely superior in number, and a great part of the retreat was through a country applicable to the manœuvre of that arm, yet we hear of no baggage being taken, no posts surprised, nor of any of those feats which must have occurred, had not the French been held in check by the British cavalry.

Surely Massena did not take with him so large a corps of cavalry as eight thousand, into a country where forage is at all times scarce, but in the hopes that he would reap great advantage from it. As we do not hear of any influence produced by the movements of the French cavalry, it is surely but reasonable to assert that they were held in check, and their effect neutralised, by the British horsemen, who, in doing so, rendered good service to the cause, although they were not able to leave any splendid memorial of their services.

Perhaps it is a fair illustration to compare the case to that of two expert cricketers. A novice at Lord's is surprised to see how rarely the batter strikes the ball, and he never gets a good honest swipe ; but a better informed hand points out the superior bowling opposed to him, and makes it evident that if he can keep his stumps up, and get an occasional run, it is all that can be expected. In all matters whatsoever, whether in games of skill, or in the business of life, a great part of the affair is to neutralise the skilful arrangements of a superior adversary; and in all such cases, the efforts of the defending party are only observed by those who pay attention to the details, and who, from experience, are able to appreciate the difficulties. When the army arrived in the lines, there was but little opportunity for the use of cavalry on either side. The retreat from Villa Franca to Santarem had been so well arranged, that nothing was seen of the French. During the occupation of the position at Santarem, a considerable party of cavalry was employed on the outposts, but as each party was desirous of repose, the advance was seldom disturbed.

Massena broke up from his position on the 5th of March. The pursuit commenced the following morning, but it was at Torres Novas, about six leagues from Santarem, that the advanced party of the British came in contact with the French ; a skirmish ensued, and the same was daily renewed. When the army reached Thomar, a corps under

General Cole was sent to Alentejo: the cavalry then remaining with Lord Wellington consisted of four regiments—viz., the 1st, 14th, and 16th dragoons, and the 1st hussars, amounting at that time to about sixteen hundred sabres. The duty committed to the cavalry from this time was most arduous—the sole charge of the outposts, with frequent patrolling to the front and flanks. The British cavalry was partially engaged every day; the French dragoons being generally supported by infantry, whose tirailleurs were mixed up with the mounted ones. The greatest evil to which the British cavalry was exposed, was the utter want of forage. During nearly a month, the commissariat did not issue twenty pounds of corn per horse: the sole provender for the horses was rye-straw, which, from its purging quality, is most unfit food for a horse at work; indeed, under any circumstances, it is a most woful substitute for hay and corn. The horses, consequently, became attenuated, and unable to perform the heavy duties imposed upon them. In illustration of the abject state to which the horses were reduced, we must mention a circumstance, of which we have a vivid recollection.

A subaltern officer had been directed to carry a despatch, and off he went at a walk. The commanding officer called out, "Mr. P., an officer never leaves the ranks at a walk." The Brummagems were applied, and a convulsive canter ensued, which lasted about half-a-dozen strides, when the animal sank down to his original walk, and no farther coercive measure was resorted to. As this officer was considered to be well mounted, and was careful of his horses, the foregoing may be deemed a fair specimen of the degraded state of the horses. In spite of this moral dismounting, the cavalry continued to do all the outpost duty, and, at least, had the good effect of performing services which, if they had devolved on the infantry, would have been most distressing. We cannot assert that any affair of posts worth noticing occurred, and we must farther say, that one or two good opportunities were afforded; one at Pegoā, a little village near Sabugal, where the French had left the 70th regiment quite unsupported. The French infantry formed squares, and were canonaded for some time with little effect, but had they been attacked by the dragoons, and at the same time canonaded with grape, there cannot be a doubt as to the issue. Lord Wellington did not come up that day, and if he had been there, he seemed so truly to despise small matters, and at the same time felt his weakness in horse so keenly, that it is doubtful if he would have done anything. The other opportunity which was lost was at the action of Sabugal, when the French might have been attacked on their retreat to Alfayates, with very great effect. The corps which had been attacked at Sabugal (Regnier's), retired during the night, got across the Agueda, was then in safety, and thus ended Massena's retreat.

The Alentejo corps meanwhile fell in with the

enemy, and a most distinguished and gallant cavalry affair took place. The French having dismantled Campo Mayor, were engaged in carrying off such of the stores as were of value—and this operation was in the course of execution, under the escort of a corps consisting of a brigade of infantry, and 700 or 800 cavalry, (Colonel Napier makes the dragoon force larger,) and thirteen guns, which probably had formed part of the Campo Mayor garrison guns; the whole under the command of the well-known General Latour Maubourg. The British advance, consisting of two squadrons of the 13th Light Dragoons, and two squadrons of Portuguese, came upon this body rather unexpectedly. The commanding officer, Colonel Head, was aware of the neighbourhood of the enemy, although he appears not to have been informed of their extreme contiguity.

The ground appears to have been what is called, in land-surveying, a hog's back. The French were ascending to the crest of the hill, or rather slope, on one side, as Colonel Head, with the 13th, were going up the other side, when he found himself in the presence of the enemy, who was equally surprised by the encounter. Without a moment's hesitation, Colonel Head wheeled up his squadrons, and charged the French, (who had time to form a line and wait to receive the charge,) drove them down the hill, reformed and charged back again; and having again formed, he made a third charge, killing, wounding, and upsetting a great number of the French; the French commanding officer having been killed in the first charge by Corporal Logan of the 13th, and the French cavalry being so completely broken that Latour Maubourg was fain to seek shelter in a square of infantry. Trusting to the heavy brigade of dragoons, which was immediately in his rear, to secure the guns and prisoners, and to deal with the infantry, Colonel Head and his gallant band galloped on, and pursued the French to the gates of Badajoz, when a salute from the rampart of that place forced him to return to review the spoil which he had left to the care of the heavy brigade—but that force had not been moved up. The French cavalry had been allowed to form again: the infantry to move to their support, the guns had been retaken, and were afterwards carried in safety to Badajoz, there to deal destruction on our gallant fellows, who so frequently and so nobly fought against that place. Latour Maubourg was allowed to withdraw himself from a shelter of bayonets which he had sought, and to take charge of his people again—no doubt his bile excited by the straits to which he had been driven —and he found an early opportunity of wreaking his vengeance at Albuera, where he charged a very material part of the position, routed the Spaniards, destroyed an English brigade, and the day was saved only by the heroism of the fusileer brigade.

Meanwhile, the 13th, on their return, found their retreat cut off, and they were only able to escape by taking a circuitous route. Colonel Head, however, had done his duty most gallantly, and, no doubt, he expected unmeasured applause. He had defeated a corps of cavalry four times more numerous than the one he commanded: he had suffered little or no loss, and had taken thirteen guns and a number of prisoners. The exploit was surely not the less to be admired, because the reserve had not secured the advantages he had gained; and in return for this service, what reward did Colonel Head receive? Less distinguished services have been nobly recompensed, but the whole of Colonel Head's merits were repaid by the information, that he had acted with great rashness, that he ought not to have charged without a support; or, in other words, that he ought to have attacked 700 or 800 French dragoons with 100 instead of 200. Although the brigade of heavy dragoons was within two minutes ride of his rear, yet Colonel Head was accused of having acted with great rashness: it is true that he had been successful; his temerity had been crowned with unexampled success; but the result did not excuse his committing himself; and it was solemnly pointed out to the British cavalry, through the medium of the orderly-book, how wrong it was to be rash; how necessary to have a support, with other valuable truisms; to which was added a pleasing compliment to the heavy brigade, and congratulation on their steadiness. Of this, we believe, the heavy dragoons were most unworthy, but they would gladly have aided their brave fellow soldiers had they been allowed to do so.

In this affair, Colonel Head had displayed the one great qualification which, above all others (always assuming the existence of personal courage), tends to make a good officer, and especially a good cavalry officer—viz., prompt decision. The moment he saw the enemy, he formed and charged. The French were aware of the vicinity of a large force, and finding themselves vigorously attacked, a panic seized them, and they fled. Colonel Head, himself an Irishman, and commanding men mostly from that country, duly appreciated their impetuous courage, and did not hesitate to attack, convinced that the enemy did not know his force, and that he would be supported. He might have done less, and escaped without blame, but he bravely took advantage of circumstances in his favour, and succeeded, as brave men generally do succeed, under similar circumstances. Had he been advancing over a plain, and had he opened the ball in the usual manner, with skirmishers, supports, &c., the enemy would have been enabled to estimate his force, and would have felt confident. Had he then charged, he would have been guilty of rashness, and, without a doubt, would have been most shamefully defeated. He used his wits as an officer ought to do; in doing so, he acted the part of an experienced soldier; as far as leading the actual charge, that service would probably have been as ably performed by Corporal Logan. After receiving the reward of his valour, we have heard that Colonel Head was addressed—" I believe, Colonel, that you would have galloped into Badajoz, if the gates had been open."

"By Gad, General, I believe I would," was the answer—and we believe so too; the boys were so fresh.

When a body of dragoons has charged, they become loose and broken, and are of little service, till they have been regularly reformed and told off. As the orderly-book very properly observes, an officer must have a support. We believe that the 13th never got over the effect of the unjust treatment they met with.

Perhaps some one of the officers who were present may honour this paper with perusal. We *know* that the leading facts are correct. If we have not done justice to the exploit, let it be attributed to want of power, and not to want of will. We have now recorded two instances in which the British cavalry were accused of rashness, instead of being rewarded for valour. A work might have been as well published, entitled, "A plan for the abasement and farther deterioration of the British Cavalry." This was not done—but the treatment experienced by the 13th and 23rd, added to the well-known advantages of a whole skin, afforded a practical lesson, which, no doubt, was profited by, although not to the extent which might have been fairly expected. Another inducement to inactivity was held out, in the absence of any reward to junior officers; an order, such as is given by all the Continental powers, would have a most beneficial effect.

It is needless to refer to the ardour produced by the Legion of Honour, although its decorations were so lavishly bestowed. With us the rewards were confined to the commanders of regiments, or distinct bodies, and were, perhaps, distributed indiscriminately enough. We cannot deny that we feel sorely, but this soreness does not arise from any private wrong. We have no unrequited claim on the service; indeed, we have no claim at all; but we feel anxious that the public should be made acquainted with the difficulties against which the British cavalry had to contend.

* * * * *
* * * * *

Lord Wellington having taken up the line of the Agueda, turned his attention to Almeida, which was occupied by a small garrison—and slenderly provisioned—and an attempt was made to lessen their means of support, by employing riflemen to fire at the oxen which were grazing upon the glacis. Little effect appeared to have been produced by this measure, but it was ascertained, from an intercepted letter, that most of the cattle had been wounded, and it became necessary to kill and salt them, which, it is well known, is done to great disadvantage in very hot weather. The place was finally blockaded. Massena retired with his army to the plains of Salamanca. The British army was placed in cantonments. Such a portion of the cavalry as was not required for the outpost, was sent behind the Coa, and allowed a repose of about three weeks, to recover from the effects of the fatigue it had undergone. The young crops of rye, then nearly three feet high, were purchased by the commissariat. The grain which had been hoarded by the inhabitants was now brought out, and the horses began to recover their flesh. Time, however, was not afforded to put them into condition—and when they came to work again, they rapidly lost the flesh which had been put on their bones by the green forage. Although twenty years have intervened, the writer of these pages looks back with horror to this period. The village in which he was cantoned, had suffered severely from the French; more than half of the houses had been destroyed, and those which remained were in the most abject state of dilapidation, and utterly devoid of furniture. The poor inhabitants were returning to their desolated dwellings, and patiently resuming their wonted avocations; suffering, with resignation, the severest penury, and being under great difficulty from the loss of their oxen and rude implements of husbandry, which had been carried off, or wantonly destroyed. The people appeared to suffer all with great patience, but their sad countenances harmonized with the surrounding scene, where melancholy reigned. Without any occupation, save stable duty, this inactive life, immediately succeeding a short but very animated campaign, generated a degree of *ennui* far beyond anything the writer has ever experienced. Still the horses got fat.

Meanwhile Massena, having received reinforcements, was making every exertion to reorganize his army, and soon found himself at the head of about 40,000 infantry and 5000 cavalry, with which he advanced to the relief of Almeida. Lord Wellington took up his position between the Coa and the Duas Casas, which small river was immediately in front of some part of his position. Sir William Erskine's division, with one squadron of dragoons, was placed near the ruins of Fort Conception, to guard the road to Almeida, the investment of which place was committed to General Packe's brigade, of Campbell's division. The village of Fuentes was strongly occupied. General Houston's division was on the right at Poso Velho, and the village of Nava-da-ver was held by the guerilla corps of Julian Sanchez. The French were allowed to pass the Agueda without molestation—and on the 3rd of May took up their position with their left opposite to Fuentes, and on that day made an attack on the village. But after varied success, and the demonstration of the greatest bravery on each side, the largest portion of the village remained in the hands of the British.

The position and prospects of the British army were such as demanded all the firmness of Lord Wellington. The French army, which was within cannon-shot of our lines, counted a *fully* equal force of infantry: in cavalry they were superior in the proportion of five to one, while their artillery was superior both in number of pieces and in calibre. The British occupied a position which was probably the best that could be obtained, but which offered no natural obstacle; while the whole of it, with the exception of the villages, was suited to the employment of cavalry. In the event of disaster, the rugged Coa lay in the rear—and the fords on that river are dangerous, and very difficult of access. By the extension of his right, Lord Wellington secured the bridge of Sabugal; but the operations of the 5th cut off the army from that line of retreat, when there only remained the bridge of Castelo Bom, which was so narrow, that it would have required many days for the passage of the army over it. There can hardly be a doubt but that defeat must have caused the destruction of the British army; but Lord Wellington felt confident, and communicated his gallant feelings to the whole army. On the afternoon of the 4th, a squadron of dragoons was sent to Nava-da-ver, to support Julian Sanchez. The commanding officer, Captain Brotherton, found that the guerillas had taken every precaution, and the outposts continued in their hands. During the night, the Spaniards sent in several reports that the French army was in motion—and as it turned out, Massena had moved his army bodily by its left.

On the morning of the 5th, Captain Brotherton, in obedience to previous orders, prepared to rejoin the cavalry, behind Poso Velho; and on its route, this squadron was the first to witness the threatening demonstrations of the French. It was a glorious sight. The morning was beautiful; the sun was gradually dispelling a thick mist which had prevailed during the night, and which seemed yet in lower grounds to dispute the solar influence. The silence of the morning was scarcely broken by the hum of the neighbouring armies, when the French advance upon our right was observed at the distance of about half a mile. The nearest columns of cavalry were only seen in parts, the continuity being broken by the partial fogs; beyond them the valley seemed filled with troops, parts of the columns only becoming visible for a moment as the mist cleared off. Farther to the rear, the enemy were on higher ground. The sun had gained the ascendancy, and shone upon the accoutrements of the squadrons; and again the view was impeded by the fog, and the sequel left to the imagination. Enough, however, had been seen to authorise the report sent in, that the French were moving upon the right in great force, as this squadron continued its march when nearly behind Poso Velho, and the advance of the French was coming nearly perpendicularly upon its wake. We observed a very fine squadron of French grenadiers à cheval, which advanced towards the wood near Poso Velho, and charged the infantry skirmishers with which it was filled—but failing to make any impression, the Frenchmen gave up that object, and continuing at the same pace (a canter), by bringing divisions right shoulder forward, the squadron was thrown into a column of divisions to the left, in which order it skirted the wood, descended into the valley of the Duas Casas, and having cleared that river, again formed squadron on the leading division, and advanced towards the British position; several other squadrons being observed coming to its support. But this part of the enemy's force does not appear to have done anything more on that day; at least, no troops of that sort were observed by the writer in the *melée* which he was called on to witness and to take part in.

By reference to the plate of the battle of Fuentes, in Colonel Napier's History, which is very good and clear, it will be observed that the rivers Turones and Duas Casas form a long plateau. The French cavalry having closed up on our side of Nava-da-ver, made an impetuous charge upon our pickets, and for a time were in possession of two of our guns; at least they were around the guns; and if the gallant Norman Ramsay had argued scientifically, he might fairly have accounted himself prisoner. Such a thought never entered his noble mind—but heading his gunners, he charged the enemy, and cleared the road for his guns. The French, who, by the by, most fortunately for us, were drunk, came on at a rapid pace, but in bad order, and were checked by different squadrons as they came up. The squadron whose progress has been related, had received orders to join the main body; and as it came on the plateau, all seemed confusion. Ramsay was still followed by the French chasseurs, and the number of chasseurs and hussars of the French appeared to be much greater than that of anything opposing them. The British, however, formed whilst the French seemed to be galloping about in detached parties, and immediately charged those nearest to us, but they gave way, and the ground being boggy, several horses fell, mine among others. When I remounted, I perceived very near me a German hussar, hammering his pistol-flint, while a French chasseur knelt before him. I asked the German what he was about. "Ah! I shoot dis fellow, den he do no more mischief." I persuaded him with difficulty to relinquish his quarry and join his squadron. I imagine that the pistol had already missed fire at the Frenchman. As soon as the German was fairly off, the chasseur knelt to me in gratitude, as he had to the hussar in supplication, and embracing my knee saluted me as his generous preserver. I asked the poor fellow for his sword, which he joyfully gave me, and which I continued to use, in preference to my own unwieldy machine. I derived farther advantage from my chasseur friend; instead of a leather sword-knot, he used a handkerchief, which I found more agreeable, and that it attached the sword more securely to the wrist. This little adventure occupied far less time than it has taken to relate. On joining my squadron, we found that the French were again coming on in force, and we were soon driven back, followed by a large body of the enemy. We were in full retreat, and it seemed doubtful when we should bring up, when we came upon the Chasseurs Brittaniques, a regiment formed of Swiss and French refugees; and had scarcely time to clear their front, when they opened their fire, and gave a tremendous volley. Not many of the French seemed to fall, but their advance was completely checked by the fire of the infantry. One soldier of the Royals was unfortunately killed by the fire : he was galloping along the line when the order to "make ready" was given; an officer called out to him to halt opposite to him; the poor fellow thought he could clear the line in time; he was mistaken, and received several bullets; but if I remember aright, his mare, which was a very valuable one, escaped. Lord Wellington having now determined to contract his position by throwing back his right, the infantry retired in squares, and the cavalry was directed to form line, with a view to shelter the squares from the French artillery, of which a heavy battery was now brought into action.

It is strange that this circumstance is not alluded to by either Lord Londonderry or Colonel Napier. It must have been well known to the former—but probably from the active and most gallant share he took in this part of the action, his lordship has not detailed the cavalry operations of that morning so minutely as might have been wished. The humble station the writer of this sketch held, relieves him of any such difficulty. It must be very apparent, from the number of horses lost by the cavalry, especially by the Royals, that they must have been exposed to cannonade, while, although the French had ten or twelve pieces in battery, the squares scarcely received a shot. The cavalry truly owed all this, and much more, to the infantry, who had been the means of their preservation. We witnessed some most ludicrous scenes : one we shall give. The British cavalry having formed line, there was a space of half-a-mile between them and the French, when a cloud of skirmishers was observed coming towards us—and a brigade of Portuguese artillery, commanded by a German, thinking it was an attack by the French infantry, as indeed it appeared to be, opened upon them with spherical case. The shells appeared to burst over the heads of the skirmishers, when a mounted officer came from the cannonaded party at a gallop, waving a handkerchief. It proved to be a body of the Brunswick Oëls, who were dressed in a peculiar manner, and something like the French. The poor German was in sad distress—" Have I shed the blood of my gallant countrymen !" he exclaimed ; while he paced to and fro in great agitation, another officer now arrived from the Brunswickers (though they were usually called the Owls.) He came to console the captain ; not a man was touched. This only changed the cause of distress ; the professional skill of the gunner was called in question, and the gallant German was in still deeper despair.

The cavalry retired behind the infantry, which was formed for the new alignment on some gently-rising ground, between the rivers Duas Casas and Turones. They had just dismounted, when a squadron of French hussars charged and broke Colonel Hill's picket of the guards; a squadron of the Royals was sent to protect the guards, but came too late, Capt. Thompson's artillery having opened with grape upon the hussars and forced them back. The Royals were now moved down in front of the guards, and posted in a valley, where they were more protected from cannon-shot, and were ready to oppose any incursions of the French cavalry. The French pushed forward some horsemen; skirmishers were thrown out on each side, which continued, and for some time nothing of consequence occurred; an attack was expected every moment, but the French remained inactive, or confined their exertions to a farther attempt upon the village of Fuentes. Towards the afternoon, a squadron, compósed of a troop of the Royals and a troop of the 14th Light Dragoons, was ordered to advance, which they did, till they were exposed to the fire of the French guns, which opened on them with grape, mortally wounded the commanding officer, Capt. Knipe, and killed and wounded a good many men and horses. The writer was with this squadron, and he never has been able to make out what was the object of this advance. Capt. Thompson, of the artillery, sent to beg that it might not be repeated, as it drew the fire upon his guns, and at least one of the gunners had been killed by grape-shot, although the distance was about 700 yards. For a considerable time, our attention was occupied in observing the practice of the French artillery and Capt. Thompson's brigade; and it was admirable on both sides. I heard our men express delight when our side fired a howitzer which made a greater volume of smoke than a gun; at last a tremendous cloud of smoke arose from our battery, and one of the dragoons called out " Hurrah! there goes a shot that will kill half the French army." It turned out to be one of the tumbrils (fortunately containing only a few rounds), which was exploded by a French shell. It is a well-known fact, that one great use of artillery is to keep up the spirits of soldiers by its noise. The French continued inactive during the three following days, and failed to take advantage of the best opportunity Wellington ever gave them, even if they were afraid to attack the army; and the reason of their not doing so, given by the French writers, is, the works we had thrown up, which were really nothing, having been formed by the soldiers in a few hours. Had they deemed it inexpedient, what was to prevent their detaching a corps of 2000 horse and 1000 foot soldiers, without their knapsacks, and with some guns, which, by crossing the Coa at Sabugal and Secieras, would have come upon our rear and stopped our supplies?

The force remaining would have been ample to retain the British, and the detached corps might have returned in perfect safety, as, even had the bridge at Sabugal been occupied by the British in consequence of any change of operation, the French, by retiring south, would have passed the Coa in safety. The cause of their inactivity may have arisen from internal dissensions—as Colonel Napier states—but we believe that it arose also from an overweening fear of Wellington, who had been rated by Regnier as worth 20,000 men to the British army. It is not difficult to point out errors when the results are already known; we are the last to undervalue British bravery, but we feel convinced that if the two armies could have changed commanders, *cæteris paribus*, the war of Portugal would have been terminated on that field.

Having risked so much to gain Almeida, Lord Wellington had to suffer a sad blow from the destruction of the place and the escape of the garrison. The precautions used by the French, and the bravery of their conduct, cannot be too highly commended. For several nights previous to the escape of the garrison, there was a tremendous explosion, as if all the guns of the place were fired at once; this occurred about midnight, and was evidently intended to calm our minds as to the occurrence, which we saw take place repeatedly without any result. It was imagined by us, that these explosions were signals to Massena.

Previous to adverting to the unfortunate destruction of Almeida, and the escape of the garrison, we must beg to offer a few remarks on the battle. As to the conduct of the infantry, nothing could have been more splendid; the fighting in the village was desperate; but in what did the cavalry fail, or what service did the overwhelming force of French cavalry perform? We feel that we are liable to the charge of presumption in disputing the authority of the Adjutant-General, and we are far from intending any disrespect to Lord Londonderry, when we say that it appears to us he has overrated the number of British cavalry at Fuentes. We find by a copy of a return in the appendix to Lord Londonderry's book, that on the 15th of February, when head-quarters were at Cartaxo, the number of horses effective, with the four regiments of cavalry, which formed the whole British cavalry at Fuentes, is as follows—

	Horses.
Royals	425
14th Light Dragoons	378
16th Light Dragoons	366
1st Hussars	361
	1530

No remounts had been received since that return, and during the intervening time the cavalry had been very hard worked, dreadfully starved, and *repeatedly* engaged; indeed, during Massena's retreat, some part of the cavalry was daily under fire; this must have reduced the strength of the regiments: one squadron of the Royals also was detached, and we feel convinced that the number of sabres present at Fuentes did not exceed 1200 —we doubt whether it was so great; a remount of forty horses joined the Royals the afternoon of the battle.

Lord Londonderry takes the force of the French cavalry at 4000; we have never heard it stated under 5000; and in referring to a French work, " Campagnes en Portugal, 1810, 1811," we find that the French army at Fuentes is stated by the author at 35,000 infantry and 5000 horsemen. This may appear tedious, but we wished to ascertain as precisely as possible the numbers on each side, that we may again ask what did the French do with their 5000 horsemen? They were in far better condition than we were; every part of the plateau between the rivers was admirably adapted to cavalry movements. They had Montbrun at their head, and a numerous artillery; yet they produced no influence on the battle; and had the cavalry on each side been withdrawn, the French would not have done one iota less than they did do. We took about 100 chasseurs prisoners—and their Colonel, Lamotte, was said to have been taken by Lord Londonderry.

The French having retired beyond the Agueda, the British army were sent into quarters, and steps were taken to secure the capture of Almeida. The cavalry was in great need of repose, as during the six days, while the army was in position at Fuentes, the dragoons were ready to act from two hours before sunrise till two hours after dark, leaving but a few hours out of the twenty-four to dress the horses, and to allow the men to prepare their own food. The work had not, indeed, been hard, and all that was required was a good sleep. On the night of the 11th a tremendous explosion took place at Almeida, the garrison sallying from the town at the same time. The result has been well described, especially by Lord Londonderry and Colonel Napier. It is unnecessary to enter into the circumstances of the failure on the part of the British in preventing the escape of the garrison; some blame was thrown on the 2nd and 4th regiments, whose emblems or crests, on the colours and appointments, are severally the lamb and the lion of England. Through some mistake the 2nd had been put into quarters. The 4th, which ought to have been at Barba del Puerco, did not receive orders till it was too late. It was said, the Lion slept—the Lamb sought green pastures—the Eagle spread his wings and fled away. A squadron of the Royal Dragoons was in the village of Villa di Yegua, through which the retreat of the French lay, but General Brennier, hearing from a Spaniard that the town was full of English Dragoons, diverged to his left, and passed through the fields. Had Brennier known the true state of the case, he might have passed through the town, and have taken most part of " the heavies" with him, for they fancied themselves in complete security. The men were going to stables when a messenger arrived to tell them what was going on.

Some of the dragoons, with a quarter-master, immediately mounted and followed the French, who were now approaching their goal, and took little notice of these few horsemen. The quarter-master however, saw an opportunity of doing a little business. Observing amongst those who lagged in the rear, one man with a ledger in the slings of his knapsack, he naturally concluded that such gear in the French, as in our service, belonged to those who carried the purse, and on the strength of this reasoning, by degrees he approached him of the ledger, and returning his sword, and advancing at speed, he pounced upon his prey, and seizing him by the collar, shook the musket out of his hands and bore him off. He proved to be paymaster's clerk, and carried sixty doubloons, then worth about four guineas each. We give the story as we heard it the same day; we will not conceal the quarter-master's name—one so appropriate to the exploit—Mr. Kite—while we bear testimony to his gallant conduct on all occasions.

Nothing further occurred. The cavalry was cantoned in the neighbourhood, and remained perfectly quiet for nearly a month. Lord Wellington went to take charge of the army in the south, leaving the light division at Gallegos, and the cavalry under command of Sir Brent Spencer. It would appear that the means and situation of the French were not very well known at this time, (*i. e.* about the 4th or 5th of June,) when the light division was withdrawn from Gallegos, and the royal dragoons were ordered to occupy their quarters. The usual quartering party, under a subaltern, was sent to take up the cantonments. As this party entered the town, they observed a patrole of French dragoons descending towards Gallegos from the other side, and some little distance in the rear was the head of a column; a report of these circumstances was sent to the regiment, which, instead of coming to Gallegos, moved to a height between that town and Nava-da-ver, where it was formed with a troop of the 14th Light Dragoons (Captain Townsend's.)

Too much time was allowed to elapse before they continued their retreat. It was evident that the French were in great force, and it proved to be a reconnoissance of 2000 horse and a strong battery of artillery, under General Montbrun; they advanced through the woods, from which they debouched with so much rapidity as to place the British force in considerable jeopardy. The French squadrons were at but a little distance, and had they once engaged with the Royals, time would have been afforded to bring up such a force as would have put the matter far beyond contention. The Old Royals bundled off with all becoming speed, and retired across the ample plain in line. The French sent out a couple of squadrons in advance, one of which extended as skirmishers;

the British, however, had the start, and every prospect of getting off, when it was discovered that a morass crossed the plain. The local knowledge of Captain Townsend was of good service; that officer pointed out a pass by which this obstacle was cleared. As some time was lost in passing this defile, it became necessary that the rear squadron should charge. This duty devolved on Captain Purves, who formed and charged the French, and broke their squadron, and by this means was able to pass the defile; but the French being well supported, pushed on and soon regained their former position in the rear of the Royals. Captain Purves's charge deserved every commendation. While in full retreat, and vigorously pressed by the enemy, the squadron halted and charged while their own party was continuing its retreat. To those who have experienced the moral influence of such circumstances, it will be plain that Purves did well to hurry on his men as he did. The writer did not belong to that squadron, and he remembers feeling well pleased that such was the case; and as he is satisfied that he saw the danger and prospect of glory in no worse light than other people, he is anxious to pay every tribute in his power to Captain Purves and his squadron.

The skirmishers now came within fifty or sixty yards of our squadron; the main body was rapidly advancing; the town of Nava-da-ver was above a mile distant; and it appeared that nothing could save the Royals, who returned rapidly, but keeping well together. On a sudden the French halted, at the moment that the crisis seemed at hand; the leading squadrons cleared off and discovered a battery of ten or twelve guns, which immediately opened and fired two salvoes, not at the retreating dragoons, but into the wood, along whose margin the Royals were retiring. Montbrun was aware that the light division had left Gallegos in the morning, and considered the delayed retreat of the Royals as a *ruse* to draw him into a snare, and that the infantry was concealed in the wood; but as soon as he discovered his mistake, the pursuit was resumed, but the moment was lost. General Montbrun's conduct was anything but daring; the wood was not thick, and could not have concealed a large body of men; but even if it had done so, the French had a much larger force than the whole British cavalry, had it all been there—and their retreat was open either by the way they came, or upon Poso-Vello, into a wooded country, or across the plain towards Fuentes-d'Onore.

* * * * *
* * * * *

Montbrun having sent a patrol into Nava-daver, retired. It had evidently been the sole object of the French, on this occasion, to make a reconnoissance—for had anything farther been intended, they would have followed up their success, at least till they found something capable of offering an efficient resistance; and had they even scoured the country in front of their right, and which was totally unprotected, a great deal of baggage would have fallen into their hands.

The following day, the cavalry, continuing its march, crossed the Coa, passing through the camp of the 52nd regiment, which was bivouacked on the left bank of the river. Probably that gallant corps was never in a situation in which it could have better set at defiance any cavalry attack than in this. In their front ran the Coa, passable by only one ford, from which the tortuous and rocky path did not admit of above two horses abreast. The steep banks, covered with brush-wood, confined horsemen to the narrow road, and we verily believe, that a single company of the 52nd would have repelled Montbrun with all his host; nevertheless, an absurd alarm was given during the succeeding night, and a report consequent on it led us for a moment to doubt that the position was so inexpugnable. Having passed through the infantry camp, the cavalry had retired to a magnificent chesnut grove, about a mile and a half from the river, and in this delightful bivouac felt itself in perfect security. There cannot be a more enchanting scene for a gipsy party than a Portuguese chesnut-grove. The majestic trees are covered by so thick a foliage as only to admit at intervals the rays of the meridian sun, and the branches grow nearly horizontally at the height of about seven or eight feet, giving the appearance of a great green awning. We have a very pleasing recollection of such scenes, and of the dramas we have seen enacted in them:—the soldiers actively employed in their several avocations around the boles of the trees, to which their horses are attached by means of a forage cord encircling the tree; others at a fire in the neighbourhood cooking; parties passing to and fro with water or forage; and the erect serjeant-major, with white gloves and rattan, walking about with circumspection. A few boughs hastily piled together, in part screen the simple toilet of an officer, who is preparing to enjoy his rice broth, as we may gather from the preparations his servant has made, by covering the canteen with a napkin, which seems intended to be occupied as a dinner-table by two performers, who are to be furnished with seats by the adaptation of bundles of forage. In the distance of this part of the scene, a Portuguese boy, with shining face, is seen blowing the fire and stirring the pot. The officer's servant is actively employed in waiting on his master, as well as attending to the horses and holding Antonio in surveillance, lest on the one hand he allow the fire to go out, or on the other, the bishop to put his foot in the pot which contains the mess of four or five hungry men. Another actor in the dinner scene is just arriving from the village with a small skin of vino generoso —two quarts of which, (Imperial measure,) one raw, the second mulled, may very safely be put under the belt of any man after his day's work.

The writer of these lines had probably indulged

to about this extent, and had early retired to what the Scotch call his naked-bed, anglicè, undressed to his shirt, a bag stuffed with straw acting as mattress, while a double blanket and sheet, in addition to the foliage of the chesnuts, sufficiently shielded from the night air in that lovely climate. He was in the temporary command of a troop— one of the serjeants of the troop commanding the camp guard. About one or two on the following morning, the latter awakened the writer, saying, with great agitation, "For God's sake, Sir, get up and form the troop ; the French cavalry has charged your friends the 52nd, and is cutting them to pieces." Military men, and especially those who served in the light division, know how strong an attachment existed between the officers who had served in the different regiments of that brilliant corps. This sad intelligence came like a thunder-clap ; two or three minutes sufficed to make the transfer from the naked bed to the back of a horse. About fifty of the troop were collected, and trotted off to the rendezvous on the high road. Here General Slade was actively employed in getting his brigade mounted. The troops were coming to the road as they formed, when it occurred to all present that the French did their work very quietly; not a shot had been heard, and the most absolute silence reigned, although the night was clear and calm. It must be allowed, that the general from the first expressed his surprise at the meekness with which the light division bore their cutting up, although he had been roused from sleep by this alarming intelligence.

The bearer of this report could not be found, but the guard declared that two or three men, nearly naked, had come to them and informed them that they had with difficulty escaped from the French cavalry, which had penetrated into the 52nd camp, and had destroyed the light division. Shortly after, an orderly who had been despatched by General Slade, returned with the information that the whole alarm had arisen from the circumstance of some mules escaping from their tethers, which galloped over some of the sleeping soldiers, and had upset some piles of arms. Two or three of the soldiers who had been thus roughly treated arose from their lairs, and running through the camp spreading alarm, continued their course till they arrived at the dragoon bivouac. The alarm was not known to a great part of the division till the following morning. We have ventured to place this little matter in our simple narrative. It may be amusing to the general reader, while the military man cannot be too frequently warned of the disastrous consequences which may arise from panic; and the foregoing anecdote is at least one proof of the facility with which it may be generated.

A very successful and brilliant affair of cavalry occurred a few days after the battle of Albuera, which we have the opportunity of giving by a quotation from a French military writer, and which is as follows :*

"Le Général Latour Maubourg, réuni le 24, à la division Godinot, au-dessus de Villa Garcia, reçoit du Général-en-chef l'ordre de se porter en avant sur Usagré, et de faire replier les postes ennemis. Usagré est située à deux lieux et demie de Villa Garcia, dans un plaine coupée et boisée. Au pied d'une soumité, sur laquelle repose ce village, coule une petite rivière dont les bords sont escarpés et difficilement accessibles. Un pont est jeté sur cette rivière au bas d'Usagré. It sert de passage au chemin de Los Santos, de Ribeira, et de la Basse Estramadure. L'ennemi avoit reconnu une position favorable, sur le revers d'un monticule placé en regard du village, de l'autre coté de la rivière : Il y place 12 à 1500 chevaux. Cachée par le terrain, cette cavalerie ne doit paraître et agir qu'au moment où les avant postes, forcés de ceder le terrain, se replieront sur Usagré et le dépasseront ensuite.

"Le Général Latour Maubourg veut s'assurer avant d'occuper ce point si l'ennemi en a évacué les environs : il ordonna, en conséquence, au Général Briche de se porter avec sa cavalerie legère, par un long détour laissant Usagré à gauche vers la rivière ; de franchir ensuite le ravin dans un endroit où il présente peu d'escarpements, et d'éclairer notre droite. L'exécution de ce mouvement, exige du

* Lapène, Conquête de l'Andalousie.—page 180.

temps, à cause des difficultés du terrain. Sans attendre cependant que le Gen. Briche paraisse de l'autre côté du ravin, les 4ᵉ et 20ᵉ de dragons, qui forment la tête de la division Latour Maubourg, traversent le village déjà abandonné par l'ennemi ; le Gen. Bron à leur tête, ils descendent la rampe qui conduit au pont, et passent brusquement sur la rive gauche ; mais à peine le 4ᵉ a-t-il mis le pied sur cette rive, que les Anglais débouchent avec impétuosité de derrière le coteau qui les a jusque-la tenus cachés. Le Gen. Bron fait dès ce moment avec le 4ᵉ le plus vigoreux efforts pour contenir l'ennemi.

"Le 20ᵉ de dragons se porte sans délai au secours des escadrons engagés, avec autant de promptitude que le passage du pont, où les chevaux ne peuvent pas défiler que par deux, le permet, mais ces deux régimens qui réunis comptent moins de 700 chevaux, sont hors d'etat de résister à la cavalrie ennemie, trop supérieure en nombre, et se replient vers le pont. Le 26ᵉ de dragons (même brigade) descend aussi la rampe, dans le dessein de porter secours aux troupes compromises, et présente la tête de sa colonne sur le pont, tandis que celles-ci fortement ramenées s'y pressent pour repasser la rivière. Cette position est rendue encore plus critique par l'artillerie Anglaise, tirant à mitraille sur nos régimens *agglomérés en avant* de ce défilé ; 3 pieces d'artillerie Hollandaise au service de France, mises en batterie à la droite d'Usagré, ne peuvent neutralizer le feu du canon ennemie, qui occupe une position plus avantageuse. Les 4ᵉ et 20ᵉ hors d'état de pouvoir repousser les Anglais et même de se dégager, se replient à la fin, ou plutôt se dispersent dans les jardins en avant du village. Le Général Latour Maubourg termine cependent ce combat inégal en préscrivant au Général Bouvier-d'éclats de faire mettre pied à terre au 14ᵉ de dragons le 1ʳᵉ de la 2ᵉ brigade, et de la disposer en tirailleur pour chasser l'ennemi des jardins. Les Anglais sont arrêtés, en effet, par cette mesure, et reprennent bientôt après la position qu'ils occupaient avant le combat, tandis que les 4ᵉ et 20ᵉ de dragons dégagés aussi, rejoignent leur division. Le Colonel Farine du 4ᵉ resta au pouvoir de l'ennemi ; 400 dragons et autant de chevaux avaient été écharpés ou pris, &c."

We really are apprehensive that any remarks we can make upon this long extract, will do little towards strengthening the claim of General Lumley and his cavalry to the highest meed of praise. The French statement seems to be a very fair one. We were not with that part of the army, and do not happen to have any detailed account of the action, nor of the loss accruing from it on the part of the British. Let it be observed that the French writer estimates the British force at 12 to 1500. It is not worth while to dispute the number; it must, however, be granted, that the Frenchman has done justice to his countrymen in not under-rating the force opposed to them. He must be supposed to be correct in his statement of the

French force, which he states to have been the division of Godinot, which, however, had no opportunity of taking a share in the action, and probably was not within reach of Usagre at the time; but that three brigades of cavalry, namely, the two heavy brigades of Bron and Bouvier-d'eclats, and the chasseur brigades of Briche, were present and employed, there can be no doubt.

The French brigades were usually very strong, and it would be a very moderate calculation to suppose that they had a force of 3000 cavalry. There can be no doubt that had the whole of this force been properly directed against General Lumley, he must have retired, or probably would have suffered severely had he been induced to engage with two-fold numbers. The general, seeing that the French began to pass the bridge, while General Briche was at too great a distance to admit of his lending any assistance, allows one brigade to pass the river, and by an impetuous charge breaks the enemy, and throws them completely into confusion; and having destroyed or taken 400 of the enemy, he is driven from the remainder of his prey by the fire of a fresh regiment of dragoons, who are dismounted on the opposite bank, and are enabled to push back the British dragoons, without being exposed to any danger whatsoever.

The French writer lays a good deal of stress on the services rendered by our artillery. We have no doubt that whatever bravery and skill could accomplish was done by Captain Lefevre's troop on this as on every other occasion, but as this troop was the whole amount of that arm which the British had at Usagré, we cannot believe but Latour Maubourg must have had a larger artillery force on this occasion, as we see that he had three brigades of cavalry : he could not have left himself so unprovided with artillery as to be bullied by five light six-pounders and a light howitzer. The truth must be, that the French, seeing the Colonel, Farine, had taken his grist to a bad mill, and expecting the English dragoons to cross the river, sent away their, artillery, which would have impeded the retreat of their troops, and perhaps might have become the spoil of the enemy. General Lumley had to congratulate himself on a most daring and completely successful attack upon a superior enemy, commanded by an officer of the greatest distinction. Latour Maubourg had separated his force, and attempted to pass a defile without clearing his front. He had transgressed the rules of war and of posts, with which he was no doubt perfectly conversant; but it is impossible to applaud too highly the conduct of the British general, who detected the errors of his opponent, and effectually took advantage of the favourable position he was placed in. General Lumley's conduct can only be appreciated by those who have witnessed cavalry affairs, and who know, therefore, how much promptitude is required, and that whatever calculations were previously made, or whatever arrangements the most watchful foresight might have suggested, still the relative circumstances are continually changing. On this occasion a very few minutes' delay might have allowed the whole of General Bron's brigade to pass the bridge, and if Bron had been able for a time to repel the British attack, General Bouvier-d'éclats (what a name for a sharpshooter!) instead of acting *en tirailleur*, would have found means to pass his brigade across the stream, (for such it was, and not a river,) either by the bridge or at some other place where the banks were accessible; General Briche would have then come up, and the British would have been in a precious mess.

We frequently hear of chess as a military game; and although it is a game we have long cultivated, we must deny, at least, that it at all tutors the mind for affairs of posts. In chess the player may take as much time as he pleases, whereas prompt decision is the desideratum in active warfare. If chess is to teach anything, it must be restricted to strategy. Practice alone can make an officer perfect in this work; but occasionally, even when the commander has not been habituated to such scenes, if he be possessed of great determination, and has confidence in his soldiers, he may, by putting on a good countenance, and by acting with vigour and promptitude, making the most of any circumstances which are favourable to him, gain an advantage over a superior enemy before his opponent has time to ascertain his force, and extricate himself from the difficulties which he is thrown into by the successful attack made upon his advanced guard.

The whole of the cavalry followed Lord Wellington to the south, where the army remained till the end of July, when it returned to the neighbourhood of Ciudad Rodrigo. During this period we do not recollect any cavalry action. The French were everywhere superior to the British cavalry in point of number.

Marshal Marmont having collected a large force, advanced to the relief of Rodrigo. A splendid affair occurred at El Bodon on the 25th of August, when General Picton's division not only repelled, but actually charged an immense host of French cavalry. The small body of British cavalry made several splendid charges, and their conduct was highly applauded; but as the French had 4000 horsemen while the British cavalry did not exceed 400 or 500, little could be expected from them, and no doubt they owed their safety to the steadiness of the infantry. Many accounts have been published of this affair, and of the gallant conduct of Picton's division, which, especially Colville's brigade, cannot be too frequently held up to the admiration of the army. But what were the French doing? they had 4000 cavalry, numerous artillery, and for a long time were only opposed by a single brigade of infantry, three squadrons of dragoons, and four guns. Surely, had their attack been energetic and repeated, they must have swallowed up this daring band. The country is open, and peculiarly suited to cavalry movements; yet all the French accomplished was, to give an opportunity to Colville's brigade to achieve fresh honours, and set an example which was not lost upon the British army.

Shortly after the affair of El Bodon, we had an opportunity of seeing a great deal of the 5th regiment, which had taken a prominent share in the glory of that day; we saw officers and soldiers who had been wounded by grape-shot while in square,—they spoke highly of the conduct of the French cavalry officers, one of whom would not surrender though left quite alone. Now, this is all very well, but what does it imply? that the French cavalry officers were brave. We willingly allow such to be the case, and add that on all occasions they shewed the greatest courage, and set a good example to their men, who nevertheless, as on this occasion, frequently left them alone. The British cavalry seldom gave their officers such opportunities of shewing their bravery. The following day, Marmont assembled an overpowering force in front of Fuente Guinaldo, and Lord Wellington withdrew his army during the night, and retired to Aldea de Ponte—and after passing the frontier of Spain, the country becomes quite unsuited to cavalry.

A great deal has been said of the inferiority of the French horse—and unquestionably he is a low-bred animal—for which reason he is the more able to endure the hardships to which the horses of light cavalry are exposed. The French horse, generally, trots well, and is sure-footed. On the retreat from Guinaldo, the writer of these pages was followed by a small party of lancers, and near Peubla d'Agava one of them deserted to him, and was immediately sent to head-quarters, escorted by a well-mounted dragoon. The Frenchman started at a banging trot, keeping his friend at a hard gallop; and had he not been called to and requested to moderate his pace, he would most assuredly have done up the heavy, ere they had accomplished the two or three miles to Aldea de Ponte. The writer purchased a horse taken at Fuentes d'Onore from the 5th Hussars; it was a little horse, but quite as fit to carry a light weight as many of our horses. The writer is no feather weight; the Frenchman carried him well, was good in all his paces, and after doing good service became the charger of the Assistant-Surgeon.

⁎ A period of considerable interest passes between the close of the campaign of 1809, and the fall of Ciudad Rodrigo on the 11th of July, 1810. During that interval, two of those glorious events which mark a hero's life had occurred, and Wellington by his passage of the Douro and victory of Talavera, had earned a military reputation, which five years afterwards was consummated by the downfall of his mighty rival at Waterloo. We merely note these military occurrences, as they will occasionally be alluded to hereafter. The Douro was crossed on the 12th of May, 1809, at Oporto. The battle of Talavera won 27th July, 1810. We may also observe that Busaco was fought the 27th of September afterwards; the retreat to Torres Vedras took place the following month; the advance from "the Lines," March 1811, and Fuentes d'Onore was fought on the 4th of May.

RECOLLECTIONS IN QUARTERS.

AFFAIR OF EL BODON.*

Soon after the battle of Fuentes d'Onore, the French army withdrew from the northern frontier of Portugal, and the Duke of Wellington, with three divisions of the British army and a corps of cavalry, blockaded Ciudad Rodrigo. In September, 1811, Marshal Marmont assembled the army of the North, consisting of 60,000 infantry and 5000 cavalry, in the neighbourhood of Salamanca, and moved on Rodrigo, for the purpose of raising the blockade. On the approach of this force, our outposts were withdrawn, and Ciudad Rodrigo relieved. The head-quarters of the Duke of Wellington were at that time established at Fuente Guinaldo, a village three leagues in the rear of Ciudad Rodrigo; and it happened that the second battalion 5th regiment, to which I belonged, was

* 25th September, 1811.

doing head-quarter duty. On the morning of the 24th of September we received orders to march to the front, and occupy a post a league from Rodrigo, where we found two brigades of guns and a squadron of cavalry. About one league to the right of that post is the village of El Bodon, which was occupied by the third division, under Sir Thomas Picton. The light division occupied the ground between the village of El Bodon and the river Agueda, on which its right rested; the fourth and only remaining division was in rear of Fuente Guinaldo, occupying different villages, and not brought into position. In consequence of guns being attached to us, I became the senior officer, and having received no orders, whether to retire if attacked (by a superior force), or to defend our post to the last extremity, I thought it prudent, in the first instance, to take the best means in my power to prevent a surprise, and planted the pickets accordingly. Feeling myself in a very responsible situation, I visited the pickets at daybreak, when I discovered large bodies of the enemy's cavalry coming out of Ciudad Rodrigo, and crossing the Agueda.

There are two roads leading from Ciudad Rodrigo; one to Fuente Guinaldo, the most practicable for guns, was that on our right, which passed through El Bodon; the other led immediately through the post we occupied. It was some time before I could form an opinion whether the enemy meant to advance by El Bodon or by the road which we occupied, the ground being so favourable to mask his movements. In this uncertainty, and still not having received any orders, I directed the guns to be unlimbered and the mules harnessed, ready to move at a moment's warning. I also placed the 5th regiment in position, occupying an elevated ridge, and its right protected by a deep defile. The approach of the enemy's cavalry left me no longer any doubts as to the object of his attack, and I ordered the guns to commence a fire upon his columns. At this moment the Duke of Wellington came from the right, and after a few minutes passed in reconnoitring, told me he approved of the arrangements I had made, and would order up a brigade of cavalry to our support. But the Duke had hardly time to move to the rear, before we were charged by a large body of cavalry, which for a moment succeeded in capturing the guns. By a well-directed running fire from the 5th regiment, followed by a charge of bayonets, the guns were retaken, and the enemy repulsed.*

Reinforcements now arrived, consisting of two regiments of British infantry and one of Portuguese. This force (now about 1500 men) main-

---

* The 5th Regiment came steadily forward in line, and after delivering a shattering volley, lowered their bayonets, and boldly advanced to charge the cavalry. This, the first instance of horsemen being assailed by infantry in line, was brilliantly successful: the French were hurried down the height, and the guns were re-captured, limbered up, and brought away.—ED.

tained the post for the space of three hours, although frequently charged by the whole of the enemy's cavalry, and exposed to a heavy fire from the guns of a division of infantry which were in reserve.—Nor was it abandoned until this body of infantry moved forward, when we were forced to recede, and the ground being very favourable for cavalry to act upon, we retired in squares of regiments, which were repeatedly charged, but from their steady conduct, no impression could be made upon them.

During these operations, the enemy pushed forward a strong body of infantry, which succeeded in cutting off the light division, but by a judicious movement of Major-General Crawford, who crossed the Agueda, that division was saved, and effected a retreat.

The Duke of Wellington now took up a position in front of Guinaldo, with the three divisions above named, from which, not being tenable,* he retired

---

* While Marmont was manœuvring 60,000 of the best troops in the world, with 110 guns, at the base of the heights, and scarcely out of cannon range, he was ignorant that the allied position was held by *two weak divisions.* The left wing of the army being at Nava-da-ver, ten miles from Guinaldo; the fifth division at Payo, twelve miles' distance; and the light troops still further off, at Cespedosa. When informed, after, Wellington had retreated and concentrated his whole army, that for six-and-thirty hours he had lain within arm's length of barely 12,000 men, and allowed them to retire unmolested, Marmont passionately exclaimed, " By Heaven! the star of Wellington is brilliant as Napoleon's!"—ED.

on the following day, and posted himself strongly behind the Coa. The enemy only having supplies for ten days, was obliged to fall back, when the British army re-occupied nearly the same ground it did previously to this attack.

The following is a copy of the General Order issued by Lord Wellington after this brilliant affair.

"G. O., 2nd Oct. 1811.

"The Commander of the Forces is desirous of drawing the attention of the army to the conduct of the second battalion 5th, and 77th regiments, and 21st Portuguese regiment, and Major Arenschild's Portuguese artillery, under the command of the Hon. Major-General Colville, and of the 11th Light Dragoons and 1st Hussars, under Major General Alten, in the affair with the enemy on the 25th ult.

"These troops were attacked by between thirty and forty squadrons of cavalry, with six pieces of cannon, supported by a division consisting of fourteen battalions of infantry with cannon.

"The Portuguese artillery-men were cut down at the guns before they quitted them, but the second battalion 5th regiment attacked the cavalry which had taken the guns, and retook them; at the same time the 77th regiment were attacked in front by another body of cavalry, upon which body they advanced, and repulsed them.

"While these actions were performed, Major-General Alten's brigade, of which there were only three squadrons on the ground, were engaged on the left with numbers infinitely superior to themselves. These squadrons charged repeatedly, supporting each other, and took above twenty prisoners, notwithstanding the immense superiority of the enemy. The post would have been maintained, if the Commander of the Forces had not ordered the troops to withdraw from it, seeing that the action would become still more unequal, as the enemy's infantry were likely to be engaged in it before the reinforcements ordered to the support of the post could arrive.

"The troops then retired with the same determined spirit, and in the same good order, with which they had maintained their post: the second battalion 5th regiment, and 77th, in one square, and the 21st Portuguese in another, supported by Major-General Alten's cavalry and the Portuguese artillery. The enemy's cavalry charged three faces of the square of the British infantry, but were beaten off; and finding from their repeated fruitless efforts, that these brave troops were not to be broken, they were contented with following them at a distance, and with firing upon them with their artillery, till the troops joined the remainder of their division, and were afterwards supported by a brigade of the fourth division.

"Although the 21st Portuguese regiment were not actually charged by the cavalry, their steadiness and determination were conspicuous, and the Commander of the Forces observed with pleasure the order and regularity with which they made all their movements, and the confidence they shewed in their officers.

"The Commander of the Forces has been particular in stating the details of this action in General Orders, as, in his opinion, it affords a memorable example of what can be effected by steadiness, discipline, and confidence. It is impossible that any troops can at any time be exposed to the attack of numbers relatively greater than those which attacked these troops under Major-General Colville and Major-General Alten, on the 25th of September; and the Commander of the Forces recommends the conduct of these troops to the particular attention of the officers and soldiers of the army, as an example to be followed in all such circumstances.

"The Commander of the Forces considers Major-General Colville and Major-General Alten, and the commanding officers of the regiments under their command respectively,—viz., Lieutenant-Colonel Cummins, Lieutenant-Colonel Arenschild, Lieutenant-Colonel Bromhead, Major Ridge, and Colonel Baccelas, of the 21st Portuguese regiment, and the officers and soldiers under their command, to be entitled to his particular thanks, and he assures them, that he has not failed to report his sense of their conduct in the action of the 25th September, to those by whom he trusts that it will be appreciated and recollected."

THE CAPTURE OF CIUDAD RODRIGO.*

BY AN OFFICER OF THE NINETY-FOURTH REGIMENT.

On the 19th of January, 1812, the third division in turn of duty entered the trenches, the relief taking place in the morning, as was usual during the siege. In the afternoon of the same day, the light division arrived in the environs of the place; but, lest the enemy should suspect, from the presence of additional troops, that an attack was in-

---

* " *Ciudad Rodrigo* is built on a rising ground, on the right bank of the Agueda, and has a double enceinte all round it. The interior wall is of an old construction, of the height of thirty-two feet, and is generally of bad masonry, without flanks, and with weak parapets and narrow ramparts. The exterior enclosure is a modern fausse-braie, of a low profile, constructed so far down the slope of the hill as to afford but little cover to the interior wall; and from the same defect of the rapid descent of the hill, the fausse-braie itself is very imperfectly covered by its glacis. On the eastern and southern sides there are ravelins to the fausse-braie, but in no part is

tended, this division was ordered to march on the Salamanca road to such a distance, that nightfall might prevent their return from being noticed by the garrison. The besieged must have supposed that the object of a march in that direction was to cover the siege from the advance of the enemy, which was to be looked for.

It was then intimated to us that the breaches were practicable, and were to be stormed that night: the third division taking the greater, and the light division the lesser, breach.

It was ordered that two battalions of Major-Gen. the Hon. C. Colville's brigade should descend into the ditches, and clear them of all hindrance that might exist on or about the main breach. For this service, Major Ridge was instructed to proceed with the 5th regiment, from the rear of the convent of Santa Cruz, to escalade the fausse-braie near where it joins the wall of the place, and to advance to the main breach by the inner ditch; and Lieut.-

---

there a covered way, nor are there any countermines. Without the town, at the distance of three hundred yards, the suburbs were enclosed by a bad earthen entrenchment, hastily thrown up. The ground without the place is generally flat and the soil rocky, except on the north side, where there are two hills, called the Upper and the Lower Teson—the one at one hundred and eighty yards from the works, rises nearly to the level of the ramparts, and the other, at six hundred yards' distance, to the height of thirteen feet above them. The soil on these hills is very strong, and during open weather in winter, water rises at the depth of six inches below the surface."—Jones's Journal of Sieges.

Colonel Campbell was directed to move with the 94th regiment, in double columns of companies, from the left of the convent of Santa Cruz, to enter the outer ditch, and, turning to the left, carry the breach in the fausse-braie, and remove all obstructions that might be found on or about that breach and the main one, and thereafter to co-operate with the storming party in entering the place. From the engineers' stores, there were given out to the 94th regiment a number of knotted ropes to assist in descending the ditch, and of felling-axes to break down and remove the impediments supposed to exist about the breach.

Lieut.-Colonel Campbell, having set his watch at the head-quarters of the division, moved his regiment forward, as soon as evening permitted, to the convent of Santa Cruz, and took post under a loop-holed wall to the left of it, along which it had been intended to form a ditch, which, however, was excavated to the depth of only a foot or two. This position was enfiladed by two light brass guns, mounted *en barbette* on a projection of the fausse-braie, but as the moon threw the shadow of the wall on this half-formed ditch, we were enabled to approach unobserved to within 120 yards of the outer defences of the place.

Here we waited until the moment arrived, at which, as Colonel Campbell had been told, the storming party would leave the trenches; for although we had less ground to pass over to reach the breach than they, it was of importance that we should be there before them, in order to perform the duty of removing whatever might embarrass the attack. Then, extending our front in the order prescribed, we passed in silence over the glacis, and reached the ditch. The bottom was not visible in the shade, but Williamson, captain of grenadiers, threw himself into it, and finding the depth not so great but that men with arms might leap into it without injury, the regiment followed him, and pushed forward at the same rapid pace to the breach in the fausse-braie, and through it to the foot of that which had been made in the rampart of the place. Here an instant sufficed to show that the breach was clear for attack, and to correct the formation of the regiment—Colonel Campbell, knowing that we must be immediately supported by the parties that were approaching the breaches in different directions, and that it was of consequence not to lose a second of time in such a situation, gave the word to fix bayonets and mount, which was so done that the front reached the top of the rampart *as one man*. No sooner had they set foot upon it, than a strong train of gunpowder was fired from the enemy's left, which, passing across the breach, kindled and exploded a great number of shells, by which many were killed and wounded, and all who had gained the top were thrown down and stunned. At the same time a brisk fire was opened from a breastwork which had been raised at a little distance from the rear of the breach, just without the line of fire of our batteries. The space between this breastwork and the interior scarp of the wall, which was entire, and sixteen feet high, was filled with carriages of different kinds, chevaux de frise, and similar articles, so put together as to make it a work of time for an individual to traverse it by daylight.

The check that had been thus given was, however, but momentary. Immediately after, all sprang to right or left to force in by either flank of the breach. Colonel Campbell and those near him attacked that on our right. On this side the enemy had prepared a double retrenchment, consisting of two ditches, (each ten feet deep, and the same in width,) and two parapets formed across the rampart. It appeared that they had been communicating with the breach from this side at the moment we mounted, by means of two strong planks laid across the ditches on the inner edge of the rampart. In the confusion of the surprise, the plank traversing the ditch next to the breach was only drawn a little back, so that one end fell to the bottom of the ditch, while the other rested on the interior lip. In this position it furnished the assailants with the means of passing. This was eagerly seized, and, by mutual assistance they rapidly cleared the first ditch. The plank laid over the second ditch having been left undisturbed, Colonel Campbell proceeded forthwith to take advantage of it. While he was on the plank, a French officer sprung forward, and, calling on his men to fire, made a lunge with his sword at the colonel; he parried the blow, and closed with the Frenchman, and both were instantaneously borne within the second retrenchment by the ardour of our men who were pressing on. At this instant, the 5th regiment reached and mounted the breach with a vehement cheer. This corresponding in the rear most opportunely with the exertions of those in front, startled and appalled the French soldiers at the critical moment at which, by supporting their brave officer, who was forced to yield his sword, they might have successfully defended their post. The advantage thus lost their assailants were too energetic to permit them, whatever efforts were made, ever to regain; but springing one after the other within the retrenchment, each, as he came up, threw himself on the enemy, of whom the foremost soon lay lifeless on the terre-plein, and the rest, who were beyond the immediate reach of the bayonet, turned and fled in panic, without a thought but to save themselves.

Colonel Campbell stopped the pursuit at a place where a street coming from the centre of the town, nearly at right angles with the rampart, is terminated by the retaining wall, but ascends by a ramp on the left to the terre-plein. Beyond this ramp, the houses encroach on the rampart, and narrow it at one point to a few paces, whence it slopes gently down as far as the Agueda gate. A post was thus formed, which those who had reached it could have defended against any number of the enemy, had they recovered themselves.

The writer of this narrative had just congratulated

Colonel Campbell on his success, when the tread of a considerable body of the enemy descending the street gave warning of their approach. A sufficient number of our men having been posted to close the rampart where it was narrowest, the rest were moved down the ramp to receive the enemy on the bayonet, as they should turn at the foot of the street. They came down at a steady step till within twenty or thirty paces of us, but then, hearing a call given to those who were on their way from the breach to move on, they all at once halted, seemed to listen for a moment, and then, throwing down their arms, fled with precipitation.

Our party was now joined successively by Captain C. Campbell, of the 94th, (brother of the colonel;) Captain Laing, of the 94th, wounded through the wrist; Major Ridge, of the 5th, lame, having sprained his ankle ; the serjeant-major of this last regiment, and several men. Still in all it did not number above forty. Patrols were sent out, who went to the old Moorish castle, to the Agueda gate, which was found strongly barricaded with stones, to remove which would have required the labour of many hours, and to the different streets and lanes which touched the rampart in this direction, and which were found deserted and strewed with arms.

A strong desire was now manifested to advance into the town, and to take the defenders of the breach in reverse ; but this Colonel Campbell would not permit, and all soon became sensible that by holding our present post, whatever might happen, the garrison would be compelled to submit; as the knowledge that we had penetrated, and established ourselves in the town, must soon reach the parties who defended the breaches, and paralyse their exertions. Whereas, should we leave the rampart, and enter the streets, we not only exposed ourselves to be cut off in them, if any body of the garrison still retained courage and discipline enough to make a last effort, but also it left free passage to them to occupy again the retrenchments we had carried, and thus enabled them, almost to a certainty, to drive the assailants from the main breach.

It being now clear that all those belonging to the 5th or 94th regiment who had turned to the right flank of the breach, had either passed the retrenchments or fallen, while single files were sent in different directions, to keep up the alarm of the enemy by discharging their arms in the streets, officers went repeatedly towards the breach, in order to bring over those who were attacking the left flank. But they were unable to gain their attention, which was entirely occupied by the fire kept up on them from the retrenchment on that flank, and from the breastwork raised in rear of the rampart. This fire had brightened up, and become very close, it having evidently been reinforced at the same instant that the parties approaching us had given way, and our troops were dropping fast, and had opened their fire in return. As the dazzling light in front, and the smoke which hung over the breach, threw the ditch and flank by which we had crossed into complete obscurity, no persuasion could prevail on them to follow in that direction.

The storming party, and the other brigade of the third division, on arriving afterwards, were in like manner attracted by the fire of the enemy, and, without searching for entrance but where that fire appeared, eagerly strove to bring their own to bear on it, which in time they did so effectively as not only to keep down the fire of the flank, but to overpower and extinguish that from the breastwork, in which the men were more exposed, and were no longer sustained by fresh supplies from the panic-struck garrison. Seeing this, those on the flank dispersed, and allowed our people to enter without further opposition.

About the same time, the light division carried the lesser breach. From the weak defence made at this breach, it seems evident that when the attack was made the enemy stationed to defend it had become aware that the town had been entered elsewhere. It appears impossible otherwise to account for French soldiers, with every means of resistance at hand, allowing a high and narrow breach to be carried, without causing a greater loss to the assailants. That which the light division sustained here did not exceed what might have been caused by a single discharge into the crowded ditch.

The town now became speedily filled with our

troops, and no Frenchman was found in any quarter under arms.

Those officers and men of the 94th and 5th regiments who attacked the retrenchment on the left flank of the main breach, clung to it to the last, and suffered severely in their constant efforts to overcome the obstacles to their entrance; but it was an utter impossibility, so long as those behind it stood firm. The instant, however, that they wavered, these brave men sprung over—and both they and the light division each thought themselves first into the town.

A little attention to the following particulars will enable one to form a tolerably correct idea of the time consumed in the operation.

The point at the Santa Cruz convent from which the 94th regiment started, by the route they followed along the ditch and through the breaches, was not further from the one within the town at which Colonel Campbell stopped the pursuit, than about 500 yards. The whole of this distance was traversed at a very rapid pace, with only a pause of a few seconds, to form at the foot of the breach, and an equally short one at the top from the explosion of shells. The retrenchments and ditches formed in the rampart were passed without a breathing-time, in a manner only to be accomplished by men under the most powerful excitement,—many badly wounded, and themselves unable to proceed—still continuing to lend their aid and support to their comrades. The struggle within was but momentary, so that five minutes had not elapsed from the regiment quitting the shade of the convent-wall before the lodgement was made in the town, and the majority of the garrison had thrown down their arms,—many never having had time to take them. The time from this until the enemy engaged at the breaches abandoned them, may, no doubt, have appeared to men in our situation much longer than it was in reality—but that it was not short will be admitted, when it is considered that after the enemy's inlying picquets had faltered and dispersed, as before mentioned, and after a patrol had gone to the castle and returned, an officer had ample time to go down to the Agueda gate, examine it, come back, make his report, and again return to the breach, before the storming party from the other brigade had entered it. When they did arrive, it still required a considerable time to overpower the fire from the breastwork at the back; and until this was done, those behind the retrenchment on the rampart held fast. In short, it is probable that altogether an hour had nearly elapsed before all resistance ceased.

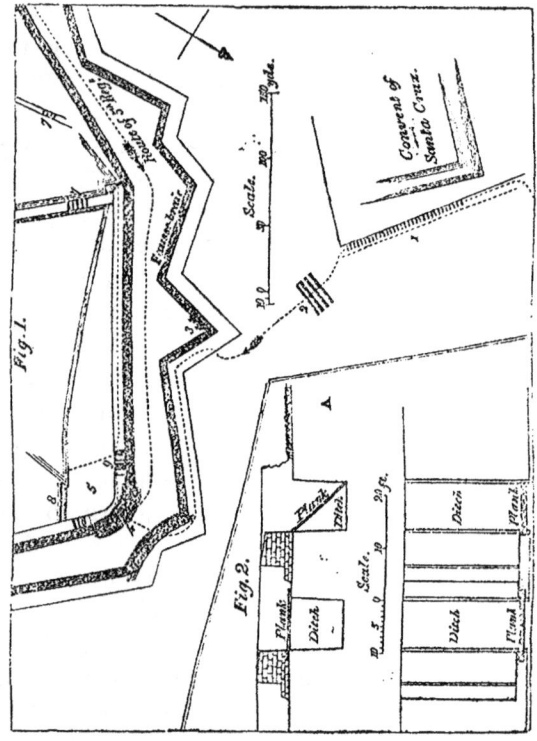

REFERENCES TO THE SKETCH.

1.—94th regiment under the high convent wall.
2.—Ditto moving to the breach.
3.—Two light guns *en barbette*.
4.—Main breach, and corresponding one in fausse-braie.
5.—Space filled with carriages, chevaux de frise, &c.
6.—Point at which the pursuit was stopped.
7.—Advance of French inlying picquets, where they abandoned their arms and dispersed.
8.—Retrenchment at the back of the breach.
9.—Ditto, carried by 94th regiment.
A—Interior retaining wall of the rampart.

* * * * *

* * * * *

The accounts of the storming of Ciudad Rodrigo contained in the "Reminiscences of a Subaltern," and in the "Sketch of the Storming" of that fortress, forcibly recal to my mind the celebrated remark of Sir W. Raleigh, (when a prisoner in the Tower,) on the degree of credit to be attached to what is called history. They have also induced me to furbish up my recollection of the event they describe—an event to which I also was an eye-witness, and therefore competent to give my version of the business; and to explain some circumstances connected with the attack which were not before sufficiently understood.

Attached to the 77th regiment in the third division, I shared the fortunes of that corps on the night of the 19th of January, 1812. We marched on the morning of that day from our quarters at Guard-a-pero, to take our turn in the trenches. It was somewhat ominous of hard knocks, that the division which we were to relieve did not return as usual to quarters for the enjoyment of its customary two days' rest, but halted in the neighbourhood. M'Kinnon's brigade went into the trenches on our arrival at our ground—and we (Campbell's) in the absence of Colville, lounged away the day by our fires, gravely or gaily moralizing, or joking, or chewing the cud of sweet or bitter fancy, as suited the anticipations of each individual, for certain symptoms plainly indicated that the assault would take place that night.

It was six o'clock—the firing on both sides had slackened, but not ceased—their instructions had been for some time in the possession of our chiefs, who were all bustle and mystery. Soon the 5th and 77th were ordered to fall in, and we proceeded some distance to the extreme right of the ground occupied by the division, where we halted; and whilst the men hammered at their flints, and made the customary preparations for business, the order was communicated to us.

"The 5th regiment will attack the entrance of the ditch at the junction of the counterscarp with the main wall of the place. Major Sturgeon will shew them the point of attack. They must issue from the right of the convent of Santa Cruz. They must have twelve axes, in order to cut down the gate by which the ditch is entered at the junction of the counterscarp with the body of the place. The 5th regiment is likewise to have twelve scaling ladders, twenty-five feet long; and immediately on entering the ditch, are to scale the *Fausse Braye*, in order to clear it of the enemy's parties, on their left, towards the principal breach. It will throw over any guns it may meet with, and will proceed along the *Fausse Braye* to the breach in the *Fausse Braye*, where it will wait until Major-General M'Kinnon's column has passed on the main attack, when it will follow in its rear.

"This regiment will make its attack at ten

minutes before seven o'clock. The 77th regiment will be in reserve on the right of the convent of Santa Cruz."

We of the 77th looked somewhat blank at the idea of remaining in reserve; and our colonel—a regular fire-eater—issued his directions with a grim countenance, and a voice fierce from disappointment. Rest your souls in peace, brave Ridge and gallant Dunkin!—though peace was little to your tastes in life. Finer fellows never cheered men to an assault; but Dunkin wanted that moderation and discretion which tempered Ridge's bravery. They alone ordered the colours to accompany their regiment—a rash act—considering that our united numbers little exceeded three hundred firelocks, and one that might have much embarrassed us in the work we had in hand: but it was Dunkin's fancy. Whilst waiting in the gloom, somewhat impatiently, for the return of the men sent for the ladders, and for Major Sturgeon's appearance, we mingled in groups of officers, conversing and laughing together with that callous thoughtlessness which distinguishes the old campaigner. I well remember how poor M'Dougall of the 5th, recently joined from the staff, was quizzed about his dandy moustaches. When next I saw him, in a few short hours, he was a lifeless and a naked corpse. Suddenly a horseman galloped heavily, but hastily towards us—it was Picton. He made a brief and inspiriting appeal to us: said he knew the 5th were men whom a severe fire would not daunt, and that he reposed equal confidence in the 77th. A few kind words to our Commander, and he bade us God speed—pounding the sides of his hog-maned cob as he trotted off in a different direction.

Major Sturgeon and the ladders having arrived, we again moved off about half before seven. The night was, if anything, dark—the stars lending but sufficient light to enable us to find our way—and where the ground permitted it—to trace the dim outline of the fortress. I do not recollect that the moon shone out during the attack. We were enjoined to observe the strictest silence; a neglect of this order occasioned great confusion and the loss of many lives, as will be seen in the course of my narrative. It was a time of thrilling excitement as we wound our way by the right; at first preserving the distance of eleven or twelve hundred yards from the town, then bending in towards the convent of Santa Cruz and the river, and gradually narrowing the space betwixt us and the fortifications. The awful stillness of the hour was unbroken save by the soft measured tread of our little columns as we passed over the green turf, or by the occasional report of a cannon from the walls, and the rush and miss of its ball as it flew past us, or.striking short, bounded from the earth over our heads, receiving our most respectful, though involuntary salaams. I have before said, that the firing had slackened, but not ceased; every two or three minutes a shot was fired at some suspicious quarter, and that by which we were moving seemed to be honoured by their peculiar attention. We had accomplished, perhaps, half our way, when a loose firing of musketry was opened from the ramparts, utterly aimless, and apparently intended as a hint that we should not catch the garrison napping; yet they subsequently acknowledged that they never contemplated the assault being made that night. Though unseen, we were quite within reach of their fire, and escaped surprisingly; yet I can distinctly remember the sharp crashing sound of a bullet, which, striking a steady old serjeant, (within a pace or two of me,) in the centre of the forehead, pierced his brain, dashing him on his back. Two or three men went back wounded.

We had approached the convent, and whilst passing under its walls, we found there the light company of the 94th, awaiting the hour of seven, when they were to commence a brisk fire against the ramparts from the glacis, to distract the attention of the enemy. After exchanging greetings with our old friends, Bogle and Griffiths, the latter gravely promising me Christian burial the next morning; we pushed on right forward to the walls, which now loomed high and near. I will not undertake to explain the circumstances or misconception which caused us (the 77th) to proceed, instead of halting at the convent according to the original plan; but I imagine there must have been some new directions communicated by Sturgeon, who led us to our point of attack, and then quitted us for the purpose of guiding some other party.

We reached the low glacis, through which we discovered a pass into the ditch, somewhat resembling a wide embrazure, heavy palisadoed, with a gate in the centre. I describe matters, not technically, but exactly according to the impressions they made at the moment, and which are still fresh in my recollection. Through the palisadoes were visible the dark and lofty old Moorish walls, whilst high over our heads was the great keep or citadel, a massive square tower which, as it was relieved against the sky, seemed like a giant frowning on the scene. We still were undiscovered, though we could distinguish the arms of the men on the ramparts, as they were levelled and fired from the parapets, in idle bluster, the balls whistling over us. Eagerly, though silently, we all pressed towards the palisadoes as the men with hatchets began to cut a way through them; the sound of the blows would not, I do think, have been heard by the enemy, who were occupied by their own noises, had it not been for the enthusiasm, so characteristic of his country, which induced a newly-joined ensign, fresh from the wilds of Kerry, to utter a tremendous war-whoop as he saw the first paling fall before our efforts. The cheer was immediately taken up by the men, and as we instantly got convincing proofs that we were discovered by our friends on the walls, (who began to pepper us soundly,) we all rushed through the opening, the two regiments mingled together. We were in the ditch heavily fired on from rampart and tower with musketry, but I do not recollect that they had any cannon bearing on us there; however, they tossed down lighted shells, and hand-grenades innumerable, which spun about fizzing and hissing amongst our feet. Some smashed men's heads in their descent, whilst others, exploding on the ground, tossed unlucky wretches in the air, tearing them asunder. I have seldom passed three or four minutes less comfortably; I think that time was consumed in bringing in and fixing the ladders against a wall to our left about twenty-five feet high, which I understood to be the extremity of the *fausse braye*. We crowded towards the ladders, and in good sooth there was little to praise in our eagerness to get out of our trap, helpless and exposed as we were.

Amongst the first to mount was the gallant chieftain of the 5th, but the love they bore him caused so many of his soldiers to follow on the same ladder, that it broke in two, and they all fell, many being hurt by the bayonets of their comrades round the foot of the ladder. Ridge's ancle was sprained, but it did not prevent his pursuing his career that night. I was not one of the last in ascending, and on raising my head to the level of the top of the wall, I beheld some of our fellows demolishing a picquet which had been stationed at that spot, and had stood on the defensive; they had a good fire of wood wherewith to cheer themselves, round which, on revisiting the place in the morning, I saw their dead bodies, stripped, strangely mingled with wounded English officers and men, who had passed the night before the fire, patiently awaiting the means of removal, the fortune of war having made them acquainted with strange bed-fellows. A few of the picquet, who fled along the ditch, bore with them an officer of the 5th, taking him into the town through a sally port in the wall. He was led to the house of the governor, who questioned him as to the assault—the reality of which he seemed to doubt—and on departing for the breach, he took the officer's parole to remain in the house. Being thus excluded from participation in the action, he amused himself in reconnoitring the premises, and repaid himself for his confinement by securing the governor's splendid case of pistols—a fair booty.

Our ascent of the ladders placed us in the *fausse braye*—a broad deep ditch—in which we were for the moment free from danger. When about one hundred and fifty men had mounted (after the little interlude with the picquet) we moved forward at a rapid pace along the ditch, or *fausse braye*, cowering in close to the wall, whilst over our heads we heard the shouts and cries of alarm and preparation. Our course was soon arrested by the massive fragments and crumbling ruins of the main breach, extending half across the ditch.

Here, then, should have ceased the operations of our little band, according to the letter of the order—and here also ought my narrative to conclude, all that followed having been so repeatedly described by able pens. But I write for my own amusement, and as an exercise of memory, and therefore shall continue my description.

The situation in which we now were placed was one of extreme danger and embarrassment. Instead of falling into the rear of a column supposed to have already carried the breach, we stood alone at its base, exposed to a tremendous fire of grape and musketry from its defences, whilst we were in danger of being assaulted in the rear by a sortie through the sally-port in the ditch already mentioned. For a minute we seemed destined to be sacrificed to some mistake as to the hour of attack, but suddenly we heard a cheer from a body of men who, crowning the summit of the counterscarp, flung down bags filled with heather to break their fall, and leaped on them into the ditch. It was the old Scotch brigade, which, like us, having been intended as a support, was true to its time, and was consequently placed in the same predicament with ourselves. On the appearance of the 94th, the fire of the garrison was redoubled—and after a moment's consultation between the seniors, it was decided that it was better to die like men on the breach, than like dogs in the ditch, and instantly, with a wild hurra, all sprung upwards, absolutely eating fire. I think the breach must have been seventy or eighty feet wide; the ninety-fourth took it on the right, we on the left extremity as you look to the country, and I affirm, it would have been a work of no small labour to have achieved the ascent under any circumstances, consisting as it did of a nearly perpendicular mass of loose rubbish, in which it was extremely difficult to obtain a footing.

As our serious intentions were now evident to them, the enemy developed and employed their entire means of defence; two guns pointed downwards from the flanks, and had time to fire several rounds of grape, working fearful destruction, partilarly on the 94th. On the margin of the breach were ranged a quantity of shells, which were lighted and rolled down amongst us, acting rather as a stimulus to push up and avoid their explosion; the top of the breach was defended by a strong body of the garrison, who maintained a heavy fire of musketry, and shewed for some time an undaunted countenance. Hand-grenades and fireballs were not wanting, nor yet the agreeable accompaniment of a heavy fire from a distant flanking demi-bastion, which bore on the foot of the breach and crest of the glacis, where the 45th and 88th, who were just arriving in time to do good service, suffered very severely by it. As we struggled up, the resistance, though not, perhaps, as determined as it might have been, was still sufficiently formidable to have daunted the bravest. However, with all its defects, a night attack has the advantage of concealing from the view much of danger and of difficulty, that if seen might shake the nerves. But there was no time then for hesitation, no choice for the timid; the front ranks were forced onwards by the pressure from the rear, and as men fell wounded on the breach, there they found their (living) grave, being trodden into and covered by the shifting rubbish displaced by the feet of their comrades. Some few, more lucky, when wounded, rolled down the slope into the ditch, where they called in vain for that assistance which could not then be afforded them, and they added by their outcries to the wildness of the scene. Such a struggle could not be of long duration—and the efforts of our men, reinforced as we were by the two last-named regiments, were in a few minutes crowned with success. The enemy's resistance slackened, and they suddenly fled from before us, escaping right and left by boards laid across cuts, through the terre-pleine, by which the breach was isolated: the boards they left behind in their panic.

It was now seven o'clock, the breach was carried, and the town virtually ours. A voice was heard to shout above the uproar, " They run, they run !" All crowded on the summit of the breach, and some spoke of forming the men on the rampart; but on that spot there was no safety, for we had scarcely attained it, when a deadly fire was opened on us from a breastwork about twenty yards distant and beneath, formed from the ruins of some houses, of loose stones, and lined with men. Many of our people threw themselves on their faces, and in that position returned the fire with good effect, as I observed, on the following morning, more than forty of the garrison lying dead behind the breastwork, shot through their heads,—the only part of them exposed to our fire.

One portion of our fellows, led by General M'Kinnon, proceeded to the left along the rampart, and turned the right flank of the breast-work, (which appuyéed against the walls,) and there firing on them, dispersed the enemy. About that time, the expense magazine blew up on the rampart, destroying the general and many with him, as well as such of the garrison as were at that end of the breastwork; behind which I saw the next day a number of blackened and mutilated corpses, hideous and shapeless, friends and foes, mingled in one common destruction. I distinctly remember the moment of the explosion, and the short pause it occasioned in our proceedings—a pause that enabled us to distinguish the noise of the attack still going forward in the direction of the little breach.

I accompanied a party which pushed across a board to our right, for the purpose of clearing the rampart (on that side) of the enemy, who still fired on us, but fled on the first demonstration of attack. Then it was that a gigantic young Irish volunteer, attached to our regiment, was said to have uttered that exclamation of surprise at the facility with which he could deprive a human being of life, that became celebrated afterwards throughout the division. Observing a gallant artilleryman still lingering near his gun, he dashed at him with bayonet fixed and at the charge. The man stepped backwards, facing his foe, but his foot slipping, he fell against the gun, and in a moment the young fellow's bayonet was through his heart. The yell with which he gave up the ghost so terrified B―― that he started back, the implement of death in his hands, and apostrophizing it, was heard to say, "Holy Moses! how easy you went into him!" As the first taste of blood rouses the latent fierceness of the tiger's whelp, so this event seemed to have altered B――'s nature, and doubtless led to his subsequent misfortunes and premature death.

No enemy being now visible on the ramparts, and the men who lined the breastwork having fled, we advanced in pursuit, dropping from the wall into the town. At first we were among ruins; but having extricated ourselves from them, we made our way into a large street leading nearly in a straight line from the principal breach to the plaza or square; up this street we fought our way, the enemy slowly retiring before us. At about half the length of the street was a large open space on our left hand, where was deposited the immense battering train of "the army of Portugal," and its matériel. Amongst this crowd of carriages, a number of men ensconced themselves, firing on

us as we passed, and it required no small exertion
on our part to dislodge them. Such of them as
were caught suffered for their temerity. In the
meantime, those of the enemy a-head of us were
lost to sight, having entered the square; for which
place we pushed on with as many men as we could
lay hands on, formed, without distinction of regiments, into two or three platoons; for the great
proportion of those who had started with us had
gradually sneaked off into the bye-streets for the
purpose of plundering, which business was already
going on merrily. As we reached the head of the
street (which entered the square at one angle),
and wheeled to the left into the open space, we
received a shattering volley from the enemy, which
quickly spoiled our array. They were drawn up in
force in the square, and under the colonnade of
the cathedral, and we were for the moment checked
by their fire, which we returned from the head of
the street, waiting for a reinforcement. At length,
when we were meditating a dash at the fellows, we
heard a fire opened from another quarter, which
seemed to strike them with a panic, for on our
giving a cheer and moving forward, they to a man
threw away their arms as if by word of command,
and disappeared in the gloom like magic. It was
the light division who entered the square by a
street leading from the little breach, and their
opportune arrival had frighted the game which we
had brought to bay, leaving the pavement of the

square covered with arms and accoutrements. Resistance had now ceased—the town was captured. The subsequent transactions of that night, the sack of the city, destruction of a part by fire, and other circumstances, have been frequently and sufficiently described by abler pens than mine. It is enough for me to relate such part of the proceedings connected with the actual fighting as I was an eye-witness to.

On reading the official account of the capture of Ciudad Rodrigo, we were all greatly chagrined to find that no mention had been made of the share which the 77th had in the business, although praise was bestowed in general terms on Colonel Dunkin, who commanded us in the absence of Colonel Bromhead, (who had gone home on leave, after having reaped a full harvest of glory by his gallantry and self-possession at El Bodon.) A respectful and explanatory letter was written to Lord Wellington, forwarded, I think, by Picton; the answer to which expressed his Lordship's regret at not having been aware of all the circumstances at the time the despatch was hastily written; that, in the plan of attack, it was not intended the 77th should have been employed in it, unless in case of necessity, and it was not until after his despatch had been sent off, that he was apprised of their having been so actively engaged. He then expressed his sense of their gallantry and good conduct, doing the regiment full justice.

Such was the purport, if not the actual words, of Lord Wellington's reply.

On recalling to mind the proceedings of that night, I feel satisfied myself, (and I think I shall be supported by the survivors of the third division,) that the 5th, 77th, and 94th were in the main breach before the light division had proceeded to assault the lesser one; and I have no hesitation in asserting that it was the prior success at the main breach of the five regiments employed there, which shook the defenders of the little one, and caused them to yield it so easy a conquest to the light division, and to seek their safety in flight. In plainer terms, I mean to say—that the light division was indebted to the third division for the ease with which it succeeded at its point of attack, and not the reverse. As to our being in a trap on the top of the breach, it is (with respect be it spoken) fudge. The breach was not cut off by traverses, but by deep ditches, over which the boards of communication were left by the enemy in their hasty flight. I think the timely escalade by the 83rd and O'Toole's Portuguese must have hastened the success of the operations of the night.

I repeat it, that no one can be more sensible than I am of the zeal, discipline, and good humour with which the light division performed the troublesome duties imposed on them; but that their merits surpassed those of their brothers in arms to the degree claimed by them, and apparently conceded by their superiors, I deny. The system of puffing histories and memoirs of the feats of the light division can only be equalled by the similar quackeries practised by the injudicious friends of the Highland regiments after Waterloo, turning the really brilliant actions of those gallant corps into burlesque and ridicule.

It will be considered, I am sure, most startling and heretical to question for a moment the superiority of the light division over the rest of the Peninsular army. I may fail in convincing others, but I am myself aware that, at Rodrigo, the merit must be divided (and in no equal portions) with the third division. I remember, that, at Badajos, when they failed, the third division, by taking the castle, gained the town; that, at Sabugal, when in a most awkward scrape, we rescued them; and where, in their whole career, can they produce one instance to equal in splendour the conduct of the 5th and 77th at El Bodon?—and yet those two regiments were not even permitted to record that event by inscribing the word upon their colours.

The disadvantages of relying solely upon two or three regiments for the performance of the outpost duties and skirmishing are obvious, and are, I trust, about to be remedied. The instruction and practice of light infantry evolutions are now insisted on throughout the army,—let us hope, with the view of enabling every regiment to take the advance when necessary, and to perform all those light duties in the field which have hitherto been entrusted to a few favoured corps.

  * * * * *
  * * * * *

The following letter was written by an officer engaged:—

I have from recollection given you a few circumstances which took place during the siege of Ciudad Rodrigo; but as I have not kept a journal, I only relate that which is still fresh in my memory.

A few days previous to the siege, the Duke of Wellington reviewed the light division on the plains of Guinaldo. He was dressed in full uniform, and merely rode down the line, looking at the troops in a cheerful manner. Just as his grace was leaving the ground, which was covered with snow, General Crawford appeared, and soon after the troops returned to their quarters. The second brigade came from Martiago, and returned that night—an immense march. I heard that they were benighted on their way home, and you know what a charming road led to that part of the country. A few days subsequent to this review, the whole division was concentrated—the first brigade being at Encina, the second at El Bodon.

On the 8th of January, 1812, the light division crossed the Agueda, *sans culotte, a cooler!* at a ford about seven miles from the town. The day was fine, and, indeed, during the operations of the siege, the atmosphere was mild, although sometimes a little frosty of a morning.

The division bivouacked for some hours two miles from the town, but when the darkness had set in, six companies drawn from the 43rd, 52nd, and 95th, moved, under the command of Colonel Colborne,* to assault the fort of Francisco. The enemy fired about two rounds; our good troops did not allow more time, and the fort was taken. It was situated on a rising ground, about six hundred yards from the town—was of a square form, with two small howitzers "*en Barbette,*" had a garrison of one officer and forty men, and was neither strong nor weak.

The parallels were immediately commenced, the earth being thrown on the town side. The land was arable; no particular military science; all plain honest digging. Oh! I forgot—we did *sap* over a gutter nearer to the town, but the reason for so doing I never could make out, and at the time I trembled, believing we were about to go under ground, and blow up the covered way.

The great convent in the suburb was carried a few days before the storming of the town, I believe, by the first division. The firing lasted a very long time. The divisions employed in the siege moved by turns from their cantonments, each taking a twenty-four hours' spell—but all this, of course,

* Now Sir John Colborne.

you know. I have never read any book of this siege; all the better! I might have got bewildered by so doing, and made more mistakes.

On the 19th of January, the light division was ordered to the assault, out of its turn. At first it was reported that they were to take both breaches, but as the third division were also throwing up earth, their general remonstrated. The truth of this you will have opportunities of finding out. During the greater part of this day, the light division remained behind a convent about four miles from the town. At four o'clock they moved towards the ground occupied by the first division, one mile and a half from the suburbs of Ciudad Rodrigo. Whether the first division remained in reserve during the night I know not, although I should rather imagine it did. The third division occupying the trenches, the garrison must have observed the march of the light division from the ramparts, extra troops! The governor should have pondered on it! The third division had relieved the first as usual in the morning, but it did not return as usual to its quarters. If the governor had kept a sharp look-out, he must have been expecting the assault; but "I guess" he was no great things. I will give you my reasons anon.

There were two breaches effected in the walls of the town; the small one being made in twenty-four hours. By this breach the large one was taken in the rear; and without doing injustice to the gallant third division, I fear that the attack on the great breach would have failed had the small breach not been carried.

At half-past six o'clock the light division was formed behind the convent in the suburb, and almost exactly opposite to the small breach, and, as I should guess, about three hundred yards from it. All was silent and still, four or five shells excepted, which were thrown by the enemy into our left battery, and fell not a great distance from our column. Now if the governor thought that the assault was preparing, he ought not to have fired at all from the ramparts, as it prevented the approach of the troops from being discovered by the ear.

I heard the town-clock strike seven, and at the same time saw a match lighted in one of the embrasures—very awful! and at that moment the forlorn hope and the storming party moved on; in two minutes they were on the brink of the ditch, and the fire of the town opened briskly on them. There was a short check, but no longer than might be expected, as they had to scramble in and out of the covered way. The storming party carried a number of bags filled with dried grass, and how the troops contrived to force the breach I know not. I can only say that it was well done. The breach was exceedingly steep, about five yards wide at the top, having a twenty-four pounder placed sideways, to block up the passage; however, there was a clear yard from the muzzle of the gun to the wall, a sufficient space for one or two men to enter at a time, besides those who could pass underneath the muzzle of the gun.

The moment the division entered, a number of men rushed along the ramparts to the large breach, (one hundred and fifty yards I should say,) and then engaged those of the French who were still firing on the third division. At this period a wooden spare magazine placed on the rampart exploded, and blew up many grenadiers, and many of the light division. Patterson of the 43rd, and Uniacke of the 95th, were of the number. This occurred just behind the traverse, which, on the enemy's right, confined and guarded the great breach.

On entering the small breach I found myself with the crowd. Col. M'Leod was collecting on the ramparts about two hundred men of the 43rd, and was exhorting them to keep together. At this time there was not any firing on us, but sharp musketry still at the great breach. While the 43rd were forming, I saw no other regiment doing the like.

I went towards the large breach, and met Uniacke of the 95th; he was walking between two men. One of his eyes was blown out, and the flesh was torn off his arms and legs. I asked who it was; he replied Uniacke, and walked on. He had taken chocolate with our mess an hour before! I returned to the regiment, which was now formed, and Colonel M'Leod immediately detached officers, with guards, to take possession of all the stores they could find, and to preserve order. These parties ultimately dissolved themselves. If they had not done so, they would have been engaged in the streets with our own troops. I will explain why hereafter.

Colonel M'Leod caused Lieutenant Madden of the 43rd to descend the small breach with twenty-five men, ordering him to continue at the foot of it during the night, and to prevent soldiers leaving the town with plunder. At eleven o'clock I went to see him. I assure you he had no sinecure. He had very judiciously made a large fire, which of course shewed the delinquents to perfection. He told me that no masquerade could, in point of costume and grotesque figures, rival the characters he stripped that night.

The fire was large, and surrounded by the dead bodies of those who fell in the first onset at the foot of the breach. The troops must have rushed up and taken it without hesitation: for had the governor of the town only tied a few baskets together, he must have stopped the entrance of the light division altogether. He had time—as the firing from our batteries ceased two hours before the assault—and then from the rampart there was only a gentle slope into the town. He was most culpable! There was no musketry from any part of the ramparts until the head of the light division column was close to the small breach. This I note down, to convince you that we were the first who got into the town; where, when the troops had sipped the wine and brandy in the stores, the extreme disorders commenced. To restore order was impossible; a whole division could not have done it. Three or four large houses were on fire—two of them were in the market-place—and the town was illuminated by the flames. The soldiers were drunk, and many of them for amusement were firing from the windows into the streets. I was myself talking to the barber Evans in the square, when a ball passed through his head. This was at one o'clock in the morning. He fell at my feet dead, and his brains lay on the pavement. I then sought shelter, and found Colonel M'Leod with a few officers in a large house, where we remained until the morning. I did not enter any other house in Ciudad Rodrigo; and if I had not seen, I never could have supposed that British soldiers would become so wild and furious. It was quite alarming to meet groups of them in the streets, flushed as they were with drink and desperate in mischief.

In the morning the scene was dreary: the fires just going out; and about the streets were lying the corpses of many men who had met their death hours after the town had been taken. At eleven o'clock, I went to look at the great breach. The ascent was not so steep as that of the small one, but there was a traverse thrown up at each side of it on the rampart; hence there was no way into the town, as the wall was quite perpendicular behind the breach. When the third division gained the top of the rampart, they were in a manner enclosed and hemmed in, and had nowhere to go, while the enemy continued to fire upon them from some old ruined houses only twenty yards distant. I am confident a plan would convince any person that the light division extricated the third division from this disagreeable situation. The very nature of the ground and the defences speaks in plain language.

I counted either sixty-three or ninety-three men of the third division lying dead on the rampart exactly between the traverses I have already described. I did not see one dead man of that division on the French side of those traverses; but I saw some of the light division.

I saw General M'Kinnon lying dead. He was on his back, just under the rampart, on the inside, that is, the town side. He had, I think, rushed forward and fallen down the perpendicular wall before spoken of, probably at the moment of receiving his mortal wound. He was stripped of everything, except his shirt and blue pantaloons; even his boots were taken off. He was a tall thin man. There were no others dead near him, and he was not on the French side of the traverse neither.

It is said that he was blown up. I should say decidedly not. There was no appearance indicating that such had been his fate. Neither his skin nor the posture in which he was lying led me to think it. When a man is blown up, his hands and face, I should think, could not escape. I never saw any whose face was not scorched. M'Kinnon's was pale, and free from the marks of fire. How strange, but with the exception of the general, I did not see a man of the third division who had been stripped! Neither was there any officer among the dead, or else they had been carried away. I should not wonder, if it is not uncharitable, that the general had been killed with all the others between the traverses, and that some *tender-hearted* soldier had taken his clothes off, and then just given him a hand over the wall, and so placed him in the position described.

On the 20th the light division returned to their quarters by regiments, having been relieved by the fifth division, which came from the rear, and took charge of the town. A few days after the assault, most of the officers of the light division attended General Crawford's funeral. He was buried under the small breach.

I may probably have made a mistake about the movements of the first and third divisions on the day of the storming. I rather think, on reflection, the third division must have left the trenches just before the assault, to take up their position behind some old houses, and within a hundred yards of the great breach. Most likely the first division supplied their place in the trench.

Without referring to the spirited and authentic pages of the Marquis of Londonderry, or those of our gifted friend, Colonel Napier, we have it in our power to throw some light on the movements of the third division on the above memorable occasion. We have before us a letter, written four days after the event, from a field-officer of distinguished bravery and intelligence,* who commanded a regiment at the storming of Ciudad, and subsequently found a glorious grave at their head in the castle of Badajoz. In this letter, the details of the assault of the *great breach* by the third division, are told with the same fidelity and manly simplicity which characterize the foregoing sketch, to which it forms, we think, an appropriate pendant. We give the writer's words, as in the former instance :—

January 24th, 1812.

MY DEAR * * *—This order† was executed to the entire satisfaction of all our superiors—you may suppose mine not less so. But instead of *following into the breach*, on our arrival at it, General Mackinnon's brigade had not arrived; the 94th only, which had also a separate route, came up, and a junction of the two weak regiments was formed, supported by the 77th—one hundred and fifty men! The enemy, on our halting as directed, opened a most destructive fire of shells, grenades, and every kind of combustible *devilment* he could bring together. This had the effect of deciding the step we must take, *as our orders said nothing about going back,*

---

* Lieutenant Colonel Ridge.
† See p. 238.

and poor Dubourdieu at the moment observing, "Major, it is as well to die in the breach as in the ditch, for *here* we cannot live," the two regiments, as by one consent, pushed up the breach, almost eating fire. But the "*Mounseers*" liked fighting best at a distance, and gave us ground; and, taking *General Funk* with them, neglected to pull away the planks they had thrown over the ditches, cut by them across the ramparts; by which neglect their preparations for defence were rendered ineffectual. *Five and ninety-four* followed them right and left, at the same time keeping, as well as we could, the centre in check, until the arrival of the intended assailants, when the town and all was ours; the enemy, one and all, throwing away their arms, and flying to their *holes*, where they endeavoured to conceal themselves until the rage of the British lion had subsided; but they had already taken the most effectual means to obtain mercy,—as it was, even here, glorious to see Britons incapable of slaying *unarmed* men, though their lives became forfeit by awaiting the assault with two practicable breaches.

Besides possession of the fortress, the whole of Massena's battering train has become prize, as well as an immense quantity of light artillery which Marmont brought against us on our retreat after El Boden. The fortress is so well supplied with warlike stores, that not an article of any kind is wanting, notwithstanding the expenditure during the siege. I have been enabled to complete the whole of our drummers present with French brass drums, and more had we wanted them.

The George and Dragon has nearly disappeared from our King's colour, by a shell passing through it, though I trust his spirit is left amongst us.

What will not the French and English now say? Ciudad invested—bombarded—and taken in twelve days, which cost Massena fifty-one days, sixteen of which he was bombarding the place. Every part of the proceeding seems to have astonished the garrison, as in erecting works, opening batteries, &c. they were always a day or two out in their calculations.

But I think I hear you ask, "How are all my friends and brother soldiers?" This, my dear friend, is the melancholy part, as our loss has been heavy indeed. Poor M'Dougall, killed; Major Grey, Dubourdieu, Johnson, Wylde, M'Kenzie, Fitzgerald, Fairtlough, Ayshford, Canch, and Volunteer Hilliard, wounded; thirty-eight men killed, and sixty-two wounded. This includes our losses during the siege, as well as in the assault.

Your poor *Light Bobs* have suffered—three killed, and ten badly wounded. The grenadiers are the greatest sufferers.

I got hold of the governor's crimson and gold saddle-cloth, of which I have entreated the acceptance of our gallant and worthy chief of division.* I possess likewise the governor's French double-

* Sir Thomas Picton.

barrelled gun. There has been a regular traffic of the plunder, but the brave fellows earned it all.

Your brother was in the thick of the business, and, I rejoice to say, came out unhurt, and slept before the same fire with me after all was over.

THE STORMING OF BADAJOZ.*

On the 3rd I gave you the little I knew of Rodrigo. T—— offered to forward it for me, and I am happy to say he approved of it, which gave me great satisfaction, as I wrote from memory.

About the middle of February 1812, the light division marched towards the Alentejo; we remained at Castello de Vida a week, and then proceeded to Elvas, when it was generally known that we were about to besiege Badajoz.

On the 17th of March, the division passed the

---

* " Badajos is situated on the left bank of the Guadiana; which river is from three to five hundred yards broad, and washes one-fourth of the enceinte, rendering it nearly inattackable. The defences along the river are confined to a simple and badly flanked rampart, with an exposed revêtement, but on the other sides consist of eight spacious and well-built regular fronts, having a good counterscarp, covered way and glacis, but the ravelins incomplete. The scarp of the bastions exceeds thirty feet in height, and that of the curtains varies from twenty-three to twenty-six feet. In

Guadiana by the pontoon bridge, which I understood was afterwards carried away, owing to the rising of the river during the siege. We bivouacked within one mile and a half on the south side of the town, our position communicating in a manner with the bridge of boats. The day was fine; but at six o'clock in the evening, the rain began to fall in torrents, and continued the whole night, which prevented the enemy hearing the troops when they commenced the first parallel, and the latter continued to work all night without being molested. Before daylight on the 18th, the parties fell in to relieve those of our division who had first broke ground. We had to make a quarter circle, which rendered the march nearly three miles to the mouth of the trench, where we arrived at daybreak, and I saw the first shot; it was fired from the Fort Picurina, and killed two poor fellows in the covering party of the 4th Division, which was formed under the slope of a hill. In a few minutes, the round shot came up the road quite

advance of these fronts are two detached works; one, called the Bardeleras, at two hundred yards distance, is a crown work; its escarps are low, its ditches narrow, and its rear badly closed; the other, called the Picurina, is a strong redoubt, four hundred yards in advance of the town. On the north-east of the town, at the angle formed by the junction of the river Rivillas with the Guadiana, rises a hill to the height of more than one hundred feet, the summit of which is crowned by an old castle, and its walls, naked, weak, and but partially flanked, here form part of the enceinte of the place."—Jones's Journal of the Sieges.

often enough to put our blood into circulation; and we immediately took our station under a small natural rise of ground, where we remained covering the workmen for twelve hours. The cannonade was pretty regular during the day, both from the town and from Fort Picurina.

We returned to camp an hour after dark, and I was surprised to find the division had been supplied with Portuguese tents. I found my friend waiting in one for me, and the canteens laid out with all the affection of a youthful soldier. I had been exposed in the rain for twenty-five hours, and this was one of the happiest moments of my life.

On the 19th, at mid-day, the firing from the town was very heavy; every one in the best position for security, which it was not difficult to obtain, as the trenches were well advanced, but everybody cried " keep down," for which truly there was no occasion. Notwithstanding this cry, Israel Wild, and another man of the 43rd, who was afterwards killed (a splendid soldier) got on the top of the trench. I caught hold of Israel's jacket to pull him down, but he turned round, and said in a most furious manner, " We know what we are about;" then looking forward for a moment, shouted with an oath that the French were coming on, and instantly sprung out of the trench like a tiger, following his comrade, just such another fine fellow. Two or three French dragoons at that instant fired their pistols into the trenches, having approached within a few yards without being perceived. We had just entered the mouth of the first parallel, and all joined in a simultaneous attack on the enemy's infantry, without regard to trenches or anything else. The French, being beaten out of the advanced lines, retired and formed line under the castle, having two field pieces on their right flank. I cannot say how they entered the town, there was so much smoke covering them, when near the walls. *Philipon knew his business well.* I should say that fourteen hundred men came out—two battalions.

We had quite abandoned the trenches, and approached near to the castle; and when we retired, I perceived two men of another division, who were stretched close to where I stood—one was quite dead, a round shot having passed through his body; the other had lost a leg, his eyelids were closed, and he was apparently dead; an adventurous Portuguese began to disencumber him of his clothes. The poor man opened his eyes, and looked in the most imploring manner, while the villain had him by the belt lifting him up. I gave the humane Portuguese a blow with my blunt sabre, that laid him prostrate for a time by the side of the soldier he was stripping.

I know not what became of the wounded man, as my attention was attracted by an extraordinary circumstance. I saw a heavy shot hopping along, and it struck a soldier on the hip—down he went, motionless. I felt confident that the wounded man was not dead, and I begged that some of his comrades would carry him off to the rear, (we were now retiring under a heavy cannonade;) my words were at first unheeded, but two soldiers, at the risk of their lives, rushed back and brought him in, or he, with many others, would have been starved to death between our lines and the ramparts of the town. His hip was only grazed, and his clothes untorn ; but of course he was unable to walk, and seemed to feel much pain, for he groaned heavily.

The sortie took place about a quarter after twelve ; (*military time quite correct ;*) this I wish to impress on you, because we were filing into the trenches. The day was fine, and the time well selected by the Governor, as he concluded that the front parallel would be vacant while the relief was coming in; but there was an order against that.

The trenches were very extensive. The weather again became bad, and our right battery was silenced ; and when the great breaching battery was completed, it fired salvos, which the enemy returned in a similar manner from a battery just under the castle-gate, on a commanding situation. One morning, at day-light, I well remember the enemy bringing a light gun out of the town to enfilade our right ; but as the relief came in at the time, I do not know the sequel of it.

The left of our lines, previous to the escalade of Picurina, ran within about a hundred yards parallel to it. One hundred of the 43rd were employed one night on the delightful job of carrying the trench across the Seville road. We commenced at the distance of one hundred and fifty yards from the Fort. The instant the enemy heard the pickaxes striking on the hard road, they opened, when, strange to relate, eleven rounds of grape were poured on us, and yet only one man was hit. The gunners could not depress their artillery so as to cover the spot we were on.

I was surprised that they used no musketry; but I imagine they had orders not to do so, unless an attempt was made to escalade the Fort.

Picurina was situated on a rising ground, without the least appearance of strength. I think it had two embrasures on each face; that towards *me*, I am sure, had, or else I used to see double. Three hundred men formed the garrison, and latterly they were obliged to block up their embrasures with sand-bags, to screen themselves from the musketry of our lines: now and then they cleared away, and got a shot.

Towards the end of the siege, the weather became beautiful. One day in particular, I call to mind, the enemy scarcely fired a shot; all our troubles were forgotten, and two or three of us amused ourselves by reading a novel in the trenches.

That excellent little soldier, Wilkinson,* was shot through the leg that day; I will tell you how. There was a path across a field, which communicated with our grand battery, and an order forbade any person to cross it in the day-time, as the French were continually firing small arms whenever any lazy fellow took that road. Poor little Wilky's

* He was killed at New Orleans, as Brigade-major, while scrambling up the enemy's lines. His horse had been killed under him. He was taken prisoner, and *died raving* mad from the agony of the wound through his body.

curiosity was excited; he made a start out of fun, was just entering the battery, when, alas! he fell.

One fine night, at half-past eight, a part of the third division, and also one hundred of the light division, carrying ladders, assailed Picurina, and for a long time without success: no wonder! the ditch was terrifically deep, and narrow at the bottom. The soldiers walked round the fort, prying into all corners, and got upon the gate, which they broke down, and then entered, bayonets in advance. The French grenadiers would not give in —a desperate bayoneting took place, and much blood was spilt; already five hundred men from the town were at hand. The struggle continued with hard-fighting, inside and outside of the fort. The enemy wished to vie with their comrades who had defended Fort St. Christoval at the former siege. Victory was some minutes doubtful; at length the fort was our own, and the reinforcements were beat back into the town.* I was sitting at the door of my tent, and witnessed all the firing.

The garrison of Badajoz fired every morning, for a few days previously to the grand assault, a cer-

* " With the capture of the Picurina, the confusion of the night might have been expected to have terminated; but the garrison, apprehending a general assault, opened a tremendous fire of musketry and cannon, while the clang of the alarm-bell, and the hissing of rockets, increased an uproar, which was continued till morning dawned."—MAXWELL's *Life of Wellington.*

tain number of rounds, as if for practice, and to measure the ground.

The first order for storming the breaches fixed it to take place on the 5th of April. I was informed that my turn for French duty fell on that evening, because the officer just preceding me was out of the way. I resolved to play a like trick, and for a like reason, namely, not to miss the assault. I therefore got a friend to persuade the adjutant to permit the men to march off without me, promising to follow. This anecdote I relate, because of the curious circumstance that it led to.

When I was quite certain that the assault was not to take place that night, I mounted my horse, and riding to the entrance of the first parallel, I gave the animal to my battman, and proceeded on foot. I had just crossed the trench, and got into a field, taking a short cut, when I observed two figures making towards me. There was not any firing; a solemn silence reigned around. I felt uncomfortable, and was about to give ground, but they gave me no time. Coming up at a half run, I put my hand to my sword, for the night was clear, and I saw they were not soldiers; they soon closed on me, demanding boldly, and in Spanish, the way out of the trenches: I pointed out the road to them in a civil manner, suspecting they were not *Spaniards*, but spies. I noticed they kept their hands behind them, and I thought it also very *civil* of them not to fire, for I am confident they were well armed. "*Buenas noches, Senhor*," said they, and hastily retired. Many might have done otherwise ; but whether the stillness of the night, the vacant trenches, the dead soldiers here and there buried and unburied, and the blue devils caused by finding myself in such a lonely spot, and addressed by two of the smallest men I ever saw in my life, with very strong voices, caused my valour to depart, I know not ; but I *do* know, that when I reached the great battery, and found every body in it asleep, I thought the place bewitched. This was my last trip to the trenches. Thirteen times I visited them during the siege.

On the 6th of April, a long order was issued relative to the positions the troops were to occupy. The day was fine, and all the soldiers in good spirits, cleaning themselves as if for a review. About two o'clock I saw poor Harvest; he was sucking an orange, and walking on a rising ground, alone, and very thoughtful. It gave me pain, as I knew he was to lead the forlorn hope. He observed, " My mind is made up ; I am sure to be killed."*

At half-past eight o'clock that night the ranks were formed, and the roll called in an under-tone. Lieutenant-Colonel M'Leod spoke long and earnestly to the regiment before it joined the division, expressing the utmost confidence in the result of the attack, and finished by repeating, that he left it to the honour of all persons to preserve disci--

---

* He was killed ; and his twin-brother, of the 52nd light infantry, fell two years after, at St. Sebastian ; also at the head of twenty-five volunteers from that regiment.

pline, and not to commit any cruelty on the poor inhabitants of the town.

The division drew up in the most profound silence behind the large quarry, three hundred yards from the breaches. A small stream separated us from the fourth division. Suddenly, a voice was heard from that direction, giving orders about ladders so loud, that it might be heard by the enemy on the ramparts. *It was horrid.* It was the only voice that broke on the stillness of the moment; everybody was indignant, and Colonel M'Leod sent an officer to say that he would report the circumstance to the General-in-Chief. I looked up the side of the quarry, fully expecting to see the enemy come forth, and derange the plan of attack. It was at half-past nine this happened, but at a quarter before ten, the ill-timed noise ceased, and nothing could be heard but the loud croaking of the frogs.

At ten a carcass was thrown from the town; this was a most beautiful fire-work, and illuminated the ground for many hundred yards; two or three fire-balls followed, and, falling in different directions, showed a bright light, and remained burning. The stillness that followed was the prelude to one of the strangest scenes that the imagination of man can conceive.

Soon after ten o'clock, a little whispering announced that the forlorn hope were stealing forward, followed by the storming parties, composed of three hundred men, (one hundred from each regiment of the brigade;) in two minutes the division followed; one musket shot, *no more*, was fired near the breaches by a French soldier, who was on the look out; we gained ground leisurely, but silently; there were no obstacles. The 52nd 43rd, and 95th closed gradually up to column of quarter distance, left in front; all was hushed, and the town lay buried in gloom; the ladders were placed on the edge of the ditch, when suddenly an explosion took place at the foot of the breaches, and a burst of light disclosed the whole scene—the earth seemed to rock under us—what a sight! The ramparts crowded with the enemy—the French soldiers standing on the parapets—the fourth division advancing rapidly in column of companies on a half circle to our right, while the short-lived glare from the barrels of powder and combustibles flying into the air, gave to friends and foes a look as if both bodies of troops were laughing at each other.

A tremendous firing now opened on us, and for an instant we were stationary; but the troops were *no ways daunted*. The ladders were found exactly opposite the centre breach, and the whole division rushed to the assault with amazing resolution. There was no check. The soldiers flew down the ladders, and the cheering from both sides was loud and full of confidence.

While descending the ladders into the ditch, a soldier of the 52nd in the hurry growled out a hearty curse, and was very angry at my preceding him, and furious blows were exchanged amongst the troops in their eagerness to get forward; while the grape-shot and musketry tore open their ranks. The first officer I happened to see down was Captain Fergusson,* who had led on our storming-party here, and at Rodrigo; he was lying to the right of the ladders, with a wound on the head, and holding a bloody handkerchief in his grasp. I snatched it out of his hand, and tied it round his head. The French were then handing over the fire-balls, which produced a sort of revolving light. The ditch was very wide, and when I arrived at the foot of the centre breach, eighty or ninety men were formed. One cried out, "Who will lead?" This was the work of a moment. Death, and the most dreadful sounds and cries encompassed us. It was a volcano! Up we went; some killed, and others impaled on the bayonets of their own comrades, or hurled headlong amongst the outrageous crowd.†

* He had also two unhealed body wounds open, which he had received at Rodrigo, and one in the trenches at Badajoz a few days before. He now commands the 52nd regiment.

† "On went the storming parties; and one solitary musket was discharged beside the breach, but none answered it. The third division moved forward, closing rapidly up in columns at quarter distance. The ditch was gained,—the ladders were lowered,—on rushed the forlorn hope, with the storming party close behind them. The divisions were now on the brink of the sheer descent, when a gun boomed from the parapet. The earth trembled,—a mine was fired,—an explosion,—and an infernal hissing from lighted fusees succeeded,—and, like the rising of a curtain on the stage, in the hellish glare that suddenly burst out around the breaches, the French lining the ramparts in crowds, and the British descending the ditch, were placed as distinctly visible to each other as if the hour were noontide!"—VICTORIES OF THE BRITISH ARMIES.

The *chevaux-de-frise* looked like innumerable bayonets. When within a yard of the top, my sensations were most extraordinary; I felt half strangled, and fell from a blow that deprived me of sensation. I only recollect feeling a soldier pulling me out of the water, where so many men were drowned. I lost my cap, but still held my sword; on recovering, I looked towards the breach. It was shining and empty! fire-balls were in plenty, and the French troops standing upon the walls, taunting, and inviting our men to come up and try it again. What a crisis! what a *military misery!* Some of the finest troops in the world prostrate—humbled to the dust.

Colonel M'Leod was killed while trying to force the left corner of the large breach. He received his mortal wound within three yards of the enemy, just at the bottom of some nine feet planks, studded with nails, and hanging down the breach from under the *chevaux-de-frise.* A few moments before he fell, he had been wounded in the back by a bayonet of one of our soldiers, who slipped. Steele told me this, and he was with the Colonel at the time.

At half past eleven the firing slackened, and the French detached men from the breaches to repulse the other attacks, and to endeavour to retake the castle. I heard the enemy calling out on the ramparts, in German, "All is well in Badajoz!" it sounded very like English.

But this repulse may be called a victory. The British soldiers did as much as *men could do.* The wood-work of the *chevaux-de-frise* was ponderous, bristling with short, stout sword-blades fastened in it, and chained together. It was an obstacle not to be removed, and the French soldiers stood close to it, killing deliberately every man who approached it. The large breach was at one time crowded with our brave troops; I mean the fourth division, the heroes of many hard-fought victories and crimsoned fields. The light division had recently been crowned with victory; but to remove such obstacles by living bodies pushing against it up a steep breach, and sinking to the knees every step in rubbish, while a firm and fearless enemy stood behind! it is too ridiculous! I must recover patience.

Two hundred and fifty officers, and nearly six thousand soldiers fell around these ramparts.* Let justice prevail! let not the foul tongue of calumny tear those laurels from the brows of men who so nobly earned them. Look on those blood-stained uniforms, gaze on those noble forms stretched on the earth, and think on their agonies!

The left breach had not been attempted at all until a quarter before twelve o'clock, when Shaw, collecting about seventy men of different regi-

* "The loss of the victors was most severe, for, in the siege and storm, nearly 5000 men were killed and wounded. Lieutenant-colonel M'Leod of the 43rd, and Major O'Hare of the 95th, died sword in hand, in the breaches; and five generals—namely, Picton, Colville, Kempt, Walker, and Bowes, were wounded."— MAXWELL'S LIFE OF WELLINGTON.

ments, and with great difficulty, as you may suppose, after such a milling for two hours, made a desperate effort to gain the top; but when halfway up, as if by enchantment, he stood alone. Two rounds of grape and the musketry prevented any more trouble, for almost the whole of the party lay stretched in various attitudes!

Captain Nicholson, of the Engineers, was of the number. He now shewed great courage; and when asked by Shaw if he would try the left breach, answered, he would do anything to succeed. A grape-shot went through his lungs, and he died three days after.

This attack was very daring. It was a forlorn hope under accumulated dangers; almost all the troops had retired, and a few moments before a great alarm was excited by a cry, from the heaps of wounded, that the French were descending into the ditch. To exaggerate this sanguinary strife, is not possible to me nor to any other person.

The small groups of soldiers seeking shelter from the cart-wheels, pieces of timber, fire-balls, and other missiles hurled down upon them; the wounded crawling past the fire-balls, many of them scorched and perfectly black, and covered with mud, from having fallen into the *lunette*, where three hundred were suffocated or drowned; and all this time the French on the top of the parapets, jeering and cracking their jokes, and deliberately picking off whom they chose,* while,

* " Gathering in dark groups, and leaning on their muskets, the assailants looked up with sullen desperation at the

I am grieved to say, the troops lining the glacis did not fire sufficiently, although, I must confess, they were terribly exposed, and could scarcely live from the cross fire of grape-shot.

General Barnard* did all in his power to concentrate the different attacks. It was in vain; the difficulties were too great. But Badajoz was not the grave of the light division's valour—nor of the fourth division either.

Shaw,† when standing near the breach, took out his watch, and said, " It is now two o'clock in the morning—what is to be done? I still hear the rolling fire. I trust all is not yet lost!" This remark he made to a wounded officer, who fell in the last attack, and who afterwards mentioned the circumstance with admiration of the self-possession and coolness displayed by it.

Philipon, the Governor, a *Frenchman*, and our enemy, gave the full particulars of this affair to a friend of mine while travelling in England. He said that he thought the great explosion would have finished the business, but he was astonished at the resolution of the British troops, and that they were fine fellows, and deserved a better fate.

The single musket-shot, fired just as the forlorn hope descended the ditch, was a signal of their

Trinidad, while the enemy, stepping out on the ramparts, and aiming their shots by the light of the fire-balls which they threw over, asked, as their victims fell, why they did not come into Badajoz?"—NAPIER.

* Sir A. Barnard, a good fellow and a first-rate soldier.
† Now Deputy-Adjutant-General at Manchester.

approach, which shews how determined the French were to have a good blow up, for not a ball was fired before the explosion. The efforts of the garrison to preserve the place does them much honour. Philipon was determined not to do as the Governor of Ciudad Rodrigo had done. Had not the Duke of Wellington wisely planned the two extreme attacks by escalade, on the castle by the third division, and on the south side of the town by part of the fifth division, and on Fort Pardoleros by the Portuguese, the result might have been very serious. Soult was within a few leagues, and opposite General Sir R. Hill. Marmont had pushed his advanced dragoons as far as the Bridge of Boats, at Villa Velha, and at length got entangled in the labyrinths of Portugal, and the river Guadiana was in our rear. I have heard and read of setting down before a town, *opening trenches, blowing up the counterscarp, and all according to rule;* but permit me to assure you " *that it was a crisis,*" and time was precious.

When the French soldiers found that the town was falling by escalade on the south side, and that the Castle, situated on a high hill, was lost to them, they made an attempt to retake the latter by an old gate, leading towards the town; that gate was pierced by their musketry in numberless places. I never saw a target better covered with holes. The third division had in return twice discharged a gun through it, which made two large holes. An old handspike was placed under its breech to depress it, and remained precisely in the same way three days afterwards. When I saw it, I wondered what the third division was about to permit a small body of Frenchmen to make such an attempt, or at least to persist in it so long as they must have done from the appearance of the gate; and I should like to know further particulars of the escalade on these terrifically high walls; the scaling ladders were well placed, *five* quite close together, against an old round tower. Many slain soldiers had evidently been pushed from off the parapet, and rolled nearly fifty yards down the hill; some lay with heads battered to pieces, whilst others were doubled up, looking scarcely human, and their broken limbs twisted in all directions.

It was generally understood their first effort failed; and that many of the enemy, contrary to General Philipon's orders, evacuated the Castle, and went to assist at the breaches. At this moment, the commanding officer of the fifth regiment called on an officer of his corps, "There, you mount one ladder, and I will lead up the other. Come on, Fifth, I am sure that you will follow your commanding officer." *He was killed, but the place was carried!*

Let us pause and reflect that this act of heroism was executed after a long and *fearful struggle*, high walls and defeat staring them in the face. The third division then filled the Castle, and there remained until daylight. On the south side of the town, a brigade of the fifth division, hearing the rolling fire at the breaches, became impatient, and with a simultaneous rush, gained (by escalade) the top of the walls, and even formed on the ramparts. On seeing a light, the cry of a *mine* was set up, and a short panic ensuing, the enemy at the time charging forward at a run with fixed bayonets and loud yells; these troops were forced to give ground. An officer informed me, that he had thrown himself over the ramparts to save the colours of his corps, while nearly surrounded by French grenadiers. This bold fellow had the choice of either being pinned to the wall, or the risk of breaking his neck: he chose the latter. However, fortunately the rear regiment stood firm. Many of the enemy then precipitately abandoned the town, accompanied by the Governor, crossed the bridge, and shut themselves up in Fort St. Christoval, on the other side of the Guadiana, and the next morning surrendered themselves prisoners of war. This brigade continued to be *hotly* engaged in the streets during the *whole night*. Some even asserted, that many of the Spaniards fired from their windows on our troops, and *held out lights* to guide the French; knowing that their property would fall a sacrifice should the town be taken. The place was eventually completely sacked by our troops; every atom of furniture broke; beds ripped open in search of treasure; and one street literally strewed with articles, knee deep. A convent was in flames, and the poor nuns in dishabille, striving in vain to burrow themselves into some place of security; however, that was impossible; the town was alive, and every house filled with mad soldiers from the cellar to the once solitary garret.

When I examined the three breaches by day, and witnessed the defences the enemy had made for their protection, I was fully satisfied that they were impregnable to men; and I do declare, most positively, that I could not have surmounted the *chevaux-de-frise, even unopposed,* in the day-time.

Some *talk* that grappling-irons would have moved it. Who would, who could have done it? thousands of warlike French soldiers standing firmly up to the points, not giving an inch, and ready for the fight. They fought in the streets to the last, and tried to retake the Castle—what would you?

The *chevaux-de-frise* were fixed after dark. Round-shot alone could have destroyed these defences, which were all chained together, and not made in a temporary manner, as most military men imagine, but strong and well finished, and the enemy, behind all, had made a deep cut, over which they had thrown planks, communicating with the town, besides three field-pieces to enfilade the centre breach, if the *chevaux-de-frise* should be seriously shaken. Had it not been for this, the divisions would have entered like a swarm of bees.

One man only was at the top of the left breach (the heaps of dead had, as a matter of course, rolled to the bottom), and that was one of the 95th (rifle corps), who had succeeded in getting his head under the *chevaux-de-frise,* which was battered to pieces, and his arms and shoulders torn asunder with bayonet wounds.

Our batteries did not play on the ramparts that night after dark; but when the explosion took place, the whole of them opened with *blank* cartridge in our rear. Probably to frighten the enemy, or to make them keep down; but they were old soldiers, and not to be so done. St. Sebastian, however, may be quoted for this expedient *at the second storm;* but that took place in the day-time. I was there. Poor M'Leod, in his 27th year, was buried half a mile from the town, on the south side, opposite our camp, on the slope of a hill. We did not like to take him to the miserable breach, where, from the warmth of the weather, the dead soldiers had begun to turn, and their blackened bodies had swollen enormously; we therefore laid him amongst some young springing corn, and, with sorrowful hearts, six of us (all that remained of the officers able to stand) saw him covered in the earth. His cap, all muddy, was handed to me, being without one, with merely a handkerchief round my bruised head, one eye closed, and also a slight wound in my leg.

The country was open. The dead, the dying, and the wounded, were scattered abroad; some in tents, others exposed to the sun by day, and the heavy dew at night. At length, with considerable difficulty, I found my friend Madden, lying in a tent, with his trowsers on and his shirt off, covered with blood, and bandaged across the body to support his broken shoulder, laid on his back, and

unable to move. He asked for his brother.—
"Why does he not come to see me?" I turned
my head away; for his gallant young brother (a
captain of the 52nd) was amongst the slain.

Captain Merry, of the 52nd, was sitting on the
ground, sucking an orange. He said, "How are
you?—You see that I am dying; a mortification
has ensued." A grape-shot had shattered his
knee; and he had told the doctor that he preferred
death rather than permit such a *good leg* to be
amputated. Another officer had just breathed his
last between these two sufferers.

The camp became a wilderness, some of the
tents being thrown down, others vacant, and
flapping in the wind, while the musketry still
rattled in the town, announcing the wild rejoicing
of our troops.

* * * * *
* * * * *

[Although the resolute though unsuccessful attacks on the *breaches* of this fortress have been well and accurately described, an authentic detail of the ESCALADE OF THE CASTLE, and actual capture of the place, has hitherto been wanting. The following brief narrative by an officer, who was among the very first to enter the castle, may be relied on as a faithful sketch, as far as the personal observation of the writer went, of that important achievement. Sir Thomas Picton, the intrepid chief of the third division, having been wounded under the walls of the castle, remained that night in the trenches.—ED.]

ON the evening of the 6th of April, 1812, as
soon as it was sufficiently dark to prevent obser-

vation from the garrison, the two British brigades of the third division, composed as follows:—The right, of the 45th, 74th, and 88th, under Sir J. Kempt; the left, of the second battalion 5th, 77th, 83rd, and 94th, under Colonel Campbell of the 94th, their light companies and three companies of the 5th battalion 60th, the whole under Lieutenant-Colonel Williams of the 60th, forming the advance, moved from the ground on which they were encamped in columns right in front. The division took a circuitous direction towards the river, and, according to a preconcerted plan, halted on the ground which had been pointed out to them, there to await the arrival of the several divisions and corps at the points allotted to each previous to the general attack. During this halt the brigades were earnestly addressed by their respective commanders on the duty they had to perform.

On the signal for the general attack, the brigades advanced in the order already mentioned. The enemy appeared fully aware of the attack, having commenced and continuing to throw fire-balls, which completely exposed the advance of the troops, particularly on their arrival at the wet ditch which covered the approach to the castle-wall. This was passed by wading or going along the top of the dam which terminated the ditch, and which was so narrow as only to admit of our passing by single files, while the enemy continued to keep up a destructive fire at this point. As soon as this obstacle was surmounted, the light companies and the right brigade, under Sir J. Kempt, moved to the left towards the principal gate of the town; the left, led by Colonel Campbell, advanced direct to that part of the castle-wall which had been bombarded the preceding year. At this point, some ladders were reared against the wall by the grenadiers of the 5th, at one of which was Colonel Campbell and Lieutenant-Colonel Ridge, who commanded the 5th regiment, and at another the officers of the grenadiers of the 5th. Colonel Ridge called to Ensign Canch of the latter to lead at his ladder, and immediately both, at their respective ladders, pushed up, followed by their men; and having succeeded in gaining the top of the wall, they joined, and found that they mustered strong enough to beat off whatever was immediately opposed to them. The gallant Ridge called out,—"Come on, my lads! let us be the first to seize the governor;" and dashed on, making his way, with those along with him, over the works which had been raised during the siege, exposed to a heavy fire, by which numbers fell, who were soon replaced by those who followed.

As the 5th advanced the enemy retired, leaving in the works a few men, who were killed or taken prisoners. Retiring from the ramparts, the French formed in an open space near the castle-gate. For a short time the firing ceased, and the regiment, headed by their commander, continued to feel their way in the dark, following the ramparts until they came to a passage leading to the centre of the castle; and on advancing a short way a column was observed, which caused a momentary hesitation in our advance. Colonel Ridge, who at the time was reconnoitring another opening, called out, "Why do you hesitate? Forward!" We again, with the greatest caution, and without firing, continued to advance, and on proceeding a little farther, the enemy were observed. We then commenced firing, which was returned by a volley. At this moment our beloved and heroic commander fell, having received a wound in the breast, which immediately proved fatal. The writer of this was so near as to be in contact with him at the instant of his fall. We left a guard by his honoured remains.

The regiment continued to advance, keeping up a fire, and being now supported by the other corps who were following them up, the enemy retiring and shutting the gates. The inner gate was forced without much difficulty, but the outer one was found strongly secured. The French, however, had left the wicket open, and kept up a heavy fire on those who attempted to pass it. Colonel Campbell now ordered the men to retire within the inner gate of the castle, and directed the 5th to form in column facing the gates, and that the other regiments should imitate that formation as they collected. The command of the whole had devolved upon Colonel Campbell, Sir J. Kempt having, as well as Sir Thomas Picton, been wounded in the assault. The regiments remained in this order of formation until a communication of their having possession of the castle was made to the Duke of Wellington, to whom, as we understood, the news of our unexpected success had given the highest satisfaction.

Having continued formed as above till morning, we received orders to advance into the town, and were cheered by the generous admission of our brave comrades—that Picton and the third division had taken Badajoz.*

*　　*　　*　　*　　*
*　　*　　*　　.*　　*

FROM THE JOURNAL OF LIEUT. P. K., 88TH REGT.

On the 6th of April (1812) the fate of Badajoz was decided. The breaches were both reported practicable by the Commandant of Engineers, and the moment fast approached which was to end our painful toils. The enemy's fire never ceased the whole morning, and seemed to thunder

---

* We have now before us a letter from an officer present, written the day after the storm, eulogizing the magnanimity of Lord Wellington on this occasion, his lordship having, it was asserted, told Sir Thomas Picton, that the "third division had saved his honour, and gained him Badajoz."—ED.

That the capture of the castle might be consummated in due form, a curious, though characteristic, emblem was substituted for the French flag. Lieutenant Macpherson, of the 45th, having got possession of the latter, immediately doffed his own jacket and hoisted it on the flag-staff. The gallant lieutenant presented the French flag to Sir Thomas Picton. —ED.

forth defiance. Lord Wellington again reconnoitred from one of the surrounding hills, and, having determined upon storming the place that night, the flank officers were assembled, and the names taken down of those daring spirits who volunteered to lead the forlorn hope; and upon this occasion, as upon all others where honour pointed to the path of glory, the 88th furnished one of the bravest of the brave, in the person of poor Whitelaw, a young Irishman, who led the advance with the ladders against the castle, and fell mortally wounded. The reader will ask, what recompence did he or his family receive? I answer, none: he died in extreme agony in a Spanish hovel, unnoticed and unknown!

The yawning breaches now seemed to call upon us to advance, and end our suspense by victory or the grave. At seven in the evening the order arrived to complete the men in ammunition and flints, (not painted sticks to resemble cartridges,) and at half-past eight we formed. The plan of attack was as follows: General Picton, with the third division, was ordered to attack the castle by escalade; a strong detachment of the 4th division was to assail the ravelin of St. Roque; General Colville, with the remainder of the 4th and the light division, was to attack the breaches which were in the bastions of La Trinidad and Santa Martha; and General Leith, with the 5th division, was to make a feint attack at the south side of the castle, which was to be made a real attack if circumstances proved favourable; and a strong body of Portuguese troops was held in reserve.

In this order, at about ten at night, the whole advanced in that profound silence that rendered the approaching storm more terrific. The 3rd division was not perceived until they arrived at a little river not very distant from the works, when we distinctly heard the entire line of French sentries give the alarm, and the whole guns of the garrison seemed, as if by signal, to open at once. The breaches soon afterwards were clearly defined by the continued blaze of fire from the enemy's musketry; and the roaring of the guns from every quarter seemed only to act as a stimulus to perform a service that perhaps no other troops would have accomplished with equal intrepidity. Incessant volleys of grapeshot were poured on our division as we advanced, accompanied by fire-balls, which too plainly shewed them our numbers and situation, and as clearly pointed out to us the difficulties we had to surmount. By quickening our pace we succeeded in getting so close under the wall that the guns could not bear upon us; but the brilliant fire-balls, which mocked all our efforts to extinguish them, burned so vividly as not only to enable them to direct their musketry, but also to hurl with fatal precision every kind of missile upon us.

The ladders being at length placed, the troops, with three cheers, courageously ascended, and nothing was soon heard but mingled cries of despair and shouts of victory. Several ladders, having too great a weight upon them, broke down, and the men were precipitated on the bayonets of their comrades below; nor did this in the least check their impetuosity; they continued to rush up in crowds, determined to reach the ramparts, or die in the attempt. The ladder I mounted, like many others, was unfortunately too short, and I found that no exertion I could make would enable me to gain the embrasure or to descend. In this unhappy state, expecting immediate death from the hands of the ferocious-looking Frenchmen in the embrasure, I heard a voice above call out, " Mr. —, is that you?" I answered " Yes." And the same voice cried out, " Oh, murther! murther! what will we do to get you up at all, at all, with that scrawdeen of a ladtherr? But here goes! hould my leg, Bill;" and throwing himself flat on his face in the embrasure, he extended his brawny arm down the wall, and seizing me by the collar, with Herculean force, landed me, as he said himself, " clever and clane," on the ramparts. In the same manner five more were landed; and thus did this chivalrous soldier, with noble generosity, prefer saving the lives of six of his comrades at the risk of his own, to the rich plunder which everywhere surrounded him. And who do you think, Mr. Reader, this noble soldier was? Why, Sir, it was the gallant Tully O'Malley, a private in my company, an Irishman, and one of the " ragged rascals."

Tully O'Malley having just landed me, as he said, on the ramparts, I found myself standing amongst several French soldiers, who crowded round the gun in the embrasure. One of them still held the match lighted in his hand, the blue flame of which gave the bronzed and sullen countenances of these warriors an expression not easily forgotten. A grenadier of the 103rd leaned on the gun, and bled profusely from the head; another, who had fallen on his knees when wounded, remained fixed in astonishment and terror. Others, whose muskets lay scattered on the ground, folded their arms in deep despair; and the appearance of the whole group, with their huge bushy mustaches, and mouths blackened with biting the cartridges, presented to the eye of a young soldier at least an appearance sufficiently formidable.

"Don't mind them fellows, Sir," said Tully; "they were all settled jist afore you came up; and, by my soul, good boys they war for a start, and fought like raal divils, so they did, till Mr. S. and the grenadiers came powdering down on them with the warwhoop. Och, my darlint, they were made smiddreens of in a crack, barring that great big fellow you see there, with the great black whiskers, bleeding in the side, and resting his head on the gun-carriage. He was the bouldest of them all, and made bloody battle with Jim Reilly; but 'tis short he stud afore Jim. He gave him a raal Waterford puck* that tumbled him like a nine-pin in a minute; and, by my own sowl, a puck of the butt-end of Jim's piece is no joke, I tell you, for he tried it on more heads nor one on the hill of Busaco."

Away then flew Tully to join his company, form-

* Reilly was a Waterford slip.

ing in double quick time, with several others, to oppose the enemy, who were collecting an overpowering force at one of the gates of the citadel, apparently with an intention of charging and driving us from the ramparts. They had already opened a most galling fire of musketry from this dark gateway, which was warmly returned by our soldiers, whose impetuosity could no longer be restrained, and they charged through the gateway, led by my gallant friend, Lieutenant Davern, of the 88th, and were received by a shower of balls; but the massive gate being closed, little impression was made. A second and third charge were likewise made without effect, when a number of the light infantry of the 74th and 88th, assisted each other to climb up on the archway over the gate, and opened such a destructive and unexpected fire down on the French (who thought themselves quite secure at the other side) that a general panic seized them, and they fled with the utmost precipitation and confusion, followed rapidly by our men, who now dashed through the gateway without opposition.

Several gallant soldiers were put *hors-de-combat* here, amongst them Major Murphy of the 88th,* whom I found quite exhausted, and unable to move from loss of blood, not having been able to bind up his wound, which I had no sooner accomplished than we moved on. However, the panic of the

* The conduct of Lieut.-Colonel Ridge of the 5th, in this escalade, and this attack, in which he fell, has been already recorded.—ED.

enemy was but momentary, for the retreating soldiers soon met a strong body of their troops advancing at the *pas de charge*, when they instantly turned round and fired into the middle of the column of their pursuers, by which many of our gallant fellows fell to rise no more. But the struggle was short, and being chiefly decided by the bayonet, the French again fled, leaving the rampart literally covered with dead and wounded, amongst whom were the most forward of their officers, whose long, narrow-bladed sabres, with brass scabbards, instantly changed masters. One who lay on his back wounded made several thrusts at the sturdy Ranger who was endeavouring to disarm him, who in the encounter had awkwardly caught the sharp sword-blade in his hand, and was so severely cut that he was preparing to rush on his antagonist, when the buckle of the Frenchman's waist-belt instantly flew open, and the sword was thrown to him. But Pat was angry, and was not now satisfied with the sword only, for perceiving a handsome silver-mounted calebash by the officer's side, he coolly transferred it to his own shoulders (first taking a copious swill) and gravely addressing the wounded man, said, while re-loading his piece, "Now, my tight fellow, you see what you lost by your contrariness." "Ah, Monsieur," said the Frenchman, "je suis grievement blessé ; rendez moi mon calebash, je vous en prie." "Grieving for your calebash; is it that you mane?" said Pat. "Why, then, I'll tell you what, no man shall say that Pat Donovan ever deprived either friend or foe of his little dhrop of dhrink; and there 'tis for you!" "Grand merci, grand merci!" said the officer. " Oh, don't bother yourself axing mercy from me," said Pat; " but take my advice," said he, as he bawled loud and slowly in his ear, so as he thought he must understand him, "keep roaring mercy, mercy, mercy, to all our fellows as they come up, and, by Gor, they'll not take the least notice of you." "Ah, merci, merci, c'est fait de moi, c'est fait de moi," repeated the poor wounded young Frenchman. Fatal presentiment! One short hour only had elapsed ere we returned. He lay on the same spot, but his spirit had winged its flight to that place " where the wicked cease from troubling, and the weary are at rest;" and the gallant, daring Frenchman was already numbered with the dead.

In the meantime, the cheering of our men, and the animating bugles sounding the charge, made those below so anxious to share the glory of their comrades, that many dreadful accidents occurred from the breaking of the ladders, in consequence of the crowds that still attempted to ascend. However, at length we had the satisfaction to see reinforcements pouring in from all points, and securing the prisoners, who scowled upon us with sullen and disappointed looks; and, although they surrendered without hesitation to their British conquerors, and perhaps, after all, with a better grace than the troops of any other nation under such circumstances, yet, when taken by the Portuguese, they could not restrain their rage, and manifested towards them a degree of contempt and indignation which cost many of them their lives.

The enemy's fire meanwhile continued with unabated fury, and those still under the castle wall were dreadfully shattered by the fire from the side batteries. In short, the carnage was so frightful, that the approach to the wall was now over the bodies of their dead and dying comrades, which caused a peculiarly revolting feeling, not easily forgotten by the fiercest soldier. At this period, also, the uproar in the town exceeded all description; great guns roaring; musketry blazing; men shrieking from the agony of their wounds; bells ringing; and dogs barking, in such numbers, and with such fury, that it would seem that all the canine species of Estramadura were imprisoned in the fortress. Add to this, the sounding of our bugles in all directions, and the French drums beating with hurried and redoubled violence the *pas de charge*, whilst a murderous fire of shot, shell, and musketry poured on the 4th and light divisions, who rushed boldly forward the second time to the breaches, nothing appalled by the carnage and failure of the first attack; but all attempts to force the breach were fruitless.

Most fortunately, the success of the 3rd and 5th divisions rendered it unnecessary to continue any further attempts to force the breach, and the troops were withdrawn on the joyful intelligence arriving that the castle was taken. The French heard the news with the utmost astonishment and dismay, and commenced a hasty retreat to Fort St. Christoval, on the opposite side of the river.*

During these operations the troops were engrossed in disarming and securing the prisoners. Among others, I happened to capture and save the life of the Colonel commanding the artillery in the citadel, at the very moment our men pursued him at the point of the bayonet. He threw himself upon me, and finding I understood French, entreated that I would save him from our infuriated soldiers, which I found it extremely difficult to do, as each successive party, on perceiving his large gold epaulettes and orders, evinced a strong anxiety to make further acquaintance with him; and upon one occasion I was obliged to use my sword to protect him from a few of the 60th, who advanced upon him in rather a suspicious and business-like manner. He was in a state of violent agitation, and kept a firm hold of my arm throughout all the changes of the fight, until I met a field-officer of the British artillery, near a short flight of steps leading to a magazine, to whom I gave him in charge, and who appeared to

* "Would that the story of that siege had ended with its capture; for now commenced that wild and desperate wickedness which tarnished the lustre of the soldier's heroism. Shameless rapacity, brutal intemperance, savage lust, cruelty and murder, shrieks and piteous lamentations, groans, shouts, imprecations, and hissing of fires bursting from the houses, the crashing of doors and windows, and the reports of muskets used in violence, resounded for two days and nights in the streets of Badajos."—NAPIER.

be in search of him, when they entered the magazine together.

The Frenchman was anxious to bring me to the bomb-proof, where his baggage was secured, to give me some token of his gratitude, and overwhelmed me with thanks; but duty called, and I could not accompany him. The British officer then hurried him away in a very abrupt and hasty manner, and I have reason to know that considerable advantages resulted to the service in consequence of that officer's life being saved, as no other individual in the citadel was so capable of giving important information relative to that hard-won fortress as that officer. The *rencontre* was a hit to the man of shot and shell, and I have no doubt he derived advantages from it much more solid than I did, as my only reward was a profusion of unmeaning thanks from the terrified Frenchman, and the consciousness of having done my duty.

The first rays of a beautiful morning discovered to us the incredible strength of Badajoz, and how dearly the capture of it had cost us. The gallant hearts that beat with devoted bravery the night before, now lay in the cold grasp of death: a comparative degree of silence had succeeded the dreadful din of arms, and rendered more awful the contemplation of this fearful scene of death and desolation. A vast number of the enemy's soldiers lay dead in a heap close by the spot where our men were forming, and whilst I gazed on these unhappy victims of a fierce and deadly fight, I was not a little astonished to observe a very young

French officer, who lay amongst them, and whom I supposed to be dead also, slowly and cautiously raise himself up, and, after looking about with a wild stare, and reconnoitering the ground, he coolly walked over to the other prisoners, and delivered himself up. This wily hero had not been wounded, nor had he received the slightest scratch, but being more frightened than hurt, he lay concealed in this manner until all apprehension of danger was over. It excited a good deal of merriment amongst our men, but the French curled their moustaches, gave him many a hearty " sacre," and looked at him with the most sovereign contempt.

THE STORMING OF BADAJOZ.

I WAS upon the hill, with the chief of the medical staff, now Sir James M'Grigor, and standing near Lord Wellington, during the night of the assault of Badajoz.* As soon as it became dark, the different divisions of the army began to move in the direction of the points to be attacked. The silence was only broken by the deep-toned sound of the cathedral clock striking the hour. The suspense was awful.

At length, fire-balls thrown by the enemy from the parapets, from the intensity of their light, enabled them to discover our advancing columns. The momentary intervals of total darkness which followed had a most imposing effect.

The conflict at last began. The parapet of the

---

* At eight o'clock in the evening an orderly serjeant entered the tent of General Leith, with whom the author of this narrative had been dining, and informed the general that his division (the 5th) was under arms. All immediately arose and separated *in silence*.

whole front, for about two hours, poured forth fire. The glare of light occasioned by explosions of gunpowder and other combustibles, by fire-balls, the firing of cannon, incessant peals of musketry, the bursting of shells and hand-grenades, gave to the breaches, and to the whole front, an awfully grand appearance.

The wounded now began to arrive: from them we could obtain no distinct information. The anxiety to receive intelligence from the scene of action became more and more intense.

At length, a staff officer galloped up, exclaiming, " Where is Lord Wellington? My Lord, I am come from the breaches: the troops, after repeated attempts, have failed in entering them. So many officers have fallen that the men, dispersed in the ditch, are without leaders; and if your lordship does not immediately send a strong reinforcement they must abandon the enterprise. Lieutenant-Colonel M'Leod, of the 43rd regiment, has been killed in the breach."

A light was instantly brought, and Lord Wellington noted the report with a steady hand. His countenance was pale, and expressed great anxiety. In his manner and language he preserved perfect coolness and self-possession. Major-General Hay's brigade was ordered to advance to the breaches.

Another staff-officer soon arrived, bringing information that General Picton had obtained possession of the castle.

" Who brings that intelligence?" exclaimed

Lord Wellington. The officer gave his name.

"Are you certain, sir?"

"I entered the Castle with the troops; have just left it, and General Picton in possession."

"With how many men?"

"His division."

It is impossible to imagine the change this produced in the feelings of all around.

"Return, sir, and desire General Picton to maintain his position at all hazards."

Having dispatched this messenger, Lord Wellington directed a second officer to proceed to the Castle to repeat his orders to General Picton.

At this moment, a youthful and gallant aid-de-camp indiscreetly put a question to the chief, for the unseasonableness of which he received a rebuke.

Here I must interrupt the narrative, to instance the fatality which befel two friends from whom I had parted on the evening preceding the assault.

Major Singer and Captain Cholwich of the Royal Fusileers, and I, had sat together for several hours upon an eminence, observing the effects produced by our breaching batteries upon the curtain of La Trinidad, which was soon reduced to a heap of ruins. The assault was expected to take place that evening. On our parting, Major Singer, shaking my hand, said "———, to-morrow I shall be a lieutenant-colonel, or in the kingdom of heaven."

Picton's division being in possession of the castle, and General Walker's brigade having entered by escalade the Bastion of St. Vincente, close to the Guadiana, on the opposite side of the town, the enemy abandoned the breaches, to visit which I set out at dawn of day. Meeting some men of the Fusileers, I inquired for Major Singer. "We are throwing the last shovels of earth upon his grave;" the brink of which, where he fell, was marked by his blood.

"Is Captain Cholwich safe?"

"In the act of climbing over that palisade (intersecting the inundation) he was wounded, fell into the water, and was seen no more."

Pursuing the course taken by the 4th and light divisions, painfully indicated by the numbers of men and officers lying dead in the line of their march, I reached the great breach. This breach I found covered with the dead from its base to its summit; many were stripped. Amongst them I recognised the countenances of several well known to me. In ascending the breach my feet receded at every step in the *débris*, so as to render my advance slow and difficult. Its summit was defended by *chevaux-de-frize*, constructed with long sword-blades firmly fixed in the trunks of trees. Behind the *chevaux-de-frize* a broad and deep trench had been cut, into which our men must have been precipitated had they succeeded in surmounting this almost insurmountable barrier. Above was a battery of 12-pounders completely enfilading the great and the small breach, near to each other, so as to render them apparently the strongest parts of the fortress.

I next visited the Castle, at the bottom of whose walls, nearly forty feet high, were lying shattered ladders, broken muskets, exploded shells, and hand-granades, with the dead bodies of many of our brave men. I ascended into the Castle by a ladder, the only one which preserved its situation against the wall. Amongst the dead I recognised the body of the gallant Major Ridge, of the 5th regiment, lying near the gate communicating with the town, in forcing which he had fallen riddled with balls. On entering the city by the Talavera gate, I found it a more difficult task than I had expected. The ditch, into which I descended, was inundated, the gate nearly built up, the approach being by a narrow causeway just raised above the water, and scarcely wide enough for two persons to pass. I met a soldier of the Connaught Rangers overpowered by excitement and brandy; the fellow looked at me suspiciously, and appeared disposed to dispute my passage. He held his loaded musket at half present, and I was prepared to close with him; but fortunately, flattery succeeded, and he allowed me to pass.

Soon after entering the town, a girl, about nine years of age, implored my protection "*por el amor de Dios*" for her mother. A number of soldiers of a distinguished regiment were in the house, armed, and under the influence of every evil passion, and the wretched woman became their victim.

I met another man of the 88th regiment dragging a peasant by the collar, with the intention, as he declared, of putting him to death in atonement for not having money in his possession. A fortunate allusion, which, as in the former instance, I made to the gallantry of his corps, and country, saved the life of his intended victim.

My object in going into the town was in the hope—vain indeed—of affording protection to a family in whose house I had resided for several months while the head-quarters of our army were at Badajoz, after the battle of Talavera. I found that the house had been plundered, the furniture destroyed, and I could not learn anything of the family.*

The town had now become a scene of plunder and devastation; our soldiers and our women, in a state of intoxication, had lost all control over themselves. These, together with numbers of Spaniards and Portuguese who had come into the city from the neighbourhood in search of plunder,

* I was an inmate of this house when the intelligence of the surrender of Flushing to the British army, under the command of the Earl of Chatham, arrived. The guns of the fortress were firing for the occasion. The lady of the house, a very kind-hearted woman, entered my apartment, exclaiming, " Senor Don Carlos, hay grandes noticias, los Ingleses tomaron Flusingo, mas grande que la Francia." (Great news, Don Charles—the English have taken Flushing, larger than France.") She considered the power of Napoleon at an end, and Spain free. When I pointed out the island of Walcheren upon a map, which she had just borrowed from a *sabio*, or wise man, her countenance changed, assuming a mixed expression of doubt and belief, disappointment and mortification.

filled every street. Many were dispossessed of their booty by others; and these interchanges of plunder in many cases were not effected without bloodshed, when the party about to be deprived of his spoils was sufficiently sober to offer resistance. Our soldiers had taken possession of the shops, stationed themselves behind the counters, and were selling the goods contained in them. These were again displaced by more numerous parties, who became shop-keepers in their turn; and thus, one set replaced another until order was restored.

In addition to the incessant firing through the key-holes of the front doors of houses as the readiest way of forcing the locks, a desultory and wanton discharge of musketry was kept up in the streets, placing others, as well as myself, literally between cross fires. Many of our own people were thus killed and wounded; and it was afterwards well known that numbers in the hospitals had been wounded by their own comrades.

I was glad to escape from this scene of infuriated licentiousness, in which all the worst passions of human nature seemed to be in unrestrained operation. An attempt was in vain made on the day following to collect our soldiers. The troops sent into the town for that purpose, however, joined in the work of plunder.

It was not until the morning of the 9th that I returned to Badajoz. The scene which presented itself on my arrival would require the pencil of a Hogarth to describe. Hundreds of both sexes were lying in the streets in a state of helpless intoxication, habited in various costume. Amongst them were those who had fallen by the hands of their comrades. Nor was it easy to discriminate between the drunken and the dead; both were often equally pale and motionless.

Churches and convents, shops and stores with wine and spirituous liquors, private houses and palaces, had all been plundered. The actors of these excesses were attired in the habits of priests, with broad brimmed hats, of monks and of nuns, and in the dresses of grandees and of ladies of rank. I quartered myself in the house of Don Emmanuel de la Rocha, a canon of the cathedral, a man of liberal opinions, and said to be in the French interest. He was glad to receive a British officer into his house. Count Phillippon, the French governor, had been my predecessor. His papers were lying scattered about the room. Amongst them I found his commission, which I sent to head-quarters, and a number of *billet-doux* of his staff.

Don Manuel, who had scarcely yet recovered from his alarm, said that he had been knocked about with the butt ends of muskets by the soldiers who had entered his house, and pricked by their bayonets, in order to force him to give up treasures they suspected he had concealed. The old and the young were equally victims to the most savage brutality, less the natural disposition of the men than the result of maddening intoxication; and subsequent inquiry left no doubt but that every woman who had not concealed herself incurred outrage.

General Walker was in the French hospital desperately wounded. After getting into the town his men deserted him in a panic, occasioned by the apprehension of the explosion of a mine. Being left alone, a French soldier, finding no opposition, turned, and fired over a traverse at the general. The shot struck his watch, suspended in his bosom, was thus diverted from its course, down the right side, breaking ribs and wounding large blood-vessels. The Frenchman afterwards inflicted several bayonet wounds, tore off his epaulettes, and was only deterred from giving the general an immediate *coup de grace*, from the conviction of his having already received a mortal wound.

The medical officers who attended the general had little expectation of his recovery; but, by their unremitting care during several months, he was, under Providence, saved.

Several wounded officers, who had been removed into the town soon after it was taken, described their having been exposed to great personal danger by the licentious conduct of their own men, who had entered the houses, plundered the rooms in which they were confined to bed, and abused the females. One in particular, who had been conveyed to the house of the Caldera family, so described his situation. Madame Caldera, formerly the *belle* of Badajoz (when the headquarters were there), had taken refuge at Elvas during the siege. She returned as soon as order was restored.

The city still continued, on the third day after the assault, in the exclusive possession of a disorganized and tumultuous soldiery; acknowledging no law, considering everything within their grasp their own, and allowing no impediments to interpose themselves between desire and gratification.

On entering the cathedral, I saw three British soldiers *literally drowned* in brandy. A spacious vault had been converted into a spirit depôt for the use of the garrison. The casks had been pierced with musket-balls, and their contents escaping, had formed a pool of some depth. These men becoming intoxicated had fallen head foremost into the liquor, the position in which I found them, and were suffocated.

I passed the night in my clothes, with a brace of pistols by my side. Every noise I heard, or thought I heard, (not sleeping, as may be supposed, very sound,) brought me upon my legs, with a pistol in my hand.

My equipage, including horses, mules, &c., of several hundred pounds value, might have been plundered in an instant, without the possibility of replacing it. On the following day, General Power marched his Portuguese brigade into the town. A gallows was erected on the *Plaça*, or Square. Its appearance alone had a magical effect—not a man was executed, and order was restored. Sentinels having been placed at my quarter, I was now relieved from further apprehension.

At the door of the cathedral, into which the wounded were now being removed from the camp, a pale, jaded, thin little woman, very shabbily dressed, accosted me. She introduced herself as the Marchioness of Innojosa; had recently emerged from a subterranean chamber in the church, where, with others, she had taken up her nightly abode for security during the siege. She requested my permission to remove a mattress, of which many had been deposited in the church for use as well as for security. I replied,—" The wounded stand in need of them." The Spanish General O'Lawler, attached to the head-quarters, interceded. At last, it was intimated that a mattress should be placed on the outside of the church door when it became dark.

The General, the Hon. Charles Colville, who so gallantly led the fourth division to the assault, was amongst the wounded who were brought into the town. I frequently visited him, and had the gratification of witnessing his recovery.

General Hay took me to the quarter of Colonel, now Sir George Elder, commanding a Portuguese regiment of Caçadores, who had received several severe and dangerous wounds. Whilst apparently doing well, he was seized with locked-jaw, which placed him in imminent danger. Contrary to all expectation, he recovered. But he has ever since been subject to severe spasms, not only extremely distressing, but very alarming whilst they continue. As soon as he was able, he gave me the following account of his own proceedings:—

Memorandum of the siege and the assault of Badajoz, on the evening of the 6th of April, 1812:—

We opened our fire on the 31st of March,* from twenty-six pieces of cannon in the second parallel, to breach the face of the bastion at the south-east angle of the fort, called La Trinidad, and the flank of the bastion, by which the face is defended, called Santa Maria: the fire upon these continued with great effect. And on the 4th of April, in the morning, we opened another battery of six guns, in the second parallel, against the shoulder of the ravelin of St. Roque and the wall in its gorge.

Practicable breaches were effected in the bastions above-mentioned on the evening of the 5th; but it appeared that the enemy had entrenched the bastion of La Trinidad, and the most formidable preparations were making for the defence of both the breaches; in consequence of which, Lord Wellington delayed the attack for another day, in order to turn all the guns in the batteries in the second parallel on the curtain of La Trinidad, in hopes that, by effecting a third breach, the troops would be enabled to turn the enemy's work for the

* "During this memorable siege, 2523 barrels of powder, each containing 90 lbs.; 31,861 round shots; 1826 common and spherical $5\frac{1}{2}$ inch shells; and 1659 rounds of grape and case shot were expended. The reduction of Badajoz required 70,000 sand-bags, 1200 gabions, 700 fascines, and 1570 entrenching tools."—MAXWELL'S LIFE OF WELLINGTON.

defence of the other two breaches. The third breach was effected in the evening of the 6th, and the fire of the face of the bastion Santa Maria and the flank of the bastion La Trinidad being overcome, Lord Wellington directed that the place should be attacked that night.

The plan for the assault was, that Lieutenant-General Picton should attack the castle of Badajoz by escalade, with the 3rd division; while the 4th division, commanded by the Honourable Major-General Colville, and the light division, commanded by Colonel Barnard, attacked the breaches in the bastions of La Trinidad and of Santa Maria, and in the curtain by which they are connected.

On this occasion I was second in command to Colonel Barnard, and in the assault on Badajoz, two regiments of Portuguese Caçadores and a few companies of the 95th Rifle Regiment were placed under my orders. Colonel Barnard commanded the remainder of the light division, composed of the 43rd, 52nd, and remaining companies of Riflemen, which he conducted to the breach. I was directed to follow the leading brigade at a respectable distance, and not to advance until the rear of the 43rd regiment entered the ditch. I therefore remained under cover until an officer of the Rifle Regiment (who very handsomely volunteered for those services) followed the 43rd regiment, and in a short time returned, and reported that he had seen the troops into the ditch. I then advanced, and on my reaching the glacis, I was astonished when I observed the frightful confusion among the troops in the ditch; and in order to ascertain the particulars, I immediately descended the ladders, at the bottom of which I met Major Broke, (now Colonel Sir Charles Broke Vere,) who was severely wounded. I understood from him, that nearly all the field-officers were either killed or wounded; and that the attack on the great breach, La Trinidad, had failed; and that he was going back to report the particulars to the Commander-in-Chief, Lord Wellington. I immediately pushed forward; and as I was endeavouring to form some of the troops near me, in order to lead them to the small breach on my left, Santa Maria, I was at that moment severely wounded; and upon my regaining the glacis, by the assistance of some soldiers, to the best of my recollection, I was a second time wounded on the glacis, and afterwards I was carried upon men's shoulders to the camp.

On the evening of the assault I invited five friends to dine with me: during dinner and after, not a single word was mentioned on the subject of the attack which was to take place that night. About eight o'clock, the orderly serjeant came into the tent to report that the parade was ready-formed. We immediately stood up, and I proposed a bumper to our success; and as my old friend, Major O'Hare, of the Rifle Corps, was named to command the forlorn hope, I shook him by the hand, and said, that I hoped we should meet the next day, when I should have the pleasure to congratulate him on his promotion to a lieutenant-colonelcy. The poor fellow thanked me, and said, "By Jove, Elder, we have seen a great deal of service together, and we have had our share of hard knocks, and I sincerely hope that we shall meet to-morrow." We then dispersed, every one to his post; but, unfortunately, our "next" meeting never took place.

Major O'Hare led the forlorn hope to the breach. He and Captain Morphew, of the 3rd Caçadores, (who likewise dined with me on that day,) were amongst the first killed; two other officers of the same dinner-party and myself were very severely wounded; and only one out of the six that sat down to dinner escaped.

I must here notice the fate of a very fine young man, Captain St. Pol, of the Royal Fusileers, who died of the wounds he had received during the assault, after amputation of the leg. I wrote to the Duke of Kent an account of this officer, to which I received the following reply:—

"I have to acknowledge with many thanks, your letter of the 25th ult., containing a statement of the case, sufferings, and death of my young friend and protegé, Captain St. Pol.

"The loss of this promising young man has been a source of great affliction to his friends, but it is some consolation to them, as well as to myself, to reflect, that his noble and heroic conduct had so justly secured to him the esteem and attachment of all those who were acquainted with him.

(Signed,) EDWARD.
"Kensington Palace, May 25, 1812."

Captain St. Pol was son of the Duke of Orleans, Louis Philippe, to whom he bore a striking resemblance.

Soon after the capture of Badajoz, General Power, Colonel Fletcher, the chief engineer, who afterwards fell at the assault of St. Sebastian, Colonel Buchan, and several other friends, were engaged to dine with me. On that morning, whilst writing a letter to England, I heard an explosion like the sound of a gun. Don Manuel, my host, rushed into my room, exclaiming, "Monsieur, votre cuisinier est mort."

I found Gonsalvez, the cook, lying extended upon the kitchen floor, covered with blood; part of one of his hands was on the opposite side of the room. The barrel of a musket, lying near the body, explained the cause of the catastrophe. The barrel, left by the soldiers who had plundered the house, probably half-filled with ball cartridges, had served the purpose of a poker. Gonsalvez had unfortunately inserted the breech end into a fire larger than usual; it exploded, and produced this fatal issue. Not a vestige of the heart could be discovered upon examining the body; it had been blown to atoms. Thus terminated the life and culinary labours of Gonsalvez.

Although not in holy orders, I possessed a degree of power over the churches rivalling, if not exceeding, that of the bishop. Becoming impatient of lay control in matters ecclesiastical, the prelate intimated his intention of paying me a visit one evening, after he had taken his siesta. Supported by the canons Caldera and de la Rocha, I received the bishop, who arrived, attended by the *cabildo ecclesiastico*.

Having partaken of chocolate and *dolces*, the bishop, after some general conversation, made known to me, through his secretary, the object of his visit, "my sanction for ringing the bells."

I replied, "the sound of the bells would disturb the wounded," with which the churches were filled. The prelate, appreciating the force of my argument, took his leave. We parted, and continued upon good terms.

During the last summer, a lady and a gentleman occupied with myself a public conveyance from Fulham to London. Perceiving my companions to be Spaniards, I addressed the latter:—"Sir, you come from a country where I passed six of the happiest years of my life."

His countenance lighted up. He had been Alcalde (mayor) of Badajoz, intimate with the Calderas, Don Manuel, and others, my old friends. From him I learned, with regret, that they, like himself, had been expatriated for their political opinions. When we parted, with an embrace, a tear stood in his eye.

THE BATTLE OF SALAMANCA.

About the 10th of June, 1812, the light division concentrated and joined the army, which commenced its march through the great forest that lies between Rodrigo and Salamanca. The division was composed of the 1st and 3rd Rifles, two regiments of Caçadores, 43rd and 52nd regiments, and a brigade of horse artillery.

The march of the light division was worthy of notice; the men were very fine, and well-seasoned to endure fatigue, having served in many campaigns.

The discipline of the division was most exact; the men were not tormented by unnecessary parades—the march was their parade; that over, the soldiers (except those on duty) made themselves happy, while those with sore feet, by such a system, had rest, which enabled them to be with their comrades, when, by a mistaken notion of discipline, it would have been otherwise: their equipment was regularly examined, nor were the men on any pretence permitted to overload themselves—one of the most serious afflictions to an army. A general may be endowed with transcendent abilities, and by a forced march place himself in a situation to overthrow his enemies; he may possess the number of divisions, and the number of regiments, but by internal bad management of regimental officers, half his army may be straggling in the rear. Again, nothing is so pernicious as keeping the soldiers under arms, while the officers are going God knows where: it destroys all *esprit*, causing the officers to forget the sufferings of their men after a weary march, and creates feelings of dislike towards them in the breasts of the soldiers. Such a system did not exist in the light division; and when a young officer fell in action, the old soldiers proffered their services with parental care.

The baggage followed the line of march in succession. The mules of each company were tied together, and conducted by two batmen in rotation, right or left in front, according to the order of march. Each regiment found an officer, and each brigade a captain to superintend. The alarm-post for them in camp was on the reverse flank of respective regiments. When the enemy were at hand, the baggage was ordered to the rear, the distance according to circumstances.

The army was four days clearing the forest, which was clothed with verdure, and supplied the most delightful bivouacs. The Sierra de Gata lay on the right hand, covered with snow, while a cloudless sky formed our canopy, with the sunshine of hope and happiness beaming on every countenance, not excepting the growling surly batmen, who were seen to smile at finding forage at hand for their animals.

On the fourth day, the division encamped within two leagues of Salamanca, and quite clear of the wood. The German hussars had an affair on that day with the enemy's cavalry. The officers of hussars described it to us, and related the conversation that took place between them and the French dragoons stationed on piquet in front of Salamanca. The enemy requested the Germans not to charge; the hussars replied, while advancing, that if the French fired, they would. The enemy then fired their carbines to stop their progress. The hussars charged, and cut most of them down.

The next morning we advanced, and pushed a body of the rifle corps to feel their way through a village near Salamanca, which they found to be unoccupied by the enemy. The division then brought up their left shoulders, and passed in open column of companies within cannon range of the forts, situated on the right bank of the Tormes, and within a short distance of the north side of the town. The enemy stood on the ramparts to see us pass; the whole plain was covered by our cavalry and infantry, crowding towards the ford of Santa Martha, where we also forded the river, and bivouacked a short distance from the town. The French army had retired, leaving eight hundred men to garrison the three forts of St.

Vincent, Gayetano, and Merced, constructed with the masonry extracted from the different handsome convents, monasteries, and colleges, which had been pulled down to be converted into bastions.

The sixth division took possession of Salamanca,* and invested the forts. Soon after we had taken up our ground, most of the officers hurried into the town; the inhabitants appeared much rejoiced to see us, and as I entered, two ladies ran towards me, each seizing a hand. My Rozinante dropped her head in search of food, as I believe she had not enjoyed a feed that day, while I looked right and left, and thought such congratulations very romantic. The *Senoras*, in black silk, put numerous questions, few of which I could understand, nor am I confident whether they were civil or military, although from the expression of their eyes, I concluded that they were on a civil subject. I much admired the female peasantry; they were healthy, well-made, with black eyes, red lips, little feet, and wore red, yellow, and blue petticoats. Soon after, I ascended

---

* Salamanca stands in a commanding situation on the right bank of the Tormes, (a river of considerable magnitude there,) which rises near the Sierra de Tablada, a mountain in Old Castile, and falls into the Douro, on the Portuguese frontier, opposite Bemposta. The country round is generally flat, without trees, and with a few villages interspersed over its surface. On the left of the Tormes there are extensive pasture lands, and on the right a corn country, open and unenclosed.—Ed.

to the top of the cathedral, to reconnoitre the forts, when I had a full view into the interior of them, and musketry might have been applied with effect from this point. I then descended, and entered into the festivities and pleasures of the place.

In the evening the town was illuminated, and resounded with music, while the merry Spanish *muchachas* were dancing boleros, and striking their castanets in the streets. The glare of light was reflected from the bright arms piled in the great square, surrounded by soldiers of the sixth division, many of whom were destined soon to fall within a few hundred yards of the fascinating scene.

Our division advanced the next day, and took up their ground a league and a half in front of Salamanca. On the 20th, a staff officer rode up to a group of us, and said, " the enemy are advancing." I rode up to the side of the position of St. Christoval, and descried them afar off in the plain. The division then fell in, and were ordered to crown the heights, which they did ; and at the same time some Spanish regiments came in our rear, with two pieces of cannon : the mules became restive ; some went one way, and some another— every way but the right. They became entangled in their harness ; some kicking, and others feeding on the uncut corn, and finally, during this mutiny of the mules, a gun was upset, and rolling over the bank into the road, quite deranged the dignity of the Spanish march.

The different divisions of the army were now

ascending the heights of St. Christoval at many points. The French army continued to advance, and soon after began to debouch from the different roads in order of battle. The view was not obstructed; the country was level, covered with a sheet of corn, as far as the eye could reach. To those fond of military evolutions, the scene was bold; to those of more tranquil habits, time was given to pray for the good of their own souls, and for the rest of the army, if charitably inclined.

At first, our division deployed on the left of the front line; then again moved and took post in the centre of the second line; the whole army were deployed into two lines to oppose the enemy, the cavalry to the right, and also some detached on the left, to scour the plain between us and Salamanca, where part of the sixth division remained to cover the forts at that place. The whole army present consisted of seven divisions, besides cavalry, artillery, the before-mentioned Spaniards, and some Portuguese infantry.

At five o'clock in the afternoon, the French cavalry approached by the valley to the left of our position, where our light dragoons began to skirmish with them, and showed some disinclination to give ground; the enemy brought up six guns, and opened on our squadrons in reserve, when the dispute ended.

Towards evening the French made an attack on part of the seventh division, occupying a village at the base, and on the right of our position: after some sharp work it was carried by the enemy. A brisk cannonade then took place to our right between the two armies; night put an end to the firing. The whole army slept on their arms in order of battle, and after dark the picquets were placed at the foot of our position. An hour before day-break, the army stood to their arms, fully expecting to be attacked. The dark shades dispersed, the sun rose; both armies tranquil, notwithstanding their proximity; the enemy were full in view, without a bush or any obstacle to prevent close quarters. Their right was thrown back in *echelon* of divisions. I suppose our General-in-chief wished them to come a little nearer, but Marmont was now cautious, for his army was inferior in numbers.

Our position was covered with uncut corn, which served the cavalry for forage, and the infantry for beds. The contending armies caused great devastation, and trampled down the ripe wheat for miles around. The river Tormes ran about two miles in our rear, with two fords. Our division was now withdrawn from the line, and placed as a column of reserve in rear and centre of the army: it protected the fords in our rear, and might be used as a moveable mass, either to resist cavalry or assist where required.

The Duke of Wellington was stationary from morning till night, watching the enemy, generally alone and on foot, at the crest of the hill, and in the centre of the position. His staff approached him one at a time to receive orders. At night the Duke slept on the ground, wrapped in his cloak.

The troops were much inconvenienced for want of water, as the river was at some distance, and only a few men could be spared, as it was impossible to know what moment the enemy might not attack. Some Spanish ladies came from Salamanca and walked through our lines. On the third night the French retired; our division took ground to the right, and were posted on the bare and conical hill of Cabrerizes. It appeared necessary that the fort and the command of the bridge at Salamanca should be secured before we made any forward movement. The Duke of Ragusa evidently wished to gain time, and to continue in the vicinity to succour the forts, also to infuse courage into the little garrisons until his reinforcements should arrive.

The Duke of Wellington remained on the hill of Cabrerizes the whole day. The sun shone with great brilliancy, and it was burning hot. One of the soldiers of the 43rd put up a blanket to keep the rays of the sun from his Grace. Our bivouac presented a droll appearance, as the whole division had hoisted blankets in a similar manner. The breaches at the forts were now considered practicable. At about nine o'clock at night the attack commenced; but after some time the firing became slack, and I saw three rockets thrown up from the forts, and immediately answered by several rounds of artillery from the French army on a rising ground two leagues on our right, which instantly satisfied me that the assault had not succeeded, and was done as a signal that they were still at hand.

The next morning, the 24th, at day-light, we heard some firing on the other side of the Tormes during a dense fog, which at first prevented the force of the enemy from being ascertained. The Duke of Wellington would not move. The soldiers laughed, and said, "Oh, they are only shaking their blankets on the other side of the water:" for, if you recollect, in heavy weather, musketry produced sounds such as I have described. As the fog cleared away, a few rounds of artillery took place; and the Duke sent a sufficient body of troops by the ford in the rear of St. Christoval to meet the enemy. When the atmosphere cleared, we saw about a division of the French moving towards Salamanca. They were opposed by our heavy cavalry, which had been placed there to secure the flank and rear of our army. At seven that evening the French recrossed, unmolested, to the right bank of the Tormes, by a ford a league to our right. I did not consider the movement a serious one, but merely to encourage the soldiers in the forts to hold out.

On the 27th, St. Vincent being in flames, the enemy permitted our troops to ascend the breaches without opposition. It was a sort of half assault and half surrender. The troops in the other forts also laid down their arms, having suffered severely; and only marched out three hundred out of eight, their original force, and many of those scorched by the flames, or otherwise hurt.

The army now moved forward. Our division supported the cavalry, and advanced toward Ruêda.

On the 2nd of July, Captain Bull's horse artillery and the cavalry overtook the enemy's rear-guard near that place. Although the country appeared open, it was unfit for cavalry, as it was intersected with small vines, the size of gooseberry-bushes. On entering the town, I observed five of the French killed from the fire of the six-pounders.

The division bivouacked round the town; and the next morning we moved about two leagues in advance, and rather to the left, where an interchange of shots took place between the left of our army and the enemy, who had no idea of permitting us to cross the Douro at that time, as Marmont wished to keep the left bank of that river for the base of his future operations. We then returned and took up our quarters in Ruêda. Pay was issued; all of which we spent in gaieties and *iced wines*. The inhabitants had all returned to their dwellings. The mayor was informed that the officers would give a ball; when he procured *Senoritas*, according to custom. It was extremely pleasant, with waltzing, and all the fascinating mazes of the Spanish country-dance in perfection. Many of the Duke's staff attended. On the evening of the 16th of July, our division was ordered to quit Ruêda, and marched the whole night over a dusty and arid country; and towards morning we took up our ground near Castréjon. Just before nightfall, the company was ordered a quarter of a league to the front on picquet; the country was open, and as the cavalry passed, I heard a staff-officer giving orders, which led me to suspect that the enemy were at hand. At break of day, on the 18th, a few shots were exchanged to our right, the firing increased, and the cheering might be distinctly heard at intervals, as the sun rose above the horizon.

Our dragoons became visible, while retiring before the enemy's horse and light artillery, which at intervals were blazing away. The scene was sublime and beautiful. Houlton said to me, "there will be a row this day; however, we had better get our breakfast, as God knows *when* we shall have any thing to eat, unless we take advantage of the present moment." The tea service being laid out, and a stubble fire kindled to warm the bottom of the kettle, we suddenly espied some squadrons of French heavy dragoons in a valley to our right, pushing for the main road at full trot. An absurd and ludicrous scene now took place. The crockery was thrown into the hampers; also the kettle, half-filled with hot water,—the other officer all the while vociferating, "God bless me! you will not desert my mule and hampers: they are worth four hundred dollars." In fact, to get off seemed impossible; the company formed column of sections, and fixed bayonets, fully determined to cover the old mule, who went off with a rare clatter, and we after him, in double-quick time. The enemy were now within two hundred yards of us, brandishing their swords, and calling out, when they suddenly drew up, on seeing some of our cavalry hovering on their right flank. A rivulet, with steep banks, ran parallel with the road; but we soon found a ford, where we drew up, intending to dispute the passage. Our division had moved forward, and had deployed to the succour of our dragoons first engaged, about half a mile to our right. Soon after this, two squadrons of our light dragoons formed on a rising ground, two hundred yards from us, with two pieces of horse-artillery on their right, when about an equal number of French heavy cavalry, handsomely dressed, with large fur caps, made rapidly towards them, our guns throwing round-shot at them during their advance. When they had arrived within one hundred yards of our squadrons, they drew up to get wind, our dragoons remaining stationary.

A French officer advanced, and invited our people to charge, to beguile a few moments, while his squadrons obtained a little breathing time. He then held his sword on high, crying aloud, "*Vive l'Empereur, en avant Francais,*" and rushed on, single-handed, followed by his men, and overthrew our dragoons. The guns had fortunately limbered up, and the horse-artillery fought round them with great spirit—the enemy trying to cut the traces, while the poor drivers held down their heads, sticking their spurs into the horses' sides with all their might, and passed the ford under cover of our picquet. The Duke of Wellington was in the thick of it, and only escaped with difficulty. He also crossed the ford, with his straight sword drawn, at full speed, and smiling. I did not see his Grace when the charge first took place, but he had a most narrow escape; he had not any of his staff with him, and was quite alone, with a ravine in his rear.

A few stragglers of each party still continued engaged, and this part of the affray took place within twenty yards of us. One of our dragoons came to the water with a frightful wound; his jaw was entirely separated from the upper part of his face, and hung on his breast; the poor fellow made an effort to drink in that wretched condition.

The round-shot now flew in various directions; one spun through a cottage behind us, and the shepherd ran out in great terror. The light division now commenced its retreat from the vicinity of Castréjon. The French had crossed the river Douro with reinforcements, and had made an amazing march to take us in flank. We had only retrograded a short way, when we obtained a view of the bulk of the French army pushing forward, on a ridge of hills to our right. The first false attack had been made at daylight on our front, merely to draw all our force to that point, while Marshal Marmont executed this movement. The fourth division were retiring in mass within range of the enemy's fire, critically situated in the valley, while the French cannon rolled on the crest of the hills above, and poured in their shot with effect on their right flank.

Our division was obliquely to the rear, in column of quarter distance, with fixed bayonets ready to form square,* surrounded by large bodies

* Six companies of the second battalion of Rifles joined us on the retreat, just arrived from England.

of our cavalry. To avoid an action seemed impossible. The enemy's infantry were almost on the run, and we were marching away from them as hard as we could. While the round-shot from a flank fire flew over us, a French division came running to engage, and detain us until others came up, and obliged us to abandon the road, and trample down a tract of wheat. The heavy German cavalry drew close round us. The country was open, and a vast sheet of corn enveloped us for many miles. The men became much distressed, owing to the rapidity of the movements and heat of the day. We were enabled to regain the road (owing to our numerical superiority of cavalry), which made a curve down a gentle descent; and the men descried, at a short distance, a dirty meandering stream, called the Guarena, near Castrillo. A buzz ran through the ranks that water was at hand, and the soldiers were impelled forward with eyes staring, and mouths open; and when within fifty yards of the stream, a general rush was made. I never saw the troops during my service so thirsty. The discipline of the division was such, that I have seen them pass clear water unbroken, suffering under fatigue, in the hottest weather, known only to those under the weight of a heavy knapsack and accoutrements.

All this took place under a cannonade, which had continued at intervals for more than ten miles. This was following up with a vengeance. We had no sooner crossed the river than some squadrons of the enemy's cavalry galloped up a hill immediately overlooking us. The division now moved more leisurely; and every one was aware that had our cavalry given way the division must have halted to repulse charges, which would have given time for the French infantry to come up; and had that been the case, the struggle must have been very sanguinary. Our reserves now being at hand, we soon halted on a round hill, and shewed front. The fourth division did the same, when a brigade of the enemy, covered with dust, came in contact with an equal number of the fourth division, who, firing a volley, charged with the bayonet, and overthrew the French in good style, taking many prisoners. The French army had done their best to overtake us, but became glad of a halt as well as ourselves, and the firing ceased. We remained stationary during the day, when I fell asleep, and after some time suddenly awoke with my lips glued together, and almost roasted by the scorching rays of the sun, and actually crawled some distance before I knew where I was. Dry biscuit was served out; but we could not get any water until eleven at night, when I obtained a draught of dirty water out of my batman's canteen. However, it cooled my inside; and I believe that many hundreds dreamed that night of limped streams.

On the 19th the troops stood to their arms an hour before day-break, but the enemy continued stationary; and well they might, as they had made the previous night and day an enormous march to cut us off in detail, according to the Duke of

Ragusa's favourite expression. However, at four o'clock in the afternoon, the Duke of Wellington rode up to Wilkinson of the 43rd, who was on picquet, and said, "What are the enemy doing?" Wilkinson replied, "The French are in motion." The Duke said, "Yes—to the right now;" and ordered the first brigade of our division to make a corresponding movement by crossing a valley to prolong our right. We ascended a high hill, and formed on our original front, when the French army issued from behind the hills, presenting a martial appearance, and a grand display of moving squadrons with brazen helmets, and a great body of infantry flanked by their cannon.

The river Guarena was nearly dried up, and was the only obstacle between the contending armies, as the face of the country continued bare and hilly, without even a tree to be seen. The Duke of Ragusa entered the valley to reconnoitre, surrounded by a numerous staff, when two guns of our horse-artillery opened, and a ball struck on the ground and knocked up the dust in the very centre of the group without killing any one. They took the hint and shifted their ground.

Eight of the enemies' guns instantly began a heavy firing on our brigade. The first shot struck an officer of the horse-artillery on the side of his helmet, and displaced him from his horse. After a short time the brigade went to the right about to get out of range. At that moment the Spaniards attached to us simultaneously started from the left of each regiment, and I do not recollect ever seeing them afterwards. It was most ludicrous to witness the flight of these patriots in disorder, while our troops retired, sloping their arms, with the utmost *sang-froid*. We soon halted and faced about, the enemies' guns ceased to play, and a large force of our light dragoons mounted the hill in our rear with sloped swords. Night coming on, we formed columns in case of accidents. An officer and myself then stole down the hill on horseback in search of water for ourselves and animals. Having passed our advanced posts some distance, and hearing strange voices, we looked at each other, and whispered that to go further would be indiscreet, and rejoining the column, we wrapped ourselves in our cloaks, and fell into a profound slumber, out of which we were awakened by a great bustle and the trampling of horses. The word passed to stand to our arms, and the Portuguese Caçadores fired some shots, and I was so overcome by drowsiness that I continued in a squatting position, rubbing my eyes, too lazy to move. The confusion was caused by two or three mules breaking their ropes and becoming lively, not unusual amongst such animals.

On the 20th, our division concentrated soon after day-light, and descended into the plain of Velesa, where we observed our whole army formed in a dense phalanx, ready to deploy in order of battle. The French army were not in sight. However, it was evident they intended to avail themselves of the high ground. A brigade of our cavalry had pushed half way up the ridge, to entice them to show front, and to develope their movements, as it appeared during the night they had moved on a quarter circle, round our extreme right flank, and were now pushing on and trying to cut off our communications. Marmont would not accept battle as long as he could gain ground without it, unless we attacked at a disadvantage, as he seemed to be a perfect master of the localities of the country.

Our army, under all these circumstances, broke up and began to retreat, the different divisions arranged in such a manner, that, should it become necessary, by facing to the left, they could show front, and be ready to engage, the more particularly as both armies were again moving parallel to each other, and in this order continued some leagues, and bivouacked. It became necessary for the troops to cook with fires of stubble, as there was not any wood in the neighbourhood. A brigade of Portuguese cavalry happened to be left at some distance in the rear, and, as it slowly retired in line, presented such an imposing *front to our rear*, that, by mistake, an artillery officer ordered them to be saluted by a couple of shot, which unfortunately did some execution.

On the 21st, two hours before day-light, we began our march, branching off towards Salamanca, and took up our ground in the valley below St. Christoval, the enemy having moved on Alba de Tormes and its vicinity. Towards evening we fell in, and crossed the Tormes by a ford, and marched in the direction of Salamanca, the river being on our right hand. Night approached, and a German Hussar passed us at full speed, and said, "She is coming," meaning the French.

The atmosphere became overspread with an unusual darkness, the thunder began to roll, the lightning was vivid, and the rain fell in torrents. During the storm a whole troop of horses galloped past at full speed without their riders, having broke loose from fright caused by the loud claps of thunder.* Continuing our march, we soon bivouacked about two miles from Salamanca, our left wing resting on the Tormes, and in vain attempted to screen ourselves from the pelting of the storm. However, the morning of the 22nd broke beautiful and serene; and at six o'clock we heard to our right, and about two miles to the front, a brisk fire of small arms, which continued for an hour, and then died away. The enemy had attacked the seventh division, to ascertain whether the Duke intended to give up Salamanca. Poor little Freer was washing his shirt, when the order came to fall in at eleven o'clock, and was

* Nothing could harbinger a bloody day more awfully than the elemental uproar of the night which preceded the day of Salamanca. Crash succeeded crash, and in rapid flashes the lightning played over height and valley, while torrents burst from the riven clouds, and swelled all the streams to torrents. Terrified by the storm, the horses broke from their picketings, and rushing madly to and fro, added to the confusion. One flash killed several belonging to the 5th dragoon-guards; and many of the men were seriously injured in their attempts to recover the infuriated animals.—ED.

under the necessity of putting it on wringing wet.

Our division advanced and took up the ground the seventh division had occupied in the morning. The wood extended a short way to our front. The division was formed in open column, concealed from the enemy, who were stationed in small force a mile to the front, with two pieces of artillery. From our situation we formed a corps of reserve, communicating with the third division placed on the top of the conical hill of Cabrerizes, on our extreme left, and rather in advance of us on the right bank of the Tormes.

We had no sooner piled arms than I began to look about me. The *Table Mountain* was a short way to our right, and a mile to the front, with a very large mass of troops formed behind it in contiguous columns, with one red regiment presenting their front towards the enemy, in *line*, at the top of it. Large bodies of cavalry, three divisions of infantry, with a proportion of artillery, composed the right of the army in the plain; also a corps of *Spanish Patriots*. Placed thus, who could have thought the Duke intended that day to retreat? I *never did*. Nor could I see any reason for it: it seemed the Duke's game to beat the French before *El Rey* Joseph made his appearance with an additional force.

The arrangement of our troops was inimitable; years could not have improved it. Bear in mind, our right had been fairly turned since the 20th, the army were presenting a new front, so that the *first* or *last*, whichever you may please to call it, of military movements was to be effected—that is, for the contending armies to *change places*. The French could not attack our left that day; if they had, the right of their army must have been either surrounded or cut to pieces. The third division would have hung on their flank, the light division would have engaged them in front, the masses behind the Table Mountain could have debouched on either side, while our cavalry, artillery, and the rest of the army, could have moved forward, and attacked the left of the French in the plain, which must have advanced to support such a movement. The Table Mountain is the mark of the French fieldmarshal's discomfiture. Military men say, the French ought to have taken possession of it; but was their army up, and strong enough to maintain it? The advance of the enemy, at six o'clock in the morning, was not that of their whole force; I should say that it was merely a *réconnoissance;* half a dozen squadrons of cavalry, and a division of infantry, must not be taken for a whole army. Nor had the French soldiers wings; for, in justice to them, more could not have been done by legs. The Duke of Ragusa might have had his army in hand, and could have placed a corps of observation where his centre stood; then, towards evening, have manœuvred with his main body at a greater distance from our right flank, and threatened to cut us off from Rodrigo (and thereby change positions with us) until nightfall; at the same time keeping his communications open with Alba de Tormes, in the event of his not deeming it advisable to follow up such a movement the next day; at all events, the French general would have gained time, which was precious to him, as reinforcements were on the road to join him. The fact was, the French marshal was completely out-generaled; the Table Mountain puzzled him; and the third division descending from Cabrerizes at twelve o'clock, and raising clouds of dust as they passed along the rear of our army, caused Marmont to imagine that we were drawing off, which I am confident led him to take hasty measures, forgetting that he had been manœuvering only on *blank* ground the four previous days. The Duke of Wellington saw his over haste and his error; knowing that to support such an extension of the left, the enemy ought to have advanced in force on the village of the Arapiles, or expose their left to a flank attack, which they did. On the other hand, had they advanced towards the Arapiles in the plain in force, our right and centre would have become engaged, and the troops concealed behind the Table Mountain could have debouched, and hovered on their right flank; however, owing to the confusion in our centre, caused by a division giving way from being attacked in front and flank, much time was lost in restoring order, and preventing the French from exhausting that part of our line : it was their only resource.

This was the first *general action* fought on the Peninsula where the Duke of Wellington *attacked*, which led Marmont still farther from his reckoning. The Duke, of course, did not wish to fritter away his army in useless skirmishes, and therefore only waited for a *fit moment* to bring it fairly in contact with the enemy, to *finish* well when once commenced; and as the French marshal brought himself to action within the precincts of Salamanca, the advantage was ours, the wounded soldiers having speedy assistance, while those of the enemy who managed to drag themselves far from the field, endured the most distressing privations.

The field of battle generally was composed of light sand, with a few straggling blades of parched grass. A very light breeze blew towards the French, which gave them the benefit of the clouds of dust and the volumes of smoke arising from the immense masses in motion, notwithstanding the heavy rain on the preceding night. Near one p. m. the third division were passing in rear of ours. The first battalion of the 5th regiment had joined them on the 20th. I was strolling about, here and there coming across a dead or wounded soldier of those who had fallen in the morning, when a Portuguese caught my attention. He was resting on his elbows, with his legs extended, suffering indescribable pain from a wound in his stomach; his face pale, his lips discoloured, and stifled groans issued from his nearly lifeless body, while an almost tropical sun was shining on his uncovered head. Soon after the third division had reached its destination, a column of French descended a hill *en masse* on our extreme right. Three eighteen-pounders opened on them, which took full effect, and spoiled their regularity. The enemy hesitated, while the discharges of our heavy ordnance were overthrowing all opposition. They went to the right-about to get out of range. Our columns, formed behind the Table Mountain, now debouched in double time, shewing the French marshal that the long-expected crisis was at hand. A sharp fire of musketry opened on the fourth division as they broke through the village of the Arapiles at half-past two. The third division had already brought up their right shoulders, and were pushing on very successfully, when the enemy's horse furiously charged the grenadiers and right of the 5th regiment while advancing in line, which they repulsed, and steadily continued their movement. The fire gradually increasing, at half past four the armies were well in contact. The musketry rolled without intermission, only interrupted by the still louder artillery. The fourth division, breathless, amidst showers of grape, musketry, and round-shot, had succeeded in planting their standards on the crest of the enemy's position; but at that moment a French division, in close column, and at a run, with fixed bayonets, forced them down the hill, whilst others advanced on their left flank, which was exposed, and carried the centre of the battle again into the valley; but our heavy cavalry, in the right centre, were bearing down all opposition, driving the left of the enemy before them, and putting them into the greatest confusion. Major-General Le Marchant was killed heading this charge. At six the battle was at the height—no cessation of musketry, and the cannon of both armies thundering away as if there were to be no end of it. The columns of smoke and dust were rolling up in dense volumes, so that the atmosphere became dark above the bloody scene; yet there was not a cloud to be descried, except those which arose from the battle. A Spanish peasant was looking on with his arms folded; I heard him exclaim, *" Que grandisimo mundo!"**

The inhabitants of Salamanca crowded the places of public worship, to offer up prayers for the success of our arms. *Apropos,* it was Sunday.

At half-past six, a brigade of Portuguese guns opened on the enemy, in front of our division. At seven, one of the Duke's *aids-de-camp* rode up and ordered our division to move on the left to attack. We moved towards the Table Mountain, right brigade in front, in open column; having passed it, we then closed to column of quarter distance. The enemy's skirmishers soon advanced, and opened a brisk fire. The shades of evening now approached, and the flashes of cannon and small arms in the centre and on the heights were still vivid, while the enemy were making their last struggle for victory. An English officer of General Pack's brigade passed us, covered with dust and

* He was the only peasant I ever saw in a battle, except one, who offered his services at Vittoria, to conduct our division over an unprotected bridge, when the second shot fired took off the poor fellow's head.

perspiration; he complained of the rough usage of the French. They allowed the Portuguese to approach nearly to the summit of the point of attack, then charged them, and used the bayonet without remorse, taking that part of the field under their especial protection.

The enemy's light infantry increased, and retired very deliberately; the ascent was gentle. The first brigade deployed, supported by the second; the first division was marching in reserve.

Our skirmishers were obliged to give ground to the obstinacy of the enemy. The line of the 43rd was one of the finest specimens of discipline I ever saw—as steady as rocks, with Colonel William Napier twenty yards in front of the corps, alone; he was the point of direction. Our skirmishers ceased firing, and the line marched over them, dead and alive. I expected to see our chief unhorsed, and carried away in a blanket.

Appearances indicated a severe fight, for we were near the enemy's reserves. The Duke of Wellington was within fifty yards of the front, when the enemy's lines commenced firing. I thought he was exposing himself unnecessarily, the more so, as I heard he had put every division into action that day. The Duke *ordered us to halt* within two hundred yards of the enemy. They gave us two volleys with cheers, while our cavalry galloped forward to threaten their right flank. At this time I heard that a musket-ball had perforated the Duke's cloak, folded in front of his saddle. As we were about to charge, the enemy disappeared. This advance was beautifully executed.

Night coming on, the firing died away. Thus ended a battle which bore on the destinies of Europe, by showing the decline of French power in Spain, leaving the British army for the first time free to pursue them at pleasure. It lasted six hours. Our line continued to advance until *midnight*. A French cavalry picquet fired on us at ten; the *ruse de guerre* would not do. We bivouacked round a village.

Marmont was badly wounded, and carried off the field by a company of French grenadiers. He had manœuvred well; from the 19th till the battle, he had moved round our flank on a half-circle.

As morning dawned on the 23rd, the light division advanced, supported by the first division, and crossing the ford, near Huerta, formed *en masse* in a valley, while the heavy Germans ascended the hill, moving on the left of the enemy; after some time we debouched. The heavy Germans made a brilliant charge, and broke the French rear guard, formed on the side of a hill near La Serna. They suffered much. The whole of the enemy had not formed square. I observed five hundred stand of muskets on their left, lying on the ground in line, as if they had been piled and knocked down, and the owners had shifted as well as they could; the muskets were not grounded to the front, but lying sideways. The enemy only formed two squares. I saw a man and horse dead, the rider still in his saddle. They must have received their mortal wounds at the same instant. On mounting the hill, the enemy's army were in full view, in one great mass. Our horse artillery threw some shot into them. The troops soon halted, and the enemy were seen no more.

EVENTS SUBSEQUENT TO THE BATTLE AND ADVANCE FROM SALAMANCA.

No battle, since that of Marengo, in 1800, which opened the gates of Vienna to the first consul of France, has been fought, whose consequences ought to be more duly appreciated than the battle of Salamanca.

While the north of Europe attracted the notice of the world by the gigantic efforts made by the French Emperor to conquer and to crush Russia, all eyes were at the same time turned towards the Peninsula, in the hope, though not exactly in the expectation, of seeing a stand made there, which might mar the designs of one who, it would appear, was determined, at all hazards, to lay prostrate at his feet the civilized world, from the port of Archangel to the bay of Cadiz.

Philosophers, historians, and statesmen, were all on the tiptoe of expectation to witness an event which, while it puzzled many as to its probable result, made nine-tenths of Europe turn pale for the consequences. Independent of any other reasons—and there were many of much heavier weight in the scale—curiosity prompted many to reason as to the probability of one extraordinary, but certainly great man, being able to wield two armies with success in climes so many hundred leagues distant from each other at one and the same moment. A war carried on on such a vast scale has not been recorded in modern times at least; and it may not come amiss to the reader if I touch on the consequences that might have followed the defeat of the British army on the plains of Salamanca, as also the results that actually followed that splendid victory.

Had that battle been lost, the disasters of the French army before Moscow would have been of little account in the scale of the south, and the Imperial Eagles would have soared with the same splendour, from Madrid to Cadiz, or perhaps to Lisbon, as if no event of importance had occurred beyond the Vistula. Portugal would have been then open to invasion—the siege of Cadiz continued—the lines of Lisbon once more invested—and what then? Why, the probable withdrawal of the British army from the Peninsula. Portugal would be thus conquered—Spain laid prostrate—England in utter dismay, and 150,000 veteran French troops marched across the Pyrenees to take a part in the combats of Leipsic and Lutzen. Those would have been the results of a defeat at Salamanca; and who is the man bold enough to say what the results in the north of Europe would have been, had such an augmentation of force, which would have been certain, joined Napoleon in the end of 1812, or even in the spring of 1813? As it was, he gained the battle of Lutzen with a "green army." Had he been backed by 150,000 veteran troops from Spain, it requires no conjuror to tell what the upshot would have been. Those are the consequences which would have followed a defeat at Salamanca. The gaining that battle placed matters on a different footing; Portugal had nothing to dread; Soult was forced to raise the siege of Cadiz; Madrid was evacuated; and Castille and Andalusia were freed from the presence of a French force; but, above all, no reinforcement of any account durst leave Spain to succour the French army in the north of Europe.

The battle of Salamanca was not only a hard-fought battle—a battle of points—but it was a parade battle in the fullest acceptation of the word. It was unlike those that had preceded it, where the bravery, and the bravery only, of the British soldier was to be called into the scale, and nothing else left to him but to defend the ground he occupied "to the death." But on this day the British soldier proved that he was as quick in movement as the redoubtable imperial veteran, and that he was able to foil him with his own weapon—rapidity of motion.*

* Of the marshals, none handled troops more beautifully than the Duke of Ragusa; and during the late operations, he had both out-marched and out-flanked the allied general; and yet, in all the variety of rapid evolutions his complicated movements had required, he had never left an opening for his

At ten o'clock at night, Lord Wellington, at the head of 12,000 infantry and 2000 horsemen, was in pursuit of the routed and discomfited army of Marmont, while the bulk of his own soldiers lay on the field of battle. The results of that battle were—prisoners, 130 officers, 7500 men, two eagles, and fourteen guns. The field of battle was heaped with the slain, and the total loss of the enemy may be estimated at 17,000; it has been reckoned by some writers as exceeding 20,000, but I apprehend I am nearer the mark, and that 17,000 was the outside. The dead and wounded on the side of the British and Portuguese (for the grand Spanish army, commanded by Don Carlos de Espana, lost but four!) were nearly 5000; but the greater number of the Portuguese either fell in their feeble attempt against the Arapiles height, or by the shot that passed over the first line, composed of British,

watchful antagonist to attack. If Wellington received a battle, the repulse of his assailant, and the winning a few trophies, would have brought no paramount advantages. Success demands a sacrifice; victory must be purchased with a loss; to cripple would be to defeat; for, when joined by the army of the centre, could Wellington, with weakened numbers, withstand an antagonist re-inforced by 12,000 men? To fight without delay, and not fight at disadvantage, was scarcely possible. Days passed. No error allowed the opportunity, for every movement was made with admirable skill. For one moment, however, Marmont's good genius was asleep—his order of march severed the left from the centre of his army. Wellington saw the mistake; the fault was flagrant, and he fixed it with the stroke of a thunderbolt."—MAXWELL's LIFE OF WELLINGTON.

which fell at random amongst the Portuguese placed in the rear.

I have already said, that at one period the battle was in doubt, and that it was prolonged until nearly ten at night. But what caused the delay, the doubt—the total annihilation of Marmont's 50,000 men? No; the failure of Pack's Portuguese brigade. Their failure caused the prolongation of the battle to ten at night, when there was a fair prospect of its successful termination at eight. Had it been finished at that hour, how was it possible for Marmont to escape in broad day with one man of his army, pursued as he was by three superb divisions that had not pulled a trigger in the battle? The thing was morally impossible.

Some there were who said, in the excitement of the moment, that Lord Wéllington was to blame, because he placed too much confidence in the Portuguese under Pack. Perhaps he was; indeed, the result proved that he was wrong in his estimate of this brigade; but how could he suppose that a body of 2000 men, opposed at most to 400, seeing the battle at all points going in their favour, and commanded, too, by such a battle-general as Pack, would allow themselves, in the view, and within hail of their gallant and victorious comrades, the British, to be beaten by a handful of men that did not count more than one-fifth of their number? Yet so it was. The fate of this momentous battle was kept in doubt, and what was, if possible, worse, prolonged for two hours; the total annihilation of the army of Portugal, which must have followed, averted, and the British general actually robbed of the fairest field he ever had of destroying, to a man, one of the most formidable and carefully-organized French armies he was ever opposed to.

I am aware that many may differ from these my opinions, but I speak from experience; and notwithstanding all that has been said and written of the Portuguese troops, I still hold the opinion that they are utterly incompetent to stand, with any chance of success, before even half their own numbers of Frenchmen; and if the front line of British at Salamanca had been worsted, every man of the Portuguese army, instead of supporting them, would have turned tail. The victory was, nevertheless, a glorious one, and was as much owing to the presumption of the French marshal, as to the bravery of the British troops, and the wise combinations of their general; because the inconsistency of the Duke of Ragusa was palpable in seizing on the line of communication of an army that had offered battle but two days before on the plains of Velosa. This confirms the maxim which has oftentimes been repeated, that those principles should never be departed from which the art of war prescribes; and that circumspection should be invariably attended to which obliges all commanders never to swerve from rules which, even when *everything favours such meditated projects*, the surest way is never so far to despise an enemy as to suppose him incapable of resistance. Good or ill fortune is decided in a moment; chance never resigns its rights; nevertheless, in this very battle, the failure of Pack was nigh being fatal to the British; yet it must be acknowledged that the description of the British troops that fought at Salamanca, and the qualities of the general who commanded them, considered, no great doubts could be entertained of the issue of the battle, notwithstanding the unlooked for failure of the Portuguese under Pack. Of forty British battalions, twenty-two only were in action, and carried the victory; and it may be said, without any great metaphorical sketch, or much alteration in the words of Frederick King of Prussia, that the world rested not more securely on the shoulders of Atlas, than England on such an army and such a general.

No one ought to be surprised that the victory was not more complete, and the French closer pursued: both were impossible. The attack against the French line was unavoidably delayed until five; it never would have taken place but for the false movement of Marmont's seventh division; and the unlooked for failure of Pack's Portuguese brigade prolonged the battle until it was too late to profit by its results. Night had set in; the wooded country near the Tormes favoured the French in their flight; and to all those circumstances is attributable the escape of a single man of the French army of Portugal.

The battle, though short, was one continued effort; and although the desperate fighting of Clinton's men re-established it towards its close, it was not possible for a single division, no matter how brave, to undo altogether what had been effected by Pack's failure. The time lost could not be recalled, and Lord Wellington saw, without being able to control it, two-thirds of the French army scrambling, in a manner, from his grasp.

The troops that had gained the victory lay buried in sleep until two o'clock of the morning following, when the arrival of the mules carrying rum aroused them from their slumber; but the parties sent out in search of water had not yet reached the field. The soldiers, with parching lips, their tongues cleaving to their mouths from thirst, their limbs benumbed with cold, and their bodies enfeebled by a long abstinence from food, and the exertion of the former day, ran to the casks, and each man drank a fearful quantity. This for a short time satisfied them; but a burning thirst followed this rash proceeding, and before any water arrived, we were more in need of it than at the close of the battle.

The inhabitants of Salamanca, who had a clear view of all that was passing, hastened to the spot, to afford all the relief in their power. Several cars, most of them loaded with provisions, reached the field of battle before morning; and it is but due to those people to state, that their attentions were unremitting, and of the most disinterested kind, for they sought no emolument. They brought fruit, and even quantities of water, well knowing how distant from us, and how scantily the country near the field of battle was provided with so necessary a relief to men who had not tasted a drop for so many hours, under a burning sun, and oppressed with the fatigue they had endured during the fight.

The soldiers, thus refreshed, forgot all their toil, and proceeded to examine those parts of the field where each battalion had been most engaged. The men of Wallace's brigade naturally turned their attention to the hill they had won, and to the flat space behind it, where Le Marchant's horse had so gallantly seconded them: at both they found ample food for reflection—for a horrible massacre had taken place there! Hundreds of human beings lying dead, or what is worse, mutilated in a frightful manner—horses mangled by shot or shell, running here and there in disorder, or lying in a helpless state, still endeavouring to eat a mouthful of grass around the spot which it was evident they could never leave. Those beautiful animals, unconscious of the cause of their agony, looked at us as we passed them, and their sufferings touched the heart of many a veteran, who never knew what it was to feel a tear moisten his cheek: but a field of battle, after a battle, is not easy of description; it is a fearful sight, even for those who are the victors. Men looking after their tried old friends and companions—women and children seeking for their husbands or fathers —looking for those whom destiny had decreed that they should never again behold, except as lifeless corpses, or as objects more to be shunned than sought after, is a frightful but too true a sketch of a battle-field. Those who but a short time before were in the prime of life and vigour, now lying dead—rode down—trampled into atoms, with not a vestige of face recognisable, is a melancholy feature in war, and a trying sight to witness, much less describe; yet, nevertheless, many of the brave men who have taken a part in those battles —who have shared in all those dangers, and some who have volunteered their services on occasions when, without such gallant men, matters might have taken a different turn—when in place of a victory being proclaimed, a defeat would perhaps have been announced—are passed over unnoticed and unrewarded!

During the battle there were many circumstances which, if related in their places at the period they occurred, would have broken in upon the narrative, but may be told with more propriety now.

When the third division under Packenham had crossed the flat, and were moving against the crest of the hill occupied by Foy's tirailleurs, a number of Caçadores commanded by Major Haddock were in advance of us. The moment the French fire opened, those troops which had been placed to cover our advance, lay down on their faces, not for the purpose of taking aim with more accuracy, but in order to save their own sconces from the French fire. Haddock dismounted from his horse and began belabouring with the flat side of his sabre the dastardly troops he had the misfortune to command, but in vain; all sense of shame had fled after the first discharge of grape and musketry, and poor Haddock might as well have attempted to move the great cathedral of Salamanca as the soldiers of his Majesty the King of Portugal.

At the time the colonel of the 22nd French regiment stepped out of the ranks and shot Major Murphy dead at the head of his regiment, the 88th, a number of officers were beside Murphy. It is not easy at such a moment to be certain who is the person singled out. The two officers who carried the colours of the regiment, and who were immediately in the rear of the mounted officers, thought that the shot was intended for either of them. Lieutenant Moriarty, carrying the regimental flag, called out, "That fellow is aiming at me!" "I hope so," replied Lieutenant D'Arcy, who carried the other colour, with great coolness —"I hope so, for I thought he had *me* covered." He was not much mistaken: the ball that killed Murphy, after passing through him, struck the staff of the flag carried by D'Arcy, and also carried away the button and part of the strap of his epaulette! This fact is not told as an extraordinary occurrence, that the ball which killed one man should strike the coat of him that happened to stand in his rear, for such casualties were by no means uncommon with us; but I mention it as a strong proof of the great coolness of the British line in their advance against the enemy's column.

The staff of the wounded pole and its companion, have been with good taste and true soldier-like feeling, preserved by Colonel O'Mally, who now commands the 88th, and he has, by special permission, been allowed to fix on the old poles —the silent evidence of many a hard-fought day —the new colours that have been presented to the 88th. It was a happy thought, and I doubt not but there are many officers at the head of regiments, who, when they hear of it, will feel regret at not having done the like. On the wounded pole there is engraved, on a plate of silver, the day, and the manner in which it was so mutilated, and when the " Connaught Rangers" again take the field against the enemies of their country, if the sight of those *bits of stick* don't inspire them with a proper recollection of the former deeds of the regiment—the sooner they go back to their native homes the better.

It may be asked why I dwell so much on the *poles* that carry the *colours?* I do so, first, because I think that the touch—the very sight of those "bits o' stick" is sufficient to inspire men who have never before fought beside them, with a feeling that they ought to look up to them, and if they cannot add to their lustre, at least never to forsake or allow them to fall into the hands of the enemy. But I turn to the *poles* in preference to the *colours*, because the former stand firm on their *own deeds!*—they may be lopped down—cut smaller—shaved to a shred !— but still, there they are, the very same identical poles that were present in every battle which the silk that out-tops them *ought* to mention ! One battle (the battle of the Pyrenees) has been withheld from the 88th; and it is a singular fact, that a part of that regiment* was in a most particular manner distinguished on the very day for which it is, in a manner, disgraced: for most unquestionably, if it be an honour for a regiment to receive a badge for a battle, it is a disgrace to them if one is withheld from them on the day they have been under fire with the enemy.

When the cavalry of Le Marchant passed through Wallace's brigade, in their advance against Foy's column, Captain William Mackie, of the 88th, the discountenanced leader of the forlorn hope at Ro-

* On the 28th of July, 1813, when the third and fourth British divisions occupied a post in the Pyrenees, the latter was warmly engaged, and every regiment belonging to it charged with the bayonet; but the third division was unmolested, although menaced, until about five o'clock in the afternoon. At this time a considerable body of the enemy's tirailleurs pressed forward to that part of the ridge occupied by the third division, and immediately in front of the 88th regiment, the light infantry company of which, commanded by Captain Robert Nickle, was ordered to drive back this force: he did so in the most gallant manner; but the enemy could ill brook such a defeat, the more annoying, as it was witnessed by our third division, as also by a considerable *portion of one of the enemy's corps d' armée*. A reinforcement, commanded by an officer of distinction, rushed forward to redeem the tarnished honour of their nation, while some of the battalion-men of the Connaught Rangers, seeing the unequal contest their light infantry company were about to be engaged in—for *the French* were upwards of one hundred to sixty of ours—hastened to take a part in the fray. The detachment of the 88th lay behind a low ditch, and waited, until the French approached to within a few yards of them; they came on in gallant style, headed by their brave commanding officer, who was most conspicuous, being several

drigo, who acted as *aid-de-camp* to Colonel Alexander Wallace, was *missing!* In the confusion that prevailed, it was thought he had fallen! No one could give any account of him; but in a short lapse of time, after the cavalry had charged, he returned, covered with dust and blood, his horse tottering from fatigue, and nothing left of his sabre—but the hilt! He joined the cavalry so soon as the fighting amongst the infantry had ceased, and those who knew the temperament of the man were not surprised at it: wherever glory and danger were to be met, there was Mackie to be

paces in front of his men. The soldiers of the two armies, posted at a distance, and lookers on at this *national trial*, shouted with joy as they beheld their respective comrades on the eve of engaging with each other. But this feeling on the part of the French was but of short duration, for at the first fire their detachment turned tail, and were what they themselves would term "culbutés," leaving their brave commandant, with many others, mortally wounded behind. Captain Robert Nickle ran up to his bleeding opponent, and rendered him every assistance in his power. He then advanced alone, with his handkerchief tied on the point of his sword, which he held up as a token of amity, and, thus re-assured, some of the French soldiers returned without their arms, and carried away their officer with them. They were delighted with the considerate conduct of Captain Nickle, and embraced our men on parting. Perhaps, for so much, there never was a more gallant exploit; and it may be better conceived than expressed what the feelings of the bystanders must have been. It may also be asked what favour was granted to the brave 88th for their distinguished behaviour? THEY ARE THE ONLY REGIMENT OF THE BRIGADE TO WHICH THEY BELONGED THAT IS NOT ALLOWED TO BEAR THE BADGE OF THIS BATTLE (termed Pyrenees) ON THEIR COLOURS!!!

found, and nothing—not even the chilling slights he had experienced—could damp his daring spirit.

At the first dawn of the morning of the 23rd of July, Lord Wellington continued the pursuit of the defeated army of Marmont. He placed himself at the head of the light division, which opened the march, followed by the heavy German cavalry under General Bock, and Anson's brigade of light horse. Those two superb brigades of dragoons had only joined the army the night before. The first division of infantry, composed of the Guards and German Legion, followed the cavalry, and Lord Wellington, at the head of 13,000 men that had not pulled a trigger, or unsheathed a sabre in the battle, followed the enemy back, but the retreat was so quick that Marmont's head-quarters were thirty miles from Salamanca the day after the battle. Nevertheless, the corps that covered the retreat, consisting of three battalions of infantry and five regiments of cavalry, were attained near the village of Lerena. The infantry formed themselves into a square, the cavalry were posted on the flanks for its support, but the panic, with which all were infected by the defeat of the preceding day, had taken such a fast hold of them, that the French horse in advance could not be prevailed upon to show a front. This threw those that were at hand to support them into disorder: confusion was communicated to the remainder, and the field of battle was precipitately abandoned by the cavalry, who, in the most unaccountable manner, left their companions, the infantry, to their fate.

The cavalry having thus fled, Bock, with his German horse, gallopped at the square, and breaking through it, slew or took prisoners the entire; and the contest ended in one dreadful massacre of the French infantry. Nevertheless, many of the troopers fell; for one regiment in particular, the 105th French, bravely stood their ground, but the ponderous weight of the heavy cavalry broke down all resistance; and arms lopped off, heads cloven to the spine, or gashes across the breast and shoulders, showed to those who afterwards passed the spot the fearful encounter that had taken place; and from this moment nothing more of the army of Portugal was to be seen.

If anything was wanting to prove what I have before said of the certainty of the total annihilation of this army on the 22nd, at Salamanca—had that battle not been prolonged until dark by the failure of the Portuguese under Pack—the overthrow of the rear-guard on the following day, after such a lapse of time, when the spirits of the enemy had a reasonable time to recruit and refresh themselves, is a sufficient evidence of the manner in which they would have behaved on the field of battle in the midst of their routed companions—in the hearing of the shouts of their victorious opponents—opposed to that invincible infantry, which no fire, poured in as it was from the formidable masses that it broke through, could shake — under the edges of those sabres that cut in piecemeal their best organized squares! Behaving as this rear-guard did on the day after the battle, when the rout had ceased, and was converted into a regular retreat—acting thus, I ask, is not the conclusion I have come to as to what might, or rather ought to have been the result of the battle of Salamanca, a fair estimate?

The overthrow of the rear-guard, which covered the flight of the army of the Duke of Ragusa, and the rapid manner in which Clausel made good his retreat from the heights of La Serena, where that army for the last time made any show of a stand against the British troops that had defeated him on the plains of Salamanca, finished the campaign, so far, at least, as regarded the army of Portugal.

The leading regiments followed the enemy's track as far as Flores de Avila, which town, distant ten leagues from Salamanca, had been evacuated by them two days after the battle. The cavalry and artillery of the northern army met them on their retreat near Arevela; but nothing—not even this reinforcement—could inspire them with confidence; and the mass of fugitives hastily followed the road leading to Valladolid.

The good generalship displayed by Clausel, and the steady front he shewed when in the presence of a victorious army, raised him considerably, and justly so, in the estimation of his own troops; but all his skill would have been of no avail, had the battle not been unavoidably prolonged until dark.

The British general continued the pursuit; but for what end? The moment for crushing, to a man, that formidable army, was lost at Salamanca; and he might, with as much chance of success, have attempted to catch the tail of a comet as the tail of the army that fled before him. The failure of Pack ruined all. One flitting hour, lost by that failure, was productive of the disastrous results which followed—but of them hereafter. War, with all its terrible accompaniments, is a fearful-sounding thing; yet it is, nevertheless, a complicated and delicate web, the meshes of which require to be as delicately handled as if they were composed of the finest materials. The least false touch may destroy all its arrangement; and that which cost so much time and labour to render perfect, may be undone by falling into hands unable to appreciate its texture. But to speak without any metaphorical aid, so it is with soldiers going into battle. Their commander makes his arrangements—allots to each corps, brigade, or division, the part they have to take in the accomplishment of his end—the defeat of his foe. If any one part give way, the whole machinery becomes unhinged—broken up; and the repairing of it oftentimes costs more than the original outlay; or, more properly speaking, *than the cost of the repair is worth*, and the end sought for—*is lost!*

So it was at Salamanca. The failure of Pack's brigade caused the loss of half the fourth division; and the bloody conflict which the sixth, under Clinton, were engaged in, to save not only Cole's troops, but the general issue of the battle, never would have taken place had the Portuguese done their duty. But the fate of a battle often hangs, as it were, by a hair. At Marengo, when the day was, to all appearance, lost to the army of the First Consul, Dessaix arrived on the field. It was two o'clock. Napoleon asked his opinion— "What do you think of it?" said the First Consul. Dessaix replied, with the bluntness of a soldier, "By G—d, it is lost!—but," said he, at the same time taking out his watch, "it is only two o'clock, and we have time enough left to gain a battle yet." Dessaix's division gained the battle of Marengo— Clinton's decided Salamanca. The former was the principal cause, by his conduct, of gaining that memorable battle; but how did the French nation pay a tribute to his memory?—by a paltry subscription of a few pounds towards the erection of a pillar which is a disgrace to the nation.

The march of the British army continued without interruption. Those divisions which followed the enemy were enthusiastically welcomed as they passed through the different towns and villages on the Valladolid road; the inhabitants flocking in vast numbers with a supply of wine, fruit, bread, and vegetables, which were all bought up by the soldiers. Arrived at Valladolid, and finding himself as far as ever from being able to overtake the army of Marmont, Lord Wellington made a full stop. Giving the army one day's rest, for the purpose of allowing the stragglers to come up, he, on the 1st of August, turned off abruptly towards the grand Madrid road; while Hill, with the second corps, reached Zafra.

Marmont being thus disposed of for the present, and Lord Wellington having formed the resolution of marching to the Spanish capital, every road leading to it was occupied, and thronged by cavalry, infantry, and artillery, baggage and commissariat mules, stores of all descriptions, the reserve parks of guns, and the followers of the camp, such as suttlers, Portuguese servants, and women who followed the soldiers. Those, when assembled together, formed one vast mass of between 60,000 and 70,000 souls. The sight was an imposing one; the weather was beautifully fine, and the advance of the army as it moved onward towards the capital, was one scene of uninterrupted rejoicing. Never was the general feeling in Spain so much in favour of the British nation, the British army, and the hero who commanded it, as on the present occasion. The news of the great victory gained by the British army only a few days before, under the walls of Salamanca, which was witnessed by thousands upon thousands of Spaniards, was spread afar; and the different routes which the army traversed were crowded almost to suffocation by the Spanish people, who vied with each other to gain a passing view of the men who had so distinguished themselves, and to supply them with every assistance in their power. Every face was cheerful; and at the termination of each day's march, our bivouacs, or the villages we occupied, were crowded with Spanish girls and young men, who either brought wine, lemonade, or fruit; the evening was wound up by boleros and fandangos; and, in short, our march to Madrid more resembled a triumphal procession—which, in point of fact, it really was—

than the ordinary advance of an army prepared for battle.

Meanwhile, the King of Spain hastily endeavoured to make arrangements to stop the torrent which threatened his capital. He had advanced upon Blasko Sancho, on the 25th of July; but there hearing of the fate that had befallen his favourite General at Salamanca, he retraced his steps, and gaining the passes of the Guadarama, retired towards the palace of the Escurial. He collected all the disposable force that could be taken from the capital; but his army, chiefly composed of *Jurementados*, (Spaniards that entered into King Joseph's service,) counted not quite 15,000 bayonets and sabres—a force, as to number, without taking into account its *morale*, not of that formidableness very likely to disconcert the grand designs of Lord Wellington. In short, the army continued its march towards the Spanish capital without molestation. On the 6th of August, the head-quarters were at Cuellar; on the 7th, at the ancient town of Segovia, so celebrated in Spanish romance; and on the 8th, the divisions destined to march upon Madrid were concentrated at Saint Ildefonso.

Saint Ildefonso is beautifully situated. The magnificent waterworks, the elegant taste with which the gardens and pleasure-grounds are laid out, and the vast concourse of people who thronged them on the day of our arrival, gave to it the appearance, in our eyes at least, of the most enchanting spot on the face of the globe. At each of the principal walks bands of music played inspiring airs; and at half-past six in the evening the water-works were in full play. Those works, situate at the base of a lofty blue mountain, cast up water to an immense height; and one in particular seemed to us to be much superior to anything we afterwards witnessed at either Versailles or St. Cloud. To me it certainly seems so; but I, in common with many others, may be wrong; for, in truth, we were so charmed with the novelty of the scene we then witnessed, and the vast contrast it presented to the scenes we had, for such a length of time, not only witnessed, but taken an active part in, that all due allowance ought to be made, if we are wrong, for our prepossession in favour of this spot.

At eight o'clock Lord Wellington, surrounded by a number of generals of different nations, a splendid staff, and many grandees of Spain, entered the gardens. All the bands, at one and the same moment, played, "See the Conquering Hero Comes," the singers joined in chorus, and the vast multitude rent the air with acclamations. The females, disregarding all form or etiquette, broke through the crowd to get a nearer view of his lordship, and many embraced him as he passed down the different alleys of the gardens. The groups of singers continued to sing; this was succeeded by bolero dancing, fandango dancing, and waltzing; and all was wound up by one of the most intoxicating and delightful nights of pleasure that we had ever witnessed, and, if I mistake not greatly, that was ever acted on the same spot. It was late before we retired to rest; and, indeed, we had need of repose. Our minds as well as bodies required it; and when the shrill note of the bugle the following morning (for that matter it was the same morning) aroused us from our sleep, all that had passed seemed but as a dream. It was no dream notwithstanding; and many an old curmudgeon of a Don little dreamt, though we might, of the gambols his wife had been acting the night before.

At six o'clock on the morning of the 9th we were again in motion. Indeed, we had been "in motion" with a vengeance the entire of the preceding night, but on the morning of the 9th we were in motion towards the centre of Spain. The night before we had also been in motion, but certainly not towards the centre of gravity! No matter. We, as I said before, were now on the high road to Madrid; before that, we were on " the road to ruin."

The causeway leading to Madrid is broad and well arranged. As we reached each league-stone, we counted with anxiety the distance we had yet to pace ere we arrived at the capital of Spain. The mountains which overhang the Guadarama passes are bold and lofty. Those passes, easy of defence, and requiring but a small force, were abandoned without a musket-shot being fired for their protection; and, in fine, on the 11th, Lord Wellington was near the village of Majalahonde, distant but one march from the capital. Thirty thousand infantry were encamped half a league in its rear; the different brigades of horse and artillery attached to the infantry were at hand. In short all was in readiness, but the advanced guard of cavalry, unfortunately intrusted to the brigade of Portuguese of D'Urban, was in front of all. Behind them, at the distance of a mile, were the two regiments of heavy German horse, while the splendid "parc" of horse-artillery, commanded by Captain Macdonald, was ready to support D'Urban.

The greatest part of the day had passed over without any event taking place between the advanced posts. Some slight skirmishing with the enemy's lancers and D'Urban's cavalry left matters as they were at the commencement. The army was preparing its arrangements for the night's repose, and the march of the following day, when the thunder of Macdonald's artillery aroused us in an instant from our occupations. It was soon manifest that the enemy's advance had attacked the Portuguese cavalry; and the vast cloud of dust that came rolling onwards towards the village where the German horse were placed in reserve, told but too plainly that the Portuguese were routed, and the Germans about to be cut off. The infantry betook themselves to their arms, and in a few moments the entire were in readiness to march to the scene of action, for so in fact it was. The Portuguese dragoons fled at the first onset, without waiting to exchange one sabre-cut with the French; and so rapid was their flight, for they rode through the village where the reserve of

Germans were posted to support them, that not more than half of the Germans were mounted. Many brave men thus fell before they could defend themselves, and their colonel was cut down while in the act of shaving himself; but his brave soldiers, forming themselves together in the best manner the time would admit of, closed with drawn sabres upon the French lancers, which turned the stream, broke the mad fury of the attack, and drove back the lancers in confusion. Up to this time the combat was one scene of desperation. An irregular and furious crowd might be seen mixed together, fighting without order or regularity; and from the confusion that prevailed, it was not possible to see distinctly to which side the victory belonged; but at a distance, far from the scene of action, the burnished helmets of the Portuguese troopers were distinguishable as they fled from the post they had deserted, and from their brave companions, the Germans, whom they left to be massacred. The din of arms, the clashing of swords, and the thunder of the cannon, mingled with shouts from every side, completed the confusion. In the hurry of the moment, some tents belonging to the 74th regiment took fire, the flames soon communicated with those of the next regiment, and the camp was enveloped with smoke. But this was soon overcome; and by the time we approached near the point in dispute, the French cavalry had been driven off the field, but not before many of the Germans had fallen. Three guns of Macdonald's brigade had also been taken; and upon the whole, it was one of the most disgraceful and unlooked-for events that had taken place during the campaign. To be beaten at any time was bad enough, but to be beaten by a handful of lancers, on the eve of our entering Madrid, almost in the view of the city, was worse than all. But what caused our defeat —our disgrace—under the eyes of the people of Madrid? The placing undue reliance on the Portuguese troops.†

* * * * *
* * * * *

ADVANCE FROM SALAMANCA.

A great portion of the French army had marched more than twelve leagues in thirty-six hours, (advancing and retreating from the field of battle,) and had also been engaged in hard fighting six hours out of that time; therefore, until the night of the 23rd, they had hardly made a halt for any considerable time for two days and a night, and I think I may venture to assert, that the rapidity of their movements, before and after the action, and

† In this unexpected and unfortunate affair, nearly two hundred men and one hundred and twenty horses were placed *hors de combat;* and the troops, who had hitherto behaved bravely in the field, deserted officers who set them a noble example, and thus occasioned a serious loss.—MAXWELL'S LIFE OF WELLINGTON.

their ultimate escape under General Clausel from the very jaws of destruction, are equally astonishing. Early on the morning of the 24th of July, we passed Panaranda, from whence the inhabitants sallied out, loaded with bread, wine, and liquors, and rent the air with their acclamations in praise of the glorious victory that we had won over the French; and even the little boys straddled out their legs and bent forward their heads in derision of the enemy's soldiers, to represent to us to what a state of distress and exhaustion they were reduced. As we passed onwards, numerous objects of commiseration lying by the side of the road, reminded us of the miseries of war in all its horrors: many of the French soldiers lay dead, exposed to the scorching rays of the sun, which had so blistered their faces and swelled their bodies, that they scarcely represented human forms, and looked more like some huge and horrible monsters of gigantic dimensions than anything else. It is impossible to convey an adequate idea of such spectacles, or the sufferings they must have endured during their last agonies. These, now inanimate, objects, had marched over sandy plains, without a tree to shelter them, while suffering from fatigue, sore feet, and want of water; then, crowding into the battle, covered with dust, and under a scorching sun, they had received severe wounds, and were finally dragged, or carried on rudely constructed bearers from the scene of action, during excruciating torture, and ultimately left to perish by the side of the roads, or on stubble land, with their parched tongues cleaving to the roof of their mouths; and to complete their miseries, before breathing their last sigh, to behold, with glazed and half-closed eyes, the uplifted hand of a Spanish assassin, armed with a knife to put an end to their existence. This dreadful fate awaited the defeated French soldiers in Spain. It was impossible to gaze on the mutilated bodies of these our enemies, without feelings of deep commiseration for our fellow-creatures, who a day or two previously had been alive like ourselves, and perhaps the admiration of their comrades.

On the 25th, we made a halt to enable the stragglers and stores of the army to come up. On the same day El Rey Joseph had arrived at Blasko Sancho, near Arevalo, with a reinforcement principally composed of Spaniards, for the purpose of joining the Duke of Ragusa; but on gaining intelligence of the defeat his troops had sustained at Salamanca, he countermarched in the evening towards his capital, leaving a picket of cavalry behind at Blasko Sancho, who were all taken prisoners, while carousing in a wine-house, by a corporal's party of the 14th light horse.* About this time Lord Hill had moved with the second division on Zafra, in Estramadura, to observe a French force in that quarter. On the 28th our division bivouacked round the ancient town of Olmedo, where the Duke of Wellington gave a ball, with a general *invite* to all those officers who liked to attend. The Alcalde selected

* *Vide* end of vol. ii.

the different ladies as usual, whose merry hearts and supple forms were always ready for the dance. The following morning, an hour before daylight, we advanced, and it was a droll sight to see the officers sleeping as they rode along, after the fatigues of the previous night, still dressed in their ball attire—such as crimson, light blue, or white trowsers, richly embroidered with gold or silver, velvet and silk waistcoats of all colours, decorated in a similar manner: dandies, ready alike for the dance and the fight; most of them had received a wound, and others more; nor can I call to mind one of the officers present at this time who had reached twenty-five years of age, including the senior officer. Owing to the heat of the weather, it was the fashion of the times to wear the jacket open, which was the only particle of dress left to denote to what nation we belonged; as to any other uniformity for the officers, it was quite out of the question, the fantastical dresses of these days would have confounded the most ancient or modern disciplinarians. The enemy still continued the flight across the Douro through Valladolid, which city the Duke of Wellington entered on the 31st, at the head of a large body of horse. The country on the banks of the Douro is remarkably sandy, and highly cultivated with vines; we forded to the left bank of the river on that day within two leagues of Valladolid. While our baggage was crossing, a batman and pony got out of their depth, and were carried down the stream a considerable distance, and so determined was the soldier to hold on, that he disdained to quit his charge at the risk of his life, and continued swimming until a rope was thrown to him, by the assistance of which he conveyed the little animal and his master's portmanteau safe on shore.

We had no sooner heard of the large town in the vicinity, than we began to prepare for the visit; however, it struck me that it would be very refreshing to enjoy a swim first, and also wishing my horse to participate in the luxury, I stripped myself, and mounted its back, and together we plunged into the stream; but, as ill-luck would have it, for a moment the provoking animal hardly made any exertion, so down he went, and thinking there was no time to be lost, I sprang from its back, but owing to his plunging I received a slanting kick on my chest, which most probably would have proved fatal, had the full weight of the blow struck me direct; the animal, however, soon recovered itself, and swimming with the current, it was with considerable difficulty I succeeded in getting it on shore. Valladolid is a fine old town, with a spacious square, containing nearly thirty thousand inhabitants, who were glad to see us, but evinced none of those rapturous and warm expressions of delight displayed by those of Salamanca.

The next morning, the 1st of August, we recrossed the river, and branched off in the direction of Madrid. Having halted a day or two, we again became in motion, and struck on a well-paved road leading to the capital. Many exclaimed, Is this the road to Madrid? are we really going to the capital of Spain, the centre of romance? My mind was filled with all sorts of illusions, and various anticipations of pleasure; my rest was disturbed, and my dreams were of Madrid; every day's march was counted, every object brought something new, and I made up my mind to dance every night when I got there. Continuing our route, we had arrived within two days' march of Segovia, and occupied a pine wood. On seeing an officer pass, who was likely to give me every information relative to the movements of the army, I issued from my small Portuguese tent, and entered into conversation with him, which lasted a considerable time; and being without my cap, I felt the top of my head extremely hot from the rays of the sun, and was about to withdraw several times for a covering, which unluckily I failed to do. When the dinner-hour arrived, composed of rice and boiled beef, without any bread or biscuit, my appetite failed, and I laid down, in hopes that a few hours' sleep would restore me. At daylight, the following morning, we were again in route, and had just cleared the sandy wood, enveloped in dust, when a sudden giddiness seized me, and I fell from my horse; on recovering my senses, I found myself supported by an officer.

There was no water to be procured, and on overtaking the division, I was advised to ride gently on to avoid the dust. For the first time in Spain, I observed a Spanish grandee travelling in a carriage drawn by eight mules, escorted by fourteen servants, clothed in long yellow coats, with cocked hats, and all regularly armed, like horse-soldiers. The costume of the peasantry now became somewhat different; one of that class was walking by my side, with a sort of spiral cloth cap, clad in dark brown, who asked me if I did not admire a little girl passing on the road, whom he called a Wappa Chica; she wore also a stiff spiral cap of cloth, perched on the top of her head, with round balls of different colours up each side of it; her hair was plaited on each side of her head, ending in a huge pig-tail, about eight inches long, and precisely similar to those worn by British sailors; the jacket was brown, laced up the front; a yellow petticoat, reaching just below the knee; blue stockings, red clocks, shoes, and silver buckles.

Having travelled some leagues, I came to a village, where I observed one of the commissaries of our division standing at the door of a cottage, who remarked that I looked very ill, and asked me where I was going. I told him about half a league further on, when I intended to lie down under a tree until the troops came up, as I concluded they would not proceed much further that day; he politely begged that I would partake of breakfast with him, as it was already prepared, which offer I thankfully accepted. My fever continued rapidly to increase, so that I could scarcely sit upright, and I soon began to talk very incoherently, which induced him to put me to bed; the division shortly afterward filed through the village, and bivouacked half a league in advance. In the evening, two other officers of the company with whom I messed paid me a visit, and said, " Why, what is the matter ?" when I replied, "That the commissary had used me very cruelly, and had been smothering me in blankets, to prevent my going on to Madrid." The assistant-surgeon having felt my pulse, asked, " Whether I would permit him to throw some water on my head ?" which I readily assented to, entreating him to do anything to make me well. Then being lifted out of bed, and divested of my linen garment, I was placed in a chair; the doctor, standing on a table, emptied two pitchers of spring water on my crown, which produced a most painful sensation. The following morning my companions assured me that I could not be permitted to proceed; but as there was a station to be established at Cuellar, it would be necessary that I should go there, when they felt no doubt that I should speedily recover, so as to be enabled soon to rejoin them. A car was accordingly procured, drawn by two fine mules, with a blanket extended over the top as an awning. At the expiration of two days' journey, I reached the entrance of Cuellar, when a soldier came forward, and intimated that no sick could enter the town until the commandant's permission was obtained, and we were actually detained nearly two hours roasting in the mid-day sun, before a free passage was granted us. Much exhausted and half-suffocated, I at length obtained a most excellent billet in a gentleman's house, where I received the greatest attention from an assistant-surgeon belonging to one of the regiments quartered there, being unable to quit my bed. At this time the army had possessed itself of the passes of Segovia and the Guadarama, and had moved forward on the 11th of August towards Madrid, from the vicinity of Galapagos, and forced the enemy's advance guard of cavalry to retire; but in the afternoon they again advanced from Malagahonda towards Rosas, to reconnoitre the Portuguese dragoons, who were drawn up on a rising ground above the latter village, who made a show of charging, but when they had arrived sufficiently near to observe the hardened-looking visages of the sturdy French heavy horse, who displayed their long, shining weapons with brass hilts, like the Highland broadsword, with the exception of being one-third longer—at such a sight our allies simultaneously wheeled about, and scampered off as fast as their Portuguese horses could trot and gallop, followed by their unmerciful pursuers, stabbing and hacking them down, and riding past three pieces of horse artillery that had been overturned. The heavy dragoons of the King's German Legion took to horse as speedily as possible, amidst the confusion, and after a good deal of savage sabreing, the enemy retired, leaving at night the captured guns behind them. Joseph had retired with his followers behind the Tagus, and the following day our army entered Madrid, where the French had injudiciously left a garrison in the Bueno Retiro, who surrendered themselves prisoners of war, just as part of the third division, and some other detachments, were about to escalade the works. A vast quantity of stores, powder, and ball, fell into our hands, besides 190 pieces of cannon, principally dismounted.

About the 20th of August, a detachment of our regiment passed through Cuellar, but as they had experienced a long march during the hot months, an enormous quantity of them died, and the sick continued to increase from the army in such numbers, that most of us were ordered to proceed to Salamanca; accordingly, on the sixth day after my arrival, I was placed in a car, drawn by bullocks, to begin another tedious journey. The sixth division was on parade, having been left at that station as a corps of observation to protect the sick and the stores of the army. That night I travelled a short way, and was billeted on a very clean house, where the patron was most anxious to have all the particulars of the late battle recounted to him; however, finding that I was not a sufficient master of the Spanish language to satisfy his curiosity, he was determined to make up for it by entering into the history of his own country. It was in vain that I exerted all my patience, and requested he would have the goodness to leave the room, pleading my indisposition in excuse for my apparent rudeness. Having maintained silence for a few minutes, he offered me everything in his house, inquired if I was better, and recommenced his volubility to such a degree, that I almost became distracted, and was under the painful necessity of calling in my servant, who, in half fun and half earnest, turned him out of the room by the shoulders. The next day I reached Arevalo, where the market was filled with fresh vegetables, a sight only to be appreciated by those who have travelled over a dry country devoid of vegetation. A smiling muchacha, who sat by the side of a well-made young Spaniard, jumped up, and handed me a large bunch of grapes, with a dignified air of affability and frankness so peculiar to the lower orders of that country. I obtained a billet on a very handsome house, situated in a luxuriant garden, and on being supported out of the car, I was so weak that I fell down, and continued in fainting fits for some time, my servant all the while sousing me with water, in imitation of the doctor. The fascinating señorita of the house, about seventeen years of age, very kindly administered every attention; and at night, with a small lamp, remained in a recess, in readiness to offer me liquids, for which I continually inquired. My recollection did not entirely forsake me, but my head was in a bad state, and I fancied I saw groups of monkeys grinning at the foot of my bed, and as I was unable to endure the slender rays of the lamp, I begged of the young lady to retire. At such a request her countenance portrayed every mark of disappointment: whether she considered me as one of the deliverers of her country, or whether so young a girl, residing in so sequestered a spot, fancied me under her especial protection, I know not; but I do know that her amiable solicitude and her lovely eyes made such an impression, that she continued the mistress of my thoughts, and heroine of my fancy, for a long period afterwards. Taking my farewell on the following morning, and apologizing to the little señorita for my want of gallantry, I proceeded on my journey, and at the end of four hours reached the middle of an extensive plain, when one of the bullocks became dead lame, and the enraged driver declared vehemently that he would go no further; my servant therefore dismounted from my palfrey, and placed me on its back; we made for the distant steeple which skirted the horizon, as the point of our destination. At the expiration of a toilsome ride we reached the Pueblo, and there sojourned until the next morning; in two more days we reached Alba de Tormes. I was quartered at an apothecary's shop, where I lay on the mattrass for twelve hours in a sort of stupor; on recovering in some degree, my servant fancied that I was dying, and proposed sending for the Spaniard, which I would by no means consent to, from the apprehension that he would bleed me to death.

The next day, while quietly passing through a wood, at a lonely spot, my horse made a sudden start, and on looking to the right, I observed a dead man, perfectly naked, placed against a large piece of rock, who had been killed at the battle of Salamanca. His hair was long and grey, his beard had grown to a considerable length, his arms and legs had been placed in an extended position; in fact, he was in an exact fencing attitude, in an extraordinary state of preservation, and presenting, of course, a dreadful spectacle. On reaching Salamanca, I obtained a billet, which on presenting, I was treated with the greatest insolence by the man of the house, who declared that I might enter, but that he had no accommodation for my servant: under these circumstances, I was under the necessity of sitting down in the street, until the soldier went to seek elsewhere for better success. After some further delay, he procured me another on a public notary, where I was civilly received; but in the middle of the day, my patron, smelling of tobacco and garlic, came in to take a siesta, in one of the two beds in a large recess. I asked him if he intended to sleep there; he replied, "Si, señor." To such an arrangement I objected, but he would not give up the point; a struggle then ensued between us, which lasted some minutes, although eventually I made him surrender. He was a little diminutive old man; but I had become so weak, and the scene so amusing, that his own son, with a smiling countenance, was quietly looking on.

An hospital mate being put in requisition, the first dose administered to me was an emetic, and whenever I complained, the same dose was repeated; therefore, whenever he visited me, I invariably declared that I was better.

I noticed, during the period that I was in Spain, that those men killed in action who were exposed to the rays of the sun, immediately became a mass of corruption, but those, on the contrary, who fell under trees, or in shady places, exposed to heavy dew or rain, their skin became as hard as leather, and they would remain in that state for a very considerable period, unless they were devoured by wild animals or birds of prey. I have often seen vultures feeding on dead horses, (that had been killed in battle,) so fat that they could scarcely take wing to raise themselves from the ground.

Our army had now occupied the heart of Spain, and the enemy, with rapid strides, were endeavouring to concentrate in the distant provinces round our centre, blowing up magazines, and eating up all before them, like a swarm of locusts. Napoleon was at this period traversing the wilds of Russia, with his grand army, and his magnificent and highly-appointed Imperial Guard. The banners of Austria, Prussia, Italy, and the Germanic States, were marching under his control; the north and south of Europe were in a blaze, and had become the extreme points of contest, which was ultimately to decide this mighty struggle for supremacy. The victory of Salamanca had shook the combinations of the enemy in all parts of Spain, and put the whole of them in motion. On the 25th of August, they destroyed their works before Cadiz, leaving behind them stores, heavy artillery, and mortars, many of the latter having been cast at Seville, by the orders of the Duke of Dalmatia, for the purpose of throwing shells into the town of Cadiz.*
Some Spaniards and British immediately advanced from the lines, and took forcible possession of Seville.

On the 29th of August, Lord Hill, with the

* One of these mortars was brought to England, and is now placed on the south side of St. James's Park.

second division, entered Illerena, and pushed on to Ayllones, on the borders of Estremadura, but finding the French were retrograding on Cordova and Granada, for the purpose of communicating with Joseph, who, in like manner, was forming a junction with Marshal Suchet, intending to make Valencia the centre and the base of his future operations against Madrid, Lord Hill, therefore, by a flank movement, marched towards the city of Medillin, on the left bank of the Guadiana, so as to be in readiness to act wherever his presence might be required, or to open his line with the third, fourth, and light divisions cantoned in the vicinity of Madrid.

The General-in-Chief no sooner saw a probability of his right flank being cleared of the enemy, than he set off from Madrid, and concentrated the first, fifth, sixth, and seventh divisions round Arevalo, (early in September,) with a force of cavalry and artillery, passed the Douro, and retook Valladolid, which had been re-occupied by the enemy for a short time. On the 19th, he crossed the Arlanzon, and laid siege to the old Castle of Burgos, bristled with cannon and the bayonets of its hardy defenders.* Various attempts by esca-

* " On being closely reconnoitered, the defences were found to occupy an oblong, conical hill, and to be of a triple nature nearly all round. The lower or outer line consisted of the old escarp wall of the town or castle, modernised with a shot-proof parapet, and flanks ingeniously procured by means of palisades, or tambours, at the salient and reentering points. The second line was of the nature and profile of a

lade, mining, explosions, and breaching were tried for a month without success, owing to the want of a sufficiency of battering artillery, and the obstinate defence made by the enemy, who firmly lined its walls, and threw their balls and bullets with deadly aim against the assailants. The enemy's vanguard was at Briviesca, and his main body behind the Ebro, during a greater part of the siege.

field retrenchment, and well palisaded. The third, or upper line, was nearly of a similar construction to the second; and on the most elevated point of the cone, the primitive keep had been formed into an interior retrenchment, with a modern heavy casemated battery, named after Napoleon. The situation of this fortified post was very commanding, except on the side of the hill of St. Michael, the summit of which, at less than three hundred yards distance, is nearly on the same level with the upper works of the castle, but separated from them by a deep ravine. This height was occupied by a hornwork of large dimensions; the front scarp of which, hard and slippery, twenty-five feet in height, stood at an angle of about 60°, and was covered by a counterscarp ten feet in depth. The branches were not perfect, and the rear had been temporarily closed, on intelligence of the fall of Madrid, by an exceedingly strong palisading. No part of the front or branches were palisaded or fraised."—JONES's JOURNAL OF THE SIEGES.

END OF VOL. I.

INDEX

(Compiled by S. Monick)

Introductory notes:

(1) The terms which comprise the Indices to Volumes I and II are selected on a keyword basis;
ie the key terms on each page are entered. As is commonly the case, these terms are ordered in an alphabetical sequence. However, it is readily apparent that the sequence incorporates main terms, beneath which subordinate entries are contained.
In Volume I the main terms are:
Badajoz; **Battles, Campaigns, Wars**; **Casualties**; **Cuidad Rodrigo**; **Lisbon**; **Spain/Spaniards**; **Tactics**; **Uniforms and accoutrements**; UNITS AND FORMATIONS; **Weapons and Ammunition**
In Volume II the main entries are:
Battles, Campaigns, Wars; **Casualties**; **Shipping/Ships**; **Spain/Spaniards**; **Tactics**; **Uniforms and accoutrements**; UNITS AND FORMATIONS; **Weapons and Ammunition**
It is equally apparent that the entries under these main headings are further sub-divided. This aspect is an especially notable feature of the heading UNITS AND FORMATIONS; due to the need for specificity in complex military organisations.

(2) The obvious relationships between terms (as in the case of geographical locations which are also the site of battles, Salamanca and Badajoz being obvious examples) necessitates the extensive use of cross references.

(3) The use of annotation has, in theory, no place within an index. However, careless editing has resulted in confusion with regard to several terms, obvious examples being:
– The references to the two Paget brothers in Volume I, no distinction being made between Generals Edward Paget and Lord Henry Paget (cf INTRODUCTORY ESSAY - **Maxwell as editor**].
– The reference to the 7th Hussars as the 1st Hussars [cf INTRODUCTORY ESSAY - **Maxwell as editor**].
– The variation in the spelling of place names (often within the context of the same chapter) [cf INTRODUCTORY ESSAY - **Maxwell as editor**].
– The misspelling of names of prominent personalities (Pack and Crauford in Volume I being obvious examples).

In the interests of historical accuracy, and with a view to providing the reader with clarity on these points, notes have thus been added in such circumstances where it has been deemed necessary.

(4) The use of square brackets indicates that the indexer has completed the name of an individual, where the Christian name, etc has been excluded in the text.

(5) Where the authorship of a particular chapter has been identified, both the author and title of the chapter are separately indexed. However, where a chapter is anonymous, it has not been indexed.

(6) Occasionally, a term has been more closely identified by the indexer. For example, where the author has referred to a division or regiment as 'our division' or 'our regiment' and it is possible to more accurately define the formation in question, the term has been more specifically identified. This practice has also been adopted with regard to place names (eg rivers, towns, etc).

INDEX TO VOLUME I

A

Abrantes, 31,103,105
Abrantes, Duke of [*see*: Junot, General Jean-Androche]
Account of the war in Spain and Portugal (Col Jones), vi
Adiga, 85
Agueda (River), 168,179,185,187,198,219, 221,225,240,254,289
  Ford, 254
Alaejos, 40
Alba de Tormes, 338,342,385
Alberche (River), 120,121,124,125, 126,127,128,139,140,145,150, 151,156
  Fords, 129
Albufera, Duke of [*see*: Suchet, Marshal Louis-Gabriel]
Alburquerque, Duke of, 109,117,165
Alcantara, 84
  Bridge, 81,103
Alcoentre, 174,175
Aldea de Ponte, 215,216
Alentejo, 179,267
Alexander I (Tsar of Russia, 1777-1825), 78
Alfayetes, 179
Almandralejo, 167
Almarez, 80,105,109,160,161,165
  Pontoon bridge, 160
  Pass, 161
Almeida, 70,105,185,187,196,197, 198,199
  Garrison, 185,196,197,199
Alten, Maj Gen (later Field Marshal) Sir Charles (Karl), 222,224
Amarante, 81,84,94,95,96
  Prior, 91
Andalusia, 167,351
Animals, 42,50,99,337
  [*see also*: specific types; eg Bullocks, Donkeys, Horses, Mules]
Anson, Gen [Sir William], 107,118, 120,129, 148,363
Aranjuez, 109,121
Arapiles (village), 342,344
  [*see also under:* **Battles,**

INDEX

Campaigns, Wars - Salamanca]
Archangel, 349
Ardour (River), [v]
Arenschild, Lt Col, 222,223
Arevala, 365,*376,*384,*388
  [*spelt 'Arevalo' on these pages]
Arlanzon, 387
Arroyo, 167
Arzobispo, 161,163
  Bridge, 80,110,159,160,164
Astorga, 61,68
Asturia, 69
Augereau, Marshal Pierre-Francois-
  Charles], 68
Austria, 67,387 [*see also*: Habsburgs]
Atlantic, 4
Aventes, 91
Aveiro (Bay), 85
Awards
  Legion of Honour (France), 61, 185
  Order of Maria Theresa (Austria),
  54
Axes, 227,238,271
Ayllones, 388
Ayshford, Maj, 265

B

Baccelas, Col, 224
Badajoz,
  166,167,184,267,279,282,308,
  309,310
  [*see also under:* **Battles,
  Campaigns, Wars**; Ramparts]
  Alcalde [*see*: Mayor]
  Bridge, 285
  Cathedral, 311,313,314
    Bishop, 320
    Canon, 311
    [*see also*: Rocha, Don Emmanuel
    de la]
    Secretary, 320
  Gate, 308
    Talavera gate, 308
  Governor, 271,285,290,311
  Mayor, 320
  [*see also*: Philipon in general section]
  Square, 313
Baggage, 12,45,50,96,97,99,102,113,

159,165,176,204,302,322,368,376
Baird, Gen Sir D[avid], 77
Ballasteros, [General Francesco], 109
Banos (mountain pass), 105,167
Barbary Coast, 110
Barba del Puerco, 199
Barnard, Col, 316
Barnard, Gen [Sir Andrew Francis],
  282
Barricades, 127
Bassecourt, General, 148,158,160
Battles, Campaigns, Wars [*see also*:
Casualties]
  Aire, [1]
  Albuera (1811), 151,181,207
  Alexandria (1801), 51
  Almonaciadid (1809), 165
  Aronches (1801), 74
  Austerlitz (1805), 60
  Austria (French Revolutionary
  Wars, 1792-1802), 52
  Badajoz (siege) (1811), 273,290,
  312,315,316,319
  Badajoz (siege) (1812), 181,253,
  263,267,275,281,288,292,302,304
  [*see also in general section*]
    Breaches, 274,277,278,279,280,
    284,286,287,292,293,294,300,
    305,307,315,316, 317,318
    Castle, 253,268,270,283,284,
    286,288,289,290,291,292,293,
    297,300,302,305,306, 308,316
    Gate, 271,273,291,297,301,302
    Tower, 284
    Citadel [*see*: Castle]
    Defences, 268,269
    Ditch [*see*: Trenches]
    Fort Pardoleros, 283
    Fort Picurina,
    268,269,271,272,273
    Garrison, 272,283,294
    Journal of French officer, 121
    Magazine, 301
    Pardoleros [*see*: Fort Pardoleros]
    Picurina [*see*: Fort Picurina]
    Ramparts, 267,270,276,277,279,
    280,282,284,285,287,290,295,
    297,298,323
    Santa Martha (bastion), 293,315,
    316,317

St Roque, 293,315
St Vincent (bastion), 307
Trenches, 268,269,270,271,272,
274,275,277,278,281,288,289,
307, 308,316,317
Trinidad (bastion), 282,293,
306,315, 316,317
Barossa (1811), [v]
Benevente (1808), 58-60,61
Beunos Aires (1807), 9
Burgos (siege) (1812), 389
[see also under: Parapets]
Busaco (1810), 170,174,[217]
Antonio de Cantara, 170
Convent Hill, 170
Cadiz (siege) (Peninsular War),
350,351
[see also in general section]
Corunna (battle) (1809), 102,
137,153
[see also in general section]
Corunna (retreat) (1808-1809),
46,47,62,85,101
[see also: individual battles; eg
Benevente, Rueda]
Cuidad Real (1809), 80
Cuidad Rodrigo (siege) (1812),
33,170,[217],218,225,237,251,
253,254,256,263,265,267,278
[see also in general section]
Breaches, 226,227,228,229,230,
231,232,233,234,235,238,244,
245,246,247,249,252,256,257,
258,259,260,262,263,264
Ditches [see: Trenches]
Sketch, 236
Traverses, 261,262
Trenches, 225,226,227,229,230,
232,234,235,237,238,242,243,
244,245,247,256, 262,264
[see also in general section]
El Bodon (1811), 214,215,218,
251,253,264
[see also in general section]
Flushing [see under: Walcheren]
French Revolutionary Wars (1792-
1802), 51
Fuentes d'Onoro (1811), 189-
190,216,[217],218
Garcia Hernandez (1812), 363-364

Italy (French Revolutionary Wars,
1792-1802), 52
Leipzig (1813), 350
Lutzen (1813), 350,351
Maida (1806), 51,52,154
Marengo (1800), 349,366,367
Medellin (1809), 80,161
[see also in general section]
New Orleans (1815), 272
Peninsular War (1808-1814),
vii,10,61,122, 168,196,342
[see also: individual battles,
campaigns]
Prussia (French Revolutionary
Wars, 1792-1802), 52
Pyrenees (1813), viii,360,362
[see also in general section]
Revolutionary Wars [see: French
Revolutionary Wars]
Roleia [see: Rolica]
Rolica (1808), vii,10,19
Rueda, 85
Russia (1812), 72,349
Moscow, 350
Sabugal (1811), 253
Sahagun (1808), 56,57,58,61
[see also under: Casualties]
Salamanca (1812), viii,321,344-
348,349,350,351,352,354,355,
363,364,365,366,367,376,385,387
Arapiles (heights), 352
Forts
Breaches, 328,329
Fort Gayetano, 324
Fort Merced, 324
Fort St Vincent, 324
Garrisons, 328
[see also in general section]
San/St Sebastian (1813), 275,287,
319
Spanish Succession (1702-1714), 74
Talavera (1809), 135,140-
151,153,160, 216,309
[see also in general section]
Torres Vedras (Peninsular War), 350
Toulouse (1814), vii
Ucles (1809), 80
Usagre (1811), 208,209,211 [see also
in general section]
Bridge, 211,213 [see also in general

section]
Villa Franca (1808), 57
Villars-en-Couche [ie Villiers-en-Couche] (1794), 52
Vimiero (1808), 15,53,137,153
Vittoria (1813), 134,345
Walcheren (1809)
  Flushing, 309
  Fortress, 309
Waterloo (1815), [217],253
Bay of Biscay, 21,22
Bay of Aveiro [*see*: Aveiro (Bay)]
Beef, 379
Belem, 14,28
  Rocio-square, 14,17
Belliard, [General Augustin-Daniel], 126
Belluno, Duke of [*see*: Victor, Marshal Claud]
Bembibre, 48
Bemposta, 324
Benevente, 46 [*see also under:* **Battles, Campaigns, Wars**]
Beresford, Marshal [Sir William Carr], 73,75, 76,84,96,100,101,105,166
Berg, Grand Duke of [*see*: Murat, Marshal Joachim]
Berthier, [Marshal Louis-Alexandre], 68
Bessier, [Marshal Jean-Baptiste], 68
Biscuit, 335,379
Blankets, 328,381
Blasko Sancho, 369,376
Bogle, - , 241
Bonaparte, Joseph [*see*: Joseph Bonaparte]
Bonaparte, Napoleon [*see*: Napoleon Bonaparte]
Boots, vi,112
Borghese, Pauline [*see*: Pauline Borghese]
Bourbons, 111,135
Bouvier-d'eclats, General, 210,213
Bowdlier, Sgt, 9
Braga, 70,71,97,98,102
  Bishop, 97,102
  Garrison, 97
Bread, 163,164
Breastworks, 127,228,229,232,233, 247,248,249

Brennier, General, 199
Briche, General, 208,209,211,213
Bridges, 90,98,99,171,172,345
  [*see also*: name of bridge; eg Arzobispo - Bridge]
Boats, 89
Brievesca, 389
Britain/British [*see*: Great Britain]
British Isles [*see*: Great Britain]
Brock, Gen, 363,364
Broke, Maj Charles, 317
Broke Vere, Col Sir Charles [*see*: Vere, Col Sir Charles Broke]
Bromhead, Lt Col, 224,251
Bron, General, 209,212
Brotherton, Capt, 188
Buchan, Col, 319
Bugio (fort) [*see under:* **Lisbon** - Forts]
Bugles, 299,300,371
Bull, Capt, 330
Bullocks, 164,383,385
Bunker, Mr
  (English Hotel), 27
Burcellas, 11

C

Cabrerizes (fort), 328
Cabrerizes (hill), 328,340,342
Cadiz, 77,349,350,387
  [*see also under:* **Battles, Campaigns, Wars**]
Caesar, Julius, 134
Caldas [*see*: Las Caldas]
Caldera (family), 312,320
Caldera (Canon of Badajoz Cathedral), 319
Caldera, Madame, 312
Cameron, Brig Gen A, 71,83,98,100, 107,141,145
Campagnes en Portugal, 1810,1811, 198
Campbell, Lt Col, 227,228,229,230, 231,234, 289,290,291
Campbell, Brig Gen Alexander, 83, 107,140,147,150,154,162,237
Campbell, Capt C, 231
Campbell, Brig Gen H, 82,107,151,154

Campo Major, 167,180
[*also referred to as* Campo Mayor]
Garrison, 180
Canch, Ensign, 290
Canch, Maj, 265
Cantonments, 15,49,185,201,255
Carden, Lt, 173
Carion, 67
Cartajol, General, 80
Cartaxo, 197
Carts, 5,113,159,162,356,381,383
Casa del Puertos, 108,116
Casa de Centinela, 108
Casa de Salinas, 127
Casaleguas, 126,127,128,129
Cascaes, 11,12
Caseres, 104
Castello Branco, 31,103,106,166
Castello Brom [spelt 'Castelo Brom' in text]
Bridge, 188
Castello de Vida, 267
Castiglione, Duke of [*see*: Augerau, Marshal Pierre-Francois-Charles]
Castille, 39,69,105,157,324,351
Castlereagh, Lord, 58
Castrejon, 330,333
Castrillo, 334
Castro Novo, 42
Casualties
Amarante
British, 94
French, 95
Badajoz
British, 287,307,314
Officers, 280
Soldiers, 280
Wounded, 305,314,320
Busaco
British, 170
French, 170
Cuidad Rodrigo
British
94th Regiment
Officers, 265
[*see also*: individual names]
Soldiers, 265
Light Infantry, 265
Grijon
British, 89

Palencia
French, 58
Rolica
British, 10
French, 10
Sahagun, 56
British
15th Light Dragoons, 57
French, 55
Salamanca
British, 352
French, 352
Portuguese, 352
Spanish, 352
Talavera
British, 150
Burial, 155
Foot Guards, 146
Wounded, 162,163
23rd Light Dragoons, 151
Horses, 151
Officers, 151
Soldiers, 151
French, 151
Wounded, 156
Spanish, 151
Cattle [*see*: Oxen]
Cavado (River), 98,99
Cespedosa, 221
Chatham, Earl of, 309
Chaves, 70,71,81,96,100,102
Chaves, Marquis de [*see*: Silveira, General]
Chinese, 74
Cholwich, Capt, 306,307
Cintra, 12
Cintra (Convention of), 54,69
Clausel, Marshal [Bertrand, 365,375
Clinton, Gen [Sir William Henry], 355,366
Coa (River), 168,186,187,188,195, 196,204,222
Fords, 188,204
Coach, 117
Cock, Capt, *172,175
[*spelt 'Cocks' on this page]
Coimbra, 82,84,85,103
University students, 8,71
Colborne, Col (later Field Marshal Sir) John, 255

Cole, Gen [Sir Galbraith Lowry], 178,366
Collier, Sir George, 78,79
Colours, 14,152,239,253,285,359, 360,362
  King's Colour, 265
Columbus, Christopher, 26
Column [see under: Tactics]
Colville, Maj Gen [later Gen Sir Charles], 214,215,222,224,226,237, 280,293,314,316
Conductors, 45,113
Confederation of the Rhine, 65
Conquete d l'Andalousie (Lapene,-), 208
Constantino, 63
Continent [see: Europe]
Convention of Cintra [see: Cintra (Convention)]
Convents*, 14,15,25,28,30,36,37, 39,155, 161,285,310,328,340,342
  [*Note: term used interchangeably with Monastery]
  [see also: Nunneries]
  Santa Cruz, 226,227,234,235,238, 239,240,241,255,256,257
  Serra, 90
Cordova, 388
Coria, 105,106
Corn, 125,178,287,325,326,327
Cornegliano, Duke of [see: Moncey, Marshal Bon-Adrien-Jeannot de]
Cortesada, 106
Corunna, 22,24,64,65,69,71,73,77, 137,163
[see also under: **Battles, Campaigns, Wars**]
  British Consul, 23
  Convicts, 23
    Criminals [see: Convicts]
    Prisoners [see: Convicts]
  Streets, 23
Cotton, Maj Gen [later Field Marshal Sir Stapleton], 82,107,140
Craddock, Gen Sir J[ohn Francis], 72,77,78, 79
Crauford, Brig Gen (later Maj Gen) R[obert], 150,161,166,168, 221,254,262
  [Spelt 'Crawford' in text]

Cuellar, 369,381,383
Cuesta, [General Don Gregario Garcia de la], 80,105,108,111,116,119, 121,122,123,125,126,145,148,153, 158,159,161,162,164,165
Cuidad Rodrigo, 32,73,81,214,219, 225,260, 321,341,361
  [see also under: **Battles, Campaigns, Wars**]
  Agueda gate, 230,231,235
  Castle, 231,235
  Cathedral, 250
  Citadel, 241
  Convent [see: Convents - Santa Maria]
  Fortress, 240,264
    San Francisco, 255
  Garrison, 226,232,235,241,245, 246,248, 255,256,265
  Governor, 244,256,257,259, 265,283
  Magazine, 248,258
  Ramparts, 226,227,228,230,231, 232,235,241,241,243,247,248,249, 256,257,258,259,260,261
  San Francisco [see under: Fortress]
  Square, 250
  Suburbs, 256,257
Cummins, Lt Col, 224

D

D'abrantes, Duc de, 15
D'Alafoes, Duc de, 74
Dalmatia, Duke of [see: Soult, Marshal Nicholas]
Dalrymple, Sir Hew, 55
Dantzic, Duke of [see: Lefebre [Lefebvre-Desnouettes], General Charles]
D'Arcy, Lt, 359
Davern, Lt, 297
Debelle, General, 56,61
De Chaves, Marquis [see: Chaves, Marquis de]
Delancey, Col, 124
De la Rocha, Don Emmanuel [see: Rocha, Don Emmanuel de la]
Deleytoza, 161,165

Del Infado, Duke [see: Infaldo, Duke del]
De Lorna, Marquis de [see: Lorna, Marquis de]
De Pombal [see: Pombal, Marquis de]
Denmark, 72
Desaix [ie Desaix de Veygoux], [General Louis-Charles-Antoine], 367
Desolles, General, 137
De Epana, Don Carlos [see: Espana, Don Carlos De]
Dogs, 17,18,300
Donovan, Pte Pat, 298
Donkeys, 40
Donkin, Col (later Gen Sir Rufane), 107,141
Douro (River), 84,89,90,94,95,96,99, [217], 324,330,333,376,377,388
Dribourg, Brig Gen, 83
Drums, 14,92,124,265,300
Duas Casas
  River, 187,190,194
  Valley, 190
Dubourdieu, Maj, 264
Duke del Infado [see: Infado, Duke del]
Duke of Abrantes [see: Abrantes, Duke of]
Duke of Albufera [see: Albufera, Duke of]
Duke of Alburquerque [see: Alburquerque, Duke of]
Duke of Belluno [see: Belluno, Duke of]
Duke of Castiglione [see: Castiglione, Duke of]
Duke of Cornegliano [see: Cornegliano, Duke of]
Duke of Dalmatia [see: Dalmatia, Duke of]
Duke of Dantzic [see: Dantzic, Duke of]
Duke of Istria [see: Istria, Duke of]
Duke of Kent, 318
Duke of Moscow [see: Moscow, Duke of]
Duke of Orleans [see: Orleans, Duke of]
Duke of Ragusa [see: Ragusa, Duke of]
Duke of Rivoli [see: Rivoli, Duke of]
Duke of Treviso [see: Treviso, Duke of]
Duke of Wellington [see: Wellington, Duke of]
Dunkin, Col, 239,251
D'Urban, [Lt Gen Sir Benjamin], 372

E

Eagles (French standards), 152,350
  Bearers, 152
Earl of Chatham [see: Chatham, Earl of]
Eben, Baron, 70,73
Ebro (River), 125
Edward, Duke of Kent [see: Duke of Kent]
Egypt, 52
El Bodon, 219,254 [see also under: **Battles, Campaigns, Wars**]
Elchingen, Duke of [see: Ney, Marshal Michel]
Elder, -, 317
  The storming of Badajoz, 304-320
Elder, Col (later Sir) George, 314
Elvas, 267,312
Encina, 254
England/English, vi,viii,[1],28,23,33, 41,47,61,65,66,67,75,76,77,78,79, 81,95,112,133,137,151,265,282, 350,387
  [see also: individual place names]
English in Spain, The (Lt Col Wilkie), [1]-20
Entrenchments, 127
Erskine, [Maj Gen] Sir William], 187
Escalona, 109,167
Escurial, 55
  Palace, 369
Esla (River), 58,59
Espana, Don Carlos De, 352
Essling, Prince of [see: Massena, Marshal Andre]
Estramadura, 104,105,208,300,376, 388
Europe, vi,vii,[1],2,18,52,64,79,104, 110,167,168,347,349,350,351,387
Evans, Pte, 260

INDEX   399

F

Fairtlough, Maj, 265
Falmouth, 22
Fane, Gen John, [Westmoreland, Gen John Fane] 107
Farine, Col, 210,212
Ferdinand VII (King of Spain, 1814-1833), 115
Fergusson, Capt, 278
Figueras (fort), 3
Fitzgerald, Maj, 265
Fletcher, [Lt Col Sir Richard], 319
Flores de Avila, 365
Food, 166
Forage, 42,165,176,178,186,205,323,327
[see also: Corn, Hay, Straw]
Fordice, Maj, 131
Fort Conception, 187
Fort St Christoval, 273,285,301
Fortifications, 240 [see also under:
Battles, Campaigns, Wars -
Badajoz, Cuidad Rodrigo;
Breastworks, Redoubts, Trenches]
Foy, [General Maximilien-Sebastien], 65,92, 358,361
Histoire de la Guerre de la Peninsule sous Napoleon, 136
France, 65,66,67,72,76,78,104,111,115,133,134,135,163,209,309
[see also: French]
First Consul, 349,367 [see also: Napoleon]
Franceschi, General, 55,71,85,106
Francis I (Emperor of Austria, 1792-1835), 52
Frank, Dr, 155
Franks, 134
Fraser, Lt Gen Alexander Mackenzie [see: Mackenzie, Maj Gen Alexander]
Frederick II (King of Prussia, 1740-1786), 355
Frederick William III (King of Prussia, 1770-1840), 78
Freer,- (officer), 339
Freire, 6
*French, 6,7,8,9,10,11,14,15,16,17,18,19,32,39,40,48,50,53,54,55,56,57,58,59,60,61,62,65,67,72,74,77,85,86,87,89,90,94,96,98,99,100,101,102,104,105,108,118,119,120,121,124,128,129,130,131,134,135,136,138,140,141,142,143,144,145,146,147,148,150,152,153,154,157,158,160,162,164,167,168,171,172,174,175,176,177,179,180,181,184,186,187,189,190,192,193,194,195,196,198,199,200,201,202,203,206,210,211,214,215,220,222,223,225,226,246,250,257,258,261,264,265,269,270,271,272,278,281,282,283,284,285,286,289,290,291,297,300,303,311,312,322,323,326,328,330,331,333,336,337,338,339,340,341,343,345,346,347,355,361,362,365,372,375,377,382,387,388
[see also: France; UNITS AND FORMATIONS - France - Army]
   Flag, 292
   Refugees, 192
   Revolution (1789), 67,88,110,136
   Spies, 32
[* Note: The term 'enemy' is entered under 'French']
Frogs, 276
Fuel, 42
Fuentes, 187,194,197,198 [see also:
Battles, Campaigns, Wars -
Fuentes d'Onoro]
Fuentes d'Onoro, 203 [see also under:
Battles, Campaigns, Wars]
Fuentes Guinaldo, 215,218,219
Fulham, 320

G

Galapagos, 382
Galestad, 106
Gallegos, 200,201,203
Gallicia, 3,66,69,70,101,102
   Mountains, 64
Garda, 33,34
Garonne, vi
Gauls, 134
Genghis Khan, 135
Germany, 104
   Germanic states, 387

Gibraltar
  Governor, 78
Ginso, 101
Gloucester, 8
Goatherders
  Paths, 101
Godinot, General, 208,211
Gonsalves (cook), 319
Gorravilla, 167
Gordon, Col, 155
Granada, 106,388
Grappling-irons, 286
Great Britain, 52,368 [see also: England]
  Government, 21,71,73
Grey, Maj, 265
Griffiths, -, 241
Grijon, 87,89
Guard-a-pero, 237
Guadiana (River), 80,105,166,267, 267,268,283,285,307,388
  Pontoon bridge, 268
Guadarama
  Mountains, 371
  Passes, 368,371,382
Guarena (River), 336
  Stream, 334
Guimaraens, 96,97,98
Guinalde [possibly variant spelling of Guinaldo]
  Retreat, 216
Guinaldo, 221 [possibly variant spelling of Guinalde]
  Plains, 254

H

Habsburgs, 67 [see also: Austria]
Haddock, Maj, 358,359
Harvest, - (officer), 275
Harvest, - (twin brother of above, killed at San Sebastian), 275
Hatchets, 242
Hay, 178
Hay, Lt, 172,173,175
Hay, Maj Gen [Andrew], 305,314
Hay, Leith, 45
Head, Col, 180,181,182
Hervey, Maj, 94

Herrerias, 62
Hill, Maj Gen [later Gen Sir Rowland], 77,82,88,90,107,130, 131,142,150,151,283,367,376,387, 388
Hillyard, Volunteer, 265
History of the war in the Peninsula and the South of France, (Lt Gen Sir William Napier), 190,192,262, 282,301
Hogarth, [William], 310
Horses, 11,45,50,62,85,97,99,100,111, 113,117,120,126,127,128,138,145, 149,154,173,174,178,179,186,187, 192,193,194,197,198,199,204,205, 206,215,216,240,272,274,313,332, 337,339,347,357,358,362,374,378, 379,382,385,387
  [see also: Forage; Pony; 'Rozinante'; UNITS AND FORMATIONS - Great Britain - Army - Cavalry - Remounts]
  Shoes, 50,62
  Stirrup leathers, 112
Hospitals, 95,143,155,158,159,160, 161,310,312
  Nurses, 155
  Orderlies, 155
Houlton, - (officer), 331
Houston, Gen, 187
Huerta, 347

I

Iberian Peninsula, 2,51,54,64,66,67,71,77,80, 104,116,153,349,350
  [see also: **Battles, Campaigns, Wars** - Peninsular War; Portugal, Spain]
Illerena, 388
India, 121
Infado, Duke del, 80
Innojesa, Marchioness of, 314
Isle of Wight
  St Catherine's Head, 78
Istria, Duke of [see: Bessieres, Marshal Jean-Baptiste]
Italy, 387

INDEX

J

Jarcejo, 166
Johnson, Maj, 265
Jones, Capt, 58
Jones, Col
   Account of the war in Spain and Portugal, vi
Jones, [Maj Gen Sir John Thomas]
   Journals of the sieges undertaken by the Allies in Spain, 226,268,389
Joseph Bonaparte (King of Naples (1806-1808) & Spain (1808-1813)), 80,126,157, 160,340,369,376,382,388
Jourdan, Marshal [Jean-Baptiste], 68,145
Journals of the sieges undertaken by the Allies in Spain
   (Maj Gen Sir John Thomas Jones), 226,268,389
Junot, General [Jean-Andoche], 15,54, 68,69,74

K

Kellerman [General Francois-Etienne], 69
Kempt, Gen [Sir James], 280,289, 290,291
Kennedy, Gen Sir James Shaw [see: Shaw Kennedy, Gen Sir James]
Kerry, 242
Kettle, 43
King of ... [see: place; eg Naples, King of]
Kite, Qmr, 200
Knipe, Capt, 194
Krauchenberg, Capt, 169,170
Kremlin, vi

L

Laborde, Gen, 9,10,53
Ladders, 238,240,243,244,273,276, 277,278,284,290,292,294,299, 308, 317
Laing, Capt, 231

La Mancha, 104,108,109,126,164
La Mata, 167
Lamotte, Colonel, 198
La Rocha, Don Emmanuel de [see: Rocha, Don Emmanuel de la]
Langworth, Brig Gen, 83,107,150
Lannes, Marshal Jean, 68
La Peubla de la Calsada, 167
Lapene,-
   Conquete de l'Andalousie, 208
Lapisse, General [Pierre-Bellon], 70, 71,81,102
Larrey, Baron, 59
La Romana, General Pedro Caro y Sureda [see: Romana, General Pedro Caro y Sureda la]
Las Caldas, 7,8
La Serna (hill), 347,365
Lavos, 3
Leaves from the journal of a veteran (Maj Patterson), 21-50
Lefebre [Lefebre-Desnouettes], General [Charles], 58,59,68
Lefevre, Capt, 212
Leigh, Col, 57
Leira, 6
   Bishop's palace, 6
Leith, [Lt Gen Sir James], 293,304
Le Marchant, Maj Gen [John Gaspard], 345, 357,361
Leon, 69,85,105,106,157
Life of the Duke of Wellington, The (W H Maxwell), 3,273,280, 315,352,374
Line [see under: **Tactics**]
Lippe-Buckenburg, Frederick, Count of, 74,75,76
Lisbon, 13,16,17,18,20,24,26,28,55, 69,72,73,77,79,82,84,166,350
   Black Horse Square, 27
   Earthquake, 18
   Forts
      Bugio, 72
      St Julian, 72
   Rocio-Square
      Palace of the Inquisition, 80
      Police, 18
   Streets, 18
Lobone, 167
Logan, Cpl, 181,183

Loison, [General Louis-Henri], 94,96,97
London, 320
Londonderry, Lord, 197,198,199
  Narrative of the Peninsular War from 1808 to 1813, 50,192,262
Lord Castlereagh [*see*: Castlereagh, Lord]
Lord Londonderry [*see*: Londonderry, Lord]
Lord Paget [*see*: Paget, Lord Henry]
Lorna, Marquis de, 72
Los Santos, 208
Louis Philippe (Duke of Orleans), 318
Lowe, Brig Gen, 107
Lugo, 45,63
Lumley, Gen [Sir William], 210,211,212

M

Macdonald, Capt, 372
Macdougall,-, 239,265
Macduff, Lord, 116
Mackenzie, Maj, 265
Mackenzie, Maj Gen (later Lt Gen) Alexander, 83,84,101,103,107,116, 120,141
Mackie, Capt William, 361,362
Mackinnon, Col, 158
Mackinnon, Maj Gen, 237,238,248, 261,262,263
Macleod, Lt Col, 258,259,260,275, 276,279,280,287,305
Macpherson, Lt, 292
Madden, Lt, 259
Madden, - (officer), 287
Madden, Capt, 288
Madrid, 68,80,104,108,119,121, 124,126,127,137,160,167,350,351, 367,368,369,371,374,378,379,382, 388,389
  Beuno Retiro, 126
  Garrison, 382
  Gate, 127
Magaron, General, 53
Majalahonda, 371,382
  [possibly variant spelling of Malagahonda]
Majedas, 109,166
Malagahonda, 382
  [possibly variant spelling of Majalahonda]
Malvern, 9
Manchester, 282
Marchant, Maj Gen [John Gaspard] Le [*see*: Le Marchant, Maj Gen John Gaspard Le]
Marches/marching, 42,43,48,50,55, 58,71,84,94,96,98,102,105,106,160, 162,204,254,268,322,325,333,335, 351,352,363,367,368,372,376,379, 383
Marchioness of Innojesa [*see*: Innojesa, Marchioness of]
Maria I (Queen of Portugal, 1777-1816), 19
Marialva (bridge), 170
Marmont [Marshal Auguste-Frederic-Louis], 68,214,215,218,221,264, 283,327,328,330,333,336,338,341, 342,343,344,347,352,353,354,363, 365,367,369,376
Martiago, 254
Massena, [Marshal Andre], 68,170,176,177, 179,187,188,196,197,265
Maubourg, General Latour, 180,181,207, 209,210,212
Maxwell, William Hamilton
  The life of the Duke of Wellington, 3,273,280,315,352,374
  Victories of the British Army, 278
Mayne, Col, 84
Medellin, 104,110,166,388
  [*see also under*: **Battles, Campaigns, Wars**]
Mellish, Capt, 96,162
Memoires sur les operations militaires des Francais en Gallice, en Portugal, et dans la Valle du Tage, en 1809, 69
Merida, 104,166
Mermet, General, 71,88
Merry, Capt, 288
Messa de Ibor, 161,165
Minho (River), 70
Miserele, 100
Modtejo, 167
Monasteries, 324

Moncey [Marshal Bon-Adrien-Jeannot de], 68
Mondego (Bay), 4
Mondego (River), vi,3,171,172,176
Moniteur, 52
Monks, 310
Montalegre, 98,100,101,102
Montbrun, General [Louise-Pierre], 175,198, 201,203,204
Montebello, Duke of [see: Lannes, Marshal Jean]
Monte Junto, 8
Monte Santa (camp), 28
Moore, Lt Gen Sir John, 20,28,43,46, 47,55,58,64,67,68,72,137
Moriarty, Lt, 359
Morphew, Capt, 318
Mortier, [Marshal Edouard-Adolphe-Casmir-Joseph], 68,69
Moscow, Duke of [see: Ney, Marshal Michel]
Mountains, 25,43,45,98,102,106,161 [see also: specific place names; eg Gallicia - Mountains]
Passes, 160,162,164
Mules, 43,45,100,113,114,116,123, 132,164,207,220,313,322,325,331, 337,356,368,379,381
Paths, 101
Murat [Marshal Joachim], 68
Murphy, Maj, 297,359
Murray, Maj, 173,174,175,176
Murray, Col [later Gen Sir George], 79,91,94,99

N

Napier, Col [later Lt Gen] Sir [William Francis Patrick], 170,176,180,196,199,346
History of the war in th Peninsula and the South of France, 190,192,262, 282,301
Naples, King of [see: Murat, Marshal Joachim]
Napoleon Bonaparte, vi,[1],15,43,55, 61,64,65,66,67,68,69,70,80,133, 134,135,136,221,309,351,367,387, 389
[see also: France - First Consul]
Narrative of the Peninsular War from 1808 to 1813 (Lord Londonderry), 50,192,262
Nava-da-ver, 187,188,190,201, 202,203,221
Naval Moral, 158,160,163
Neufchatel, Prince of [see: Berthier, Marshal Louis-Alexandre]
Newcastle, 21
Ney,[Marshal Michel], 68
Nicholson, Capt, 281
Nickle, Capt Robert, 361,362
Nunneries, 34,37 [see also: Convents]
Santa Clara, 34,36
Nuns, 36,285,310

O

Obidos, 7,8
Ocana, 168
O'Donnel, Mrs, 27
O'Hara, Maj, 280,317,318
O'Lawler, General, 314
Olimedo, 376
Olivenza, 167
O'Malley, Pte Tully, 295,296
O'Mally, Col, 359
Opera, 19
Oporto, 69,70,72,73,81,84,85,89, 90,95,96,103,[217]
Garrison, 103
O'Reilly, General, 110
Orense, 70
Orleans, Duke of [see: Philippe, Louis]
Oropesa, 109,114,116,158,159,160,162
O'Toole, -, 252
Otway, Col, 59
Ovar, 85,88,90
Oxen, 185,186

P

Pack, [Maj] Gen [Sir Denis], 187, 345,353,355,356,364,366
[*Spelt 'Packe' on this page]
*Paget, Gen Sir Edward, 40,83,84, 91,93

*Paget, Lord Henry, 55,56,57,58, 59,60,61
 [***Note**: Gen Sir Edward Paget was the brother of Lord Henry Paget, 2nd Earl of Uxbridge. The latter did not serve in the Peninsular following Wellington's return in 1809. Confusingly, both served under Wellington during the period preceding the Convention of Cintra; Gen Sir Edward Paget leading the reserve division and being severely wounded (losing his arm). Gen Sir Edward Paget Paget returned to the Peninsula in 1812. In the text no distinction is made between the two].
Pakenham, [Maj Gen Sir Edward Michael], 358
 [misspelt in text as 'Packenham']
Palencia, 58
Panaranda, 375
Parapets
 Badajoz, 278,281,304
 [*see also*: Badajoz in general section]
 Burgos, 388
 Cuidad Rodrigo, 225
 [*see also*: Cuidad Rodrigo in general section]
Paris, vi,68,120
Patrollings/patrols, 103,156,201,203,231,235
Patterson,-, 258
Patterson, Maj
 Leaves from the journal of a veteran, 21-50
Pauline Bonaparte [*see*: Pauline Borghese]
Pauline Borghese [sister of Napoleon], 68
Paye, 221
Payne, Capt, 9
Payne, Lt Gen, 84
Pedro de Regoa, 96
Pegoa, 179
Penafiel, 81,96
Penalonga, 13
Peninsula [*see*: Iberian Peninsula]
Penrice, Lt, 175
Peretada da Gabern, 161

Philip V (King of Spain, 1700-1746), 111
Philipon [ie Phillipon, General Armand], 270, 282,283,284,311
 [*see also*: Badajoz - Governor]
Pickets, 7,16,56,58,59,99,172,173, 190,194,219,235,243,244,323,327, 330,332,336, 347,376
Picton, [Lt] Gen [Sir Thomas], 214, 219,239,251,265,280,288,291,292, 292,293,305,316
Pigs, 40
Placentia, 105,106,108,109,116, 158,160,162,166
 Bishop's palace, 106
 Cathedral, 106
Plough, 40
Pombal, Marquis de, 74
Ponto Novo (bridge), 98
Pontoons
 [*see*: Almarez - Pontoon bridge; Guadiana - Pontoon bridge; Villa Velha - Pontoon bridge]
Portsmouth, 21,52,78,95
Portugal, 9,24,53,54,66,69,70,71, 74,77,78,81,102,103,104,158,160, 161,162,153,163,166,283,350,351
 [*see also*: **Battles, Campaigns, Wars** - Peninsula War; individual place names (eg Lisbon); Iberian Peninsula in general section]
 Fortresses, 54
 Frontier, 105,151,164,167,218,324
 Nobility, 75
 Peasantry, 75,89,97,102
 Regency Council, 72,80
Portuguese, 72,90,94,205,269,309
 [*see also*: UNITS AND FORMATIONS - Portugal]
Poso Velho, 187,188,189,203
Pouissin, Gaspar, 7
Power, Gen, 313,319
Praza d'Arcos, 13
Prince of Essling [*see*: Essling, Prince]
Prince of Neufchatel [*see*: Neufchatel, Prince of]
Prince Regent, 78
Prisoners-of-War, 41,285
Provisions, 11,96,113,157,163,165, 166,356 [*see also*: Stores]

INDEX

Prussia, 387
Puebla d'Agava, 216
Pueblo (River), 387
Puente del Arzobispo, 109,117
Purves, Capt, 202
Pyrenees, 68,350,361 [*see also under:* **Battles, Campaigns, Wars**]
Romana, General, 70

Q

Queluz, 13

R

Ragusa, Duke of [*see*: Marmont, Marshal Auguste-Frederic-Louis Viesse de]
Raleigh, Sir W[alter], 237
Ramsay, Capt (later Maj) [William] Norman, 190,191
Rations
  Spirits, 166 [*see also*: Rum]
Redoubts, 164,165
Regnier, General, 179,196
Reilly, Pte Jim, 296
Reminiscences of a subaltern, 237
Ribeira, 208
Ridge, Maj (later Lt Col), 224,226, 231,239,243,263,290,291,297,308
Riding, 112
Rio Mayor, 174
Rivillas, 268
Rivers, 105,106,170,198,209,211 [*see also*: name of river (eg Tagus)]
Rivoli, Duke of [*see*: Massena, Marshal Andre]
Roads/routes, 28,31,32,42,43,45,47, 63,70,85,86,87,90,92,94,96,98,99, 100,101,103,106,117,119,124,127, 159,160,161,162,165,166,167,171, 187,204,206,219,226,254,268,271, 325,334,365,367,368,371,375,378, 379
Rocha, Don Emmanuel de la, 311, 319,320
Rochelle, 69
Rodrigo [*see*: Cuidad Rodrigo]

Roleia [*see*: Rolica]
Rolica, 7 [*see also under:* **Battles, Campaigns, Wars**]
Romana, General Pedro Caro y Sureda, 70,72
Roman Gardo, 161
'Rozinante' (horse), 324
Rueda, 329,330
Ruffin, [General Francois-Amable], 130,142,148
Ruivaens, 97,98
  Pass, 100
Rum, 356
Russia, 387
Rye, 186

S

Sabugal, 179,195
  Bridge, 188,196
Sahagun, 43,56
Saint...[*see*: St... at end of this letter sequence]
Salamanca, 28,31,36,37,42,55,58,69, 105,160,167,218,226,321,323,324, 325,326,328,338,339,343,345,349, 356,363,365,368,374,378, 383,385
  Bridge, 328
  Cathedral, 325,359
  Mayor, 330
  Plains, 185
  [*see also under:* **Battles, Campaigns, Wars**]
Salamonde, 98,102
Salt, 62
Sanches, Julian, 187,188
Santa Cruz (reglious order of nuns), 29
Santa Maria, 167
Santarem, 28,31,77,84,177
Sarzedas, 106
Sebastiani, [Marshal Horace-Francois-Bastien], 104,126,137,139,165
Secieras, 195
Segovia, 369,379
  Mountain passes, 382
Severn (valley), 8
Seville, 106,271,387
Shaw, [Gen Sir James], 280,281
Shaw Kennedy, Gen Sir James [*see*:

Shaw, Gen Sir James]
Sherbrooke, Gen [Sir John], 77,84, 107,123,131,145
Shipping/Ships, 3,4,12,15,21,72, 81,92,95
   Boats, 3,91,92,93
   Collier, 21
   Frigate, vii,24,26,27,78,79
   Transports, 3,4,21,24,64
Shoes, vi,61,113
Sicily, 53
Sierra de Gata (Mountain), 322
Sierra de Santa Catherina (Mountain), 96,98
Sierra de Tablada (Mountain), 324
Sierra Morena (Mountain), 80
Silveira, General, 70,72,81,84,95, 96,100
Singer, Maj, 306
Sketch of the storming, 237
Slade, Gen, 206,207
Sontag, Brig Gen, 83
Soult, Marshal [Nicholas], 65,68,69, 70,71,79,81,88,92,95,96,97,100, 102,103,104,105,106,158,159,160, 283,351,387
Southey, [Robert], 8
Spain/Spaniards, [1],5,15,20,22,23, 24,33,38,41,45,55,66,67,69,74,77, 80,81,104,105,106,111,115,122, 144,147,156,159,162,167,199,274, 285,309,320,325,340,347,350,351, 368,371,376,379,384,385,386
[*see also*: **Battles, Campaigns, Wars** - Peninsular War; individual place names; UNITS AND FORMATIONS - Spain]
   Aristocracy [*see*: Nobility]
   Constitution, 70
   Cortes, 115,123,165
   Farmers, 115,118
   Frontier, 101,164,215
   Gentry, 110
   Insurrection (1827), 70
   King [*see*: Joseph Bonaparte]
   Ladies, 328
   Nobility, 110,379
   Parliament [*see*: Cortes]
   Peasantry/peasants, 43,70,113,115, 308, 345,380
   Soldiers serving in King Joseph's army, 369,376
Spencer, Gen Sir Brent, 3,200
Square [*see* under: **Tactics**]
Standards [*see*: Colours, Eagles]
Stanhope, Capt Fitzroy, 95
Stewart, Brig Gen (later Lt Gen Sir William), 40,58,79,83,85,86,87, 107,119,142
Stores, 3,11,113,180,227,258, 264,368,376,383,387
[*see also*: Provisions]
Storming of Badajoz, The (Elder,-), 304-320
Straw, 178
Sturgeon, Maj, 238,239,240,241
St Christoval (hill), 325,326,329,340
[*see also*: Fort St Christoval]
St Christoval (valley), 338
[*see also*: Fort St Christoval]
St Cloud, 370
St Ildefonso, 369
   Gardens, 369,370
   Waterworks, 369,370
St Jago, 70
St James's Park, 387
St Julian (fort) [*see under*: Lisbon]
St Michael (hill), 389
St Ollala, 151,156
St Pol, Capt, 318
Suchet, [Marshal Louis-Gabriel], 68, 388
Suttlers, 368
Swiss
   Refugees, 192

T

Table Mountain, 340,341,342,344,345
Tactics
   Column, 99,100,101,119,124, 131,139,140,141,142,148,149,154, 162,167,169,175,189,190,201,209, 220,227,277,278,289,304,323,331, 337,340,344,345,359,361
      Attack, 145
      March, 97
   Line, 88,145,192,193,220,270,340, 344,347

Skirmishing, 253
Square, 169,179,181,192,193,215, 221,223,250,333,347,363,364
Tagus (River), 3,26,31,69,72,73,77, 79,80,82,101,104,109,117,120,121, 125,129,139,153,160,161,164,166, 382
Talbot, Col, 101,169
Talaquela, 109
Talavera, 120,127,132,140,158,159
[*see also under:* **Battles, Campaigns, Wars**]
Talavera de la Real, 167
Talavera de la Reyna, 108,109,117
Talleyrand-Perigord, Prince Charles Maurice de, vii
Tamega (valley), 70,81
Tamerlane, 135
Taylor, Lt Col, 53
Teitar (River), 108,109
Tents, vi,5,269,287,288,373,379
Teson (hills)
  Lower Teson, 226
  Upper Teson, 226
Thames, 21
Thiebault [General Paul Charles], 54
Thomar, 75,177
Thompson, Capt, 194,195
Tilson, Maj Gen, 82,84,107,142
Toledo, 126,164,165
Tomkinson, Lt, 175
Tormes (River), 323,324,327,328, 329,334,338,339,340,355,378
  Fords, 327,329,332,338,347
  Santa Martha, 323
Toro, 40,55
  Prison, 40,41
Torre Major, 167
Torres Novas, 177
Torres Vedras, 11,[217]
Torrijos, 125,126
Townsend, Capt, 201,202
Transport, 159,162,163
[*see also:* Carts, Horses, Mules]
Trant, Col [(later Maj Gen Sir) Nicholas], 71
Tras os Montes, 73,74,102,103,163
Trenches, 283
[*see also under:* **Battles, Campaigns, Wars** - Badajoz,

Cuidad Rodrigo]
Treviso, Duke of [*see:* Mortier, Marshal Edouard-Adoplphe-Casmir- Joseph]
Truxillo, 166
Trumpets, 124
Tumbrils, 195
[*see also:* Carts; **Weapons and Ammunition** - Ammunition - Waggons]
Turones (River), 190,194
Tuy, 70

U

Uniacke,-, 258
Uniforms and accoutrements, 147
[*see also under:* UNITS AND FORMATIONS - France - Army - Cavalry - Hussars; Portugal - Army; Spain - Army]
Accoutrements, [vi],50,251,334
[*see also:* Canteens, Haversacks, Pouches]
Belts, 113
Canteens, vi,269
Caps, 332
Cloaks, 337
Epaulette, 359
Greatcoats, vi,113
Haversacks, vi,42,137,195,334
Helmets, 373
Knapsacks [*see:* Haversacks]
Pouches, vi
United Kingdom [*see:* Great Britain]
UNITS AND FORMATIONS
  Allied Army (Peninsular War), 109,127, 129,138,145,221
  [*see also:* Great Britain, Portugal, Spain]
    Lusitanian Legion, 12,72,84, 106,107
  Europe, 168
  France [*see also:* French, in general section]
    Armies, 13,16,20,43,52,55,60, 66,68,70,80,98,104,105,125,127, 135,136,151,152,153,158,160, 163,167,185,187,188,198,218,

323,326,327,328,333,336,337,
338,341,344,345,348,350,351,
353,354,356,362, 363
[*see also*: Tactics - Column]
Army of the North, 218,365
Army of Portugal, 353,355,364,
365
Artillery, 65,70,164,188,192,195,
198,212,214,223,264,331,365
   Batteries, 141,146,192,193,
   201,203,271
   Battering train [*see*: Siege
   artillery]
   Dutch artillery, 209
   Gunners, 249
   Horse artillery, 129
   Siege artillery, 264
Barracks, 15
Battalions, 171,222,270
Brigades, 56,148,149,180,181,
211,335
   Cavalry, 212
      1st Cavalry Brigade, 210
      2nd Cavalry Brigade, 210
Camps, 125,128
Cavalry, 15,53,54,57,59,60,61,
69,70,71,80,88,117,120,124,129,
139,146,148,149,150,161,168,170,
174,176,180,181,182,187,188,189,
190,194,195,197,198,201,202,203,
206,207,208,211,214,218,219,220,
221,222,223,323,326,331,332,334,
336,341,344,347,363,364,365,373,
376,382
[*see also*: under Brigades; *see also*:
Imperial Guard]
   Chasseurs, 56,58,59,60,61,173,191,
   198,211
   [*see also*: Imperial Guard]
   ★ Cuirassiers, 53,182,331
   [★Note: Referred to as 'Heavy
   Dragoons'on these pages. However,
   the French heavy cavalry consisted
   of Cuirassiers and Carabiniers
   (distinguished by their breastplates).
   The Dragoons represented medium
   cavalry, in contrast to the British
   horse formations].
   Dragoons, 54,58,178,180,181,201,
   210,211,269,283,323

[*see also*: individual regiments]
   'Heavy Dragoons' [*see*: Cuirassiers]
   Grenadiers-a-cheval, 189
   Heavy cavalry, 332,382
   [*see also*: Cuirassiers]
   Hussars, 173,191,194
   Uniform, 106
   Lancers, 216,372,373,374
   Light cavalry, 106 [*see also*:
   Chasseurs, Hussars, Lancers]
   Squadrons, 86
Chasseurs [*see* under: Cavalry]
Commanders, 68,79,351
[*see also*: individual names]
Conscription/Conscripts, 10,88
Corps, 68,71,88,97,102,105,137,
145,158,159,162,167,179,
180,182,195,361
   1st Corps, 69,70
   2nd Corps, 69,70,71,160
   4th Corps, 69,126
   5th Corps, 159,160
   6th Corps, 68,159,160
   8th Corps, 69
Cuirassiers [*see* under: Cavalry]
Deserters, 138,155
Divisions, 10,70,71,88,130,139,142,
158,190,208,222,329,334,341,
344,367
   7th Division, 355
   Light Divisions, 171
Dragoons [*see under*: Cavalry]
General officers, 44,115 [*see also*:
Commanders]
Grand Army (Russia), 387
Grenadiers, 273,285,296,347
Grenadiers-a-cheval
   [*see under*: Cavalry]
Imperial Guard, 58,59,68,126,
137,139,387
Infantry, 15,54,60,86,87,119,128,
149,169,170,171,178,179,180,
181,187,188,193,195,198,214,
218,222,223,270,334,335,341,
362,364
Light Infantry, 87,99,148,346
[*see also*: Skirmishers, Tirailleurs]
Italian army, 137
Joseph Bonaparte's army, 369
Lancers [*see under*: Cavalry]

INDEX

Marshals [see: Commanders]
Northern Army, 365
Officers, 58,61,99,125,134,136,
 146,156,173,175,215,229,230,
 298,302,303,332,361
Portuguese Legion, 72
Regiments, 69,71,93,137,174
 Foreign, 65
 Westphalian, 155
 4th Dragoons, 209,210
 5th Hussars, 216
 9th Regiment, 130
 14th Dragoons, 210
 17th Regiment, 93
 20th Dragoons, 209,210
 22nd Regiment, 359
 24th Regiment, 130
 26th Dragoons, 209
 31st Regiment, 71,88
 47th Regiment, 88
 70th Regiment, 93,179
 96th Regiment, 130
 103rd Regiment, 296
 104th Regiment, 304
Sharpshooters, 44
Skirmishers, 117,173,174,183,189,
 193,201,202,345
[see also: Tiraillers, Sharpshooters]
Soldiers, 40,98,100,129,134,136,
 145,175,190,212,230,233,234,
 270,277,278,280,283,286,294,
 295,298,299,302,312,341,348,
 350,352, 354,362, 375,376
Tirailleurs, 99,118,120,139,178,
 213,358,361
Troops [see: Soldiers]
Great Britain
 Army, vi,28,32,39,43,46,51,52,53,
 54,55,61,64,65,69,71,77,78,79,
 81,82,84,85,86,95,96,97,98,100,
 102,105,106,108,121,122,123,
 126,127,129,131,133,137,140,
 152,153,156,157,158,160,161,
 162,163,166,167,170,171,174,
 177,180,185,187,188,191,195,
 196,198,199,201,210,212,213,
 214,215,221,222,224,253,299,
 304,309,321,325,326,327,329,
 330,335,336,337,338,340,341,
 343,344,345,347,350,352,353,
 354,355,362,363,367,368,369,
 372,376, 379,382,383,387
Adjutant, 274
Adjutant General, 85,119,197
Adjutant General's Department,
 79,89,131
 Deputy Adjutant General, 282
Army Corps [see: Corps]
Artillery, 72,93,94,145,174,174,
 194,195,209,211,301,326,338,
 341,368
 [see also: Regiments - Royal
 Horse Artillery]
 Batteries, 145,195,229,257,259,
 265,270,272,275,287,300,306,
 307, 315
 Brigades, 143,195,219,372
 Gunners, 195,272
 Horse artillery
 [see: Regiments - Royal Horse
 Artillery]
Bands, 14
Batman, 274,323,377
Brigades, 3,20,71,107,128,129,131,
 141,145,181,206,214,215,223,
 226,233,235,237,263,284,285,
 289,305,306,316,322,345,361,
 362
 [see also under: Artillery; King's
 German Legion]
 Cavalry, 82,107,220,222,223,
 337, 363,372
 [see also: specific brigades]
 Heavy Cavalry, 84,103,148
 Fusilier, 181
 [see also: Regiments - 7th
 Regiment]
 Guards, 154 [see also under:
 Regiments]
 Light Brigade, 161
 Scots Brigade, 245
 1st Cavalry Brigade, 107,140
 1st Brigade (Light Division),
 336,346
 1st Infantry Brigade, 82,90,107,
 254
 2nd Brigade (Light Division),
 346
 2nd Cavalry Brigade, 107
 2nd Infantry Brigade, 83,85,

107,254
3rd Cavalry Brigade,
　107,118,120, 124,148
3rd Infantry Brigade, 82
4th Infantry Brigade, 83
5th Infantry Brigade, 83
6th Infantry Brigade, 83,86,94
7th Infantry Brigade, 83,98,100
Brunswick-Oels Corps, 193
Cavalry, 15,50,51,52,53,55,58,61,
　62,65,72,84,86,87,88,91,94,97,
　98,99,100,120,124,127,129,141,
　142,148,168,170,171,172,174,
　175,177,178,179,182,183,184,
　185,188,190,192,193,194,197,
　200,203,204,210,214,215,218,
　219,223,323,326,327,329,330,
　331,332,334,335,340,346,351,
　357,361,362,363,368,372,377
　[*see also*: Dragoons; Hussars;
　individual regiments; *see also
　under*: Brigades]
　Heavy Cavalry, 329,344
　Light Cavalry, 363
　Remounts, 197,198
　Troopers, 364
Commissariat, 108,125,178,186,
　368,380,381
Corps (ie Army Corps)
　2nd Corps, 367
Corps of observation, 83,383
Corps
　Engineers, 108,126,227,281,319
　[*see also*: Pioneers]
　　Commandant, 292,319
　　[*see also*: Fletcher, Lt Col Sir
　　Richard]
Divisions, 3,20,45,107,126,127,
　129,187,218,221,222,270,286,
　304,325,326,327,338,340,342,
　346,353,355,367,369
　1st Division, 107,124,140,141,
　　145,147,167,255,256,262,346,
　　363, 388
　2nd Division, 107,124,130,141,
　　167,376,388
　3rd Division, 107,116,120,123,
　　161,167,214,219,225,226,227,
　　233,237,238,249,252,253,256,
　　258,260,261,262,263,273,278,

　　283,284,288,289,292,293,294,
　　300,306,316,340,342,343,344,
　　358,361, 382
　4th Division, 107,124,140,147,
　　167,219,222,268,276,280,282,
　　293,300,307,314,316,333,335,
　　344,361,366
　5th Division, 127,128,221,262,
　　283,284, 293,300,304,388,
　6th Division, 324,325,326,366,
　　383,388,
　7th Divisiion, 326,339,340,388
　Light Division, 150,200,201,203,
　　206,207,219,221,225,226,233,
　　234,250,252,253,254,255,256,
　　257,258,259,261,262,267,268,
　　269,273,275,276,277,278,280,
　　282,293,300,307,316,320,322,
　　323,325,326,327,328,329,330,
　　332,333,334,335,336,337,340,
　　341,345,347,363,376,379,380
Doctors [*see under*: Medical staff]
Dragoons, 51,53,59,94,168,170,
　176,179,187,188,195,199,211,
　212,214,216,331,332,333
　[*see also*: individual regiments]
Light dragoons, 59,326,332,
　337,363
　[*see also*: individual regiments;
　King's German Legion -
　Regiments]
Drummers, 265
Hussars, 62,170,191
　[*see also*: individual regiments;
　King's German Legion -
　Regiments]
Infantry, 15,51,58,65,99,126,174,
　175,179,192,193,194,197,203,
　214,220,223,323,327,340,352,
　362,363,364,368, 371
　[*see also under*: Brigades]
　Battalions, 91,137,108,226,355,
　　357,363
　　[*see also*: individual battalions
　　under Regiments]
　Companies, 49,108,227,255,277,
　　289,316,322,323,330,331,333,
　　361
　　[*see also*: Tactics - Column]
　Grenadier, 100

INDEX   411

Light Companies, 100,108,241,
  289,290,361
Riflemen, 108 [*see also*:
  Riflemen]
Grenadiers, 116,228,258,265,
  290,296,344
  [*see also under:* Companies]
Light infantry, 10,86,98,131,132,
  253,297
Platoons, 250
Sections, 45,331
King's German Legion, 96,98,
  100,130,131,141,191,363,382
  Battalions, 86,100
    2nd Bn, 107
  Brigades, 83
  Cavalry [*see also*: individual
    regiments]
  Dragoons
    Heavy Dragoons, 382
Heavy cavalry, 334,347,363,372
  [*see also*: Dragoons – Heavy
  Dragoons]
Infantry
  Light Infantry, 86
  Regiments, 83
  1st Hussars, 107,149
  3rd Hussars, 55
  3rd Light Dragoons, 82
Marines, 3
Medical staff, 108,155,158,304,
  312
  Assistant Surgeon, 216,381
  Chief, 304 [*see also*:
    MacGrigor, Sir James]
  Doctors, 288
Officers, 5,15,22,28,29,36,44,
  52,55,60,73,76,89,101,111,116,
  118,119,123,126,129,131,132,
  138,147,150,155,156,163,171,
  172,174,178,179,183,192,215,
  224,232,234,235,239,244,258,
  260,262,274,276,282,284,285,
  288,290,292,302,305,306,307,
  312,316,317,318,322,323,324,
  325,330,331,336,337,338,345,
  359,360,374,376,377,379,381
  Flank, 293
Pioneers, 14 [*see also*: Engineers]
Quartermaster General, 158

Quartermaster General's
  Department, 79
Quartermasters, 40,48,200
Regiments, 48,107,108,131,137,
  142,156,166,220,221,250,253,
  262,281,285,340,360,361,365,
  373,372,381
  [*see also under:* King's German
  Legion]
'Buffs' [*see*: 3rd Regiment]
Cavalry, 363,368
  [*see also*: individual regiments]
Commanders, 185
Chasseurs Britanniques, 192
Connaught Rangers [*see*: 88th
  Regiment]
Foot Guards, 82,94,98,100,107,
  132,137,140,141,145,146,155,
  194,363
  [*see also*: individual regiments]
Fusiliers [*see*: 7th Regiment]
Guards [*see*: Foot Guards]
Highland, 253
Rifle Regiment [*see*: 95th
  Regiment]
Royal Dragoons [*see*: 1st Dragoon
  Guards]
Royal Fusiliers [*see*: 7th
  Regiment]
Royal Horse Artillery, 150,171,
  321,330,332,336,348,372,382
  Brigades, 321,373
  Drivers, 332
  Gunners, 190
Scots Guards *see*: 3rd Foot
  Guards]
1st Dragoon Guards, 173,178,
  192,194,197,198,199,200,201,
  203,207
1st Hussars, 107,149
2nd Regiment, 199
3rd Dragoon Guards, 59,103,107,
  147,149,153
3rd Foot Guards, 79
3rd Hussars, 55
3rd Light Dragoons, 82
3rd Regiment, 82,91,92,93,94,
  107,142
4th Dragoon Guards, 103,107,149
4th Regiment, 199

5th Dragoon Guards, 339
5th Regiment, 215,220,226,230, 232,234,238,243,244,252,253, 264,284,290, 291,297,308,344
  1st Bn, 343
  2nd Bn, 218,222,223,289
7th Hussars, 55,178*,197*,222*
  [*Note: Referred to as 1st Hussars on these pages. The 7th Hussars was the senior Hussar regiment, but no regiment of light dragoons (subsequently Hussars) was numbered 1].
7th Regiment, 83,107,147,306,307
  [see also: Brigades - Fusilier]
9th Regiment, 83,131
10th Hussars, 55,56,57,59
11th Light Dragoons, 222
13th Light Dragoons, 180,181,184
14th Light Dragoons 72,82,101,107, 168,169,*175,194,197,201,202,375
  [*referred to as '14th Heavy Dragoons' on this page]
15th Hussars [see: 15th Light Dragoons]
15th Light Dragoons, 52,55,56
16th Light Dragoons, 80,82,88, 107,172,173,174,175,197
18th Hussars, 55,58
18th Light Dragoons [see: 18th Hussars]
20th Light Dragoons, 53,54,82
20th Regiment, 83
23rd Light Dragoons, 107,148,149,184
23rd Regiment [see: Brigades - Fusilier]
24th Regiment, 107
27th Regiment, 83
29th Regiment, 87,107,131
31st Regiment, 83,107,128
42nd Regiment, 49
43rd Regiment, 150,255,258,259, 269,271,277,280,305,316,321, 328,336,346
45th Regiment, 9,83,107,246,289, 292
48th Regiment, 82,93,107,131, 142,146
50th Regiment, 21
52nd Regiment, 150,204,206, 207,255, 275,277,278,288,321
53rd Regiment, 83,107,147
60th Regiment
  5th Bn, 82,83,107,289,301
61st Regiment, 107
66th Regiment, 82,93,107,142
74th Regiment, 289,297,373
77th Regiment, 237,238,239,240,241, 243,251,252,253,263,264,289
  2 Bn, 222,223
83rd Regiment, 83,107,146,155,252
87th Regiment, 82,107,155
88th Regiment, 82,107,246,247, 289,292,293,297,308,359,360, 361,362
94th Regiment, 225,227,228,231, 232,234,235,241,243,245,246, 248,252,263,264,289
95th Regiment, 150,255,258,277, 280,286,316,317,323
  1st Bn, 321
  2nd Bn, 333
  3rd Bn, 321
97th Regiment, 83,107,147
Riflemen, 7,44,185
  [see also: Regiments - 60th Regiment - 5th Bn; 95th Regiment; under Companies]
Skirmishers, 119,173,194,346
Soldiers, 21,36,39,43,44,46,47,48, 49,50,51,52,53,54,56,77,84,101, 103,116,120,121,128,129,130, 131,132,133,134,137,142,143, 144,145,147,148,154,156,157, 162,163,164,171,174,194,199, 207,215,224,232,234,244,259, 260,262,269,271,273,274,275, 279,282,286,287,295,301,305, 307,308,309,310,311,313,317, 319,321,325,328,329,334,337, 339,343,351,354,355,356,357, 362,365,367,368,374,381
  [see also: Cavalry - Troopers]
Militia, 5,108,137
  London trained bands, 37
  Pay stoppages, 166
Staff, 239

INDEX 413

Troops [*see*: Soldiers]
Royal Navy
  Fleet, 22,72,73,78
  Sailors, 180
Holland, 65
India
  Commanders, 121
  Sirdars [*see*: Commanders]
Italy, 65
Naples, 65
Netherlands [*see*: Holland]
Portugal, 8,110,116
  [*see also*: Allied Army (Peninsular War) - Lusitanian Legion]
  Army, 70,72,73,74,75,76,84,86, 98, 105,252,283,294,299,352,354
    Artillery, 74,76,222,223
      Battering train [*see*: Siege artillery]
      Brigades, 345
      Siege artillery, 249
    Battalions, 93,108
    Brigades, 108,193,313,353, 355, 364,366,372
      [*see also under:* Artillery, Cavalry]
    Cacadores, 77 [*see also under:* Regiments]
    Cavalry, 74,76,85,180
      Brigades, 338
      Dragoons, 372,382
      Troopers, 373
    Divisions, 19
      Grenadiers [*see* under: Infantry]
    Infantry, 74,154,220,326
      Grenadiers, 82
      Light infantry, 8,108 [*see also*: Cacadores]
    Officers, 12,19,20,75
    Regiments, 74,76,77,85,103, 220
      Cacadores, 314,316,321, 337,358
      [*see also*: specific regiments]
      3rd Cacadores, 318
      10th Regiment, 83
      16th Regiment, 76,83,86
      21st Regiment, 222,223,224
  Soldiers, 75,76,270,343,354,359,374

  [*see also*: Cavalry - Troopers]
  Uniform, 20
  Irregulars, 76
  Militia, 76
Rome
  Legions, 108
  Principes, 108
  Triarii, 108
  Velites, 108
Spain, vi [*see also*: **Spain/Spaniards** in general sections]
  Army, 69,70,72,80,81,108,109, 110,111,113,114,115,116,118, 119,120,121,123124,125,126, 127,132,140,153,157,159,160, 161,163,164,165,167,168,181, 325, 326,336,352,387
    Artillery, 113
      Batteries, 113,127,164
      Brigades, 145
    Battalions, 14,113
    Brigades, 111 [*see also under:* Brigades]
    Carabineers [*see under:* Cavalry]
    Cavalry, 80,81,110,112,114, 117,119,124,147,149,164, 165
      Carabineers, 111
      Heavy cavalry, 111,112
        Dragoons, 111
      Light Cavalry, 111,112
        Hussars, 111
    Divisions, 109,148,160,164
    Dragoons [*see under:* Cavalry - Heavy Cavalry]
    Garde du Corps, 111
    Grenadiers, 123
    Hussars [*see under:* Cavalry - Light Cavalry]
    Infantry, 80,81,107,110,112,114, 147,164
      Irish Brigade, 112
      Walloon Guards, 112
    Irish Brigade
      [*see under:* Infantry; *see also*: Regiments - Hibernia, Ultonia, Yrlanda]
    Militia, 161

Officers, 110,111,114,153,163
  Irish, 113
  Regiments, 111,132,147,325, 336
    Hibernia, 112
    Regiment del Rey, 111
    Sagantum, 111
    Ultonia, 112
    Yrlanda, 112
  Soldiers, 114,115,122,153, 160,163
  Swiss troops, 6
  Troops [see: Soldiers]
  Uniforms, 112,113,114
    Walloon Guards [see under: Infantry]
  Guerrillas, 115,116,118,187,188
Usagre, 208 [see also under: **Battles, Campaigns, Wars**]
  Bridge, 208 [see also under: **Battles, Campaigns, Wars** - Usagre]

V

Valencia, 388
Valongo, 92,94
Valladolid, 40,365,367,377,378,388
  Square, 378
Vanegas, General, 80,109,126,164,165
Velesa (plain), 337,354
Vere, Col Sir Charles Broke
  [see: Broke, Maj Charles]
Versailles, 370
Victor, [Victor-Perrin], [Marshal Claud], 68,69,70,81,82,84,97,98, 102,103,104,105,125,126,139,159
Victories of the British Armies (W H Maxwell), 278
Vienna, 349
Vigo, 81
Villa da Ponte, 100
Villa del Rey, 105,167
Villa di Yegua, 199
Villa Franca, 28,62,177
Villa Garcia, 207
Villa Nova, 71,88,90,97
Villa Velha, 283
  Pontoon bridge, 283

Villa Vicosa, 126
Villele, General, 148
Vimiero, 11,15 [see also under: **Battles, Campaigns, Wars**]
Viseu, 84
Vistula (River), 350
Voyage en Espagne, et de lettres philosophiques, 104
Vouga (River), 71,85,88,106
Vultures, 33,387

W

Waggons, 50
Walker, Gen, 280,306,312
Wallace, Gen [Sir John Alexander], 357,361, 362
Water, 109,205,328,334,337,356, 379,381,384
Waters, Col (later Lt Gen Sir John), 89,91,162,165
Weapons and Ammuntion
  Ammunition, 11,50,108,293
    *Bullet, 241
    [*Note: A term used interchangeably with musket ball]
    Caissons [see: Waggons]
    Cannister shot [see: Case shot]
    Cannon balls, 93,120,141,145, 194,240,242,270,286,300,302
    Case shot, 193,315
    Grape shot, 179,194,195,215, 245,246,272,278,281,282,288, 294,315,344,358
    Gunpowder, vi,228,277,305, 315,383
    Musket balls, vi,6,89,100,154, 155,260,283,297,308
    Cartridges, vi,16,100,150,287, 293,296
    Round shot [see: Cannon balls]
    Shell, 93,129,130,145,195,228, 243,246,257,263,265,300,302, 305,308,315,357, 387
    Fuses, 145
    Shot [see: Case shot, Round shot, Grape shot]
    Waggons, 96,113,165 [see also: Tumbrils]

INDEX 415

Artillery, 3,10,33,45,108,119,120, 129,162,169,195,272
  Cannon [*see*: Guns]
  Field artillery, vi
  Guns, 15,46,54,70,72,87,93,95, 96,130,131,132,141,143,145, 147,152,165,172,173,174,175, 180,181,182,190,194,195,196, 203,214,219,220,221,222,227, 240,243,246,270,271,273,278, 283,286,294,296,300,305,309, 315,325,326,332,333.336,337, 340,345, 368,373,382,383,388
    3 pr, 86,98
    4 pr, 86,120
    6 pr, 96,142,212,330
    8 pr, 143
    12 pr, 113,143,145,307
    18 pr, 344
    24 pr, 257,258
    Carriages, 96,296
    Howitzer, 120,195,212,255
  Siege artillery
    Battery, 389
    Mortars, 387
    Rockets, 273,328
Bayonet, 16,76,87,131,145,147, 154,169,181,220,228,230,231, 243,249,273,278,279,285,287, 295,298,301,311
Cannon [*see*: Artillery - Guns]
Carbine, 8,111,323
Fireballs, 246,276,278,279,281,282, 289,294,304,305
Firelocks [*see*: Musket]
Grenade, 243,247,263,305,308
Guns [*see under*: Artillery]
Hand-grenade [*see*: Grenade]
Mine, 278,285,312
Musket, vi,6,200,276,281,296,301, 308,311,319,345,347
  Flints, 293
Ordnance [*see*: Artillery]
Pike, vi
Pistol, 45,269,313
Powder [*see*: Gunpowder]
Rockets [*see* under: Artillery]
Sabre [*see* under: Sword]
Small arms, 272 [*see also*: Bayonet, Carbine, Musket, Pistol]

Sword, vi,61,191,230,274,279,280, 331,332,362,373,382
  Broadsword, 382
  Sabre, 56,59,80,270,298,358,362, 363,364,372,373
  Sword-knot, 191
Wellesley, Sir Arthur [*see*: Wellington, Duke of]
Wellington, Duke of, 3,10,15,20,33, 53,61,64,78,79,80,82,84,87,89,90, 93,95,97,101,102,103,104,108,109, 116,117,120,121,122,123,125,126, 127,128,133,138,139,144,145,146, 150,155,156,159,160,166,170,178, 179,185,187,188,192,195,196,200, 214,215,217,218,220,221,222,251, 252,254,276,283,292,293,304,305, 306,315,316,317,327,328,329,330, 332,336,339,340,342,343,345,346, 352,353,354,355,356,362,365,367, 368,369,370,371,376,377
  General Order (2 October 1811), 222-224
Westmoreland, Gen John Fane [*see*: Fane, Gen John]
Wheat, 125,327,334
Whitehall, 152
Whitelaw, - (officer), 293
Wilde, Pte Israel, 269
Wilkie, Lt Col
  The English in Spain, [1]-20
Wilkinson, - (officer), 336
Wilkinson, Bde Maj, 272
Williams, Lt Col, 289
Williams's English Hotel, 18
Williamson, Capt, 228
Wilson, [Gen] Sir Robert, 72,73,81, 106,109,167
Women, 308,309,368

Z

Zafra, 367,376
  Alcalde [*see*: Mayor]
  Mayor, 376
Zagalo (guerrilla leader), 3
Zarza Major, 106
Zobreira, 106

www.ingramcontent.com/pod-product-compliance
Lightning Source LLC
Chambersburg PA
CBHW071618170426
43195CB00038B/1344